# Antitrust Settlements

## International Competition Law Series

VOLUME 80

*Editor*

In its series editor, Alastair Sutton, Kluwer is fortunate to engage and benefit from the experience and expertise of one of the world's outstanding authorities on European Union and international economic law.

*Introduction*

In their efforts to regulate competition in an increasingly complex business environment, competition authorities face a daunting task. The European Commission and Courts, as well as national courts and legislatures, policymakers, and regulators, are constantly proposing, enacting, reviewing, and enforcing new legal measures, often addressing novel situations. Every industry and service is affected.

*Contents/Subjects*

With many titles currently available and new ones appearing regularly, the series' coverage includes detailed analyses of relevant legislation and case law in major global trading jurisdictions, defences used in cases involving the digital network economy, state aid cases, enforcement methodologies and a great deal more.

*Objective & Readership*

The purpose of Kluwer's International Competition Law Series is to follow the ever-changing contours of this dynamic area of the law, keeping the practice in sharp focus so that practising lawyers (including in-house counsel) and academics can be assured of the most up-to-date guidance and sources, in the widest possible range of applications.

*The titles published in this series are listed at the end of this volume.*

# Antitrust Settlements

## How a Simple Agreement Can Drive the Economy

Giovanna Massarotto

Wolters Kluwer

*Published by:*
Kluwer Law International B.V.
PO Box 316
2400 AH Alphen aan den Rijn
The Netherlands
E-mail: international-sales@wolterskluwer.com
Website: lrus.wolterskluwer.com

*Sold and distributed in North, Central and South America by:*
Wolters Kluwer Legal & Regulatory U.S.
7201 McKinney Circle
Frederick, MD 21704
United States of America
Email: customer.service@wolterskluwer.com

*Sold and distributed in all other countries by:*
Air Business Subscriptions
Rockwood House
Haywards Heath
West Sussex
RH16 3DH
United Kingdom
Email: international-customerservice@wolterskluwer.com

ISBN 978-94-035-1133-7

e-Book: ISBN 978-94-035-1111-5
web-PDF: ISBN 978-94-035-1122-1

# About the Author

Dr. Massarotto is an international expert on antitrust law and economic regulation in the field of information technology. She is affiliate of the UCL Centre for Blockchain Technologies (UCL CBT) and she serves as an Adjunct Professor at the University of Iowa. Dr. Massarotto has held seminars and has been a speaker in several international conferences at Harvard Law School, Fordham University of New York, at Italian Antitrust Authority (AGCM), at the University of Münster (Germany) and the University of Liege (Belgium). Dr. Massarotto was Academic Visitor at the University of Oxford after spending two years in the United States for her PhD in New York at Fordham University and in Washington D.C. working for the economic consulting firm—Criterion Economics LLC—specializing in antitrust, intellectual property and regulatory law issues related to telecommunication and digital industries. She also worked for the Journal of Competition Law & Economics, published by Oxford University Press.

She has taught as Adjunct Professor Competition Law at Bocconi University and worked at the Italian Antitrust Authority (AGCM) and for some international law firms in Milan. Having obtained a degree in law with honours, in May 2014 Dr. Massarotto attained a PhD in Law at Bocconi University. She also has education experience in Brussels, London, and in Paris at Univerisitè du Pantheon.

# Table of Contents

# Acknowledgments

I am extremely grateful for all the support I have received throughout my journey of creating this book. First, I owe a huge thank you to my family and close friends for their steadfast support during these years. Carla Picardi, Andrea Lively, Angela Danieli and Marialaura Pintonello have believed in me, possibly more than myself, on the idea and completion of this book. I especially thank Richard P. Bogusz III who was willing and enthusiastic to proofreading the entire manuscript, as well as all Cimba Staff, particularly Professor Al H. Ringleb and Professor Dennis O'Toole, whose comments and suggestions were invaluable. I also thank Professor Kim Petrone for being so excited about my research and inviting me as a guest speaker in her class, which enabled me to share my passion and thoughts with her students. As a result, Michael Catt, one of her students, introduced me to blockchain technology, for which I am very thankful.

I owe a special thanks to Professor Ariel Ezrachi for hosting me at the University of Oxford as an Academic Visitor where I conducted my research for the European part of this book.

I am also grateful for my students' support and enthusiasm regarding my research and topics covered in classes. You are the target audience of this book.

My biggest thanks goes to my father who has always encouraged me to study abroad and immerse myself in different cultures. His greatest gift to me was the opportunity to explore the world. It is from this gift that my curiosity and passion for research and writing stem.

I could not have ever written this book without the help and support of all these great people. Everyday I feel honored and grateful for that.

*With gratitude and appreciation,*
*Giovanna*

# Introduction

The most attractive thing in research is that you know exactly what you are looking for, but you have no idea what you will find. In 2012, when I started studying European commitment decisions, that topic was quite fashionable. The goals of antitrust law were secure, and antitrust enforcement became the main topic of the antitrust debate. Antitrust settlements (named *commitment decisions* in Europe and *consent decrees* in the U.S.) soon stole the show from other antitrust enforcement tools, fines and leniency programs. In 2012, the European Commission (EU Commission), similarly to U.S. Federal Trade Commission (FTC) and the Department of Justice (DOJ) antitrust intervention, adopted antitrust settlements to resolve approximately 90 percent of the abuse of dominant position cases.

The European and the U.S. antitrust agencies through antitrust settlements saved time, money, and regulate markets; undertaking, in exchange of some (often minor) commitments, avoided the risk of uncertain and expensive litigations, fines and reputation damages. Antitrust settlement as a tool, with no clear winners or losers, seemed to achieve a happy ending for both U.S. and European antitrust enforcement. And, while in medicine science researchers studied how to improve chemotherapy for cancer; the antitrust community strives to promote antitrust settlements addressing its contraindications.

As a PhD in law, what first struck me was how a simple agreement (which in my mind was a contract) could regulate markets and drive our economy by changing the dynamics of the affected markets. At least in Europe, antitrust settlements involve no regulators, or court examination: but private parties and watchdogs. Second, given that no finding of liability is made and no fine imposed, the increasing adoption of antitrust settlements seemed to sacrifice deterrence of competition law.

Looking for insights into the U.S. antitrust context and its century of experience on antitrust settlements, it turned out that the context where such bargaining tools were applied was completely different. In contrast to the European Competition Authorities, the FTC is a regulatory agency and the agreements reached with the DOJ to settle civil antitrust proceedings are enshrined in a judge act—the consent decree. The regulation effects of consent decrees are undisputed and the legitimacy powers of the FTC and courts to regulate markets is not an issue, as well it is in Europe.

Furthermore, the deterrent effect of the U.S. antitrust law was ensured through private enforcement mechanism and not the public one; thus, antitrust settlements did not necessarily sacrifice antitrust deterrence.

Here seemed to be all my answers. Commitment decisions are *de facto* regulatory tools, and the legitimacy issue of European competition agencies can be solved requiring the courts' revision of commitments. Despite the fact that commitment decisions do not find liability or impose any fines, deterrence of competition law can be better preserved reinforcing private enforcement, having any private party as an antitrust enforcer.

However, the U.S. experience provided me more questions than answers. While my initial inquiries were addressed, there remained an unresolved challenge for the U.S. consent decrees' success story. How do consent decrees who prevent judge's rulings preserve the enunciating effect of antitrust law? Legal rules are public goods, and private judges are not well suited to providing an authoritative interpretation or creating law.

In summary, the U.S. antitrust experience, along with remedies for promoting the main antitrust enforcement tool, urges us to explore a more critical question. The judicial system must establish rules, and this duty is not discharged through settlements, which conversely rapidly and surgically regulate markets. This gives rise to the question: Is competition law truly a law, or does it more closely resemble an economic regulation policy?

Law typically serves to recognize and protect rights. Contract law, for example, recognizes and protects the rights of parties who enter into in an agreement. Regulation is neither a law nor best practice, but "the pattern of government intervention in the market,"[1] which aims to achieve market efficiency. In 1890 the U.S. Congress, probably affected by the Adam Smith's concept of competition and cartels, recognized competition as a right, enacting the first competition law. At that time, nobody—not even Senator Sherman—would have predicted the evolution of competition law; the main concern was to contrast the increasingly powerful Standard Oil trust.

But since 1890 antitrust law goals have changed. The current antitrust core mission is consumer welfare protection, ensuring low prices, and even higher quality products through innovation.[2] The evolution of markets that are dynamic and unpredictable requires competition law to be flexible and dynamic to be effective. Antitrust settlements appear to be exactly the tool that competition law needs.[3] But, law must be certain, and by definition law is neither dynamic nor flexible.

Moreover, as Richard A. Posner observed, the legislative production is a costly bargaining process among a large group.[4] Yet, legislation does not seem to suit in

1. Richard A. Posner, *Theories of Economic Regulation*, 5 Bell J. of Eco. Management Science 335 (1974).
2. Herbert Hovenkamp, *Antitrust Enterprises* (Harv. U. Press 2009).
3. *See*, e.g., FTC, Speech of Deborah L. Feinstein, *The Significance of Consent Orders in the Federal Trade Commission's Competition Enforcement Efforts* (2013), https://www.ftc.gov/sites/default/files/documents/public_statements/significance-consent-orders-federal-trade-commission%E2%80%99s-competition-enforcement-efforts-gcr-live/130917gcrspeech.pdf at 4.
4. Posner, *supra* n. 1, at 335, 343.

markets that constantly change, always including even larger groups of individuals. And, Barry Hawk's suggestion that competition law is an economic law where "economics must play a predominant (if not exclusive) role in the examination of particular agreements"[5] is of little help. Elaborating a law that works as an economic regulation and defining it "economic law" is misleading. If competition law strives to strike consumer welfare in markets that are even more dynamic, there is a little room for law—economic regulation is a better fit. Judges deal with law, economists deal with markets and economic regulation; thus instead of wasting time and effort teaching economics to judges and law to economists, would it not make more sense to leave judges to create and interpret law and economists to grow our economy through the determination of the appropriate tool?

In summary, antitrust settlement is not a mere tool to enforce antitrust law, and this book is not merely a book on antitrust settlements. This book is a springboard to further investigate how a simple antitrust enforcement tool, having turned competition law into an economic regulation policy, can drive our economy leading both the antitrust and regulatory intervention in markets. In contrast to the most familiar competition law book, this book does not discuss competition law, but it rewrites competition law to enable competition authorities to pursue its goals in tackling today's market challenges.

In 2019, markets are no longer children as they were in 1890, but they grow up and evolved in something that is so dynamic and unpredictable that is difficult to manage preserving efficiency. Maybe, Adam Smith and the Schools which have been inspired by his theories are right again and as adults markets are better off with self-regulation. But also adults sometimes fail and need rules as well as markets, maybe shared rules, and antitrust settlements exactly respond to such a need. Perhaps, markets will evolve again passing also the adult age, and antitrust settlements will not be the appropriate cure anymore, as the cancer will not be the next day's illness. But if we do not know the disease, it is hard to find a cure. Thus, let us start from this book to put the puzzle together as best we can. And in reply to those who want to abolish competition law because it is vague and general, we can say that they are partially right. Antitrust law does not necessarily need to be abolished, but rather should be fully exploited as an economic regulation led by antitrust settlements.

In summary, the reason why I have written this book and I urge you to read it is that a simple tool within the framework of competition law drives our economy and seems to constantly be overlooked. As I said, the most attractive thing in research is that you know exactly what questions you are asking, but you have no idea what answers you will find, nor what other questions will emerge in the process. I was researching to develop a tool that would improve enforcement of competition law, and I have discovered how this tool was curing our economy from possible diseases day-by-day. Antitrust settlements need to be protagonists and deserve attention from the entire community of economists, not only the minority antitrust one.

5. Barry E. Hawk, *System Failure: Vertical Restraints and EC Competition Law*, 32 Common Market L. Rev. 973, 986 (1995).

This book is divided into three Parts. Part I provides a comparative analysis between U.S. consent decrees and European Union (EU) commitment decisions, which includes the analysis of the U.S. and EU antitrust law enforcement framework. Part II focuses on an economic analysis on the adoption of antitrust settlements in both the U.S. and EU markets from 2013 to 2018, investigating the different economic outcomes. Part III investigates the fundamental role of antitrust settlements in regulating the current digital markets, in addition to question the future of both antitrust law and antitrust settlements. Part III also examines the role of antitrust law in grappling with AI and blockchain technology providing some insights for the future. Antitrust settlements need to be considered beyond antitrust law as a fundamental tool in other economic areas such as data economics. Finally, some conclusions need to be drawn on the role of antitrust settlements and antitrust law in nowadays industries. My conclusions look at antitrust settlements as an economic driver and antitrust law as a subject that should be enforced more as an economic regulation rather than a law in all jurisdictions as well as markets.

PART I

# A Comparative Analysis Between U.S. Consent Decrees and EU Commitment Decisions Within the U.S. and EU Antitrust Law Enforcement Framework

When I started studying commitment decisions in Europe, as a PhD in law what first struck me was the idea that a simple agreement between the antitrust agency and the company subject to an antitrust investigation regulated the markets driving our economy. It took me a while to understand that in the United States the regulation effects of consent decrees were not only undisputed, but also quite obvious for U.S. antitrust scholars. In contrast to the EU Commission, the FTC is a regulator[6] and consent decrees reached between the DOJ and the companies subject to a civil antitrust litigation are enshrined into a judge order. Despite the similarities between the EU and U.S. antitrust enforcement tools, the context where commitment decisions and consent decrees are applied is completely different. After having compared the function, procedures, and characteristics of U.S. consent decrees with those of EU commitment decisions, an analysis of U.S. and EU antitrust laws' history and ideological framework is necessary.

Part I of this book is divided into three Chapters: Chapter 1 explains the characteristics of U.S. consent decrees, their functioning, and procedure emphasizing how the increase in the adoption of consent decrees led to a shift from an enforcement model of law into a regulatory regime. Chapter 2 examines the characteristics of EU commitment decisions, their functioning and procedure analyzing similarities and differences with U.S. consent decrees. Chapter 3 explores the U.S. and EU antitrust

6. The FTC "was designed to supplement the work of the Department of Justice and the courts under the Sherman Act. The job of the Department was to be primarily that of the prosecutor. The Commission, on the other hand, was meant to practice preventive law through administrative and regulatory activities as well as by the initiation and conduct of adversary proceedings." Edward F. Howrey, *Section of Antitrust Law of the New York State Bar Association, the Federal Trade Commission and the Administrative Process*, 1 (Jan. 28, 1954).

enforcement framework. Differing historical context along with disparate legal systems and approaches of enforcing competition law have led to the development of two very distinct antitrust law cultures in the U.S. and Europe, which in turn affect the practice of antitrust settlements (U.S. consent decrees and EU commitment decisions).

In summary, Part I engages in a comparative analysis between the U.S. consent decrees and the EU commitment decisions that explains the similarities and differences between U.S. and EU antitrust tools through the investigation of their differing antitrust framework.

CHAPTER 1

# A Century of U.S. Antitrust Law and Economic Regulation Marked by Consent Decrees

In 1890 when the first U.S. federal antitrust law had been enacted, there were not consent decrees. The introduction of consent decrees was the result of the evolution of U.S. antitrust law which, as outlined in Chapter 3, constantly promoted the role of economics and economic analysis in enforcing antitrust law.

Consent decrees are agreements between the FTC or the DOJ and companies to settle civil antitrust investigations. These decrees soon become the main (if not the only one)[7] tool of enforcing civil antitrust law provisions. Although the procedure to end an antitrust investigation by means of consent decrees before the two antitrust agencies diverge, the reasons behind the adoption of such a bargaining solution converge. Through consent decrees, antitrust agencies save time and money by imposing behavioral or structural remedies on the investigated companies, which appear as a form of regulatory regime.[8] Companies, in exchange for particular remedies, are able to avoid the risk of uncertain and expensive litigation, fines and damage to reputation. Through the adoption of consent decrees, antitrust agencies seek market efficiency goals directly by imposing procompetitive structural or behavioral remedies rather than requiring adjudication by courts.

With no clear winners or losers nowadays, consent decrees represent the main tool to enforce antitrust law and regulate markets as they are adopted to settle more

---

7. Joshua D. Wright & Douglas H. Ginsburg, *The Economic Analysis of Antitrust Consents*, 3 Eur. J. of L. and Economics, Forthcoming (Mar. 14, 2018). Available at SSRN: https://ssrn.com/abstract=3140736.
8. *See* Giovanna Massarotto, *The Deterrent and Enunciating Effects of Consent Decrees*, 11 J. Comp. L. & Econ. 493, 497 (2015); Giovanna Massarotto, *Antitrust Agencies, Watchdogs or Regulators?* 7 Geo. Mason J. Int'l Com. L. 39 (2015).

than ninety percent of civil antitrust lawsuits filed by the U.S. government (excluding mergers).[9]

Chapter I investigates the shift from an enforcement model of agency to a regulatory regime through the increased adoption of the *antitrust consent* examining remedies enshrined in some of the most crucial *antitrust consent* decrees. The procedure and the role of antitrust enforcers (agencies and judges) are also analyzed.

## §1.01 FROM AN ENFORCEMENT MODEL OF AGENCY TO A REGULATORY REGIME

Since the adoption of the first *antitrust consent* decree in 1906,[10] it has been clear that a bargaining antitrust solution, as well as a judge's ruling, would have affected the dynamics of markets. Different from judge rulings, consent decrees intervene in markets in a shorter period of time and with the consent of the company subjected to an investigation. Consent decrees have enabled the FTC and the DOJ to directly attain an antitrust solution without the uncertainty of a lengthy and costly trial given that the investigated company agreed with the terms of the final decision.

In 1914, with the enactment of the Clayton Act, consent decrees became more appealing and were adopted more readily.[11] Section 5 of the Clayton Act exempted consent decrees from being used as *prima facie* evidence in any proceeding against the same defendant[12] to seek treble damages. Specifically, as explored in paragraph *a*, § 1.02, under Section 5 of the Clayton Act no finding of liability is made and no fine imposed through a settlement solution.

In the period between 1906 and 1940, more than a quarter of the antitrust suits were settled by means of a consent decree.[13] In 1978, the adoption of consent decrees increased to eighty percent;[14] and nowadays civil antitrust lawsuits filed by the U.S. government (excluding mergers) are nearly entirely settled through consent decrees.[15] In the light of the regulation effects of consent decrees outlined below, the extensive use of such a bargaining solution led antitrust law to closely resemble a form of government regulation.

9. Wright & Ginsburg, *supra* n. 7, at 3.
10. Andrea Berger Kalodner, *Consent Decrees as an Antitrust Enforcement Device*, 23 Antitrust Bull. 277 (1978); Walton Hamilton & Irene Till, *Antitrust: The Reach after New Weapon*, 26 Wash. U. L. Q. 1 (1940)
11. Victor H. Kramer, *Modification of Consent Decrees: A Proposal to the Antitrust Division*, 56 Mich. L. Rev. 1051 (1958).
12. *See*, Phillip E. Areeda & Herbert Hovenkamp, *Consent Decrees*, Phillip E. Areeda & Herbert Hovenkamp, *Antitrust Law: An Analysis of Antitrust Principles and Their Application* 327, c) (Aspen Publishers, Supp. 2009). *See also* Kramer, *supra* n. 11.
13. Maxwell S. Isenbergh & Seymour J. Rubin, *Antitrust Enforcement Through Consent Decrees*, 53 Harv. L. Rev. 386, 387 (1940); William J. Donovan & Breck P. McAllister, *Consent Decrees in the Enforcement of Federal Anti-trust Laws*, 46 Harv. L. Rev. 885 (1933).
14. Kalodner, *supra* n. 10, at 277.
15. Massarotto, *The Deterrent and Enunciating Effects of Consent Decrees*, *supra* n. 8, at 493. Wright & Ginsburg, *supra* n. 7, at 3.

### [A] Consent Decrees as Rules of Regulation

*Antitrust consent* decrees usually occur in monopolization cases (typically concerning market leaders) and impose on the firms subject to an investigation behavioral or structural remedies[16] which establish a kind of regulatory regime.[17] In contrast to Europe, U.S. scholars have deeply investigated the regulation effects of antitrust settlements. Professor Douglas A. Melamed observed that by imposing mandatory obligations on the investigated companies, consent decrees represent a "new form of government regulation."[18] Similarly, Professor Richard A. Epstein defined consent decrees as "an opaque form of government regulation,"[19] confirming the fact that antitrust settlements regulate U.S. markets. In contrast to the EU Commission and EU commitment decisions, the FTC is a regulatory body and the DOJ's consent decrees are judicial acts.

Consent decrees primarily establish remedies to preserve competition, which *de facto* govern markets.[20] In contrast to the traditional rules of regulation, consent decree remedies are tailored to the competitive harm by providing a customized and time-sensitive solution for markets.[21] According to Professor Seymour J. Rubin and Maxwell S. Isenbergh, an extensive use of consent decrees reflects the adoption of "a more realistic approach to antitrust law enforcement."[22]

#### *[1] Structural Versus Behavioral Remedies*

Consent decrees can impose structural and behavioral remedies. The following analysis of some crucial *antitrust consent* decrees will show how remedies enshrined in such settlement solution *de facto* regulate markets. In contrast to rules enacted by a regulator such as the Federal Communications Commission (FCC), consent decree remedies are tailored to competitive harm and provide a targeted solution for markets.[23] Both the DOJ and the FTC modify firms' behavior and/or structure to encourage competitive conduct that increases consumer welfare[24] through such remedies.

The main structural remedies are the divestiture of a division, facility or product, while behavioral remedies usually require a firm to change the terms of its contracts or

16. *See* Daniel L. Rubinfeld, *Settlements in Antitrust Enforcement: A U.S. Economic Perspective*, in Claus-Dieter Ehlermann & Mel Marquis (eds.), *European Competition Law Annual 2008: Antitrust Settlements Under EC Competition Law*, at 90 (Hart Publishing, 2009). *See also* 3 Areeda & Hovenkamp, *supra* n. 12, at 151, 154.
17. Massarotto, *The Deterrent and Enunciating Effects of Consent Decrees*, *supra* n. 8, at 497.
18. Douglas A. Melamed, *Antitrust: The New Regulation*, 10 Antitrust 4, 14 (1996). ("[A]ntitrust has evolved in recent years, subtly and almost imperceptible, toward a new form of regulation.") *See also*, Michael L. Weiner, *Antitrust and the Rise of the Regulatory Consent Decree*, 10 Antitrust 4, 4 (1996).
19. Richard A. Epstein, *Antitrust Consent Decrees in Theory and Practice* vii (AEI, 2007).
20. Weiner, *supra* n. 18, at 6.
21. *See*, e.g., FTC, Speech of Deborah L. Feinstein, *supra* n. 3.
22. Isenbergh & Rubin, *supra* n. 13, at 386.
23. *See*, e.g., FTC, Speech of Deborah L. Feinstein, *supra* n. 3.
24. Weiner, *supra* n. 18, at 6.

business policies.[25] In price-fixing cases, for example, consent decree provisions can require price variation of its products,[26] while in antitrust cases that involve patents, the antitrust agency may require compulsory licensing.[27]

As behavioral antitrust remedies usually concern dynamic markets that are by nature dynamic, the DOJ often agrees to limit the time frame of the consent decree in addition to requiring a periodic supervision.[28] Ten years is generally the time limit imposed by the DOJ.[29] Furthermore, consent decrees usually require the defendant to send periodic reports to the DOJ to monitor and ensure the defendant's compliance with the terms.[30] These reports are sent annually for a period of ten years as well.[31] Thus, in contrast to structural remedies, behavioral remedies require constant monitoring, implying high costs and significant time required by the DOJ.[32] However, behavioral remedies that were originally criticized in the 2004 version of the DOJ/FTC Merger Guidelines were favored in the 2011 version.[33] Today, as the Roundtable on Consent Decrees of April 2018 revealed, the DOJ gives preference to structural remedies,[34] at least in the context of mergers.

To understand how in practice consent decrees regulate markets/industries and their impact on the affected markets/industries an analysis of remedies enshrined into

25. American Bar Association's (ABA) case provides a good example of behavioural remedies enshrined into a consent decree that regulated the ABA accreditation process. According to the DOJ, the ABA process for accrediting law schools would have been "misused to inflate faculty salaries and benefits" of law faculties, instead of guaranteeing quality legal education. To remedy such an antitrust concern, the consent decree imposed detailed behaviour remedies on the process for accreditation, regulating matters, such as membership criteria. The consent decree, for example, prohibited "fixing faculty salaries" and "[r]efusing to allow ABA-approved law schools to accept credits for classes at schools that are state-accredited but not ABA-approved." Department of Justice, Justice Department and American Bar Association Resolve Charges that ABA's process for Accrediting law schools was Misused (Jun. 27, 1995), https://www.justice.gov/archive/atr/public/press_releases/1995/0257.htm.
26. *See also* ABA Section of Antitrust, *Antitrust Law Developments*, 238 (ABA Book Pub., 7th ed., 2012).
27. *See* Areeda Phillip & Louis Kaplow, *Antitrust Analysis-Problems, Text, and Cases*, 416 (Aspen, 5th ed., 1997); *See* 3 Areeda & Hovenkamp, *supra* n. 12, at 149.
28. *See* ABA Section of Antitrust, *supra* n. 26, at 238.
29. *Ibid.*
30. *Ibid.*
31. *Ibid.*
32. With respect to behavior remedies, even if it concerns mergers, *see* Robert B. Bell, *Regulation by Consent Decree*, ABA Section of Antitrust, *supra* n. 26, at 73ff. In particular, see the author's considerations at 77. ("For many years the Division has taken the position that, with a few exceptions, regulatory remedies cost too much to administer, are easy to evade, and move the Division away from its proper mission as a law enforcement agency into a regulatory role for which it is ill suited. Recent decrees and the 2011 Remedies Guide reject that position.") *Ibid.*
33. *See* John E. Kwoka & Diana L. Moss, *Behavioral Merger Remedies: Evaluation and Implications for Antitrust Enforcement*, 2 (Nov. 14, 2011). https://papers.ssrn.com/sol3/papers.cfm?abstract_id=1959588.
34. DOJ, Public Roundtable Discussion Series on Regulation & Antitrust Law, Transcript Part One, 2 (Apr. 26, 2018) https://www.justice.gov/atr/page/file/1067496/download. ("[W]e've announced a renewed emphasis on seeking structural relief when possible as opposed to regulatory behavioral conditions.")

some of the most important *antitrust consent* decrees adopted from 1906 to date appears necessary.[35]

### *[a] The Telecommunication Industry and AT&T Consent Decrees*

Since the formation of the telecommunications industry it has been considered a natural monopoly in which a regulator—the FCC[36]—was necessary.[37] The U.S. government, however, considered the presence of a specific regulatory body insufficient to preserve a workable and competitive U.S. telecommunication market. Antitrust agencies in conjunction with the FCC have constantly monitored such a market, enforcing several antitrust regulatory consent decrees mainly to limit the monopoly of AT&T.[38]

In 1949, the DOJ filed a suit against AT&T, alleging that AT&T and its subsidiary Western Electric monopolized the telephone equipment market.[39] The DOJ argued that AT&T illegally foreclosed rivals from the equipment market, earning monopoly profits by means of terminations of purchasing contracts and acquisitions.[40] According to the complaint, AT&T violated Sections 1 and 2 of the Sherman Act, restraining competition in the manufacturing, distribution, sale and installation of telephones, telephone apparatus, equipment and materials and supplies.[41] Through its subsidiaries, AT&T supplied about 90 percent of all domestic and international long-distance service. By means of Western Electric, AT&T was also the largest producer of telephone equipment,[42] monopolizing all aspects of the telecommunications marketplace.

The antitrust investigation started in 1949 and ended in 1956 with a consent decree which required only conduct remedies. Section 5 of the decree, for example, established that AT&T was "enjoined and restrained from engaging, either directly, or indirectly through its subsidiaries [other than Western and Western's subsidiaries,] in

35. Melamed, *supra* n. 18, at 15.
36. FCC, *What We Do*, available at http://www.fcc.gov/what-we-do.
37. Paul W. MacAvoy & Kenneth Robinson, *Winning by Losing: The AT&T Settlement and Its Impact on Telecommunications*, 1 Yale J. on Reg. 2 (1984). *See also* Theon Van Dijk, *General or Specific Competition Rules for Network Utilities?*, 2 J. Network Ind. 93, 95 (2001); Nicholas Economides, *The Telecommunications Act of 1996 and Its Impact*, 11 Japan and the World Economy 455, 458 (1999). The main idea behind regulation was that it was necessary because the market for telecommunications services was a natural monopoly, and therefore a second competitor would not survive. *See* W. Kip. Viscusi, John M. Vernon & Joseph E. Harrington Jr., *Economics of Regulation and Antitrust*, 365 (MIT Press, 2005). ("To deal with the technologically progressive communications market, the Federal Communications Commission was established in 1934 to regulate broadcasting and to take over the duty of regulating the intercity telecommunications market from the ICC.") *Ibid.*
38. Brian M. Hoffstadt, *Retaking the Field: The Constitutional Constraints on Federal Legislation that Displaces Consent Decrees*, 77 Wash. U. L. Q. 53 (1999).
39. *See* Fred W. Henck & Bernard Strassburg, *A Slippery Slope, the Long Road to the Breakup of AT&T*, 57 (Greenwood Press, 1988).
40. *See* Barry G. Cole, *After the Breakup: Assessing the New Post-AT&T Divestiture Era*, 59 (Columbia U. Press, 1991).
41. The complaint is reprinted *in Consent Decree Program of the Department of Justice Hearings Before the Antitrust Subcommittee (No. 5) of the Committee on the Judiciary pt. I1 Vol. I, 85th Cong., 2d Sess. I, 54 (1958)*, at 1719. The complaint was primarily the result of a report by the FCC following a four years investigation of the telephone industry in the United States.
42. *See*, e.g., MacAvoy & Robinson, *supra* n. 37, at 1, 3.

any business other than the furnishing of common carrier communications services."[43] Nevertheless, this section was not applicable to several services, such as furnishing services or facilities for the plaintiff or any agency thereof, or experiments for the purpose of testing or developing new common carrier communications services. In short, the consent decree precluded AT&T from providing unregulated services.[44] Furthermore, it included the retention of the courts' jurisdiction to modify or terminate the decree in case circumstances would have changed.[45]

The AT&T consent decree of 1956 was crucial in the development of Unix, the first and most important universal computer operating system.[46] Although AT&T developed the Unix operating system for private use in 1969, AT&T could not sell Unix because the terms of the consent decree of 1956 prevented AT&T from selling software, such as Unix.[47] As a consequence, AT&T decided to freely license the Unix operating system to universities, which soon became the most important universal operating system[48] due to its network effects and the underlying language of the Internet.

In 1974, the DOJ filed a new antitrust suit against AT&T, Western Electric, and Bell Telephone Laboratories, Inc., seeking the vertical divestiture of Bell operating companies (BOCs).[49] This phase was called "the AT&T divestiture era." At that time, William F. Baxter, a renowned law professor at Stanford University, was the Assistant Attorney General and Charles L. Brown the AT&T chairman. Charles L. Brown worked for AT&T since the age of eighteen, almost all of his working life, and became chairman in April 1977.[50] Brown's approach to competition was curious. Brown was far from being a strong opponent of competition. "Competition is here and it is growing," and AT&T, said Brown, "is ready without preconceptions to explore alternative futures."[51]

The trial began on January 15, 1981, before the District Court. Judge Harold H. Greene, who actively participated in the determination of the terms of the decree, stated that AT&T:

> [was] violating the antitrust laws by various monopolistic practices ... [and] as a consequence of these practices (1) defendants have achieved and ... maintain[ed] a monopoly of telecommunications service and equipment; (2) competition in these areas ha[d] been restrained; and (3) purchasers of telecommunications service and equipment ha[d] been denied the benefits of a free and competitive market.[52]

43. *United States v. American Tel. and Tel. Co.*, 552 F. Supp. 131, 178 n.196 (D.D.C. 1982).
44. *Ibid.*, at 138. *See also*, Stanley M. Besen & John R. Woodbury, *Regulation, Deregulation, and Antitrust in the Telecommunications Industry*, 28 Antitrust Bull. 39, 50 (1983).
45. *United States v. Western Electric Co., Inc.*, 1956 Trade Cas. (CCH) 68, 246 at 71,143 (D.N.J. 1956).
46. David McGowan, *Between Logic and Experience: Error Costs and United States v. Microsoft Corp.*, 20 Berkeley Technology L. J. 1186, 1208 (2005).
47. *United States v. AT&T*, 552 F. Supp. 131, 138 (D.D.C. 1982).
48. Laura Lambert, *Internet: A Historical Encyclopedia*, 138 (MTM Pub., 2005). The development of Berkley Unix "helped pave the way for the way for the open-source movement." *Ibid.*
49. Paul W. MacAvoy, *The Failure of Antitrust and Regulation to Establish Competition in Long-Distance Telephone Services*, 8 (AEI Press, 1996).
50. *See* Cole, *supra* n. 40, at 5.
51. *Ibid.*
52. *United States v. AT&T*, 461 F. Supp. 1314, 1318 (1978).

AT&T's defense was extremely onerous, involving around two hundred fifty witnesses, tens of thousands of pages of documents, [53] and over 24,000 pages of trial transcript. A year later, William F. Baxter and Charles L. Brown reached an agreement to settle the government's suit which leads to the largest corporate separation since 1911—the dismantling of Standard Oil.[54]

As the 1982 consent decree was a modification of the 1956 version, it was referred to as the Modification of Final Judgment (MFJ). The MFJ required AT&T to divest seven subsidiaries out of its twenty-two BOCs that provided long-distance service. The theory underpinning that consent decree was the Baxter "quarantine theory,"[55] according to which the solution to AT&T's monopolization was to "separate—quarantine—the competitive and potentially competitive from the monopoly portion of AT&T." Furthermore, the theory considered it necessary that AT&T "divested [its] local exchange companies to provide all long-distance carriers equal access and service to their bottleneck local facilities."[56]

In addition to the divestiture, the MFJ established that "[t]he Bell operating Companies are prevented from engaging in any 'non monopoly' business in an effort to eliminate their ability to abuse their position of dominance."[57] Moreover, it "specifically barred the divested telephone companies from manufacturing or marketing customer premises equipment, providing long-distance service, providing directory advertising such as the Yellow Pages, and from offering services where they controlled the information content."[58] After the divestiture, AT&T continued to operate the long-distance and manufacturing units of its remaining BOCs. The MFJ is recognized as the first of two major regulatory interventions in the U.S. telecommunications industry.[59]

---

53. *United States v. AT&T*, 522 F. Supp. 131 at 140.
54. *See* Cole, *supra* n. 40, at 5.
55. *See*, e.g., Gregory J. Sidak & Daniel F. Spulber, *Deregulatory Takings and Regulatory Contract, the Competitive Transformation of Network Industries in the United States*, 55–99 (Cambridge U. Press, 1997); Howard A. Shelanski & Gregory J. Sidak, *Antitrust Divestiture in Network Industries*, 1 U. Chi. L. Rev. 1, 68 (2001); *see also* William J. Baumol & Gregory J. Sidak, *Toward Competition in Local Telephony*, 130 (MIT Press, 1994).
56. *See* Cole, *supra* n. 40, at 7.
57. *See* e.g., Harry M. Shooshan III, *Disconnecting Bell: The Impact of the AT&T Divestiture*, 19 (Pergamon Press, 1984). Moreover, Judge Greene "barred AT&T from using the Bell name or logo except in connection with Bell Labs, leaving that trademark in the hands of the divested local operative companies." *Ibid.*
58. *Ibid.*
59. *See*, e.g., Damien Geradin & Gregory J. Sidak, *European and American Approaches to Antitrust Remedies and the Institutional Design of Regulation in Telecommunications* (Dec. 18, 2003), Handbook of Telecommunications Economics, Vol. 2, Technology Evolution and the Internet, 517-553 (Sumit K. Majumdar, Ingo Vogelsang, and Martin E. Cave, eds., Elsevier B.V., 2005). ("If a single firm is the object of the antitrust case, and if it is prominent enough in its industry (we will avoid using the loaded term 'dominant'), then the consent decree becomes the *de facto* asymmetric regulation of the entire industry. The most obvious example is the Modification of Final Judgment, by which the federal judiciary governed the telecommunications industry after the antitrust breakup of the Bell System in January 1982 until Congress enacted the Telecommunications Act in February 1996. A more recent example, of course, is the Microsoft case.") *See also* Hoffstadt, *supra* n. 38. ("[A]t the time Telecommunication Act became law, the major participants in the telephone industry were already governed by a series of consent decrees administered by the District Court of the District of Columbia: the AT&T Consent Decree

AT&T is the exemplary case representing the regulation effects of consent decrees and likely the most studied U.S. antitrust case, which divided scholars into two camps. For the reason that the AT&T consent decree created "a vertically fragmented industry structure",[60] Robert W. Crandall considered it unsustainable and unnecessary. Similarly, Gregory J. Sidak noted that the introduction of ever-new technologies constantly change telecommunications market and structural remedies in that market are both unnecessary and unworkable.[61] According to Richard A. Epstein, the AT&T case is "the most vivid illustration of a consent decree process gone wrong."[62] However, AT&T's consent to divestiture "was the most successful antitrust structural remedy in history",[63] according to Richard A. Posner.

Although the MFJ is often criticized, it does deserve credit for marking the end of the AT&T monopoly era which started at the beginning of 1900s.[64] Following the MFJ, AT&T's market share decreased significantly and the telecommunications market never looked the same. The MFJ might not be the best procompetitive relief, but it was time-sensitive and perhaps the only way to *de facto* interrupt a monopoly in one of the most fundamental markets.

The AT&T divestiture, for example, led to a decrease in the price of distance calls. According to the FCC, the price of a long distance call dropped "from 32 cents per minute to 7 cents per minute"[65] from 1984 to 2006, more than 85 percent. Despite the fact that the AT&T's market share has been decreasing, according to the FCC's 1995 study, AT&T increased its output by two-thirds over 1984 levels.[66] In other words, since

regulated the participation of AT&T and its Bell operating companies in various telecommunications markets.") *Ibid.*, at 55; Christopher S. Yoo, *The Enduring Lessons of the Breakup of AT&T: A Twenty-Five Year Retrospective*, 61 Fed. Comm. L. J. 1 (2008). ("The breakup of AT&T represents an ideal starting point for examining the major threads of telecommunications policy that have emerged over the past quarter century.") *Ibid.*, at 2; *See also* Kenneth A. Nickolai, *The AT&T Divestiture: For Whom Will the Bell Tool?*, 10 William Mitchell L. Rev. 507 (1984). ("The breakup of The American Telephone & Telegraph Company (AT&T) has caused a revolution in the structures used to provide telecommunications service to American families and business.") *Ibid.*, at 507-508.

60. Robert W. Crandall, *The Remedy for the "Bottleneck Monopoly" in Telecom: Isolate It, Share It, or Ignore It?*, 72 U. Chi. L. Rev. 3, 4 (2005).
61. *See* Gregory J. Sidak, *How Does the Experience of U.S. Telecommunications Regulation Inform the Forced Sharing of Intellectual Property Rights under Global Competition Law?* (May 17, 2012) available at SSRN: https://ssrn.com/abstract=2061895 or http://dx.doi.org/10.2139/ssrn.2061895; Gregory J. Sidak, *The Failure of Good Intentions: The WorldCom Fraud and the Collapse of American Telecommunications after Deregulation*, 20 Yale J. On Reg. 207 (2003).
62. Richard A. Epstein, *The AT&(and)T Consent Decree: In Praise of Interconnection Only*, 61 Federal Communications L. J. 149 (2008).
63. Richard A. Posner, *Antitrust Law*, 111 (Univ. Chicago Press, 2d., 2001).
64. Regulation of the U.S. telecommunications market was marked by two important antitrust lawsuit that the U.S. DOJ brought against AT&T. The AT&T case filed in 1949, and second one started in 1974.
65. FCC, Trend in Telephone Service—Industry Analysis and Technology Division Wireline Competition Bureau (August 2008), https://archive.org/stream/FccTrendsInTelephoneService/FCC-Trendsintelephoneservice_djvu.txt. The FCC specified that "[t]he average price of 7 cents per minute represents a mix of international calling (10 cents per minute) and domestic interstate calling (6 cents per minute)." *Ibid.*
66. FTC, Measurements of Market Power in Long Distance Telecommunications, 4 (April 1995) available at https://www.ftc.gov/sites/default/files/documents/reports/measurements-market-power-long-distance-telecommunications/232316_0.pdf.

AT&T's break-up, industry output (measured by the number of calling minutes) has nearly tripled. Furthermore, the AT&T divestiture reduced prices for customer equipment and services which became more competitive.[67]

### *[b] Microsoft and the Market of Operating Systems*

In 1975, a few years later the IBM *unbundling decision* of 1969,[68] Bill Gates and Paul Allen funded the Microsoft partnership.[69] The IBM *unbundling decision* required IBM to sell its hardware and software separately,[70] allowing software development companies to enter the operating systems market and compete with IBM.[71] The IBM unbundling decision led to the creation of the operating systems market.

Microsoft's true stroke of luck was developing the operating system for IBM's personal computers (IBM PC). According to the DOJ, at the time of the unbundling decisions, IBM held 70 percent of the market share in the domestic market of computers.[72] By 1983, 30 percent of the world's computers ran Microsoft's software. On November 20, 1985, Microsoft released Microsoft Windows and on May 22, 1990, launched Windows 3.0. In 1990, Microsoft Windows held over 90 percent of the world's personal computers (PC) market. As the company resembled a quasi-monopoly, the U.S. antitrust watchdogs started investigating Microsoft's business strategy.[73]

On July 15, 1994, the DOJ filed a complaint against Microsoft (*Microsoft I*), alleging that Microsoft engaged in exclusionary and anticompetitive conduct. Certain Microsoft licenses required Original Equipment Manufacturers (OEMs) to pay a "per-processor" licensing fee for all units they shipped, whether or not these used Microsoft's operating system. Microsoft also backed up its exclusive-dealing regime, negotiating OEMs' minimum purchase amounts. The result was that any OEM who

---

67. *Ibid.*
68. *See*, e.g., James Pethokoukis, *Taking a Second Look at the Idea that Antitrust Action Created the US Software Industry* (Jan. 12, 2018) http://www.aei.org/publication/taking-a-second-look-at-the-idea-that-antitrust-action-created-the-u-s-software-industry/. ("IBM implemented a software unbundling policy due to scrutiny from the antitrust suit. This allowed a software industry to emerge.") *Ibid.*
69. *Ibid.*
70. According to the DOJ, at that time IBM held 74 percent of the market of general-purpose digital computers. *See* John E. Lopatka, *United States v. IBM: A Monument to Arrogance*, 68 Antitrust L. J. 145, 147 (2000).
71. Martin Campbell-Kelly, William Aspray, Nathan Ensmenger & Jeffrey R. Yost, *Computer, a History of the Information Machine* (Westview Press, 3rd ed., 2014).
72. *See* Martin Campbell-Kelly, *From Airline Reservations to Sonic the Hedgehog: A History of the Software*, 109 (MIT Press, 2004).
73. *See United States v. Microsoft Corp.*, Memorandum Opinion (Feb. 14, 1995); *United States v. Microsoft Corp.*, 56 F.3d. 1448, 1451 (1995). *See also* Richard J. Gilbert & Michael L. Katz, *An Economist's Guide to U.S. v. Microsoft*, 15 J. Economic Perspective 25, 26 (2001). "After nearly three years of investigation, the five-member Commission failed to support the legal staff's desire to bring a suit against Microsoft (the vote was 2-2; one commissioner had not participated.)" Daniel L. Rubinfeld, *Maintenance of Monopoly: U.S. v. Microsoft (2001)*, in John E. Kwoka Jr. & Lawrence J. White, eds., The Antitrust Revolution: Economics, Competition, and Policy 532 (Oxford U. Press, 2004).

adopted a rival operating system was obligated to pay twice the fee for the privilege. On July 15, 1994, the DOJ and Microsoft filed a consent decree to settle that case. The proposed settlement prohibited Microsoft "from entering into per processor licenses, licenses with a term exceeding one year [], licenses containing a minimum commitment, and unduly restrictive nondisclosure agreements."[74] For example, Microsoft could not condition or tie the Microsoft operating system license to the license of a different operating system product. In addition, the agreement banned Microsoft from adopting certain arrangements, such as variants of per-processor licensing and lump-sum pricing.[75]

On August 21, 1995, the *Microsoft I* case was concluded in court by means of a consent decree that imposed the above-mentioned behavioral remedies which focused on limiting certain Microsoft license practices intended to foreclose competition.[76] However, Microsoft launched a new operating system tied to the latest version of its browser (Internet Explorer 4)[77]—this was the beginning of the *Microsoft II* case. When Microsoft released its new operating system tied to Internet Explorer, there was concern that Microsoft was violating the terms of the 1995 consent decree which banned Microsoft from tying its operating system to the license of other operating system products.

On October 20, 1997, the DOJ considered Microsoft's conduct a violation of the 1995 consent decree terms and petitioned the District Court seeking civil contempt.[78] On December 11, 1997, Judge Jackson ordered Microsoft to offer Internet Explorer and the Windows 95 operating system separately. However, on May 12, 1998, the Court of Appeal reversed the District Court's order recognizing that Internet Explorer and Windows 95 constituted an "integrated product."[79]

On May 18, 1998, the DOJ filed a new suit against Microsoft—*Microsoft III*—claiming that the technological giant had both monopolized the market of operating systems for PC and used its monopoly power to monopolize other markets. According to the DOJ, Microsoft violated Section 1 of the Sherman Act by engaging in a number of anticompetitive practices related to operating system licenses with OEMs and contracts with Internet Service providers (ISPs). Furthermore, Microsoft tied its

74. *United States v. Microsoft Corp.*, 56 F.3d. 1448, 1452 (1995).
75. *Ibid.*
76. Microsoft could "not enter into any License Agreement in which the terms of that agreement [were] expressly or impliedly conditioned upon: (i) the licensing of any other Covered Product, Operating System Software product or other product ... or (ii) the OEM not licensing, purchasing, using or distributing any non-Microsoft product." *United States v. Microsoft Corp.*, No. 94 1564 (Aug. 21, 1995) available at https://www.justice.gov/atr/case-document/file/628481/download at 7.
77. Microsoft had previously required OEMs to install IE 4's prosecutor, IE 3, as part of Windows. According to Microsoft the merging of Microsoft Windows and Internet Explorer was the result of innovation and competition, that the two were now the same product and were inextricably linked together and that consumers were now getting all the benefits of IE for free.
78. Nicholas Economides, *The Microsoft Antitrust Case*, 4 (2001) available at http://www.stern.nyu.edu/networks/Microsoft_Antitrust.final.pdf.
79. *United States v. Microsoft Corp.*, 147 F.3d 935, 947 (D.C. Cir., 1998).

operating system (Windows) to its browser (Internet Explorer),[80] in violation of Section 2 of the Sherman Act.

At the same time, twenty states and the District of Columbia filed a complaint against Microsoft, alleging that Microsoft engaged in a range of practices to protect and maintain its monopoly in the operating system market, violating both federal and state antitrust laws. The DOJ's and the states' complaints were consolidated.[81] The court released its findings on November 5, 1999.[82] The court issued its conclusions on April 3, 2000, two days after settlement conversations had ceased.[83] The District Court was in favor of the DOJ on almost all points.[84] Ultimately, the court recognized that Microsoft violated Sections 1 and 2 of the Sherman Act.[85]

In 2001, the D.C. Circuit affirmed in part and reversed in part the District Court's decision, remanding the case to the District Court (but to a different trial judge) for defining a proper remedy consistent with a more limited scope of Microsoft liability.[86] The case was settled on November 12, 2002, after two years of litigation, through a consent decree that again imposed only behavioral remedies. The 2002 consent decree prohibited Microsoft to "retaliate against an OEM by altering Microsoft's commercial relations with that OEM, or by withholding newly introduced forms of nonmonetary consideration ... from that OEM."[87] Microsoft was not allowed to "restrict by agreement any OEM licensee from ... installing, and displaying icons, shortcuts, or menu entries from, any Non-Microsoft Middleware or any product or service that distributes, users, promotes."[88] Another set of prohibitions concerned non-discrimination and disclosure obligations.

In summary, the U.S. Microsoft Trilogy (*Microsoft I, II, III* cases) provides not one, but three symbolic examples of conduct remedies enshrined in consent decrees. Microsoft I, II, and III significantly affected the computer industry, changing the dynamics of a number of crucial markets, such as the operating system, browser, and

80. Microsoft's practices included giving its browser away "forever free," coercing third parties not to deal with or support competitive browsers, and to carry its browser in ways that disadvantaged rivals, and paying other browser suppliers' customers and distributors not to carry other browsers or to do so only on disadvantageous terms. (DOJ Complaint). The purpose of Microsoft was to limit "the commercial viability of the Netscape browser." Rubinfeld, *supra* n. 73, at 534.
81. Jay L. Himes, *Exploring the Antitrust Operating System: State Enforcement of Federal Antitrust Law in the Remedies Phase of the Microsoft Case*, 11 Geo. Mason L. Rev. 37 (2002). In particular "This was the first time that DOJ and the States went to trial together in an antitrust case. The DOJ and the States submitted joint papers throughout the liability and remedy proceedings before the District Court in the 1998-2000 period". *Ibid.*, at 51.
82. *United States v. Microsoft Corp.*, 84 F. Supp. 2d 9 (D.C.C., 1999).
83. *United States v. Microsoft Corp.*, 87 F. Supp. 2d 30 (D.C.C., 2000). *See also* Economides, *supra* n. 78, at 6.
84. *United States v. Microsoft Corp.*, 87 F. Supp. 2d 30 (D.C.C., 2000).
85. *Ibid.*, at 56. *See also* Rubinfeld, *supra* n. 73, at 535.
86. *United States v. Microsoft Corp.*, 253 F. 3d 34, 119 (D.C. Cir. 2001).
87. *United States v. Microsoft Corp.*, *final judgement*, No. 98-1232 (D.C.C. Nov. 12, 2002), available at https://www.justice.gov/atr/case-document/file/503541/download.
88. *Ibid.* The final judgment authorized the creation of an expert and neutral three person technical committee to oversee Microsoft activities including powers to interview personnel and examine documents.

PC application markets—in a pro-competitive way. In 1990, Windows held an overwhelming market share of over 90 percent,[89] while between January and April 2016 online usage of Apple systems, Google system and GNU/Linux (hence the usage of Unix-line kernel derivates) was higher than online usage of Windows.[90]

The DOJ argued that since the application of the consent decree in 2002, competition in middleware and PC operating systems markets significantly increased. For example, "[t]he increased competition Microsoft's Internet Explorer faces from web browsers such as Mozilla's Firefox, Opera, and Apple's Safari,"[91] or "[t]he decision by Dell and Lenovo to offer the option of computers pre-loaded with a Linux operating system rather than Windows."[92]

### *[c] Intel and the CPU Market*

On December 16, 2009, according to the FTC's complaint preceded in June 2008 by a subpoena, Intel had engaged in a series of anticompetitive behaviors in violation of Section 5.[93] In 2009, Intel was the undisputed leader in the markets for Central Processing Units (CPU), holding a market share of 75 to 85 percent. According to the FTC, Intel would have done to the still diversified market for Graphics Processing Units (GPUs), what it did to the CPU markets (of those chips for which Intel was the only supplier).[94] In other words, Intel preserved its monopoly in the market for x86 CPUs and, by leveraging its position in such a market, created a new Intel monopoly in the market for graphic processing units.

To monopolize a market a firm with dominant power can undertake several actions that violate antitrust law. These actions include predatory pricing, refusal to deal or tying conduct. Intel was seemingly engaged in all of these. According to the FTC Complaint, Intel increased prices or interrupted the supply to those OEMs that offered

89. DOJ, *U.S. v. Microsoft*: Proposed Findings of Fact (Updated August 2015) available at https://www.justice.gov/atr/us-v-microsoft-proposed-findings-fact-0.
90. *See* W3Counter, Browser & Platform Market Share (January 2016), https://www.w3counter.com/globalstats.php?year=2016&month=01; StatCounter Global Stats, Top 8 Operating System on April 2016, http://gs.statcounter.com/#all-os-ww-monthly-201604-201604-bar. *See also* Tim Worstall, *Microsoft's Share Drops From 97^ to 20% in Just over a Decade*, Forbes Tech (Dec. 13, 2012, 11:16 am), http://www.forbes.com/forbes/welcome/?/sites/timworstall/2012/12/13/microsofts-market-share-drops-from-97-to-20-in-just-over-a-decade/&toURL=http://www.forbes.com/sites/timworstall/2012/12/13/microsofts-market-share-drops-from-97-to-20-in-just-over-a-decade/&refURL=https://www.google.it/&referrer=https://www.google.it/.
91. DOJ, *Justice Department Tells Court that Microsoft Settlement Promotes Competition and Consumer Choice* (Aug. 30, 2007), https://www.justice.gov/archive/opa/pr/2007/August/07_at_673.html.
92. *Ibid.*
93. Complain, In the Matter of Intel Corp., No. 9341 (F.T.C. 2009), available at https://www.ftc.gov/sites/default/files/documents/cases/091216intelcmpt.pdf) (hereinafter FTC Complain in *Intel*).
94. *See* Justin Whitesides, *The FTC's Competition Policy after the Intel Settlement*, 9 DePaul Bus. & Com. L. J. 555, 565 (2011). In particular, the Intel complaint concerned four categories of conduct: (1) the chipmaker's exclusive agreements with computer manufacturers, (2) the deceptive software design, (3) the conduct in the GPU market, which includes tampering with interoperability, deceptive software design, and bundling to accomplish predatory pricing, and (4) Intel's misrepresentations in the standard-setting process.

non-Intel products, the production, and technology collaborations, reducing also the marketing support. In addition, Intel proposed "market share or volume discounts selectively to OEMs"[95] based on OEM market share.[96] Although there were no technical reasons for doing so, in 2003 Intel also redesigned its software library and compiler (the computer program that converts source code in a different computer language named object code or target language), which reduced the performance of rival CPUs related to Intel's CPUs. Intel also induced, or even paid, the suppliers of complementary hardware and software products to reduce and refuse providing assistance for non-Intel CPU products. Despite the fact that it was not common practice for independent software vendors (ISVs) to label their products as compatible with a specific microprocessor product, ISVs did so for Intel under Intel's pressure.

In August 2010 the FTC reached an agreement with Intel to settle the case and close the investigation. According to the FTC, the settlement went "beyond the terms applied to Intel in previous actions against the company,"[97] restoring competition and leaving Intel room to provide competitive pricing and innovation. The Intel consent decree, in addition to prohibiting Intel from offering market-share based discount and retailing against computer manufacture that used non-Intel products, imposed several conduct remedies on Intel:

> Intel had to:
> (1) "modify its intellectual property agreements with AMD, Nvidia, and Via [three of its major competitors] so that those companies have more freedom to consider mergers or joint ventures with other companies, without the threat of being sued by Intel for patent infringement;"[98]
> (2) "extend Via's x86 licensing agreement for five years"[99] which would have otherwise expired in 2013;
> (3) "maintain a key interface, known as the PCI Express Bus, for at least six years in a way that will not limit the performance of graphics processing chips;"[100]
> (4) "disclose to software developers that Intel computer compilers discriminate between Intel chips and non-Intel chips, and that they may not register all the features of non-Intel chips."[101]

Moreover, Intel was ordered to reimburse[102] all software vendors who wanted to recompile their software by using a non-Intel compiler.[103] Intel also agreed to pay AMD, its main competitor, USD 1.25 billion to settle all their antitrust and patent disputes.[104] In summary, the FTC imposed on Intel (who agreed) some specific and

95. FTC Complain in *Intel* at 3.
96. *Ibid.*
97. FTC, FTC Settles Charges of Anticompetitive Conduct Against Intel, Press Release (Aug. 4, 2010), http://www.ftc.gov/news-events/press-releases/2010/08/ftc-settles-charges-anticom petitive-conduct-against-intel.
98. *Ibid.*
99. *Ibid.*
100. *Ibid.*
101. *Ibid.*
102. *Ibid.* The FTC has the power to impose the award of monetary relief.
103. Decision and Order, *In the Matter of* Intel Corp., No. 9341 (F.T.C. 2010), at 15, http://www .ftc.gov/os/adjpro/d9341/101102inteldo.pdf.
104. *Ibid.*

quite significant conduct remedies that affected the dynamics of the CPU market in a pro competitive sense. In 2010, Intel held more than 80 percent global market share in computer microprocessors, while in 2014 Intel market share decreased to 67 percent[105] reaching 58 percent market share in 2018.[106] Despite the fact that Intel's market share decreased, Intel's revenue significantly increased: from USD 38.3B in 2007 to more than USD 62.76B in 2017[107] and USD 70.85B in 2018.[108] According to Intel reports, Intel revenue increased up 13 percent year-over-year.[109]

### [B] Some Considerations

An extensive adoption of consent decrees to settle antitrust investigations opened by both the DOJ and the FTC has turned antitrust law into a regulatory policy. Antitrust law increasingly resembles a form of economic regulation based on tailored remedies defined through the *antitrust consent*. Antitrust settlements are regulatory tools that have the benefit of being flexible.[110] Market players have knowledge of markets that an antitrust agency might ignore, and their involvement in the definition of appropriate markets' rules could turn out to be essential.

Regulation and antitrust are not separate issues. As Walton Hamilton and Irene Till observed, the *antitrust consent* decree is "an instrument of industrial government,"[111] which became the main antitrust enforcement tool in the U.S.

## §1.02 THE CONSENT DECREES PROCEDURE

Section §1.02 of this chapter investigates and compares the DOJ procedure with the FTC procedure to settle an antitrust investigation by means of consent decrees. While the DOJ is a prosecutor that needs a federal judge to evaluate and approve the terms of the consent decree (which is a judge's act), the FTC is an administrative agency[112] and administrative judges evaluate its decisions. Section §1.02 intends to emphasize the role of the DOJ, the FTC and courts in designing the terms of consent decrees.

105. Grafic Speak, AMD jumps 11 percent in GPU shipments in Q2, Intel up 4 percent, Nvidia slips (Aug. 19, 2014) https://gfxspeak.com/2014/08/19/shipments-intel-nvidia/.
106. Supantha Mukherjee, Intel shares slip on fears of AMD data center chip challenge (Jul. 27, 2008) https://www.reuters.com/article/us-intel-results-stocks/intel-shares-slip-on-fears-of-amd-data-center-chip-challenge-idUSKBN1KH1OT; Austin Buttler, *Ryzen v. Coffee Lake*: AMD loses market share at Mindfactory (January 2018), https://digiworthy.com/2018/02/06/amd-share-mindfactory-coffee-lake/.
107. Statista, Intel Dossier (2018), https://www.statista.com/topics/1877/intel/.
108. *Ibid.*
109. Intel, Reports First-Quarter 2018 Financial Results (Apr. 26, 2018) https://www.intc.com/investor-relations/investor-education-and-news/investor-news/press-release-details/2018/Intel-Reports-First-Quarter-2018-Financial-Results/.
110. *See* Hamilton & Till, *supra* n. 10, at 11, 18.
111. *Ibid.*, at 8.
112. Howrey, *supra* n. 6.

### [A] Consent Decrees Procedure Before the DOJ

At any time during a civil antitrust investigation before the DOJ, both the investigated company(-ies)[113] and the DOJ can ask to reach a settlement solution to close the investigation.[114] There is no deadline or precise time schedule to observe for settling a case through a consent decree and the DOJ can negotiate a consent decree with only some defendants in the same proceeding.[115] Despite the fact that a consent decree can occur "soon after the complaint is filed, after discovery but before trial, after the trial begins, after an adjudication of liability, or even after an adjudication of nonliability,"[116] the DOJ usually starts negotiating once the complaint is ready to be filed.[117] The DOJ Antitrust Division alleged its willingness to embrace consent decrees when the litigation would have led "to obtain no more for the public than [it would have] obtained by the entry of a consent decrees in the beginning,"[118] requiring the investigated parties to propose "constructive proposals which are in the public interest and which go beyond what the law required."[119]

Again, in contrast to the FTC consent orders, courts are involved in determining antitrust remedies enshrined in the consent decree[120] and their role has been increased over the years, in particular since the Tunney Act of 1974.[121] Originally, judges only certified an agreement already reached between the DOJ and the investigated

113. *See* Areeda & Hovenkamp, *supra* n. 12, at 25.
114. *See* Sigmund Timberg, *A Primer on Antitrust Consent Judgments and FTC Consent Orders*, 39 Brook. L. Rev. 567 (1972-1973); ABA Section of Antitrust, *supra* n. 26, at 719.
115. *See* U.S. Ebook case, *Chapter 6* at 127.
116. *See* Phillip & Kaplow, *supra* n. 27, at 53.
117. ABA Section of Antitrust, *supra* n. 26, at 238. In case the prospective defendant requests pre-filing negotiations, the DOJ policy's on civil antitrust cases to avoid undue delay in pre-filing negotiations, concludes such negotiations within thirty days. Usually "the complaint and the decree are entered simultaneously." Charles F. Phillips Jr., *The Consent Decree in Antitrust Enforcement*, 18 Wash. & Lee L. Rev. 39, 54 (1961).
118. Isenbergh & Rubin, *supra* n. 13, at 387, 388 *citing* Rep. Att'y Gen. 34 (1926).
119. *Ibid.*, at 388, *citing* Speech of Wendell Berge, Special Assistant to the Attorney General, *quoted in* (1938) 6 U. S. L. WEEK 282.
120. Consent orders "entered in FTC antitrust proceedings are far from ceremonial: they involve an elaborate process of negotiation and are scrutinized by the full Commission in order to determine whether they are in the public interest." *See* Timberg, *supra* n. 114, at 568.
121. *See* Janet L. McDavid, William A. Sankbeil, Edward C. Schmidt & Berry J. Brett, *Antitrust Consent Decrees: Ten Years of Experience under the Tunney Act*, 52 Antitrust L. J. 883, 885 (1983). Authors observed that "[i]n *Sam Fox Publishing Co. v. United States*, the Supreme Court rejected a prospective intervenor's claim that a consent decree provided inadequate relief and re-emphasized the government's autonomy in negotiating consent decrees: 'sound policy would strongly lead us to decline appellants' invitation to assess the wisdom of the Government's judgment in negotiating and accepting the ... consent decree, at least in the absence of any claim of bad faith or malfeasance on the part of the Government is so acting." *Ibid.*, at 888. *See* Phillip & Kaplow, *supra* n. 27, at 53. *See also* Gordon F. Hampton, *Current Antitrust Consent Decree Procedures: Should They Be Changed?*, 42 Antitrust L. J. 129 (1973).

company[122] through a judicial act,[123] and the judicial review of the agreement was considered their rubber stamp. In *Swift and Co. v. United States*, for example, the litigants submitted the reached agreement to the court on the same day that they entered the consent decree.[124]

In 1974, the U.S. Congress enacted the Tunney Act which required the judicial review of antitrust settlements to guarantee that the remedies offered in the consent comply with the public interest. Since the Tunney Act, courts started analyzing the reached agreement on merit,[125] and in several cases, such as Microsoft, courts denied the antitrust remedies proposed by the DOJ and refused to enact the consent decree.[126] In other cases, including the AT&T case,[127] the court identified the compliance with public interest in only a part of the agreement, not in the whole proposed terms.[128]

The AT&T case was one of the first cases in which courts experienced the Tunney Act provisions.[129] Though in the AT&T case, the Supreme Court summarily affirmed the court's evaluation of the antitrust agreement. Still, the case is helpful to understand the judge's approach in analyzing consent decrees after 1974. From an informal procedure of negotiations and agreements between private and public litigants to

122. *See* Thomas M. Mengler, *Consent Decrees Paradigms: Model Without Meaning*, 29 B. C. L. Rev. 291, 301 (1988). ("The Court thus viewed the consent decree as essentially a contract between the parties, which the approving court had properly rubber-stamped and which the interpreting court consequently should construe only narrowly.") *Ibid. See also* Timberg, *supra* n. 114, at 577. ("Because they are usually entered without any prior testimony or factual record and the parties have waived their constitutional right to trial, the courts tend to interpret or enforce them on the basis of their literal language, rather than in light of the basic purposes of the parties in agreeing to the consent settlement.") *Ibid.* Lawrence M. Frankel, *Rethinking the Tunney Act: A Model for Judicial Review of Antitrust Consent Decrees*, 75 Antitrust L. J. 549 (2008). ("Congress was concerned about judicial 'rubber stamping' of proposed decrees.") *Ibid.*, at 553.

123. *See*, e.g., Frankel, *supra* n. 122, at 549-622; Himes, *supra* n. 81, at 38.

124. *Swift & Co. v. United States*, 276 U. S. 311, 320 (1928). Isenbergh & Rubin, *supra* n. 13, at 387.

125. *See* Mengler, *supra* n. 122, at 298. (Justice Frankfurter agreed with the majority's resort to the judicial act paradigm: "Of course, the District Court had the power to modify the consent decree in order to effectuate its basic purposes. The fact that the decree embodied the agreement of the parties no more limited the power of the court than if it had been a contested decree.") *Ibid. See also* McDavid, Sankbeil, Schmidt & Brett, *supra* n. 121, at 889.

126. Sanford I. Weisburst, *Judicial Review of Settlements and Consent Decrees: An Economic Analysis*, 28 J. Legal Stud. 55, 59 (1999). ("The court may reject the settlement, leading to a new round of settlement negotiations (and if those fail, to a trial). Taking into account the effects of this process on the parties incentives *ex ante*, settlement negotiations become more difficult for the parties if they cannot predict what the court expects.") *Ibid. See also* Natalie L. Krodel, *The Tunney Act: Judicial Discretion in United States v. Microsoft Corp.*, 62 Brook. L. Rev., 1293 (1996). *See also* Celillianne Green, *The 1982 AT&T Consent Decree—Strengthening the Antitrust Procedures and Penalties Act*, 27 Howard L. Journal 1611, 1628 (1984).

127. 460 U.S. 1001 (1983); *United States v. American Tel. &Tel. Co.*, 552 F. 131 (D.D.C. 1982).

128. *See* Mengler, *supra* n. 122, at 308. ("Judge Greene found that although most of the decree's provisions served the public interest, some did not. He consequently refused to approve the proposed decree unless the parties agreed to several changes, which they did."). *See also* Green, *supra* n. 126, at 1611.

129. *See* Frankel, *supra* n. 122, at 551; Mengler, *supra* n. 122, at 308. ("Because Judge Greene was uncertain whether the Tunney Act actually governed the proposal by the Justice Department and AT&T, he followed Tunney Act procedures without deciding whether the Act actually applied to the proposal.") *Ibid.*

settling antitrust investigations, the Tunney Act of 1974 formalized the procedure of consent decrees by providing rules that are still applied today.[130]

### *[1] The Tunney Act of 1974 and the Role of Federal Judges*

In 1974, the Tunney Act regulated the procedure of consent decrees by amending Section 5 of the Clayton Act.[131] The Tunney act required the court's evaluation on the merit of the agreement reached between the DOJ and the defendant and granted third parties of the agreement the possibility to submit their comments on the terms and conditions of the agreement before the court's revision and approval.[132] The Tunney Act[133] aimed to restore the public trust in the government antitrust program by increasing the role of both federal judges and third parties affected by the antitrust agreement.[134]

#### *[a] Section 5 of the Clayton Act*

According to Section 5 of the Clayton Act, when the DOJ files its proposal of the consent decree with the district court, the text of the consent decree is published in the Federal Register for a period of at least sixty days before the court's final judgment. During these sixty days, third parties can submit their comments to the decree,[135] and both comments and the relevant governmental replies are published in the Federal Register.[136]

The DOJ has the duty to provide anyone, upon request, a communication on the competitive impact of the decree, which has to specify:

(a) the nature and purpose of the proceeding;
(b) a description of the alleged antitrust violations;
(c) an explanation relating to the proposed decree including extraordinary circumstances, which led to the submitted agreement and pre-empted the competitive effects of the proposed remedies;

---

130. This regulation seems recognized unlimited judge discretion over *consent decrees*. *See* Frankel, *supra* n. 122, at 549. ("The Act appears to yield almost unlimited discretion to district judges, and different judges have approached their task under the Act in very different ways.") *See also*, E. Thomas Sullivan & Herbert Hovenkamp, *Antitrust Law, Policy and Procedure*, 126 (Michele Company Law, 1, 1989).
131. McDavid, Sankbeil, Schmidt & Brett, *supra* n. 121, at 915. ("The Tunney Act was enacted to ensure that consent decrees are in the public interest. The act is essentially procedural; even prior to its enactment, many courts recognized their obligation to protect the public interest. The Tunney Act established mandatory and discretionary procedures to assist the courts in making their public interest determination.") *Ibid.*
132. *Ibid.*, at 884.
133. "The Tunney Act expanded and codified the judicial role in overseeing the entry of consent judgments in antitrust cases." *Ibid.*, at 885. *See also*, Mengler, *supra* n. 122, at 308.
134. *See*, e.g., Sullivan & Hovenkamp, *supra* n. 130, at 126; Deborah A. Garza, *The Court of Appeals Sets Strict Limits on Tunney Act Review: Microsoft Consent Decree*, 10 Antitrust L. J. 21 (1996).
135. Sullivan & Hovenkamp, *supra* n. 130, at 126, 127.
136. *See* Section 5(b), Clayton Act 1914. 15 U.S. Code §16(b).

(d) a description of the remedies available to private claimants that may have been affected by the antitrust violation;
(e) a description of the available procedures to amend the proposed decree;
(f) and, in conclusion, an evaluation and a specification of the alternative measure to the proposed decree.[137]

Furthermore, Section 5 requires that it be published "commencing at least 60 days prior to the effective date of the judgment described in subsection (b) of this section, for 7 days over a period of 2 weeks in newspapers of general circulation of the district in which the case has been filed, in the District of Columbia, and in such other districts as the court may direct"[138] a summary of both the terms incorporated into the proposed consent and the competitive impact statement, in addition to a list of the documents and materials considered meaningful for public comments.[139] During the sixty-day period or for an extended time period granted by the Court,[140] the United States (hence the DOJ) receives and records all submitted comments on the proposed consent decree.[141]

Before approving any consent decree, the court must determine whether the decree complies with the *public interest*,[142] considering: (*i*) the competitive impact; (*ii*) the enforcement and the provisions for modification, as well as the duration of the proposed relief; (*iii*) the effects of alternative remedies; (*iv*) public impact in general or, more specifically, on individual parties directly damaged by the investigated conducts;

137. *Ibid. See also* McDavid, Sankbeil, Schmidt & Brett, *supra* n. 121, at 885.
138. 15 U.S. Code §16(c). *See United States v. AT&T*, 552 F. Sup at 131, 147 (D.D.C. 1983). ("The legislative history shows that Congress was particularly concerned that the 'excessive secrecy' of the consent decree process deprived the public of the opportunity to scrutinize and comment upon proposed decrees, thereby undermining confidence in the legal system. In addition, the legislators found that consent decrees often failed to provide appropriate relief, either because of miscalculations by the Justice Department or because of the 'great influence and economic power' wielded by antitrust violators. The history, indeed, contains references to a number of antitrust settlements deemed 'blatantly inequitable and improper' on these bases.") *Ibid.*
139. Section 5(c), Clayton Act 1914. 15 U.S. Code §16(c).
140. That term cannot be reduced, except for exceptional cases justified by the Attorney General or his appointed. Section 5(d) statues that "[t]he Attorney General or his designee shall establish procedures to carry out the provisions of this subsection, but such 60-day time period shall not be shortened except by order of the district court upon a showing that (1) extraordinary circumstances require such shortening and (2) such shortening is not adverse to the public interest. At the close of the period during which such comments may be received, the United States shall file with the district court and cause to be published in the Federal Register a response to such comments. Upon application by the United States, the district court may, for good cause (based on a finding that the expense of publication in the Federal Register exceeds the public interest benefits to be gained from such publication), authorize an alternative method of public dissemination of the public comments received and the response to those comments."
141. *See* Section 5(d), Clayton Act 1914.
142. *See* Frankel, *supra* n. 122, at 555. ("The court 'has an independent duty to assure itself that entry of the decree will serve the interests of the public generally.' But 'public interest' is never defined, nor are judges given any real guidance on how to measure a decree against the public interest or when to use the additional procedures.") *Ibid. See also*, Hampton, *supra* n. 121, at 133.

(*v*) further antitrust considerations concerning the adequacy of the consent judgment;[143] (*vi*) and how the judgment would affect competition in the relevant markets. Section 5 does not require a court's evidentiary hearing or imply the court's permission to intervene in the proceeding.[144]

To evaluate the compliance of the agreement with the public interest, the Court has also the right to: (a) obtain witness statements by governmental officers and experts;[145] (b) appoint experts or advisors; (c) authorize the participation of third parties as *amicus curiae* in a phase or for the whole duration of the proceedings; (d) amend the written comments, replies and objections; and (e) carry out any activities deemed necessary by the judge to the public interest.[146] Not later than ten days from the sixty-day term mentioned above, each defendant must submit to the Court "a description of any and all written or oral communications by or on behalf of [the] defendant ... relevant to such proposal."[147]

Section 5 of the Clayton Act[148] also exempted consent decrees from being used as *prima facie* evidence[149] in any proceeding against the same defendant[150] to seek treble damages. Under Section 5 of the Clayton Act, no finding of liability is made and no fine imposed through a settlement solution. In the 1960s, the DOJ attempted to circumvent the Section 5 of the Clayton Act exemption by including the *asphalt* clause in consent decrees,[151] which allowed privates to use consent decrees as *prima facie* evidence in treble damages suits.[152] Because the U.S. Congress in the Section 5 of the Clayton Act

143. Section 5(e), Clayton Act 1914. 15 U.S. Code §16(e).
144. *Ibid.*
145. *See* Frankel, *supra* n. 122, at 611. ("A court ought to take if it needs more information is to invite the parties in for a hearing") *Ibid.* However, taking a testimony represents a residual relief. ("If the court's concern with the decree relates to clarity, enforcement, harm to third parties, or efficacy, it should seek evidence of the type on which the DOJ relied (for example, documents, party and third-party witnesses) rather than seeking to compel testimony directly from an official.") *Ibid.*, at 615.
146. *See* Section 5(f), Clayton Act 1914. The court, for example, can ask for "an additional written sub-mission from the DOJ to, for example, clarify its position, explain its reasoning, or provide information supporting a particular choice made in adopting the settlement." Frankel, *supra* n. 122, at 613.
147. 15 U.S. Code §16(g). However, an exemption exists. The exemption is "that any such communications made by counsel of record alone with the Attorney General or the employees of the Department of Justice alone shall be excluded from the requirements of this subsection." *Ibid.*
148. The Clayton Antitrust Act explicitly statues that: "any person who shall be injured ... by reason of anything forbidden in the antitrust laws may sue therefor in any district court of the United States ... ." 15 U.S.C. § 15(a).
149. *See* Section 5(h), Clayton Act 1914.
150. *See* Areeda & Hovenkamp, *supra* n. 12, at 327, c). *See also* Kramer, *supra* n. 11.
151. *See* Bernard Kaplan, *The Asphalt Clause—A New Weapon in Antitrust Enforcement*, 3 Boston College L. Rev. 355 (1962). The "asphalt clause" refers to the provision under which the consent decree has "a specified *prima facie* effect in favor of the plaintiffs in certain subsequent private treble damage actions for the same violation." *Ibid.*, at 355. *See also*, William Barnabas McHenry, *The Asphalt Clause—A Trap for the Unwary*, 36 N.Y.U. L. Rev. 1114 (1961).
152. Robert W. Stedman, *Consent Decrees and the Private Action: An Antitrust Dilemma*, 53 Cal L. Rev. 627, 638 (1965).

explicitly exempted consent decrees from being used as *prima facie* evidence,[153] the *asphalt* clause had a short life.[154] Judges simply ignored the *asphalt* clause when it was provided.

There is, however, no provision that prevents privates from using a consent decree in antitrust suits, and despite the fact that courts cannot consider consent decrees as *prima facie* evidence, such decrees could serve as a simple clue.[155] In *Michigan v. Morton Salt Co.*,[156] for example, the district court ruled in a treble-damage suit that a consent decree could not be precluded and the Government's initial action was admissible apart from *prima facie* effect of the decree.[157]

### *[b] The Role of Federal Judges*

The experience in enforcing the Tunney Act rules shows that judges have no clear idea of what their role is in the consent decree procedure. In AT&T case, Judge Greene played a fundamental role in determining the terms of the decree; Greene conditioned its approval on several changes. In *Microsoft I*, judge Sporkin refused to approve the proposed consent decree[158] because, according to him, it was too narrow and insufficient to reply to the antitrust concerns of the case.[159] Nevertheless, the Court of Appeal

153. *See* Areeda & Hovenkamp, *supra* n. 12, at 327, c) ("[W]hile Clayton Act §5(a) allows a litigated decree to be used as *prima facie* evidence of liability in subsequent private actions against the defendant, it explicitly prohibits that use of pretrial consent decree.")
154. Clark E. Walter, *Consent Decrees and the Judicial Function*, 20 Cath. U. L. Rev. 312, 319 (1971). In 1982, in *United States v. Brunswick- Balke-Collender Co.*, "[t]he court approved the decree without the 'asphalt clause' characterizing the government's apparent policy of seeking to advance the cause of private litigants as an 'unauthorized attempt on the part of an administrative agency to avoid Congressional intent as clearly set forth in the proviso in § 5 of the Clayton Act." *Ibid.*
155. *See Comments. Section 5(b) of the Clayton Act: The Tolling Effect of Government Antitrust Actions on Unnamed Parties*, 34 U. Chi. L. Rev. 906 (1967).
156. *State of Michigan v. Morton Salt Company*, 259 F. Supp. 35 (D.C. Minnesota, 1966). ("The Government's initial action may aid the private litigant in a number of other ways [apart from the prima facie effect of the judgment or decree]. The pleadings, transcripts of testimony, exhibits and documents are available to him in most instances.") *Ibid.*, at 45. The Supreme Court in "*3M* points out that the private litigant may receive invaluable aid from the pleadings, transcript, exhibits and documents in the Government suit, apart from the prima facie effect, if any, of these materials." *Ibid.*, at 48.
157. *Ibid.*
158. *See United States v. Microsoft Corp.*, Memorandum Opinion (Feb. 14, 1995); *United States v. Microsoft Corp.*, 56 F.3d. 1448, 1451 (1995). *See also* Garza, *supra* n. 134, at 22 (1996). ("Judge Sporkin stunned Microsoft and the DOJ by refusing to enter the decree.") *Ibid.*
159. The District Court did not initially found the consent decree was in the public interest and refused to enter it. It determined: (1) the DOJ had not provided it with sufficient information to make the required public interest determination; (2) the scope of the proposed consent decree was too narrow; (3) the proposed decree was not an effective antitrust remedy; (4) the proposed enforcement and compliance mechanisms were not sufficient. U.S. District Judge Stanley Sporkin took a very expansive view of his role under the Tunney Act. However, on appeal the court reversed this decision and held that the purpose decree was in the "public interest". ("The main issue was whether the district court had exceeded its authority under the Tunney Act in refusing to enter the decree.)" Paula L. Blizzard, *United States v. Microsoft Corporation*, 13 Berkeley Tech. L. J. 355, 361 (1998). *See also* Garza, *supra* n. 134. "Judge Sporkin insisted on opening up the DOJ's decision-making process. He demanded that the DOJ

recognized that the "court is not empowered to review the actions or behaviour of the [DOJ]; the court is only authorized to review the decree itself,"[160] during the Microsoft cases.[161] When parties proposed a settlement solution "there are no findings that the defendant has actually engaged in illegal practices."[162] In particular, the Court of Appeal stated that the Tunney Act "cannot be interpreted as an authorization for a district judge to assume the role of Attorney General."[163]

The judicial review is essential because it provides a precedent and guidance to comply with the law and to determine future antitrust remedies.[164] As the Court of Appeal for the Second Circuit recognized, consent decrees are of a public nature[165] and can, therefore, represent a model for the later decrees.[166] Although the court's review has increased for private litigants the costs of consent decrees' procedures,[167] approximately ninety percent of DOJ's civil antitrust cases (excluding mergers) are settled by means of consent decrees.[168]

### *[c] The Role of the Third Parties*

Section 5 of the Clayton Act, as modified by the Tunney Act, also allows the third parties injured by an anticompetitive conduct[169] to provide comments to the proposed consent as *amicus curiae,*[170] informing litigants about their interest in the proceedings

address alleged conduct—'vapoware,' in particular -not challenged in the complaint, and that the DOJ, in effect, show cause why the decree should not include relief sought by Microsoft's competitors". *Ibid.*, at 22-23. *See also,* Lloyd C. Anderson, *United States v. Microsoft, Antitrust Consent Decrees, and the Need for a Proper Scope of Judicial Review,* 65 Antitrust L. J. 1 (1996).

160. *United States v. Microsoft Corp.*, 56 F.3d. 1448, 1457 (D.C. Cir. 1995). ("The [district] court's authority to review the decree depends entirely on the government's exercising its prosecutorial discretion by bringing a case in the first place.") *Ibid.*, at 1460.
161. *See* Garza, *supra* n. 134. *Microsoft* contains limitations not explicitly stated in the Tunney Act.
162. *United States v. Microsoft Corp.*, 56 F.3d. 1448, 1461 (1995).
163. *Ibid.*, at 1461. *See also* Garza, *supra* n. 134, at 23.
164. *See* Weisburst, *supra* n. 126, at 66. ("The judicial review mechanism enables the court to expose the settlement to public view. Further, the judicial review mechanism allows for creation of 'precedents' of a sort—the court's opinion approving or rejecting the proposed settlement—that not only deter but also provide guidance to parties seeking to conform to the law.") *Ibid.*
165. 801 F.2d 578, 584, 585 (2d Cir. 1986).
166. Mengler, *supra* n. 122, at 317.
167. *See* Frankel, *supra* n. 122, at 596. ("[S]ome of the costs imposed by the Act are unavoidable, for instance, the cost to the DOJ of preparing the CIS, publishing the required documents, and responding to comments ... This additional cost, uncertainty, and delay can have an adverse impact on antitrust enforcement, and on the very public interest that the Act was meant to protect.") *Ibid.*, 596-597.
168. *See*, e.g., Massarotto, *The Deterrent and Enunciating Effects of Consent Decrees, supra* n. 8; Wright & Douglas H. Ginsburg, *The Economic Analysis of Antitrust Consents, supra* n. 7.
169. *See* Kramer, *supra* n. 11, at 321; Susan B. Dorfman, *Mandatory Consent: Binding Unrepresented Third Parties Through Consent Decrees,* 78 Marq. L. Rev., 153 (1994). *See also* Walter, *supra* n. 154, at 319; Mengler, *supra* n. 122, at 315.
170. McDavid, Sankbeil, Schmidt & Brett, *supra* n. 121, at 892. ("Although the courts typically deny third-party intervention in consent decree proceedings, they generally permit prospective intervenors to participate as *amici curiae.*") *Ibid.*, at 896.

and the nature of their claims. Courts have to consider third-party objections,[171] approving only those consent decrees that have no harmful ancillary effects on third parties' interests.[172]

Despite the fact that the Government tends to object third parties participation in the proceedings or in the definition of the agreement,[173] the so-called *outsiders*[174] have the right to become party in the proceedings. The Federal Rule of Civil Procedure 24(a)(2), states that "[o]n timely motion, the court must permit anyone to intervene who: ... (2) claims an interest relating to the property or transaction that is the subject of the action, and is so situated that disposing of the action may as a practical matter impair or impede the movant's ability to protect its interest, unless existing parties adequately represent that interest."

The Supreme Court has recognized the legitimate participation and right of intervention of private parties[175] directly affected by the antitrust violation; because the decree will not bind any outsiders,[176] courts usually deny third parties' contribution in settling or modifying the terms of the decree.[177] Consent decrees do not impede third parties to act in subsequent litigations, and in that respect, consent decrees are more similar to "private settlements than litigated decrees."[178]

In summary, the Tunney Act[179] has significantly changed the Courts and third parties' role in the consent decrees' procedure by allowing courts to evaluate the merit of the agreement reached among litigants and third parties to comment on that agreement.[180]

171. *See* Weisburst, *supra* n. 126, at 64.
172. Mengler, *supra* n. 122, at 316.
173. *See*, Areeda & Hovenkamp, *supra* n. 12, at 327 c). *See also*, McDavid, Sankbeil, Schmidt & Brett, *supra* n. 121, at 893. ("Efforts by third parties to intervene in consent decree proceedings have been regularly denied by the courts, both prior to and after enactment of the Tunney Act.") *Ibid.*, at 895.
174. In an antitrust procedure the parties are the United States, namely the DOJ or the FTC, and the defendant/s. Hence, with the term *outsider* I mean third parties, namely all the subjects that are not considered parties in the procedure.
175. 386 U.S. 129 (1967). *See also*, ABA Section of Antitrust, *supra* n. 26, at 240, 241.
176. ABA Section of Antitrust, *supra* n. 26, at 240.
177. *Ibid.*
178. Mengler, *supra* n. 122, at 317.
179. The Tunney Act was modified in 2004. That modification entailed that "the 2004 legislation made it clear that courts need to look at the substantive competitive effects of a decree, and not simply at ambiguity, enforcement, potential harm to third parties, and 'mockery of the judicial function.'" *See* Frankel, *supra* n. 122, at 570.
180. With respect to the role played by courts, *see* e.g., Frankel, *supra* n. 122, at 562. ("The court acknowledged that a district judge should not 'assume the role of Attorney General' by substituting its prosecutorial judgment for that of the Executive Branch, but recognised that even where the 'government is challenged for not bringing as extensive an action as it might' there could be extreme circumstances under which a court should decline to enter a decree—where entering the decree would 'make a mockery of judicial power.' ") *Ibid. See also*, Phillips, *supra* n. 117, at 41.

### *[2] Is it Possible to Modify a Consent Decree?*

The debate over the nature of consent decrees reflects on the possibility to amend the consent decree. There are those who consider the consent decree as a contract and those who consider the consent decree as a judicial act (thus amendable by courts).[181]

In 1932, the Supreme Court recognized in *Swift* that there were no doubts about "the power of a court of equity to modify an injunction in adaptation to changed conditions though it was entered by consent."[182] The party (the DOJ or the defendant) who seeks a change of the decree must provide a "clear showing of grievous wrong evoked by new and unforeseen conditions ...[183] [n]othing less than a clear showing of grievous wrong evoked by new and unforeseen conditions should lead us to change what was decreed after years of litigation with the consent of all concerned."[184] Thus, *Swift* clarified that courts can amend a consent decree on the condition that the requiring party presents clear and undisputed facts in support of the necessary and desirable amendment.

Ten years later in 1942, the Supreme Court ruled again on the amendment of consent decrees issue in *Chrysler Corp. v. United States*.[185] The DOJ required modifying a decree entered in 1938, which would have been rejected under the *Swift* test.[186] The Supreme Court embraced the DOJ's request through a different and more flexible test, questioning whether it was easier for the government than for the defendant to amend a consent decree.[187] In 1967, the Supreme Court clarified that the DOJ "has no authority to circumscribe the power of the courts to see that our mandate is carried out. No one except this Court, has authority to alter or modify our mandate."[188] Thus, judges could

181. The main school of thought argued for identified *consent decree* as a hybrid institution locates between a contract and a judge order. This position embraces both stances, namely who identifies *consent decree* as a contract, and who is inclined to consider it as a simple order of judge. The first position would limit the judge's discretion; hence the chance to modify the consent decree, on the contrary, the second perspective would make broader the judge power and easier its participation in the procedure. On this issue, Easterbrook alleged that "the terms of the consent decree should be adhered to absent a breakdown of 'some fundamental supposition of the contract.' If such a breakdown occurs, the decree should be dissolved and the case returned to the trial court. In the usual situation where the dispute involves smaller, unanticipated matters, modification is not justified unless the decree itself could be *interpreted* as providing for such modification." Jef Golfarb, *Keeping Rufo in Its Cell: The Modification of Antitrust Consent Decree after Rufo v. Inmates of Suffolk County Jail*, 72 N.Y.U.L. Rev., 625, 631 (1997).
182. In *United States v. Swift & Co.*, 286 U.S. 106 (1932), Justice Cardozo held that "we are not doubtful of the power of a court of equity to modify an injunction in adaptation to changed conditions though it was entered by consent." *Ibid.*, at 114.
183. *Ibid.*, at 119.
184. *Ibid.* McDavid, Sankbeil, Schmidt & Brett, *supra* n. 121, at 887. ("In United States v. Swift & Co., the court established procedures to assist it in determining whether a proposed modification of a consent decree was in the public interest.") *Ibid.*
185. 316 U.S. 556 (1942).
186. *Swift*, 286 U.S. at 119.
187. *See* Sullivan & Hovenkamp, *supra* n. 130, at 127.
188. *Cascade Natural Gas Corp. v. El Paso Natural Gas Co.*, 386 U.S. 129, 136 (1967).

choose either to appeal to the strict *Swift* test[189] or adopt the more flexible test used in *Chrysler*.[190]

In 1968, the Supreme Court intervened again on such an issue in *United States v. United Shoe Machinery Corp.*, recognizing that the *Swift* test does not preclude the government to require an amendment to decree in case the decree failed "to achieve the [pursued] establishment of *workable competition*."[191] Consistent with this assumption, the court's attitude changed in favor of any possible amendment to the decree.

In 1992 during *Rufo v. Inmates of Suffolk County Jail*,[192] which is not an antitrust case, the Supreme Court added something else stating that "a party seeking modification of a consent decree bears the burden of establishing that a significant change in circumstances warrants revision of the decree. If the moving party meets this standard, the court should consider whether the proposed modification is suitably tailored to the changed circumstance."[193] In 1995, in *Kodak* case[194] the Second Circuit, rejecting the *Swift* test applied a combination of principles stated in *Rufo* and *United Shoe*.[195] Under this combination, the court can modify or conclude a consent decree "guided by equitable considerations"[196] (*Rufo*) and the antitrust defendant need to be able to show that the antitrust violation pursued by the decree has been eliminated (*United Shoe*).

In short, courts recognized the judicial nature of the consent decree and the power of courts to amend the decree in the light of equitable considerations. To avoid misunderstandings many consent decrees now provide a specific clause that establishes the court jurisdiction to modify the decree if it is requested by one or both parties.[197] In particular, both the investigated company[198] and the

189. *See* Timberg, *supra* n. 114, at 572. "This standard was followed by two experienced antitrust judges in denying defendants' requests for modification: Judge Kloeb in *United States v. Owens-Corning Fiber Glass Corp.*, and Judge Ryan in *United States v. International Boxing Club of New York, Inc.*" *Ibid.*, at 572-573.

190. *See* Mengler, *supra* n. 122, at 299. "Unhappy with their restricted roles under *Swift*, some lower courts have relied on Chrysler or its progeny to modify a consent decree. *Chrysler*, like *Swift*, is alive and well." *Ibid.*, at 572-573.

191. *United States v. United Shoe Machinery Corp.*, 391 US 244, 249 (1968).

192. *Rufo v. Inmates of Suffolk County Jail*, 502 U.S. 367, 383 (1992).

193. *Ibid. See* Mengler, *supra* n. 122, at 298.

194. *United States v. Eastman Kodak Co.*, 63 F.3d 95 (2d Cir. 1995). This case concerns two decrees considered as relief against the antitrust violations carried out by Eastman Kodak from 1921 to 1954. Those decrees impeded companies to sell the private label of films or bundling selling of films and developing and printing service. *See* Golfarb, *supra* n. 181, at 642.

195. *See*, ABA Section of Antitrust, Antitrust Law Developments, 714 (6th ed., 2007).

196. *United States v. Eastman Kodak Co.*, 63 F.3d 95, 101 (2d Cir. 1995). *See also* Areeda & Hovenkamp, *supra* n. 12, at para. 327b).

197. *See* Section of Antitrust Law, ABA, Antitrust Consent Decree Manual, 60 (1979), which established the so-called *retention-of-jurisdiction clause* according to, "[j]urisdiction is retained by this Court for the purpose of enabling any of the parties to this Final Judgment to apply to this Court at any time for such further orders and directions as may be necessary or appropriate for the construction or carrying out of this Final Judgment, for the modification of any of the provisions hereof, for the enforcement of compliance therewith, and for the punishment of violations thereof." *Ibid.*

198. Specifically, the investigated company will seek to mitigate the restrictions imposed by the consent decree asking for its modification. David S. Konczal, *Note: Ruing Rufo: Ramifications of a Lenient Standard for Modifying Antitrust Consent Decrees and an Alternative*, 65 Geo. Wash. L. Rev. 130, 140 (1996).

DOJ[199] may request that the court who issued the consent decree make an amendment to the agreement for different reasons.[200] For example, the DOJ or the antitrust defendant can show that the markets affected by the decree were changed significantly making the consent decree obsolete or too expensive for company to comply with.

### [B] Consent Decrees' Procedure Before the FTC

The FTC, as well as the DOJ, can settle an antitrust proceeding through an agreement with the investigated company. Such an agreement is enshrined into an FTC order/decree and is not a proper judicial act.

The Supreme Court recognized the FTC as "the expert body to determine what remedy is necessary to eliminate the unfair or deceptive trade practices which have been disclosed" in *Jacob Siegel Co. v. FTC.*[201] Courts should not interfere unless the proposed remedy is unreasonable with respect to the investigated conduct.[202] Similar to consent decrees, FTC consent orders allow the FTC to quickly achieve an antitrust relief and resolve antitrust concerns, saving time and money in expensive and intensive litigations.[203]

Litigation is expensive and uncertain for the defendant, thus the FTC and the investigated company have incentives in settling a case by means of an agreement solution. The FTC antitrust settlement practice appears significant concerning 90 percent of FTC procedures.[204]

199. Usually the DOJ ask for a modification of the terms of the decree. *See Chrysler Corp. v. United States*, 316 U.S. 556 (1942).
200. *See* e.g., Konczal, *supra* n. 198, at 130; *See also*, Areeda & Hovenkamp, *supra* n. 12, at ¶327b); Golfarb, *supra* n. 181, at 625.
201. 327 U.S. 608, 612-613 (1946). *See also*, Paul G. Bower, *New Developments in FTC Remedies*, 41 Antitrust L. J. 465, 466 (1972).
202. *Ibid.*
203. *See* FTC, Remarks of Deborah L. Feinstein, *supra* n. 3. "And this example should make clear that our consent orders enable us to obtain relief as effective as what we can obtain through litigation." *Ibid.*, at 20.
204. FTC, Competition Enforcement Database, https://www.ftc.gov/competition-enforcement-database. *See also*, Douglas H. Ginsburg & Joshua D. Wright, *Antitrust Settlements: The Culture of Consent* (Feb. 27, 2013). William E. Kovacic, *An Antitrust Tribute—Liber Amicorum (Vol. I); George Mason Law & Economics Research Paper No. 13-18.* Available at SSRN: https://ssrn.com/abstract=2225894 ("By the 1950s, 87 percent of all civil antitrust cases brought by the Division were settled by consent decrees. By the 1980s, 97 percent of civil cases filed by the Division resulted in a consent decree, and that percentage remained relatively constant at 93 percent in the 1990s. This trend has continued, with the Division resolving nearly its entire antitrust civil enforcement docket by consent decree from 2004 to present. The Federal Trade Commission has experienced a similar increase in the use of consent decrees as a proportion of enforcement activity. FTC consent decrees more than tripled in number from 1992 to 1995. Since 1995, the FTC has settled 93 percent of its competition cases."). *Ibid.*, at § 1. *See also* Kalodner, *supra* n. 10; Steven C. Salop & Lawrence J. White, *Economic Analysis of Private Antitrust Litigation*, 26 J. Reprints Antitrust L. & Econ. 11 (1996).

### *[1] The Contents of the FTC Consent Orders*

Similarly to the DOJ consent decrees, consent orders do not impose any criminal sanction against a company.[205] FTC consent orders aim to prevent the reiteration of unlawful conduct[206] through an agreement entered among parties.[207] Again, the settlement solution imposes a kind of regulatory procompetitive regime by means of behavioral or structural remedies. The FTC consent order usually includes both a cease and desist order and behavioral or structural remedies.[208] For example, the FTC imposed a behavior remedy in *Rambus* when it ordered the company to fix maximum royalties for licensing its dynamic random-access memory (DRAM).[209] In the *Google* consent order of January 2013, Google agreed "to allow competitors access—on fair, reasonable, and non-discriminatory terms—to patents on critical standardized technologies needed to make popular devices such as smart phones, laptop and tablet computers, and gaming consoles."[210]

Again, the Supreme Court in *Jacob Siegel Co. v. FTC*[211] recognized the wide discretion of the FTC[212] in determining remedies enshrined in a consent order, and in *FTC v. Ruberoid* Co. clarified that "courts cannot take over the discretionary functions of the Commission."[213] In protecting competition, the FTC could require industry restructuring remedies by mandating a divestiture.[214] Despite the fact that in *FTC v.*

205. Phillip E. Areeda & Herbert Hovenkamp, *Antitrust Law, an Analysis of Antitrust Principle and Their Application II*, 21 (Wouters Kluwer, 4th ed., 2013).
206. This is provided by both the FTC Act and Commission orders, which, if violated, do not provide the right to claim against privates.
207. The Administrative Procedure Act (5 U.S.C. 554(c)). Specifically, it specified that "where time, then nature of the proceeding, and the public interest permit, every person with an interest in an adjudicative proceeding shall be granted the opportunity to submit facts, arguments and offers for settlement or adjustment. It is the policy of the Commission to make this opportunity available during or upon completion of the investigation (Rule 2.31(a)) as well as during adjudication (Rule 3.25)." FTC, Operating Manual, Chapter 6, at 1.
208. *See* ABA Section of Antitrust, *supra* n. 26, at 657. ("Section 5(b) of the FTC Act empowers the Commission, after notice and a hearing, to issue an order requiring a respondent found to have engaged in unfair methods of competition or unfair or deceptive acts or practices to 'cease and desist' from such conduct.") *See also* FTC, Operating Manual, *supra* n. 207, at 3.
209. FTC, FTC Issues Final Opinion and Order in Rambus Matter, Press Release (Feb. 5, 2007) https://www.ftc.gov/news-events/press-releases/2007/02/ftc-issues-final-opinion-and-order-rambus-matter. ("[T]he order requires Rambus to license its SDRAM and DDR SDRAM technology and sets maximum allowable royalty rates it can collect for the licensing, bars Rambus from collecting or attempting to collect more than the maximum allowable royalty rates from companies that may already have incorporated its DRAM technology, and requires Rambus to employ a Commission-approved compliance officer to ensure that Rambus's patents and patent applications are disclosed to industry standard-setting bodies in which it participates.") *Ibid.*
210. FTC, In the Matter of Motorola Mobility LLC, and Google Inc., Jul. 24, 2013, available at https://www.ftc.gov/enforcement/cases-proceedings/1210120/motorola-mobility-llc-google-inc-matter.
211. 327 U.S. 608 (1946).
212. Bower, *supra* n. 201.
213. 343 US 470, 493 (1952).
214. For further information on the structural remedies that imposes a divestment and their procedure, *see* FTC, *A Study of the Commission's Divestiture Process* (1999), available at https://www.ftc.gov/sites/default/files/attachments/merger-review/divestiture.pdf.

*Eastman Kodak Co.*[215] the Supreme Court recognized the FTC's lack of authority to order a divestiture of certain Kodak's entities, the Supreme Court later stated the opposite recognizing that the FTC has the power to impose a divestiture order.[216]

Furthermore, the FTC can order forms of restitution to consumers. For example, in the *Intel* consent decree, the FTC ordered Intel, which agreed, to reimburse software vendors interested in recompiling their software through a non-Intel compiler.[217] Consent orders and consent decrees that include orders of restitution to antitrust defendants in favor of consumer damages by antitrust investigations are rare.[218] Section 13(b) explicitly authorizes the FTC to seek and obtain injunctions from federal district court. Courts recognized that the power of the FTC to seek monetary remedies derives from an extensive interpretation of the equitable powers provided under Section 13(b). Monetary remedies are not explicitly foreseen.

Finally, the consent order can specify that the proposed remedies do not constitute an admission of guilt, but the agreement is for settlement purposes only.[219]

### *[2] Procedure for Consent Orders*

The FTC has exclusive authority, under Section 5 of the FTC Act to regulate "unfair methods of competition ... and unfair or deceptive acts or practices."[220] Under Section 6 of the FTC Act, the FTC has extensive power to investigate conduct that might be anticompetitive.[221] Before a complaint is issued, the FTC allows "any individual, partnership, or corporation being investigated" the opportunity to submit "a proposal for disposition of the matter in the form of a consent order agreement executed by the party being investigated."[222] The FTC is free to accept or refuse the consent agreement.[223] The FTC's Bureau for Competition and Bureau of Economics review the

215. 274 U.S. 619 (1927).
216. *FTC v. Procter & Gamble Co.*, 386 U.S. 568 (1967). *See also* Sullivan & Hovenkamp, *supra* n. 130, at 152.
217. FTC, FTC Settles Charges of Anticompetitive Conduct Against Intel, Press Release (Aug. 4, 2010), https://www.ftc.gov/news-events/press-releases/2010/08/ftc-settles-charges-anticompetitive-conduct-against-intel.
218. Spencer Weber Waller, *The Past, Present and Future of Monopolization Remedies*, 76 Antitrust L. J. 11, 19 (2009) ("In a small number of situations, the Federal Trade Commission and the courts have required antitrust defendants, including monopolists, to provide restitution to consumers who were overcharged by reason of an antitrust violation. The FTC's restitution power is derived from Section 13(b) of the FTC Act and is often invoked in consumer fraud matters, but only more recently has been invoked in a handful of competition cases.") *Ibid.*
219. FTC, Operating Manual, *supra* n. 207, at 3.
220. 15 U.S.C. § 45(a).
221. To initiate the investigation activity it is not required an authorization of the Commissioners, but the authorization of directors, vice-directors, assistants or assistants or associate directors of one of the regional office. *See* ABA Section of Antitrust, *supra* n. 26, at 665.
222. 16 CFR §2.31.
223. 16 CFR §2.34. The consent order agreement usually includes "a proposed order, an admission of proposed findings of fact, admissions of judicial fact, and a waiver of the FTC's obligation to make findings of fact and conclusion of law. It also generally contains a waiver of all rights to judicial review." *See* ABA Section of Antitrust *supra* n. 26, at 675. Similarly, *see also*, FTC, Operating Manual, *supra* n. 207. ("[C]onsent agreements are used by the Commission to secure an effective and legally enforceable order to cease and desist, to divest, or for other corrective

proposed consent, and the majority of the FTC Commissioners can provisionally accept the agreement.[224] In that case, the FTC releases the order which contains the complaint and the consent agreement for thirty days (or other period specified by the Commission) to enable interested parties to send their comments on the terms of the agreement.[225] The Commission can instead accept the agreement proposal on the condition that parties accept certain revisions or return it, providing general or specific directions on how to continue negotiations.[226]

In conjunction with the consent agreement, the FTC also released "an explanation of the provisions of the order and the relief to be obtained thereby,"[227] and any further information that the Commission considers helpful for the public to understand the terms of the Act. Once the comment period is concluded, the FTC "may either withdraw its acceptance of the agreement"[228] or "issue and serve its complaint in such form as the circumstances may require."[229]

The FTC could also decide that on the basis of its received comments, the final decisions and orders issued before the comment period "should be modified."[230] In case the respondents do not comply, the FTC may reopen the proceeding, modifying its decision.[231] Once the final version of the consent order is determined, with the received comments taken into account, that order is published.

Contrary to the DOJ's consent decrees in which only the judge can modify the decree, the FTC can amend, pursuant to FTC rule 2.51, a consent order if any party show that facts or law's conditions are changed.[232] The FTC represents "both the public prosecution system and the judge of the proceedings,"[233] not a plaintiff or a defendant.

In deciding whether or not the consent order needs to be modified, the FTC adopts a simple test based on "public interest." Section 3.72(b)[234] of FTC's rules sets

---

action without expending time and resources required to fully prepare and adjudicate a case.") *Ibid. See also* Sullivan & Hovenkamp, *supra* n. 130, at 128.

224. Shepard Goldfein & Thomas Pak, *Negotiated Antitrust Settlements: Some Perspectives from U.S. Defendants*, in European Competition Law Annual 2008, 205, 214 (Hart. Publ., 2008).
225. 16 CFR §2.34. *See also* FTC, Operating Manual, *supra* n. 207, at 10; Goldfein & Pak, *supra* n. 224, at 214. ("[The] proposed FTC consent orders are not filed with or approved by a district court. Instead, the proposed consent is reviewed and vetted by supervisors within the FTC's Bureau of Competition and Bureau of Economics and then provisionally accepted by a majority of the five FTC commissioners. Such proposed consent are not subject to the Tunney Act, but must satisfy the requirements of the FTC Rule 2.32. Similar to the DOJ consents, most FTC consents are agreed to during the FTC's investigation phase and prior to the commencement of any administrative adjudication.") *Ibid.*
226. FTC, Operating Manual, *supra* n. 207, at 10.
227. 16 CFR §2.34.
228. *Ibid.*
229. *Ibid.*
230. *Ibid.*
231. *Ibid.*
232. 16 C.F.R. §2.51.
233. *See* ABA Section of Antitrust, *supra* n. 26, at 683. ("The rule that govern FTC adjudications are designed to separate functions that are adversarial (and therefore not impartial) from those that are adjudicative (and therefore must remain impartial).")
234. 16 C.F.R. §3.72(b).

forth that an FTC's order can be amended if the changes of circumstances or of the law require it consistently with the protection of public interest.[235]

## §1.03 CONCLUSIONS

Having explored the functioning, characteristics and the procedure of both DOJ and FTC consent decrees, some considerations can be drawn. Since the first *antitrust consent* decree of 1906,[236] the bargaining antitrust solution became the perfect tool in the U.S. to regulate markets with the knowledge and consent of the companies subject to an antitrust investigation. Markets inefficiencies are corrected through a specific and time-sensitive solution, which avoids the costs of a government regulation extended to all market participants, as well as the uncertain and expensive litigations. Intel, Microsoft and AT&T consent decrees clearly show how much potential exists in enforcing antitrust law by means of antitrust settlements.

The analysis of both the DOJ and FTC consent decree/orders procedure demonstrates the wide discretion of antitrust agencies in determining the terms of such decrees/orders and therefore the structural or behavioral remedies grounded in economics. Judges deal with law while economists deal with market and economic regulation. Thus, it seems appropriate to leave judges to create and interpret law and economists (like those who work at the FTC and DOJ) to regulate markets through the determination of the most efficient remedies. However, as it is outlined in Chapter 4, the adoption of antitrust settlements requires a comprehensive economic analysis both before and after their adoption to be effective.

235. Timberg, *supra* n. 114, at 576.
236. The first *antitrust consent* decree dates back to before the Clayton Act. In 1906, the DOJ reached a settlement with the Otis Elevator Co., the first antitrust case to be settled by means of a consent decree. Kalodner, *supra* n. 10; Hamilton & Till, *supra* n. 10.

CHAPTER 2

# How Commitment Decisions Converge and Diverge with the U.S. Consent Decrees

Similar to the U.S. antitrust enforcers, the EU Commission and National Competition Authorities (NCAs) can settle antitrust investigations by means of agreements reached regarding the undertakings subject to investigations—*commitment decisions*. In particular, those undertakings can offer to the EU Commission some commitments, which aim to address the EU Commission's antitrust concerns defined in the complaint/preliminary assessment.[237]

Such a bargaining procedure was initially informal.[238] Before 2003, the EU antitrust settlements were neither binding nor had a transparent procedure to preserve rights of the interested third parties.[239] In 1984, the EU Commission settled its first antitrust case through an informal agreement achieved with IBM.[240] In 1989 Coca Cola also agreed to close some EU competition law investigations by accepting unilateral undertakings.[241] In 1994, Microsoft reached an agreement with the Commission accepting modification of its licensing practices to avoid the risk of an antitrust

237. EU Commission, Communication from the Commission to the European Parliament and the Council, Report on the Functioning of Regulation 1/2003, COM(2009)206 final, §13.
238. *See*, e.g., Richard Whish, *Commitment Decisions under Article 9 of the EC Modernisation: Some Unanswered Questions*, in M. Johansson, N. Wahl & U. Bernitz (eds.), *Liber Amicorum in Honour of Sven Norberg: A European for All Seasons* (Bruylant, 2006) at 555.
239. Wouter P.J. Wils, *Settlements of EU Antitrust Investigations: Commitment Decisions under Article 9 of Regulation No. 1/2003*, 29 World Competition 345, 347 (2006).
240. *See*, e.g., John Temple Lang, *Commitment Decisions and Settlements with Antitrust Authorities and Private Parties under European Antitrust Law*, in Barry Hawk ed., 2005 Annual Proceedings of the Fordham Corporate Law Institute 267 (2006); Whish, *supra* n. 238.
241. EU Commission IP/90/7, Competition, Press Release, http://europa.eu/rapid/press-release_IP-90-7_en.htm?locale=en.

condemnation for abuse of dominant position.[242] In 1996, AC Nielsen,[243] and in 1997, Digital Equipment and other EU antitrust investigations were settled by means of an informal commitment decision. Again, such antitrust settlements lacked a transparent procedure to preserve rights of the interested third parties, and the Commission did not have power to enforce such commitments in case of failure to comply.[244]

Article 9 of Regulation 1/2003 established commitment decision procedure[245] making such commitments binding.[246] Article 5 of Regulation 1/2003 also enables NCAs to close an investigation through commitments offered by the investigated company.[247] In other words, Regulation No. 1/2003 formalized the practice of commitment decisions before adopted under Regulation No. 17.[248] Article 23(2) (c) and Article 24(1) (c) of Reg. 1/2003 empowered the Commission to fine a company in case of failure to comply with commitments ex Article 9.[249] By imposing a fine of 561 million of euros on Microsoft,[250] in March 2013, the EU Commission demonstrated their intent to take serious any noncompliance with binding commitments under Article 9.

Article 30 of Regulation 1/2003 stated that commitment decisions, as well as the Commission's prohibition decisions, had to be published so that aware third parties have the opportunity to provide comments on the terms of commitments. Despite the fact that Mario Monti had the clear goal of matching the EU competition enforcement mechanism to the U.S. antitrust enforcement mechanism by enacting Reg. 1/2003, significant differences remained between the two antitrust regimes and their antitrust settlement practices. With respect to the settlement antitrust solution, these differences—as outlined below—mainly concern the role of courts and antitrust agencies within commitment decision procedure.

242. EU Commission IP/94/653, Competition, Press Release (Jul. 15, 1994) http://europa.eu/rapid/press-release_IP-94-653_en.htm. *See also* Francois Leveque, *The Application of Essential Facility and Leveraging Doctrines to Intellectual Property in the EU: The Microsoft's Refusal to License on Interoperability*, Working Paper at 8 (2004), available at http://www.cerna.ensmp.fr/Documents/FL-WP-ComVsMS.pdf; Lang, *supra* n. 240, at 267.
243. EU Commission IP/96/1117, Competition, Press Release (Nov. 28, 1996) http://europa.eu/rapid/press-release_IP-96-1117_en.htm?locale=en.
244. Wils, *supra* n. 239, at 347.
245. Council Regulation (EC) No. 1/2003, Article 9.
246. John Davies & Manish Das, *Private Enforcement of Commission Commitment Decisions: A Steep Climb Not a Gentle Stroll*, 29 Fordham Int'l. J. 917, 923, 926, 927 (2005); Florian Wagner-Von Papp, *Best and Even Better Practices in Commitment Procedures after Alrosa: The Dangers of Abandoning the "Struggle for Competition Law"*, 49 Common Market L. Rev. 929 (2012).
247. EU Regulation 1/2003, Article 5. *See also* Alison Jones & Brenda Sufrin, *EU Competition Law: Text, Cases, and Materials* 274 (Oxford U. Press, 5th ed., 2014).
248. *Ibid.*
249. *Ibid.*
250. EU Commission IP/13/196, Antitrust: Commission fines Microsoft for noncompliance with browser choice commitments, Press Release (Mar. 6, 2013) http://europa.eu/rapid/press-release_IP-13-196_en.htm.

## §2.01 DO COMMITMENT DECISIONS REGULATE MARKETS AS WELL AS U.S. CONSENT DECREES?

Similar to the U.S. consent decrees, the proposed commitments/remedies can be of behavioral or structural nature requiring, for example, a supply obligation or a business divestiture.[251] Do commitment decisions similar to U.S. consent decrees regulate markets? To answer this question, an analysis of at least two relevant commitment decisions (*Bulgaria* and *Visa*) appears necessary. In *Bulgaria* the EU Commission imposed on the Bulgarian incumbent in the electricity market a divestiture remedy similar to the U.S. AT&T case; in *Visa*, the EU Commission imposed merely behavioral remedies.

### [A] *EU Bulgaria v. U.S. AT&T Case*

The Bulgaria case is an example of an antitrust issue that has been closed by means of a commitment decision which imposed structural remedies similar to the ones defined in the U.S. AT&T case. On December 3, 2012, the EU Commission started a formal investigation on Bulgaria Energy Holding ("*Bulgaria*") to determine whether *Bulgaria* was abusing its dominant position in the wholesale electricity market in Bulgaria.[252] *Bulgaria* is the state-owned vertically integrated incumbent in the energy market of Bulgaria, which engaged in both electricity and gas production supply and transmission. *Bulgaria*, also owned the only Bulgarian licensed power exchange administrator, IBEX EAD. According to the EU Commission, Bulgaria hindered competition in the wholesale electricity market in Bulgaria and neighboring Member States through some territorial restrictions, in violation of Article 102 TFEU. On June 19, 2015, *Bulgaria* proposed some commitments to address the EU Commission's concerns.[253] Surprisingly, such commitments were not limited to a mere removal of territorial restrictions; *Bulgaria*'s commitments went much further.

*Bulgaria* offered to "divest the ownership of IBEX EAD from its structure ... and transfer the capital of IBEX EAD to the Ministry of Finance."[254] In addition, *Bulgaria* undertook action to ensure full support in the IBEX EAD activities "towards establishing an operational DAM Platform and to continue to provide IBEX EAD with the necessary funding and Key Personnel that have the necessary competence and

251. EU Commission, Antitrust Manual of Procedures 183 (March 2012) available at http://ec.europa.eu/competition/antitrust/antitrust_manproc_3_2012_en.pdf. Commitments can also include the appointment of a trustee to assist the DG COMP during the implementation of commitments. A trustee is often appointed in a divestiture commitment, which usually follows the Standard Model for Divestiture Commitments developed for merger remedies.
252. EU Commission, IP/12/1307, Antitrust: Commission Opens Proceedings against Bulgaria Energy Holding, Press Release (Dec. 3, 2012).
253. Commitments Submitted by Bulgarian Energy Holding Ead Natsionalna Elektricheska Kompania EAD Thermal Power Plant Maritsa East 2 EAD Nuclear Power Plant Kozloduy EAD, AT.39767-BEH Electricity (Jun. 19, 2015), available at http://ec.europa.eu/competition/antitrust/cases/dec_docs/39767/39767_1505_3.pdf.
254. *Ibid.*, at 4

knowledge for establishing the DAM Platform until the end of the Divestiture period,"[255] five years. Thus, *Bulgaria* commitments focused on ensuring the independence of the power exchange by implementing a structural unbundling remedy. On December 10, 2015, the EU Commission was satisfied with the commitments' terms and made those terms legally binding.[256]

### [B] *EU Visa v. U.S. Microsoft/Intel Case*

The *Visa* case provides a good example of an EU antitrust case settled through a commitment decision that stated only behavioral remedies, similar to the U.S. Microsoft and Intel cases. On April 6, 2009, the Commission sent a Statement of Objection to Visa Europe Limited, Visa Inc., and Visa International Services Association, which alleged that Visa applied multilateral interchange fees (MIFs) that were likely to restrain competition in the payment market between merchants' banks. In reply to the Commission's Statement of Objection, Visa offered some commitments. On December 8, 2010, the EU Commission made the revised Visa commitments binding for four years.[257] The key terms of the commitment decision were to reduce "the maximum weighted average MIF applicable to debit card cross border transactions and to national debit transactions in those countries where MIFs are set directly by Visa Europe [_] to 0.2 percent of the value of the transaction. This represents a reduction of about 60 percent on average for domestic MIFs and 30 percent for cross-border MIFs."[258]

However, on July 31, 2012, the EU Commission informed Visa of additional competition issues concerning MIFs by means of a Supplementary Statement of Objections (SO).[259] The EU competition agency questioned whether MIFs were necessary to preserve efficiency in the payment sector. Visa offered some commitments to close the investigation with no finding. In particular, Visa agreed to "simplify[ing] its inter-bank fee structure and make the invoicing of card acceptance services more transparent to merchants,"[260] in addition to reducing cross-border inter-bank fee and capping its credit card MIFs. On February 26, 2014, the EU Commission made Visa's commitments legally binding, which again imposed a reduction of MIFs to 0.3 percent of the value of the transaction for credit card and 0.2 percent for debit card transactions. Visa also agreed to reform its rules to encourage cross-border competition.[261]

---

255. *Ibid.*
256. EU Commission, IP/15/6289, Antitrust: Commission Accepts Commitments by Bulgaria Energy Holding to Open up Bulgarian Wholesale Electricity Market, Press Release (Dec. 10, 2015).
257. EU Commission, Summary of Commission Decision, Case COMP/39.398 (Dec. 8, 2010).
258. EU Commission, Antitrust: Commission makes Visa Europe's commitments to cut interbank fees for debit cards legally binding, Press Release, IP/10/1684 (Dec. 8, 2010), http://europa.eu/rapid/press-release_IP-10-1684_en.htm?locale=FR.
259. EU Commission, IP/12/871, Antitrust: Commission Sends Supplementary Statement of Objections to Visa, Press Release (Jul. 31, 2012).
260. EU Commission, IP/14/197, Antitrust: Commission makes Visa Europe's commitments to cut interbank fees and to facilitate cross-border competition legally binding, Press Release (Feb. 26, 2014).
261. *Ibid.*

On March 10, 2015, the European Parliament enacted the Interchange Fees Regulation, revised in November 2015, which has determined cap interbank fees for all card-based payments for intra-EEA card payments (without regulating inter-regional transaction).[262] Therefore, the *Visa* commitment decision in some way anticipated rules later imposed through an EU Regulation on the payment sector and a standardization across the industry of the approach agreed in the Article 9 decisions. In setting the rate of interchange fees, the Regulation made binding by European legislators knowingly adopted the fee levels that had been agreed with Visa.[263] Thus, the regulation effects of the Visa commitment decision are undisputed—the EU Parliament and Council implemented similar terms of the agreement in the payment sector regulation.

Therefore, despite the fact that the EU Commission is not a regulator, both Bulgaria and Visa cases demonstrate how commitment decisions *de facto* regulate the affected markets similarly to U.S. consent decrees. Article 9 of Regulation 1/2003 allows the EU Commission to enforce competition law in a regulatory manner.[264]

## §2.02 COMMITMENT DECISIONS PROCEDURE BEFORE THE EU COMMISSION

Although a company does not have a defined term or specific time frame to offer commitments to the EU Commission for settling a case, the EU Commission urges undertakings to offer commitments in the early stages of the procedure.[265] When undertakings show their interest in the commitment procedure, the EU Commission sets a meeting between the Directorate-General for Competition (DG COMP) and the company subject of the investigation.

Here, the EU Commission provides a well-structured explanation of competition concerns to make the company aware of the underlying factual evidence and the theory of harm in the proceeding.[266] After providing its preliminary assessment, the EU Commission evaluates the (possible) offered commitments and whether they address the antitrust concerns expressed to the undertaking. The Commission can decide to make such commitments binding and end the investigation.[267] However, as the same

262. EU Commission, Regulation (EU) 2015/751 of the European Parliament and of the Council of 29 April 2015 on Interchange Fees for Card-Based Payment Transactions, OJ L 123, 19.5.2015.
263. *Ibid.*, at Articles 3 and 4.
264. Michael Hofmann, *Commitment Decisions in the European Energy Sector: Implementation of Sector-Specific Regulation via Competition Law*, 2 Eur. Networks L. & Reg. Q. 131, 132 (2014).
265. *See* Christopher J. Cook, *Commitment Decision: The Law and Practice under Article 9*, 29 World Competition 209-228 (2006); KJ Cseres, *The Impact of Regulation 1/2003 in the New Member States*, 6 Competition L. Rev. 145-182 (2010); Davies & Das, *supra* n. 246; J. Temple Lang G, *Commitment Decision under Regulation 1/2003: Legal Aspects of a New Kind of Competition Decision*, 8 European Competition L. Rev., 347–356 (2003); Luis Ortiz Blanco, *EU Competition Procedure*, 579 (Oxford, 3rd., 2013).
266. Blanco, *supra* n. 265, at 579.
267. EU Commission, EU Competition Law, Rules Applicable to Antitrust Enforcement, Vol. I, General Rules 31 (July 2013) available at http://ec.europa.eu/competition/antitrust/legislation/handbook_vol_1_en.pdf.

Regulation 1/2003 specified, commitments should not be proposed or accepted to close a case when a fine would be appropriate.[268]

Commitment decisions' procedure is neither based on full investigations nor does it involve all the steps provided for a final decision under Article 7. For example, there is no hearing or access to the file.[269] However, Regulation 1/2003 introduced a transparency procedure to guarantee third parties participation, through the so-called *market test*.[270]

### [A] Preliminary Assessment

The procedure of commitment decisions is simple compared to the procedure of the final decision under Article 7. Instead of the Statement of Objection, commitment decisions foresee a simpler step, the Preliminary Assessment.[271] However, when the parties have already received a Statement of Objections, the EU Commission can still accept the parties' commitments.[272]

The parties that signal an interest in exploring commitments' procedure will be invited to attend a State of Play meeting. At this meeting, the DG COMP presents its competition concerns, providing a preliminary assessment. The parties can ask questions about the presented assessment and concerns.[273] The preliminary assessment is an act adopted by the Competition Commissioner that is shorter than a Statement of Objections and is not available to third parties.[274] In case the Statement of Objection has been already issued, no preliminary assessment is necessary.

The preliminary assessment usually represents the base for the parties to formulate their commitments in addressing the DG COMP's concerns.[275] The DG COMP provides the time frame within which the debate on commitments should end. Typically, the parties have one month to signed and submit commitments.

### [B] Types of Commitments

The parties need to convince the DG COMP that their commitments effectively address the competition concerns, and although commitments are voluntarily submitted by the parties, the EU Commission can make its proposals on the content of commitments. Similar to U.S. consent decrees, the proposed commitments can be of behavioral or

268. Regulation n. 1/2003 at (13) states that "[c]ommitment decisions are not appropriate in cases where the Commission intends to impose a fine." *See also* Wils, *supra* n. 239, at 346-347.
269. EU Commission, Antitrust Manual of Procedures, *supra* n. 251, at 177.
270. Wils, *supra* n. 239, at 347.
271. *See*, e.g., Philippe Chone, Said Souam & Arnold Vialfont, *On the Optimal Use of Commitment Decisions under European Competition Law*, 37 Int'l Rev. L. & Econ. 169, 170 (2014).
272. EU Commission, Antitrust Manual of Procedures, *supra* n. 251, at 177.
273. *Ibid.*, at 179.
274. *Ibid.*, at 180; Blanco, *supra* n. 265, at 580, 581.
275. *Ibid.*

structural nature, requiring, for example, a supply obligation or a business divestiture.[276] Behavioral commitments require long-term monitoring compared to structural commitments.

In theory, commitments should be proportionate to harm and address the competition concern. However, the European Court of Justice (ECJ) recognized that the proportionality test under Article 9 is less strict than in the case of remedies imposed under Article 7.[277] In any case, the commitments offered should not be ambiguous and self-executing, namely the implementation should not be based on the will of a third party.[278] Commitments that appear incomplete or contradictory are rarely accepted by the EU Commission, and the parties can rarely make corrections to the commitments once proposed. Commitments can also include the appointment of a trustee to assist the DG COMP during the implementation of commitments. A trustee is often appointed in a divestiture commitment, which usually follows the Standard Model for Divestiture Commitments developed for merger remedies.[279]

The commitments offered refer to specific time frames[280] that vary from market to market considering the principle of proportionality. In addition, the terms of commitments should also foresee the circumstances that are likely to occur during the adoption of the commitments offered.[281]

### [C] Market Test and the Role of the Third Parties

When the text of the commitments adequately addresses the competition concerns, that text will then require the approval of the Competition Commissioner. Once the text of commitments is approved, the Commission can discuss with specific third parties the content of commitments prior to publishing a notice under Article 27(4). Then, before making the commitment proposal binding, the Commission under Article 27 must publish a summary of the case along with the main substance of the commitment proposal in the *Official Journal*. This is necessary to enable third parties to submit their comments and observations within a term that cannot be less than one month. The non-confidential version of the full text of the commitment proposal is published on the DG COMP website. This phase is well-known as *market test*.[282]

The Commission is not obligated to consider the third parties' observations, but those observations can help the Commission understand how to improve the terms of the commitments. The Commission can require parties to modify the content of

276. EU Commission, Antitrust Manual of Procedures, *supra* n. 251, at 183.
277. *Comm'n v. Alrosa*, Case C-441/07, 2010 E.C.R. I-5949, § 35 and 46. *See also* EU Commission, Antitrust Manual of Procedures *supra* n. 251, at 183. *See also* Blanco, *supra* n. 265, at 583.
278. Blanco, *supra* n. 265, at 581.
279. *Ibid.*
280. EU Commission, Antitrust Manual of Procedures, *supra* n. 251, at 184. "Commitments should provide that a lasting improvement of the market structure is achieved within a foreseeable timeframe." *Ibid.*
281. *Ibid.*, at 183.
282. *See*, e.g., EU Commission, Antitrust Manual of Procedures, *supra* n. 251, at 184; Chone', Souam & Vialfont, *supra* n. 271.

commitments in light of the third parties' observations.[283] The Commission starts a new market test if commitments are significantly modified.

### [D] The Role of Courts: Alrosa Ruling

*Alrosa* is the landmark decision within the framework of the EU Regulation 1/2003, which determined the limits of the Commission's extended discretion in the postmodernization regime.[284] Under Articles 102 TFEU and 263 TFEU, the courts have the capability to annul commitment decisions to prevent misuse of power, infringement of an essential procedural requirement or the Treaties, or any rules concerning their application, or the lack of competence.[285] Despite the fact that the EU courts have a broad power in the definition of judicial review standards, there are two limitations in the courts' judicial review of Commission decisions. First, the EU courts judicial review is limited to legality of Commission decisions. Second, in the field of competition law, which involves complex economic analysis, the EU courts have little room for challenging the economic analysis and the evaluation of the Commission.[286]

In *Alrosa*, the General Court reversed the Commission's commitment decision on the grounds that the Commission failed to enforce the principle of proportionality. Moreover, the Commission would not have respected Alrosa's right to be heard with respect to the commitments proposed by De Beers.[287]

The General Court recognized that "the Commission is obliged to comply with [the] principle [of proportionality] when it adopts decisions on the basis of Article 9,"[288] although the Article 9 does not explicitly refer to it. The General Court found that De Beers' commitment decision manifestly went "beyond what the Commission could have required if it were to comply with the principle of proportionality,"[289] annulling the Commission's decision.

The Commission appealed the General Court's ruling. The Court of Justice recognized that the principle of proportionality under Article 7 of Regulation 1/2003 has different extent and content than that applied in the Article 9 of the same Regulation.[290] Under Article 9 of Regulation 1/2003, the Commission needs only to evaluate whether the proposed commitments address the concerns of the Commission expressed in its preliminary assessment.[291] Thus, the Commission does not need to

283. EU Commission, Antitrust Manual of Procedures, *supra* n. 251, at 186.
284. Firat Cengiz, *Judicial Review and the Rule of Law in the EU Competition Law Regime after Alrosa*, 7 Eur. Competition J. 127, 129 (2011).
285. *Ibid.*, at 141.
286. EU Commission, Antitrust: Commission welcomes Court judgment in Alrosa/De Beers diamond case, Press Release (Jun. 29, 2010), http://europa.eu/rapid/press-release_MEMO-10-285_en.htm. In particular, "the ECJ held that the General Court had erred by substituting its own assessment of complex economic circumstances for that of the Commission." *Ibid.*
287. *Alrosa v. Comm'n*, Case T-170/06, 2007 E.C.R. II-02601.
288. *Ibid.*, at §92.
289. *Ibid.*, at §140.
290. *Comm'n v. Alrosa*, Case C-441/07, 2010 E.C.R. I-05949.
291. *Ibid.*

compare those commitments with measures which it would have imposed itself under Article 7.

The Court of Justice alleged that the court's review of commitment decision should be limited to assess whether the Commission's decision was manifestly incorrect, confirming the Commission decision.[292] In *Gasorba*, the Court of Justice specified that closing an investigation with commitment decisions does not preclude national agencies and courts from prosecuting companies for the same conduct.[293] Otherwise, commitment decisions would legalize possible anticompetitive conduct.

In summary, EU Commission has broad discretion in assessing and defining the terms of commitment decisions. Those commitments, however, leave national authorities free to prosecute companies for the same conduct at a national level.

### [E] Some Considerations

Like U.S. consent decrees, EU commitment decisions create no finding of a violation or admission of guilt by the party subject to investigation. However, in contrast to the EU commitment decisions, the DOJ can impose litigation costs by means of a consent decree and the FTC ask for a disgorgement. Moreover, the U.S. procedure appears more transparent than the European procedure of commitment decisions as, during the market test, the EU Commission provides very few details on its antitrust concerns. Differently to the EU Commission, the DOJ publishes a competition impact assessment regarding the implementation of the consent decree and its answers to the third parties' comments.

Furthermore, U.S. consent decrees foresee the judicial review process and—at least those that involve the DOJ—is *de facto* a judge order. In contrast to EU judges to whom analysis is limited to the legality of the EU Commission[294], U.S. judges can evaluate antitrust remedies enshrined in consent decrees on the merit. Finally, principles stated in consent judgments constitute rules and standards not only accepted by private litigants but also authorized by courts.[295] The U.S. consent decrees establish a kind of precedent for following agreements between the U.S. antitrust agency and companies subject to an investigation to settle antitrust proceedings while EU commitment decisions do not.

## §2.03 COMMITMENTS OR PROHIBITION DECISION—HOW DO THEY DIVERGE?

The College of the EU Commissioners adopts the commitment decision, and the process of adoption pursuant Article 9 is similar to the process for a prohibition

292. *Ibid.*
293. *Gasorba et al. v. Repsol*, C-547/16, CG UE 23-11-2017, C:2017:891, § 26.
294. *See*, e.g., Wagner-Von Papp, *supra* n. 246, at 967-68. As Professor Florian Wagner-Von Papp observed, "[t]he Court of Justice had the opportunity in *Alrosa* to provide for an effective proportionality review at least in those few cases that *are* appealed" but the ECJ opted for forgoing this opportunity. *Ibid.*
295. American Enterprise Institute, Antitrust Consent Decrees 1906-1966 American Enterprise Institute *viii-ix* (1968).

decision under Article 7.[296] However, as the *Alrosa* case revealed,[297] the differences between these two antitrust decisions are significant. In addition to a different application of the principle of proportionality in these two articles,[298] the procedure for a prohibition decision entails more steps than a commitment decision's procedure and therefore generally takes longer. Furthermore, the prohibition decision finds the liability of the parties while commitment decisions should find "that there are no longer grounds for action by the Commission without concluding whether or not there has been or still is an infringement."[299]

Thus, third parties damaged by the antitrust violation can use prohibition decisions under Article 7 as evidence of the infringement, while the commitment decision does not show any antitrust violation[300] and do not preclude national authorities from prosecuting companies for the same conduct.[301] As explained in Chapter 5, commitment decisions enable antitrust agencies to regulate markets. The effects are different than decisions made under Article 7, as these commitment decisions do not create antitrust case law.[302]

In case the parties breach the terms of the commitment decision, the Commission can sanction the company pursuant Article 23(2)(c) of Regulation 1/2003 for having breached the commitments. For example, in 2013, the Commission fined Microsoft EUR 561 million for violating the terms of commitment decision taken in 2009 to settle an antitrust investigation for abuse of dominant position.[303]

The Commission can also reopen the procedure, imposing a fine for the violation of Article 101 and/or 102 of the TFEU by enacting two different decisions: (1) a decision to reopen the case and (2) a decision regarding the violation of commitments. On its

---

296. EU Commission, Antitrust Manual of Procedures, *supra* n. 251, at 187.
297. *Comm'n v. Alrosa*, Case C-441/07, 2010 E.C.R. I-5949.
298. *Ibid*. "There is therefore no reason why the measure which could possibly be imposed in the context of Article 7 of Regulation No 1/2003 should have to serve as a reference for the purpose of assessing the extent of the commitments accepted under Article 9 of the regulation, or why anything going beyond that measure should automatically be regarded as disproportionate. Even though decisions adopted under each of those provisions are in either case subject to the principle of proportionality, the application of that principle none the less differs according to which of those provisions is concerned." *Ibid.*, at 47
299. Wouter P.J. Wils, *The Use of Settlements in Public Antitrust Enforcement: Objectives and Principles*, 31 Word Competition 335, 339 (2008).
300. *See* Davies & Das, *supra* n. 246, at 917, 920. Although the White Paper on Modernization of the Rules Implementing Articles 85 and 86 of the EU Commission Treaty stated that was useful to make commitments binding "to rely on them before their national courts." And, similarly the Explanatory Memorandum specified that third parties could be used commitment decisions before the national courts, the final text of Regulation 1 of 2003 did not implement such principle.
301. *Gasorba*, *supra* n. 293, at §26. *See also* Vasiliki Fasoula, *The Legal Effects of Commitment Decisions under Article 9(1) of Regulation 1/2003 on Antitrust Proceedings before the National Courts*, 2 Eur. Competition & Reg. L. Rev. 60, 63 (2018).
302. Giovanna Massarotto, *Antitrust Agencies: Watchdogs or Regulators?*, 7 J. Int't Commercial Law 39, 52-55 (2015).
303. EU Commission, Case AT.39530, Mar. 6, 2013. In 2009 Microsoft offered to provide Internet users a browser choice that allows to choice their preferred web browser to settle an antitrust investigation. The Commission made binding Microsoft's commitments until 2014, and the company violated the commitment relating to the browser choice from May 2011 until July 2012. *See also* Chone', Souam & Vialfont, *supra* n. 271.

own initiative or upon request, the Commission can reopen a proceeding settled by means of a commitment decision when the material on which the decision was based is changed. The Commission can also reopen the proceeding when the commitment decision was based on misleading, incorrect or incomplete information offered by the parties.[304] Moreover, it is not precluded to NCAs and courts to find liability of the same parties for an antitrust violation pursuant Articles 101 and 102 TFEU.[305] As the ECJ recognized, although national courts cannot ignore commitment decisions, these do not "create a legitimate expectation in respect of the undertakings concerned as to whether their conduct complies with" the EU competition law provisions.[306]

## §2.04 THE INCENTIVES TO SETTLE AN ANTITRUST DISPUTE AND THE TREND IN THE ADOPTION OF COMMITMENT DECISIONS

The incentives behind the use of commitment decisions in the EU converge with those analyzed for the adoption of U.S. consent decrees. Through this bargaining solution, the EU Commission and NCAs save time and money by avoiding litigations and are able to reach a more procompetitive result.[307] Companies understand the markets where they are active better than anyone and know how to encourage fair competition that benefits consumers.[308] EU competition enforcers need to understand how far undertakings can go in offering procompetitive remedies/commitments and carefully weigh the advantages and disadvantages of adopting a commitment decision in each case.[309]

As the Court of Justice recognized, undertakings through commitment decision procedure accept that "the concessions they make may go beyond what the Commission could itself impose on them in a decision adopted under Article 7 of the regulation after a thorough examination."[310] In contrast to prohibition decisions under Article 7, commitment decisions do not identify the infringement, stating only that there are no reasons for the EU Commission to act.[311] In March 2015, however, the Commercial Court of Paris ruled that claimants can seek compensation of damages due to anticompetitive conduct where the pursued company settled the case by means of a commitment decision.[312] This made the incentives under commitment decisions less secure than those stated for consent decrees in the Section 5 of the Clayton Act. The ECJ

304. *See*, e.g., Frederic Jenny, *Worst Decision of the EU Court of Justice: The Alrosa Judgement in Context and the Future of Commitment Decisions*, 38 Fordham Int'l L. J. 701, 707 (2015).
305. *Ibid.*, at 706; Davies & Das, *supra* n. 246, at 917, 919.
306. *Gasorba*, *supra* n. 293, at §28.
307. *See*, e.g., Lang, *supra* n. 240, at 275, 274; Jenny, *supra* n. 304, at 712.
308. *See*, e.g., Lang, *supra* n. 240, at 271-272.
309. EU Commission, Antitrust Manual of Procedures, *supra* n. 251, at 177.
310. *Comm'n v. Alrosa*, Case C-441/07, 2010 E.C.R. I-5949, § 48.
311. Blanco, *supra* n. 265, at 578.
312. *See*, e.g., OECD, *Commitment Decisions in Antitrust Cases, Note by France*, 11 (Jun. 15-17, 2016), available at http://www.oecd.org/officialdocuments/publicdisplaydocumentpdf/?cote=DAF/COMP/WD(2016)33&docLanguage=En; Noëlle Lenoir, Marco Plankensteiner & Mélanie Truffier, *France: Private Antitrust Litigation*, Eur. Antitrust Rev. 137 (2016).

also recognized that in *Gasorba*, the preliminary assessment performed by the Commission in a case ended with a commitment decision needs to be considered "if not *prima facie* evidence, of the anticompetitive"[313] conduct then at least as an *indication* of that.

The EU Commission can settle an antitrust investigation by means of a commitment decision only once it has evaluated whether the company subject of the investigation is willing to provide commitments that effectively remove antitrust concerns.[314] Commitment decisions are precluded when the EU Commission intends to fine the undertaking.

In Europe, serious interest in commitment decisions procedure arose after April 2006. Before that, the EU Commission had adopted only two commitment decisions—*Bundesliga*[315] and *Coca Cola*.[316] In 2006, *De Beers*,[317] *FA Premier League*,[318] and *Repsol*[319] antitrust cases were settled by means of commitment decision.[320] In Europe, such a settlement solution became similar to the U.S., a critical tool to enforce competition law.[321] In 2007, over 35 percent of EU Commission antitrust cases were settled by commitment decision, relative to 42 percent in 2013 increased.[322]

Since 2014, however, this trend in the adoption of commitment decisions seems to have changed. By 2015, the percent of cases settled by a commitment decision had fallen to 37 percent,[323] and there is now the perception from reading recent EU Commission's decisions—such as the Google's double convictions—[324] that the EU Commission is returning to favor prohibition decisions under Article 7. In 2018, commitment decisions appeared to be a residual antitrust enforcement tool rather than a critical one.

313. *Gasorba*, *supra* n. 293, at §29.
314. Blanco, *supra* n. 265, at 578.
315. Case COMP/C-2/37.214, Commission Decision of 19 January 2005, 2005 OJ L 134/46.
316. Case COMP/A.39.116/B2, Commission Decision of 22 June 2005, 2005 OJ L 253/21.
317. EU Commission, Competition: De Beers' commitment to phase out rough diamond purchases from Alrosa made legally binding by Commission decision, Press Release IP/06/495 (Feb. 22, 2006) http://europa.eu/rapid/press-release_IP-06-204_en.htm?locale = en.
318. EU Commission, Competition: Commission makes commitments from FA Premier League legally binding, Press Release IP/06/356 (Mar. 22, 2006) http://europa.eu/rapid/press-release_IP-06-356_en.htm?locale = en.
319. EU Commission, Competition: Commission increases competition in Spanish service station market, Press Release IP/06/495 (Apr. 12, 2006) http://europa.eu/rapid/press-release_IP-06-495_en.htm?locale = en.
320. Cook, *supra* n. 265, at 209, 214.
321. *See*, e.g., Yves Botteman & Agapi Patsa, *Towards a More Sustainable Use of Commitment Decisions in Article 102 TFEU Cases*, 1 Antitrust L. Enforcement 347 (2013).
322. EU Commission, Annual Reports on Competition Policy, available at http://ec.europa.eu/competition/publications/annual_report/index.html. *See also*, EU Commission, DG COMP website, http://ec.europa.eu/competition/elojade/isef/index.cfm?clear = 1&policy_area_id = 1.
323. EU Commission, Competition, Cases, http://ec.europa.eu/competition/elojade/isef/index.cfm?fuseaction = dsp_result (last visited Apr. 10, 2016).
324. EU Commission, Antitrust: Commission fines Google € 2.42 billion for abusing dominance as search engine by giving illegal advantage to own comparison shopping service, Press Release IP/17/1784 (Jun. 27, 2017). EU Commission, Antitrust: Commission Fines Google €4.34 billion for Illegal Practices Regarding Android Mobile Devices to Strengthen Dominance of Google's Search Engine, Press Release IP/18/4581 (Jul. 18, 2018).

## §2.05 CONCLUSIONS

In Europe, the trend toward the adoption of bargain solutions appears to juxtapose the trend in the U.S. In the U.S. more and more antitrust investigations are settled by means consent decrees, while in Europe the EU Commission seems increasingly skeptical of enforcing competition law through a bargain solution. A natural question is: Why? First, the primary incentive linked to the adoption of consent decrees in the U.S., namely the avoidance of treble-damages, does not make sense in Europe. In Europe no treble-damages rule exists, thus there is no benefit linked to avoid treble-damages. Not to mention that actually no EU rules of law clearly state that commitment decisions cannot be used as evidence of an anticompetitive conduct in court to seek antitrust damages. Rather, the ECJ recognized that the preliminary assessment of the Commission performed in a case ended with a commitment represents an *indication* of the anticompetitive conduct.[325] The lack of a straightforward rule on the use of commitment decisions in European court makes uncertain for companies the benefits linked to such an antitrust enforcement tool. As John Hicks reminds us "the best of all monopoly profits is a quiet life"[326]—hence monopolies are risk-averse and their skepticism on commitment decisions appears justified in Europe.

Second, in Europe, as the EU Commission's imposition of a huge fine is the main mechanism of enforcing competition law, the increasing adoption of antitrust settlements (where no fine is imposed and no violation identified) compromises competition law deterrence. In the U.S. deterrence is exerted primarily through private action. When a firm engages in an antitrust violation, private parties can bring both class action and individual suits for treble damages.[327]

Third, commitment decisions, as well as the FTC consent decrees, lead to a lack of judges' rulings,[328] sacrificing the benefit of having courts explain the content of competition law. Last but not least, the EU Commission does not have regulatory power and an increasing use of commitment decisions can lead to a lack of competence of the EU Commission in enforcing competition law.

325. *Gasorba*, *supra* n. 293, at §29.
326. J.R. Hicks, *Annual Survey of Economic Theory: The Theory of Monopoly*, 3 Econometrica 1, 8 (1935).
327. *See* Massarotto, *The Deterrent and Enunciating Effects of Consent Decrees*, *supra* n. 8, at 493, 495.
328. Jan M. Rybnicek & Joshua Wright observed that "Section 5 enforcement has resulted in no litigated cases" focusing on regulatory settlements defined by the Commission. Jan M. Rybnicek & Joshua D. Wright, *Defining Section 5 of the FTC Act: the Failure of the Common Law Method and the Case for Formal Agency Guidelines*, 21 Geo. Mason L. Rev. 1287, 1305 (2014). *See also* William E. Kovacic & Winerman Marc, *Competition Policy and the Application of Section 5 of the Federal Trade Commission Act*, 76 Antitrust L. J. 929, 936-937 (2010).

CHAPTER 3

# Antitrust Settlements Within the U.S. and EU Antitrust Law Enforcement Framework

Antitrust settlements are a by-product of the consolidation of law and economics. These settlements are the result of economic thinking. The reason behind the adoption of a negotiated solution, as well as the remedies identified in an antitrust agreement, are based on economic analysis and reasoning. As a consequence, the development of antitrust settlements in the U.S. and EU reflects differences in the approach of enforcing antitrust law—economic or formalistic—and their different origins. While antitrust law originated in the U.S. as an economic tool of regulation to monitor monopolies, the European competition law first served as a tool to integrate the markets of its Member States. Europe needed to create a single European economy before increasing competition within markets. Moreover, at the time of the first European competition provisions in Europe there were state monopolies.

An understanding of the above foundation reveals how different historical reasons, along with diverging legal systems and approaches of enforcing competition law, have led to the development of two very distinct antitrust law cultures. These differing legal cultures affect the practice and the role of antitrust settlements.

## §3.01 THE U.S. ANTITRUST LAW FRAMEWORK

When the Sherman Act was enacted, the U.S. economy was in its infancy. In the nineteenth century, with the development of the railroad, U.S. companies started producing and selling goods in a larger geographic context.[329] Benefiting from

329. *See* George J. Stigler, *The Origin of the Sherman Act*, Working Paper n. 027, 3 (August 1983) available at http://www.chicagobooth.edu/assests/stigler/27.pdf. According to Stigler, "the railroad helped to bring the midwestern farm area into the world market." *Ibid.*, n. 8.

economies of scale, U.S. companies increased in size and, to expand their profits, began merging with each other,[330] or operating together through a set of *trusts*.[331]

The most significant example of the *trust* phenomenon is the *Standard Oil* trust.[332] The same railroads that had made the creation of the U.S. market possible also allowed for the creating of the largest U.S. oil refinery—Standard Oil. Standard Oil's monopoly was possible by means a set of mergers and trusts with its competitors and the railroads. The trust agreement between Rockefeller's refinery and the railroads enable Standard Oil to benefit of favorable railroad rebates which made the selling of oil unattractive for other refineries.

The Standard Oil Trust, even bigger and more powerful, became a model that would shape the U.S. markets and U.S. economy. The economic disparities between a few powerful people, such as Rockefeller,[333] and a number of others led to the creation of a free competition philosophy[334] and a federal law to challenge large trusts/monopolies.[335] *Antitrust law* originated in the U.S. as a remarkable tool for *economic democracy*.[336]

330. *See* Naomi R. Lamoreaux, *The Great Merger Movement in American Business* 1895-1904 (Cambridge U. Press, 1985).
331. David Crane & Herbert Hovenkamp identify *trusts* "in every case in which a single person or association of persons has the power of fixing either the amount of a commodity that is offered for sale or the price at which it is offered." David A. Crane & Herbert Hovenkamp, *The Making of Competition Policy: Legal and Economic Sources* 78 (Oxford Univ. Press, 2013). *See also* 1 Areeda & Hovenkamp, *supra* n. 205, at 44. (*citing* Senator Turpie, who defined "trust" as "a combination formed with the intention of holding and selling [commodities] at an enhanced price, by suppressing or limiting the supply and by other devices, so that the price of such trust commodity shall depend merely upon the agreement made about it by those in the combination, without reference to the cost of its production").
332. John D. Clark, *The Federal Trust Policy*, 17 (Johns Hopkins Press, 1931) available at http://babel.hathitrust.org/cgi/pt?id=coo.31924013937473;view=1up;seq=5. *See also* Giuliano Amato, *Antitrust and the Bounds of Power*, 8 (Hart Pub., 1997). ("It was John D. Rockfeller who promoted the use of trusts for anti-competitive ends. The trust was a traditional institution of common law whereby one delegated to a trustee *inter alia* one's own right to vote on the board of a company. Through 'criss-crossing' voting proxies on companies their respective boards, the managers of several competing companies together decided price and market policies, each remaining under the control of the others. This created in reality cartels, distinguished through the use of trustee-ships.")
333. Harold F. Williamson, *The Growth of the American Economy, an Introduction to the Economic History of the Unites States*, 16 (Prentice-Hall, 1944).
334. Amato, *supra* n. 332, at 7.
335. In 1884, Regan, a Representative of Texas, urged Congress to take action to prevent the *trust* phenomenon. Regan made Congress aware of how U.S. companies, "enrich[ing] one corporation to a fabulous extent, as they have the Standard Oil Company," were destroying competition and the U.S. economy. *Ibid.*, at 20, *citing* 16 Cong. Rec. 43, p. 287. "In the legislative investigation in New York three years ago it was shown that the railroad companies had allowed and paid rebates to the Standard Oil Company to the amount of USD 10,000,000 in sixteen months, and yet we have no legislation to prevent these great wrongs committed by this vast power." *Ibid.*
336. Hamilton & Till, *supra* n. 10. Myron L. Erickson, Thomas W. Dunfee & Frank F. Gibson, *Antitrust and Trade Regulation, Cases and Materials* (John Wiley & Sons, 2nd ed., 1977). *Standard Oil Co. of NJ v. United States*, 221 U.S. 1, 50 (1911). "[T]he main cause which led to the legislation was the thought that it was required by the economic condition of the times, that is, the vast accumulation of wealth in the hands of corporations and individuals, the enormous development of corporate organization, the facility for combination which such organizations afforded, the fact that the facility was being used, and that combinations known as trusts were

## [A] From a Formalistic Approach to an Economic Approach

To secure competition and counteract the evil of restrictions on trade in markets by means of trusts or monopolization phenomena, U.S. legislators saw in the Sherman Act the means at hand. Different from traditional rules of law, the Sherman Act was based on Adam Smith's economic theories on competition and agreements in restrain of trade.[337] According to Smith, when there is a monopoly or a secret trade agreement between the manufacturers, the market is kept regularly under-stocked, leading to commodity prices being set "much above the natural price."[338] The monopoly's price is the highest price that can be acquired for a good or service; whereas the price within a free competition environment is the lowest price for any particular goods. As a consequence, a law to promote the concept of competition and the price of free competition would have to be focused on market price and economic analysis of markets. The initial attempt to enforce antitrust law through a pure formalistic approach (a rigid literal interpretation of the rules of law) soon turned out to be unworkable.

### *[1] The Failure of the Formalist Approach*

Senator John Sherman admitted it was hard to determine in legal terms (not economic terms) the boundary between lawful and unlawful agreements that were regulating U.S. markets and shaping the U.S. economy. Several critics noted that the language of the Sherman Act was *vague* and *general*, thus unclear to companies.[339] The Supreme Court's decision of creating an important precedent could have represented fundamental milestones[340] in enforcing antitrust law by clarifying the vague and general terms of antitrust law.[341]

The Supreme Court started enforcing antitrust law through a purely formalistic approach of antitrust legal provisions. In 1895, the Supreme Court ruled its first antitrust judgment in the case of *United States v. E.C. Knight Co.*[342] recognizing that because the Sherman Act "only authorized the circuit courts to proceed by way of

---

being multiplied, and the widespread impression that their power had been and would be exerted to oppress individuals and injure the public generally." *Ibid.*, at 221.

337. Adam Smith, *The Wealth of Nations*, 60 (Oxford U. Press, 2008).
338. *Ibid.*
339. Phillip E. Areeda, Louis Kaplow & Aaron S. Edlin, *Antitrust Analysis, Problems, Text, and Cases*, 38 (Aspen 6th ed., 2004). *See also* Hans B. Thorelli, *The Federal Antitrust Policy, Origination of an American Tradition*, 164 (John Hopkins Press, 1955). ("The prohibitions of the Sherman Act were not stated in terms of precision or of crystal clarity and the Act itself does not define them.") *Ibid. See also* Robert H. Bork, *The Antitrust Paradox, a Policy at War with Itself*, 20 (Basic Books, 1978). According to Robert H. Bork, "the language of the statute, which is singularly opaque, was chosen not merely a cause it employed familiar common law terminology but also to allay fears that the law might go beyond the then narrowly conceived commerce power of Congress." *Ibid.*
340. R. Hewitt Pate, *Antitrust Law in the U.S. Supreme Court* (May 11, 2004), available at https://www.justice.gov/atr/speech/antitrust-law-us-supreme-court.
341. Areeda, Kaplow & Edlin, *supra* n. 339, at 38.
342. *United States v. E. C. Knight Co.*, 156 U.S. 1 (1895).

preventing and restraining violations of the Act in respect of contracts, combinations, or conspiracies,"[343] the American Sugar Refining Company's acquisition of four Philadelphia refineries was lawful. Two years later, the Supreme Court ruled on the *United States v. Trans-Missouri Freight Ass'n,*[344] condemning as illegal *per se* an agreement to fix prices entered into by eighteen railroads.

In both cases the court's analysis related to the fact that those agreements were or were not covered by the text of the Sherman Act. No room was left for assessing the possible positive economic effects of the conduct on competition and overall markets. In sum, it did not matter whether a practice was effectively jeopardizing competition and harming consumers by increasing the price of goods. It only matters whether or not the agreement fell within the scope of the Sherman Act. However, the Supreme Court's preference for a purely formalistic approach in enforcing competition law turned out to be unworkable and was short-lived.

### *[2] The Economic Approach*

In the field of antitrust, May 15, 1911, is probably as important as July 2, 1890, when the Sherman Act was enacted. On May 15, 1911, the Supreme Court ruled the same day on *Standard Oil,* and *American Tobacco.*[345] Their rulings included economic evaluations/concepts in determining anticompetitive conduct. In other words, the Supreme Court that had initially adopted a pure formalistic approach, for the first time made room in its decision for economic concepts and analysis.

The Supreme Court, in *Standard Oil Co. of NJ v. United States,* recognized "monopoly" and "restraint of trade" as interchangeable terms;[346] Standard Oil embodied the "single evil of restriction of output"[347] that needed to be defeated on behalf of consumers. Although consumers were mentioned during the enactment of the Sherman Act;[348] the Supreme Court, as *United States v. E.C. Knight* and *United States v.*

343. *Ibid.*, at 17. The Supreme Court citing *State v. Glidden.* alleged that: "[a]ny one man, or anyone of several men acting independently, is powerless; but when several combine and direct their united energies to the accomplishment of a bad purpose, the combination is formidable." *Ibid.*
344. *United States v. Trans-Missouri Freight Ass'n,* 166 U.S. 290 (1897).
345. Bork, *supra* n. 339, at 33.
346. *Standard Oil Co. of NJ v. United States,* 221 U.S. 1, 55, 59 (1911).
347. *Ibid.*, at 55. ("Generalizing these considerations, the situation is this: 1. That by the common law monopolies were unlawful because of their restriction upon individual freedom of contract and their injury to the public. 2. That as to necessaries of life the freedom of the individual to deal was restricted where the nature and character of the dealing was such as to engender the presumption of intent to bring about at least one of the injuries which it was deemed would result from monopoly, that is, an undue enhancement of price. 3. That, to protect the freedom of contract of the individual not only in his own interest, but principally in the interest of the common weal, a contract of an individual by which he put an unreasonable restraint upon himself as to carrying on his trade or business was void. And that, at common law, the evils consequent upon engrossing, etc., caused those things to be treated as coming within monopoly, and sometimes to be called monopoly, and the same considerations caused monopoly, because of its operation and effect, to be brought within and spoken of generally as impeding the due course of, or being in restraint of, trade.") *Ibid.*, at 54-55.
348. Senator Sherman argued that trusts controlled the market imposing a "law of selfishness, uncontrolled by competition," which disregard "the interest of the consumer." 21 Cong. Rec. at

*Missouri Freight Ass'n* revealed, did not consider consumer welfare in its initial rulings. However, in *Standard Oil,* consumers became a prime consideration of antitrust law. Thus, in Standard Oil, the Supreme Court adopted the maximization of consumer welfare as the yardstick to evaluate anticompetitive behavior and other unlawful, agreements.[349]

In *American Tobacco*,[350] the Supreme Court introduced the *rule of reason* in antitrust law which remains the core of U.S. antitrust analysis today. The Supreme Court, as Robert H. Bork observed, determined the *three-part rule of reason*, namely three tests by which a form of conduct is examined to identify possible anticompetitive effects.[351] The first test is the "inherent nature" test, under which any course of conduct, being exclusively a means of restricting output without any positive economic effect, is *per se* illegal.[352] In *United States v. Missouri Freight Ass'n* the Supreme Court applied the "inherent nature" test, recognizing price fixing to be illegal *per se.* Only when the analyzed practice can produce some positive effects must the courts apply the remaining two tests: "inherent effect" and "evident purpose." The "inherent effect" test refers to additional facts, such as the market share of the parties, which can affirm the damaging effects of a course of conduct. The Supreme Court specified that mergers are not illegal *per se*, and have to pass the "inherent effect" test,[353] which requires showing additional facts to prove that a merger is unlawful; increase of market share is not enough. Lastly, the "evident purpose" or "specific intent" test evaluates whether the analyzed conduct intentionally aims to achieve or maintain a monopoly to restrain competition.[354]

In summary, the Supreme Court understood that a formalistic approach for enforcing a law to guarantee free competition pricing and increase consumer welfare was unworkable. As a result, the Supreme Court started using economic evaluations and concepts, such as consumer welfare, to define whether a business's conduct was unlawful. Because the scope of the Sherman Act appeared vague and broad to companies, the Supreme Court's rulings through applying the *rule of reason* test did not make the distinction between lawful and unlawful contracts any easier. The U.S. legislators continued to enact legal provisions to clarify the Sherman Act's terms, but as it is outlined below, the results were largely inadequate.

---

2457 (1890). *See* 1 Areeda & Hovenkamp, *supra* n. 205, at 45. *See also* Thorelli, *supra* n. 339, at 227. Hans B. Thorelli also argued that the Congress that passed the Sherman act had the consumers as the ultimate beneficiary, who would have enjoyed an increase of production and higher quality products at lower prices.

349. *Ibid. See also* Bork, *supra* n. 339, at 36. As Robert Bork noted, *Standard Oil* ruling, not only put an end the most serious trust, but also determined the maximization of consumer welfare as the only purpose of the Sherman Act.

350. *United States v. American Tobacco Co.*, 221 U.S. 106 (1911).

351. Bork, *supra* n. 339, at 36. *See* also, Herbert Hovenkamp, *Federal Antitrust Policy*, 57 (West Pub., 3d. ed., 2005). In *Standard Oil* and *American Tobacco* the Supreme Court developed the *rule of reason*.

352. Bork, *supra* n. 339, at 36.

353. *Ibid.*, at 36.

354. *See*, e.g., Viscusi, Vemon & Harrington, *supra* n. 37, at 135.

On June 5, 1914, Congress approved the Clayton Act,[355] and several months later, the FTC Act.[356] The Federal Trade Commission Act (FTC Act),[357] enacted on September 26, 1914, created the FTC,[358] the second public body in charge of enforcing antitrust law. Before that, the Bureau of Corporation conducted general investigation on markets and reporting its findings to the DOJ, the only U.S. antitrust enforcer.

The FTC Act not only transferred to the FTC the functions originally granted in 1903 to the Bureau of Corporations [359] but also authorized the FTC to open general investigations of trade conditions under the Clayton and the FTC Act. In particular, the FTC Act empowered the FTC to enforce the still much-criticized U.S. antitrust rule: Section 5 of the Federal Trade Act. This rule prevents persons, corporations or partnerships from using "unfair methods" [360] of competition in commerce. In addition, the act gave the FTC governance as an administrative agency with regulatory powers—not a mere prosecutor as the DOJ.

Instead of becoming clearer, the antitrust framework was becoming more complicated. Congress was seeking to provide detail for the broad and vague provisions of the Sherman Act but created at the same time an equally broad and vague provision—Section 5 of the FTC Act. The new FTC has concurrent authority with the DOJ and private individuals for enforcing the Clayton Act.[361]

Another even more unsuccessful attempt to enforce competition principles as formal law was the *Patman Bill,* derived from the draft of E.B. Teegarden, counsel for an organization of small grocers, that had the clear intention to protect small retailers, not competition overall.[362] The Robinson-Patman Act aimed to protect small firms and local economies but without interfering with the efficiency-based advantages connected with economies of scale and scope.[363]

355. 15 U.S.C. §§ 12-27. *See* Mark Winerman, *The Origins of the FTC: Concentration, Cooperation, Control, and Competition,* 71 Antitrust L. J. 1, 59 (2003). ("The bill became law on October 17.") *Ibid.,* at 92.
356. 15 U.S.C. §§ 41-58.
357. Richard A. Posner, *The Federal Trade Commission,* 37 Univ. Chicago L. Rev. 47, 49 (1969). *See also* FTC, *Annual Report of the Federal Trade Commission,* 1 (1915); Hovenkamp, *supra* n. 351, at 595-597; Barry Mohun, *The Federal Trade Commission Law, the Clayton Antitrust Law, the Webb Export Law and Rules of Practice Before the Federal Trade Commission* (Washington, 1919).
358. President Woodrow Wilson by and with the advice of the Senate appointed the fist five FTC Commissioners: Joseph E. Davies, Edward N. Hurley, William J. Harris, Will H. Parry & George Rublee, who took the oath of the office on Mar. 16, 1915. FTC, *Annual Report of the Federal Trade Commission,* 1 (1915). *See also* Richard A. Posner & Frank H. Easterbrook, *Antitrust—Cases, Economic Notes and Other Materials,* 33 (West Publishing, 1980). ("Not more than three of the commissioners shall be members of the same political party.")
359. ABA Section of Antitrust Law, *FTC Practice and FTC Procedure Manual,* 3 (2007). The Bureau of Corporations is "a unit within the Commerce Department created (along with the Commerce Department itself) at Roosevelt's behest." *Ibid.*
360. Kovacic & Marc, *supra* n. 328, at 930.
361. *Ibid.*
362. *See* Terry Calvani & Gilde Breidenbach, *An Introduction to the Robinson-Patman Act and Its Enforcement by the Government,* 59 Antitrust L. J. 765, 769, 776 (1991). ("The original bill was unabashedly called the 'Wholesale Grocer's Protection Act.'"). *Ibid.,* at 769.
363. Mark A. Glick, David G. Mangum & Lara A. Swensen, *Towards a More Reasoned Application of the Robinson-Patman Act: A Holistic View Incorporating Principles of Law and Economics in Light of Congressional Intent,* 60 Antitrust Bull. 279, 280-282 (2015). ("The RPA was the

The Robinson-Patman Act has been seriously criticized over the years.[364] Robert Bork described it as "the child of the depression"[365] representing "antitrust's least glorious hour."[366] Even the Supreme Court recognized that this legislation was "complicated and vague, in itself,"[367] and over the years it has been relied upon less and less by antitrust bodies and private litigants. So, the strategy to use rigid legal provisions, such as those introduced by the *Patman Bill*, to clarify the terms of antitrust law had failed once again.

In the 1950s, the Supreme Court, assisted by economic models offered by the Harvard, Chicago and Post-Chicago Schools, almost completely abandoned the formalistic approach related to the *per se rule*. Economic analysis started determining when, under antitrust law, a conduct was unlawful and a market inefficient.[368] In addition, as this book emphasizes, flexible regulatory tools—antitrust settlements—that enshrine regulatory remedies based on economic theories and reasoning soon overshadowed not only legal provisions but also judges' rulings and ultimately replaced both.

### *[3] Harvard, Chicago and Post-Chicago Schools*

Terms such as restraint of trade, monopolization, market power,[369] and consumer welfare which are typically used in political economics, all appear in the lexicon of competition law. Over the years, both U.S. courts and scholars have agreed that placing economic thinking within the framework of antitrust law is fundamental.[370] Professor

culmination of a wide-ranging political struggle between wholesalers and small retailers and large chain store.") *Ibid.*, at 282. Bork, *supra* n. 339, at 383.

364. *See*, e.g., Christina DePasquale, *The Robinson-Patman Act an the Consumer Effects of Price Discrimination*, 60 Antitrust Bull. 402, 403 (2015); Glick, Mangum & Swensen, *supra* n. 363, at 280.
365. Bork, *supra* n. 339, at 382.
366. *Ibid.*
367. *FTC v. Ruberoid Co.*, 343 U.S. 470, 483 (1952).
368. *See* A.D. Neale, *Fair Competition. The Law and Economics of Antitrust Policy*. By J.B. Dirlam & A.E. Kahn, *The Attack on Big Business by J. D. Glover*, 65 Econ. J. 679-682 (1955). "It has been urged that the '*rule of reason*' in anti-trust law—the judicial requirement that the Sherman Act prohibition ... should involve a through economic analysis of each case in order to determine whether alleged restarints are 'unreasonable' by reference to tests of economic performance." *Ibid.*, at 680.
369. Jean Tirole, *Market Failures and Public Policy*, 105 American Econ. Rev. 1665 (2015). Market Power is "the firms' ability to raise price substantially above cost or to offer low quality." *Ibid.*
370. *See*, e.g., Sullivan & Hovenkamp, *supra* n. 130, at 68; Bork, *supra* n. 339, at 90; Robert H. Bork, *Legislative Intent and the Policy of the Sherman Act*, 9 J. L. & Econ. 7 (1966) *citing United States v. Aluminum Co. of American et al.*, 148 F.2d 416 (1945) 429. "[w]e have been speaking only of the economic reasons which forbid monopoly; but, as we have already implied, there are others, based upon the belief that great industrial consolidations are inherently undesirable, *regardless of their economic results*.") *Ibid.*, at 8. *See also* Herbert Hovenkamp, *The Sherman Act and the Classical Theory of Competition*, 74 Iowa L. J. 1019 (1989). ("One of the great myths about American antitrust policy is that courts first began to adopt an 'economic approach' to antitrust problems in the relatively recent past—perhaps as recently as the late 1970s.") *Ibid.*

Herbert Hovenkamp and E. Thomas Sullivan noted that the introduction and application of economics into antitrust law is probably the most important factor affecting antitrust analysis.[371]

The Chicago, Post-Chicago and Harvard Schools—the leading antitrust doctrines—promoted different types of economic models to enforce antitrust law. The Harvard School, which has significantly influenced the U.S. antitrust policy from the 1950s to the early 1970s,[372] focuses on the analysis of market structure and market power. In the 1950s, Edward S. Mason and Joe S. Bain developed the Structural, Conduct, Performance (SCP) paradigm[373] according to which[374] the structure of an industry can lead to market failure. Antitrust remedies in this paradigm are mainly directed to alter the structure of the market.[375] Government regulation of market structure is probably the most important corollary of the SCP paradigm:[376] Philip E. Areeda, Louis Kaplow and Aaron S. Edlin argue that "[w]ise government intervention through varied and mixed devices may be appropriate."[377]

While the Harvard School was promoting SCP, economists from the University of Chicago sought to challenge the paradigm and present an alternative approach.[378] The Chicago School is based on the assumption that the goals of antitrust policy can be achieved through the neoclassical price theory model; that is, market price will determine whether a market is competitive, not its market structure.[379]

The main contributors of the Chicago school are Robert Bork, Frank H. Easterbrook, and Richard A. Posner and their thinking is that generally, markets work better "when left alone;" and government intervention is rarely justified.[380] Frank H. Easterbrook observed that "in most cases legislation is designed to defeat the market"[381] rendering it not only unnecessary, but often, also harmful.[382] In the history of

371. Sullivan & Hovenkamp, *supra* n. 130, at 1.
372. *See, e.g.*, Patrick Van Cayseele & Roger Van den Bergh, *Antitrust Law*, in Boudewijn Bouckaert & Gerrit De Geest, ed., Encyclopedia of Law & Economics, 474 (1999) available at http://encyclo.findlaw.com/5300book.pdf.
373. *See, e.g.*, Sherrill Shaffer, *Structure, Conduct, Performance, and Welfare*, 9 Rev. Indus. Org. 435 (1994). *See also* Hovenkamp, *supra* n. 351; Perloff, Jeffrey M., Karp, Larry S., Golan, Amos Golan, *Estimating Market Power and Strategies*, 3 (Cambridge U. Press, 2007). Cayseele & Van den Bergh, *supra* n. 372, at 473.
374. Hovenkamp, *supra* n. 351, at 43. ("[T]he Cournot theory of oligopoly pricing, first developed in 1838, predicts an inverse relationship between the number of firms in the oligopolized market and the resulting price: the fewer the firms that must coordinate their behavior, the closer they will come to mimicking the price and output of a single-firm monopolist.")
375. Daniel Crane observed that "Harvard School tends to focus on the institutional limitations of governmental actors—regulators, judges, and juries—to correct" as the cause of an antitrust intervention. Daniel A. Crane, *Chicago, Post-Chicago, and Neo-Chicago*, 76 U. Chi. L. Rev. 1911, 1919 (2009).
376. Hovenkamp, *supra* n. 351, at 43.
377. Areeda, Kaplow & Edlin, *supra* n. 339, at 9.
378. Hovenkamp, *supra* n. 351, at 44.
379. Herbert Hovenkamp, *Antitrust Policy after Chicago*, 84 Mich. L. Rev. 213, 226 (1985).
380. Crane, *supra* n. 375, at 1923, *citing* Hovenkamp, *supra* n. 2, at 124.
381. Frank H. Easterbrook, *Antitrust and Economics of Federalism*, 26 J. L. & Econ. 23 (1983).
382. Frank H. Easterbrook, *Limits of Antitrust*, 63 Texas L. Rev. 1, 2 (1984). ("If the court [or government] errs by condemning a beneficial practice, the benefits may be lost for good. Any other firm that uses the condemned practice faces sanctions in the name of *stare decisis*, no

regulation, Easterbrook noted, that antitrust interventions are often the result of speculation of specific interest groups.[383] According to Robert Bork, government suits like *IBM* and *AT&T* were not based on either economics nor law.[384] Easterbrook observed that the limits of antitrust are the costs of action and the quality of information available to judges who are responsible for decision-making.[385] He also noted that that "[n]o question should be answered without adequate data."[386]

As Herbert Hovenkamp observed, however, "nothing—not even an intellectual structure as imposing as the Chicago School—lasts forever."[387] Nowadays the cutting edge of antitrust approach is offered by critics of the Chicago School. The major critics of the Chicago School feel that the Chicago School's thinking is too simple, theoretical and speculative.[388] In short, the Chicago School is considered unempirical by its critics.[389] The merit of the post-Chicago School thinking is the recognition that markets are much more complex and varied than the picture originally put forward by the Chicago School.[390] Therefore, the major distinction between Chicago and Post-Chicago doctrine is the fact that, under the latter, the market is treated as working on the basis of a set of complex underlying assumptions.[391]

The Nobel Prize winner, Jean Tirole, is recognized as the leading Post-Chicagoan. Tirole exemplified how economists use game-theory models for analyzing different markets and business strategies.[392] Tirole treats "firms as single decision makers that maximize profits"[393] and uses game theory, namely, "the study of mathematical models of conflict and cooperation between intelligent rational decision-makers,"[394] to analyze market and competitive conditions. Jean Tirole has also developed studies on network effects that characterized network industries and today's two-sided markets.

Although the Post-Chicago doctrine has rehabilitated the idea that antitrust authorities' intervention under particular circumstances is legitimate,[395] it did not shed

---

matter the benefits. If the court [or government] errs by permitting a deleterious practice, though, the welfare loss decreases over time.") *Ibid.*, at 2.

383. Frank H. Easterbrook, *Workable Antitrust Policy*, 84 Mich. L. Rev. 1696, 1701 (1986).
384. Bork, *supra* n. 339, at 163.
385. Easterbrook, *supra* n. 382, at 4.
386. Easterbrook, *supra* n. 383, at 1701. ("The costs of erroneous prohibitions (and the losses as people trim the vigor of their competition to avoid such prohibitions) are apt to be greater than the losses involved in waiting for better data and analysis before acting"). *Ibid.*
387. Hovenkamp, *supra* n. 379, at 216.
388. Herbert Hovenkamp, *The Antitrust Enterprise: Principle and Execution*, 38 (Harvard U. Press, 2005); Robert Pitofsky ed., *How the Chicago School Overshot the Mark: The Effect of Conservative Economic Analysis on U.S. Antitrust* (Oxford U. Press, 2008).
389. Crane, *supra* n. 375, at 1924.
390. Damien Geradin, Anne Layne-Farra & Nicolas Petit, *EU Competition Law and Economics*, 74 (Oxford U. Press, 2012).
391. Crane & Hovenkamp, *supra* n. 331, at 448.
392. As Steven C. Salop & Carl Shapiro observed, Tirole's work provided "the rigorous intellectual foundations for many of the game-theoretic models and ideas that modern antitrust economists employ." Steven C. Salop & Carl Shapiro, *Jean Tirole's Nobel Prize in Economics: The Rigorous Foundations of Post-Chicago Antitrust Economics*, 29 Antitrust 76 (2015).
393. Jean Tirole, *The Theory of Industrial Organization*, 4 (MIT Press, 1988).
394. Roger B. Myerson, *Game Theory: Analysis of Conflict*, 1 (Harvard U. Press, 1991).
395. Crane & Hovenkamp, *supra* n. 331. The Post-Chicago School "has a significantly restored faith in the efficacy of government intervention." *Ibid.*, at 267.

light on how often we need to consider those particular circumstances.[396] Furthermore, the Post-Chicago School failed to deal with the serious problem of judicial or agency administration.[397] Richard A. Posner and Daniel A. Crane observed that modern antitrust law represents the alliance of Chicago and Harvard School.[398] Therefore, Judge Posner and Professor Crane seem to argue that neither the structure nor the price strategy is alone able to fully exploit consumer welfare. The conjunction between these two theories and schools, however, does seem to be the relief that markets need.[399]

Although U.S. antitrust scholars have recently offered a new set of theories,[400] the Chicago School should still be considered the dominant one as it focused on the neoclassical price theory model. As outlined above, the Sherman Act was based on the Adam Smith's economic theories on competition and agreements in the restrain of trade,[401] emphasizing the importance of free competition and its benefits on price and output.

Smith created markets to justify the so-called market price that is above or equal to the natural price governed by the proportion between the supply and the demand for a good.[402] Smith explained that, where there is a monopoly or a secret trade agreement between the manufacturers, the market is kept regularly under-stocked, leading to commodity prices being set "much above the natural price."[403] The monopoly's price is the highest that a good can acquire, whereas the price of free competition is the lowest price attainable for any particular goods.

As a consequence, the neoclassical price theory model and economic analysis of markets promoted by the Chicago School seems to better exploit legal & economic regulation that aims to promote the price of free competition.

### *[4] The Role of the Neutral Economic Expert*

Economists and their theories began not only influencing U.S. antitrust agencies, but also judges' rulings, and therefore had a disproportionate influence on antitrust case law. Because antitrust litigation often requires a careful and complex analysis of data, it is routine that each party involved needs economic witnesses to testify at the trial.[404] Rule 702 of the Federal Rules of Evidence enables parties to use witnesses qualified "as

396. Geradin, Layne-Farra & Petit, *supra* n. 390, at 76. *See also* Giorgio Monti, *EU Competition Law*, 69 (Cambridge U. Press, 2007).
397. Antonio Cucinotta, Roberto Pardolesi & Roger Van den Bergh, *Post-Chicago Developments in Antitrust Law*, 5 (Edward Elgar, 2002).
398. Richard A. Posner, *The Chicago School of Antitrust Analysis*, 127 Univ. Pen. L. Rev. 925 (1979); Daniel A. Crane, *linkLine's Institutional Suspicious*, Cato Sup. Ct. Rev. 111, 131 (2009).
399. Einer Elhauge, *Harvard, Not Chicago: Which Antitrust School Drives Recent U.S. Supreme Court Decisions?*, 3 Competition Policy Intern. 59 (2007); Crane, *supra* n. 398, at 131.
400. *See*, e.g., Lina M. Khan, *Amazon's Antitrust Paradox*, 126 Yale L. J. 564 (2016).
401. Smith, *supra* n. 337.
402. *Ibid.*, at 54.
403. *Ibid.*
404. Gregory J. Sidak, *Court-Appointed Neutral Economic Experts*, 9 J. Competition L. & Eco. 359 (2013).

an expert by knowledge, skill, experience, training, or education,"[405] to submit expert opinions.

Ordinarily, judges do not have economic training to ask the right questions or to decide without economic explanations. This is why Judge Frank H. Easterbrook considers antitrust law "an imperfect tool for the regulation of competition."[406] Easterbrook observed that "neither judges nor juries are particularly good at handling complex economic arguments"[407] and the challenge for judges is to adapt the language of antitrust law to changing economic and social conditions. However, there is neither an obligation nor rule that requires lawyers to provide the courts with all data or economic analysis useful to assess the case. Economic experts do assist parties in supporting their conduct[408] and it is likely that these experts provide evidence only in favor of their clients.

As Daniel L. Rubinfeld and Gregory J. Sidak observed, a possible solution to fill the gaps in economic cases and impartially evaluate the expert opinion filed by parties might be the appointment of a judge as its own neutral economic expert.[409] In the United States, Rule 706 of the Federal Rules of Evidence states that courts have broad discretion in appointing an expert testimony "[o]n a party's motion or on its own."[410] Courts, under Rule 706, can require the parties to specify why "expert witnesses should not be appointed and may ask the parties to submit nominations."[411]

Because a neutral expert can be crucial in determining results in a trial, parties rarely file a motion to appoint a neutral expert who could question their evidence. Despite the fact that Rule 706 does not limit the situations where intervention of a neutral witness is required, judges occasionally enforce this rule of appointing a neutral expert.[412] Besides being costly, courts also fear that the "neutral" experts may not be "truly neutral," and that they might affect jury deliberation.[413] Furthermore, the appointment of a neutral expert increases the work for judges, not only in terms of "finding, interviewing, and appointing" the expert but also in shepherding and protecting them during the trial.[414]

However, judges such as Richard A. Posner and Stephen G. Breyer seem to be in favor of appointing their own neutral economic expert under Rule 706 in order to recognize possible contradictions in testimonies offered by experts of the opposite

405. Fed. R. Evid. 702.
406. Easterbrook, *supra* n. 382, at 39.
407. *Ibid.*
408. Joseph E. Fortenberry, *Antitrust Litigation and the Court-Appointed Economic Expert: A Modest Proposal*, 12 Antitrust L. & Econ. Rev. 41 (1980).
409. Daniel L. Rubinfeld, *Econometrics in the Courtroom*, 85 Colum. L. Rev. 1048, 1049 (1985); Sidak, *supra* n. 404, at 360.
410. Fed. R. Evid. 706(a).
411. *Ibid.*
412. The U.S. district courts for the Southern and Eastern District of New York, for example, argue that the use of the neutral expert is rarely convenient. In re Joint E. & S. Dist. Asbestos Litig., 830 F. Supp. 686, 693 (E. & S.D.N.Y. 1993).
413. Sidak, *supra* n. 404, at 363. *See also*, William J. Travis, *Impartial Expert Testimony under the Federal Rules of Evidence: A French Perspective*, 8 Int'l L. 492, 493 (1974).
414. Richard A. Posner, *Reflections on Judging*, 287-328 (Harvard U. Press, 2013).

parties.[415] Indeed, Posner and Breyer see Rule 706 as an effective method in evaluating admissibility of expert witnesses before cross-examination at a trial.[416] In several countries, such as Italy, judges frequently appoint a neutral expert to cross-examine parties' experts. Otherwise, the report and deposition of parties'experts would not constitute an evidence.

In summary, terms such as restraint of trade, abuse of dominant position, monopolization and market power,[417] which are typically used in the political economy, appear in the lexicon of antitrust law. Antitrust law requires sophisticated economic evaluations and the use of economic experts seems recommendable.

In case there is no expert appointed by judges, judges tend to rely on expert witnesses appointed by parties. Judges' decisions often result from economic experts' assessments rather than a pure decision made independently. The question that arises is whether the few antitrust cases that go to trial create judges' case law or if they are merely the result of economic experts' evaluations. As around 90 percent of civil U.S. antitrust cases are settled by means of consent decrees and the few remaining trials mostly depends on economic witness testimonies, one can wonder if it makes sense to focus on enforcing antitrust as a law. Or, should we teach economics to judges and law to economists?

Easterbrook noted the very challenging task of judges to adapt the language of antitrust law to changing economic and social conditions. As explored in Chapter 1, this could be the main reason why U.S. antitrust agencies started settling most antitrust cases through antitrust settlements. Expecting judges with no economic background to make markets more efficient does not seem like a reasonable policy option.

### [B] Conclusions

Antitrust law arose in the United States to contrast the trust and monopolization phenomena in markets, as was recommended by Smith in his book *The Wealth of Nations*. The first attempt to adopt a formalistic approach for enforcing antitrust law was a failure. Soon the U.S. courts and antitrust agencies understood that antitrust law needed economic analysis to be fully exploited. Economic analysis started determining when, under antitrust law, a conduct was unlawful and a market inefficient.

Amongst the three main economic antitrust institutions—the Chicago, Post-Chicago and Harvard Schools—the neoclassical price theory model promoted by the Chicago School remains the most cutting edge and valuable antitrust economic theory. The few antitrust cases that go to trial are essentially the result of economic experts' evaluations as judges generally do not have sufficient economic training to ask the right economic questions or to decide without economic explanations.

415. Sidak, *supra* n. 404, at 360.
416. *Ibid.*
417. Tirole, *supra* n. 369.

In summary, U.S. antitrust law originated from Adam Smith's economic theories and has developed based on sophisticated economic analysis and price evaluation. As explored in Chapter 1, this could be the main reason behind the U.S. antitrust agencies' tendency to settle most antitrust cases by means of antitrust settlements. Through the adoption of consent decrees, antitrust agencies seek market efficiency goals directly by imposing procompetitive structural or behavioral remedies based on economic analysis rather than requiring adjudication by courts. Constraining judges with no economic background to make markets more efficient seems not only inappropriate but also inefficient.

## §3.02 THE EU COMPETITION LAW IN THE EUROPEAN SINGLE MARKET

The origin of European competition law has very little in common with the origin of U.S. antitrust law. Competition was the reason why Belgium, France, Italy, Luxemburg, the Netherlands and West Germany signed the Treaty of Rome on March 25, 1957.[418] The creation of the European Economic Community (EEC) was the answer to the competitive tension amongst states. Prior to the Treaty, in the post-world war period, the United States and United Kingdom (UK) wished to set a climate of cooperation and peace among Western European States in order to counterbalance the increasing power of the Soviet Union.[419] As far back as 1946, Churchill had addressed the concept of economic union within Europe by referring to "The United States of Europe."[420]

In order to effectively create a common market, the EEC would first find it necessary to remove any obstacles in the free movement of people, capital, goods and services.[421] This removal of barriers was driven by the philosophy of competition law.[422] In this context, the European Community immediately recognized the

418. *See* Koen Lenaerts, Piet Van Nuffel & Robert Bray, *European Union Law*, 12 (Sweet & Maxwell, 3d., 2011).
419. *Ibid.*, at 4.
420. "The idea of 'European integration' was brought back to the attention of the public on September 19, 1946 by a speech made by Churchill at the University of Zürich in which he called for the establishment of 'a kind of United States of Europe' on the continent." *Ibid.*
421. Stephen Broadberry & Kevin H. O'Rourke, *The Cambridge Economic History of Modern Europe*, 281 (Cambridge U. Press, 2010). *See also* Lenaerts, Nuffel & Bray, *supra* n. 418, at 12. ("Article 2 announced ambitious aims to be achieved through the establishment of a common market and the progressive approximation of the Member States' economic policies. Article 3 EEC specified those object by listing the task of the Community"). *Ibid.*
422. David Gerber, *Law and Competition in Twentieth-Century Europe: Protecting Prometheus* (Oxford U. Press, 2001). ("The process of European integration has further enhanced competition law's importance. The core of that process has been the creation of a unified market in Europe, and its success has depended on establishing norms and institutions that make that market both economically effective and politically desirable.") *Ibid.*, at 2. *See also* Vivien Rose & Davis Bailey, *EU Competition Law and Its Territorial Reach*, in Bellamy & Child ed., European Union Law of Competition 1.001 (Oxford U. Press, 7th ed., 2003). ("The Court of Justice has recognized that the EU rules on competition are 'fundamental provisions' which are essential for the accomplishment of the tasks entrusted to the EU and, in particular, for the functioning of a single, internal market.") *See also* Barry E. Hawk, *Antitrust in the EEC—The First Decade*,

need to monitor private agreements in restraint of trade within the new single market.[423]

In 1955, Jean Monnet observed that:

> the body of consumers will not enjoy the benefits of the Community unless discriminatory arrangements are prohibited and unless all activities are placed on the same footing and are given the same chance to develop.[424]

In summary, six very different economies and markets were combined to create a single economic entity and a law to prohibit discrimination practices and agreements in restrain of trade among European companies appeared as an essential component.[425]

The first commitment to protect competition was embodied in Articles 85-86 (now Articles 101 and 102 TFEU) of the Treaty of Rome of 1957,[426] which created direct implications in each Member State.[427] Articles 101 and 102 of the TFEU still represent the core provisions of EU competition law.

### [A] The EU Formalistic Approach in Enforcing Antitrust Law

While U.S. antitrust enforcers soon started adopting an economic approach in enforcing antitrust law, European competition law developed in a "fairly formalistic manner."[428] The legal formalism of EU competition law provisions "contrast starkly with U.S. antitrust,"[429] Barry E. Hawk noted. The contrasting European approach depended not only on the different reasons behind the enactment of the EU Competition law but also on the European legal system. The civil law reasoning typical of the European legal

---

41 Fordham L. Rev. 229, 231 (1972); Eleanor M. Fox, *The Competition Law of the European Union in Comparative Perspective* (West, 2009). *See also* Mario Monti, *Strengthening the European Economy Through Competition Policy* (Oct. 29, 1999) available at https://europa.eu/rapid/press-release_SPEECH-99-146_en.htm?locale=en. ("The competition rules have been since the very beginning a cornerstone of European integration and of the Treaty of Rome.") *Ibid.*

423. *See* Doris Hildebrand, *The Role of Economic Analysis in the EC Competition Rules*, 10 (Kluwer Int., 3d ed., 2009).

424. *See* Joaquin Almunia, *Competition Enforcement in the EU: Beyond the Integration of Markets* (Oct. 18, 2012) available at http://europa.eu/rapid/press-release_SPEECH-12-742_en.htm (*citing* Jean Monnet).

425. *See* Richard Whish & David Bayle, *Competition Law* §2.09 (Oxford U. Press, 8th ed., 2015). ("[I]t is important to stress that EU competition law is applied by the Commission and the EU Courts very much with the issue of single market integration in mind.")

426. Kiran Klaus Patel & Heike Schweitzer, *The Historical Foundations of EU Competition Law*, 11 (Oxford U. Press, 2013).

427. *Ibid.* In particular, *Costa v. Enel*, Case 6/64, judgment of 15.07.1964, the Court of Justice emerged the rules of the Treaty of Rome, such as Articles 85 and 86, as particular *supranational* rules. The Court of Justice stated that "[t]he executive force of Community law cannot vary from one State to another in deference to subsequent domestic laws, without jeopardizing the attainment of the objectives of the Treaty ... The precedent of Community law is confirmed by Article 189, whereby a regulation 'shall be biding' and 'directly applicable in all Member States.' This provision, which is subject to no reservation, would be quite meaningless if a State could unilaterally nullify its effects by means of a legislative measure which could prevail over Community law." *Ibid.*

428. Richard Whish & David Bailey, *Competition Law* ¶1.04 (Oxford U. Press, 2015).

429. Hawk, *supra* n. 5.

system is based on legal categories and on solving only interpretation issues through the authoritative decisions of judges.

However, once the goal of creating a single European market was achieved, economic analysis began to significantly affect antitrust intervention by the EU Commission and the EU Courts.[430] The EU competition law was approaching the U.S. antitrust law.

### *[1] From the European Market Integration to the Economic Growth Goal*

On April 21, 1956, the Messina (or *Spaak*) Report,[431] proposed that the Treaty included provisions that would have prevented agreements in restraint of trade and abuse of dominant position practices that would limit the creation of the Common Market.[432] The reply to the Messina Report was Article 3(f) of the Treaty of Rome, which set out the Community's need to establish "a system ensuring that competition in the Common Market is not distorted." Furthermore, European competition law provisions embodied in Articles 85 and 86 of the Treaty of Rome (now Articles 101 and 102 of the TFEU) determined which forms of conduct, being "incompatible with the Common Market," were prohibited. In the *Grundig* case,[433] the Court of Justice[434] recognized that, because agreements between producers and distributors "might tend to restore the national divisions in trade between member states" and may threaten "the most fundamental objectives of the Community,"[435] they could be prohibited.

Indeed, the market integration goal was clear to judges[436] who used it to interpret several aspects of competition law including the issue of parallel imports.[437] Among Member States there were significant price differences for many products and services. Parallel imports enabled companies to buy goods that traded cheaply in one Member

430. Geradin, Layne-Farra & Petit, *supra* n. 390, at 2.04.
431. This Report was made by the intergovernmental committee composed of delegates from the six governments appointed by the Conference of Messina. The chairman of this committee was the Belgium Foreign Minister in Belgium Paul-Henri Spaak. The Spaak Committee aimed to reply to the questions raised at the Messina Conference about the choice between a general common market and partial sectorial integration. The Spaak Report published on Apr. 21, 1956, set out the broad lines of a future EEC and European Atomic Energy Community. *See* Arved Deringer, *The Competition Law of the European Economic Community*, 1 (Commerce Clearing House Inc., 1968).
432. Deringer, *supra* n. 431, at 1. Hildebrand, *supra* n. 423. ("The Spaak report contains in Title II the rules concerning competition"). *Ibid.*, at 8.
433. Judgment of the Court of 13 July 1966, *Grundig-Verkaufs-GmbH v. Comm'n* ("*Grundig*").
434. Cucinotta, Pardolesi & Van den Bergh, *supra* n. 397, at 36; Geradin, Layne-Farra & Petit, *supra* n. 390, at 24.
435. In *Grundig* at 8. Monti, *supra* n. 396, at 41. ("This case is also an illustration of the Community's irrational understanding of market integration.")
436. Cucinotta, Pardolesi & Van den Bergh, *supra* n. 397, at 36. *See also*, Monti, *supra* n. 422.
437. Cucinotta, Pardolesi & Van den Bergh, *supra* n. 397, at 36. ("In Europe, territorial market partitioning and parallel imports clearly dominated law enforcement until the accomplishment of the programme to create an internal market by the end of 1992. In contrast, in the USA, the need to curtail the power of large trusts was the main issue in the first decades of antitrust enforcement.") *Ibid.*

State and resell them in other Member States where the price was higher, mitigating price discrimination strategies among Member States.

To limit parallel imports and maximize their profit, EU manufactures reached selective distribution agreements with distributors, restricting, for example, their rights to sell outside of their own Member State. The Court of Justice soon declared such agreements to be unlawful. In *Ford Werke AG*,[438] the Court specified that the Commission does not need to conduct detailed analyses to balance *pros* and *cons* of a selective distribution system if it "has good reason to believe that a manufacturer has used such a system to prevent parallel imports ... to partition the common market."[439]

Once the market integration goal had been achieved,[440] economic goals and economic analysis in enforcing competition law started becoming even more familiar to European antitrust enforcers. Building a competitive Europe became the prominent EU goal, and competition policy was identified as a crucial economic driver.[441]

### *[2] European Economic Growth and the Economics Based Approach*

The legal formalism of the European competition law provisions were strongly criticized, especially by U.S. scholars.[442] European competition enforcers started using a "more economic" approach at the end of 1990s.[443] In July 1991, for example, the

438. Case Joined 24-26/84, *Werke AG & Ford of Europe Inc. v. Comm'n*, 1985 E.C.R. 02725.
439. *Ibid.*
440. At the time of the Treaty of Maastricht Member States the creation of a common market benchmark was considered fulfilled. Eur-lex, *Summary of the Treaty of Maastricht on European Union*, http://eur-lex.europa.eu/legal-content/EN/TXT/?uri = URISERV:xy0026. ("With the Treaty of Maastricht, the Community clearly went beyond its original economic objective, i.e. creation of a common market.") *See also* Hildebrand, *supra* n. 423, at 21.
441. Neelie Kroes, *Speech Building a Competitive Europe—Competition Policy and the Relaunch of the Lisbon Strategy, Milan* (Feb. 7, 2005); Mario Monti, *EU Competition Policy after May 2004, Fordham Annual Conference on International Antitrust Law and Policy* at VII (Oct. 24, 2003), available at http://europa.eu/rapid/press-release_SPEECH-03-489_en.htm. In 2004 Mario Monti clarified that the future of competition policy enforcement was ("to contribute through competition policy instruments to foster market oriented reforms in the EU economy and, therefore, to improve its capabilities for sustainable growth.") *Ibid. See also*, Hildebrand, *supra* n. 423, at 17. ("The promotion of *effective* competition in the Community can be regarded as a major EC policy goal, which is related to economic considerations.")
442. *See* e.g., Hawk, *supra* n. 5, at 986. In vertical restraints context, Barry E. Hawk noted that ("[i]t is shocking how little time is devoted to assessing the competitive risks and benefits of the vertical restraints at issue. The practice under the Sherman Act is exactly the opposite. It is difficult to believe that EC competition policy is furthered where there is far more attention and intellectual resources devoted to doctrinal formalisms than to substantive analysis.") *Ibid.*
443. Geradin, Layne-Farra & Petit, *supra* n. 390, at 2.04; Nicolas Petit, *New Challenges for 21s Century Competition Authorities*, 13 Comm. L. Rev. 10, 15 (2012). ("This means that antitrust cases are no longer ruled by 'slogan'. *Per se* prohibition standards that inferred anticompetitive effects on the basis of an analysis of the formal features of a given course of conduct, for instance the duration or scope of an exclusivity clause, are no longer relevant. Rather, in each and every case, agencies focus on market facts, and conduct is judged in that light. The merit of the more economic approach is to limit 'error costs', in particular type I errors—false convictions–and type II errors—false acquittals.") *Ibid. See also*, Hildebrand, *supra* n. 423, at 4. ("The Commission, as the policy maker, started to recognize this need to adapt its *previously more legalistic approach*. The old-fashioned way of analyzing markets and discussing dominance has been overruled by the speed of technological development, by the trend toward

Court of Justice in the *Akzo case*[444] accepted a price-cost comparison as the yardstick to determine whether the conduct of price undercutting was lawful or unlawful.[445]

The transition toward a more economic approach was even more evident in the context of vertical restraints. On January 22, 1997, in its Green Paper on vertical restraints,[446] the EU Commission highlighted the necessity to review the current policy on vertical restraints in the light of "the current economic thinking"[447] which "stresse[d] the importance"[448] of considering market structure and applying economic analysis to vertical restraints. In 1998, the Commission, following up on the Green Paper, published a Communication on the application of Community competition rules to vertical restraints, and the "need for a more economics based approach"[449] was laid down. Furthermore, in 2004 the reviewed European Merger Control Regulation provided a new test to assess mergers—the Substantial Lessing of Competition Test—for bridging the gap between economics and law.[450]

The former Commissioner Mario Monti recognized that, in reviewing block exemption regulations and producing guidelines, the Commission "shifted from a legalistic based approach to an interpretation of the rules based on sound economic principle."[451] Mario Monti admitted that the development of an economic interpretation of European competition provisions was one of his main goals since he was appointed as Commissioner for Competition.[452] In fact, during his term, the Commission created a new position to reinforce the DGCom's economic capabilities—the Chief

globalization as well as by the rapid convergence of whole sectors. The insufficiency of the old method of applying economics became obvious in particular in the application of the Merger Regulation in the early nineties. Karel van Miert, at that time Member of the European Commission responsible for competition policy, recognized this need for policy change and initiated one of the most comprehensive reforms in EC competition law. Karel van Miert postulated the policy that a solid picture of the markets in question should be drawn and that a fact-based analysis is required to determine what the real situation is.") *Ibid.*

444. *AKZO Chemie BV v. Comm'n*, Case C-62/86, 1991 E.C.R. I-3359 §§ 71-74.
445. Cucinotta, Pardolesi & Van den Bergh, *supra* n. 397, at 45.
446. *Commission Green Paper on Vertical Restraints*, COM(1996) 721 final (Jan. 22, 1997).
447. Luc Peeperkorn, *Commission Adopts Green Paper on Vertical Restraints in EU Competition Policy* (Jan. 20, 1997), http://ec.europa.eu/competition/speeches/text/sp1997_002_en.html.
448. Commission Green Paper on Vertical Restraints, *supra* n. 446, at 17.
449. Communication from the Commission on the Application of the Community Competition Rules to Vertical Restrains—Follow-up to the Green Paper on Vertical Restraints, COM(1998) 0544 final O.J. C 365 (Nov. 26, 1998).
450. *See* Giorgio Monti, *The New Substantive Test in the EC Merger Regulation—Bridging the Gap Between Economics and Law?*, Working Paper n. 10 (2008) available at http://eprints.lse.ac.uk/24601/1/WPS2008-10_Monti.pdf; Werner Berg, *New EC Merger Regulation: A First Assessment of Its Pratical Impact, The Symposium on European Competition Law*, 24 Northwestern J. Intern. L. & Bussiness 683 (2004); Mario Monti, *Speech at the Fordham Annual Conference on International Antitrust Law and Policy*, *supra* n. 441, at 2. ("The need to ensure legal certainty while at the same time developing greater sophistication in the economic analysis also applies to the merger control field.") *Ibid.*
451. Mario Monti, *Speech at the Fordham Annual Conference on International Antitrust Law and Policy*, *supra* n. 441, at 2.
452. *Ibid. See also* Hildebrand, *supra* n. 423, at 4. ("Mario Monti ... developed further the modernization process initiated by van Miert. Legal certainty, the need to concentrate scare resources quickly on the most important issues and the will to shed bureaucracy were the buzzwords at this time. Mario Monti was convinced that the actual impact of the competition

Competition Economist.[453] More importantly, during the Monti's term as Commissioner for competition Regulation 1/2003 was enacted which formalized the procedure for commitment decisions.

Mario Monti's plan was continued by the succeeding Commissioners for Competition. Neelie Kroes agreed that European competition rules should be based on economic analysis;[454] Joaquin Almunia also confirmed the necessity to enforce competition through "sophisticated economic analysis."[455]

In 2009, the Guidance on the Commission's enforcement priorities in applying Article 82 of the EU Commission Treaty[456] confirmed increasing attention to economic analysis.[457] Here, the Commission introduced a new test based on economic principles, the "as efficient competitor" (AEC) test, used as a yardstick to evaluate conditional rebates.[458] To determine whether a firm's conduct has anticompetitive effects, the EU Commission compares costs and the efficient price instead of applying a formal-based analysis.[459]

To conclude, the progression from a legal formalistic approach to an economic one in applying European competition rules is clear, particularly with Monti's term as Commissioner for competition. What remains unclear is why today, as outlined below, the EU Commission seems to favor a purely formalistic approach, effectively reverting to an approach used thirty years ago.

---

rules on European society is determined by their efficient implementation ... [and] ... [t]he Commission's reform was centred on the 'more economics-based approach' in the EC competition rules.") *Ibid.*

453. "Professor Lars-Hendrik Röller has been nominated to this post in July 2003. He will be assisted by a team of specialized economists. In antitrust, merger and state aid cases, the Chief Economist will offer an independent economic viewpoint for policy development and provide guidance in individual cases throughout the investigation process. In cases requiring sophisticated quantitative analysis, a member of his team of economists may be seconded to work in the case team." Mario Monti, *EU Competition Policy after May 2004*, Fordham Annual Conference on International Antitrust Law and Policy at V, *supra* n. 441. *See* Lars-Hendrik Röller, *Economic Analysis and Competition Policy Enforcement in Europe* 11, in Peter A.G. Van Bergeijk & Erik Kloosterhuis, Modelling European Mergers: Theory, Competition Policy and Case Studies (Edward Elgar, 2005). ("The office of the CCE consists of 10 specialized economists, the Chief Economist Team ('CET'), all of which hold PhDs in Industrial Organization. Approximately, half of the members are permanent EU officials, while the others are temporary agents.") *Ibid.*, at 14.
454. Kroes, *supra* n. 441, available at http://europa.eu/rapid/press-release_SPEECH-05-78_en.htm?locale=en.
455. Joaquin Almunia, *EU Antitrust Policy: The Road Ahead, Speech at International Forum on EU Competition Law* (Mar. 9, 2010) available at http://europa.eu/rapid/press-release_SPEECH-10-81_en.htm?locale=en.
456. Communication from the Commission—Guidance on the Commission's enforcement priorities in applying Article 82 of the EU Commission Treaty to abusive exclusionary conduct by dominant undertakings, C45/7 (Feb. 24, 2009).
457. Richard Whish & David Bailey, *Competition Law*, 10.004 (Oxford U. Press, 2015). The guidance ("aims to provide greater clarity and predictability as regards the general framework of analysis that the Commission will employ when determining whether to pursue cases. It introduces a more economics-based approach to the Commission's enforcement of Article 102 while purporting to remain within the constraints of the case law of the EU Courts.") *Ibid.*
458. Julia Molestina & Peter Georg Pitch, *Conditional Rebate Schemes and the More Economic Approach: Back to the Future?*, 46 Int'l Rev. Intell. Prop. Competition L. 203, 204 (2015).
459. *Ibid.*, at 205.

### *[3] Intel and Google Decisions: EU Commission Versus Court of Justice*

Despite the fact that the adoption of a "more economic" approach is recognized as one of the most fundamental developments of EU competition law, Nicolas Petit predicted that the twenty-first century could be marked by the end of the "more economic" approach.[460]

In examining a possible return from an economic approach to a formal one in the enforcement of EU competition law by EU Commission, the *Intel* and *Google* cases are significant. Those decisions seem to compromise the *rapprochement* between U.S. and EU competition law by favoring prohibition decisions rather than settlement solutions in addition to affirming a formalistic approach in enforcing competition principles. In 2017 the ECJ reversed the Intel decision, affirming the importance of economic analysis in assessing anticompetitive conduct. The EU Commission's decisions regarding Google Search and Google Android have been appealed and might be reversed by EU judges in a similar manner affecting the future EU Commission's policy.

#### *[a] Intel*

On May 13, 2009, the Commission fined Intel EUR 1.06 billion for engaging in abuse of dominant position conduct under Article 102 of TFEU. The Commission found that Intel gave wholly or partially hidden rebates to original computer equipment manufacturers (OEMs) only if they purchased all, or almost all, of their x86 CPUs from Intel. Furthermore, Intel was paying OEMs directly to stop or delay their launch of products containing a competitor's x86 CPUs as well as to limit the sales channels available to those products.[461]

The crucial point in Intel is the definition of rebates. The General Court upheld the Commission's decision distinguishing three categories: quantitative rebates, exclusive rebates, and "other" rebates.[462] While quantitative rebates could have competitive effects and were likely to be lawful, exclusive rebates granted on the condition that the client purchased all or almost all the supply from the dominant firm, were, by their nature, anticompetitive rebates. The "other" rebates were those that have a fidelity-building effect, by granting financial incentives not conditioned on an exclusive or quasi-exclusive supply by the leader of market.[463] These rebates were not "anticompetitive" in nature and therefore deserved a deeper analysis.[464]

460. Nicolas Petit, *New Challenges for 21st Century Competition Authorities*, 14 (2013) available at http://papers.ssrn.com/sol3/papers.cfm?abstract_id = 2207886.
461. Summary of Commission Decision of 13 May 2009, 2009 O.J. (C 227) 13. *See also* Massarotto, *The Deterrent and Enunciating Effects of Consent Decrees*, *supra* n. 8.
462. *Intel Corp. v. Comm'n*, Case T-286/09, 2014 ECLI:EU:T:2014:547.
463. *Ibid.*, para. 78. *See also* Richard Whish, *Intel v. Commission: Keep Calm and Carry on!*, 6 J. Competition L. & Prac. 1 (2014).
464. The Intel decision has divided scholars into two camps: Damien Geradin, for example, has criticised the Court's formalistic approach because it is not consistent with economic teachings. Richard Whish, on the other hand, considers the General Court's decision completely reasonable, observing that Article 102, which deals with dominant undertakings only, is form-based in nature, and that such rules enable lawyers, judges, economists, and businesses to predict

The "formal" distinction provided by the General Court, which made exclusive rebates as "*per se*" illegal, appears as a return to a more formalistic approach by European courts.[465] In September 2017, the Court of Justice[466] surprisingly reversed the General Court ruling applying the *rule of reason* in rebate practices under Article 102 TFEU.[467] The Court of Justice recognized that "the General Court wrongly failed to take into consideration Intel's line of argument seeking to expose alleged errors committed by the Commission in the AEC test"[468] welcoming a more economic approach in the enforcement of Article 102 TFEU.

The Court of Justice's ruling in the Intel case will be "one of the most important on competition law for many years,"[469] as Professor Richard Whish noted. The Court of Justice is clearly challenging the current approach adopted by the EU Commission by standing for an economic approach in enforcing Article 102 of the TFEU.

### *[b] Google Search and Google Android*

On November 30, 2010, the EU Commission opened a formal investigation against Google concerning alleged unfavorable treatment of rival services in Google's unpaid and sponsored search results.[470] According to the EU Commission, Google intentionally manipulated its algorithm by altering both organic and paid search results to favor Google's own services at the expense of rivals.[471]

On June 27, 2017, the EU Commission fined Google EUR 2.42 billion for abusing its dominant position in the search engine market by giving illegal preference to its own comparison shopping service. That decision was the result of seven years of investigation by the EU Commission, which rejected twice the commitments offered by Google to settle the case without imposing a fine.[472] According to the EU Commissioner Margrethe Vestager, Google abused its market dominance because its search engine "does not position and display in the same way results from Google's comparison shopping service and from competing comparison shopping services."[473]

---

and distinguish lawful from unlawful conducts. *See* Whish, *supra* n. 463. Damien Geradin, *Loyalty Rebates after Intel: Time for the European Court of Justice to Overrule Hoffman-La Roche*, 11 J. Competition L. & Econ. 579 (2015).

465. Geradin, *supra* n. 464, at 579. ("the GCEU decides to stick to the quasi-per se rule of illegality contained in Hoffman-La Roche.") *Ibid.*, at 581.
466. *Intel Corp. v. Comm'n*, C-413/14 P, 2017 EU:C:2017:632.
467. Nicolas Petit, *The Judgment of the EU Court of Justice in Intel and the Rule of Reason in Abuse of Dominance Cases* (Dec. 12, 2017). European Law Review, October 2018 Forthcoming. Available at SSRN: https://ssrn.com/abstract=3086402 or http://dx.doi.org/10.2139/ssrn.3086402.
468. *Intel Corp. v. Comm'n*, C-413/14 P, 2017 EU:C:2017:632, at 147.
469. Whish, *supra* n. 463, at 2.
470. EU Commission, Antitrust: Commission probes allegations of antitrust violations by Google, Press Release IP/10/1624 (Nov. 30, 2010).
471. *Ibid.*; James D. Ratliff & Daniel L. Rubinfeld, *Is There a Market for Organic Search Engine Results and Can Their Manipulation Give Rise to Antitrust Liability?*, 10 J. Competition L. & Econ. 517 (2014).
472. EU Commission, Joaquin Almunia, The Google Antitrust Case: What Is at Stake?, Press Release (Oct. 1, 2013).
473. EU Commission, Google Search (Shopping) (Jun. 27, 2017) § 662 ("Google Bias Decision").

By doing so, the EU Commission seems to treat Google Search as an essential facility platform and requires Google to treat rivals' search results the same as its own, although the essential facility doctrine does not appear applicable in this case. Google Search platform is both reasonably replicable and not precluded to rivals. If consumers still use Google despite the fact that Google does not provide a pure organic search, perhaps most consumers still perceive Google Search as the best search engine. Perhaps Google is manipulating consumers how newspapers manipulate their readers through advertisement. This is not a violation under Article 102 of TFEU. The only justified regulatory intervention in cases like Google seems to be one aimed at improving data treatment and privacy protection.[474]

Google has appealed the EU Commission's decision.[475] The ECJ decision in Intel, which emphasizes ECJ's favoritism for an economic approach in enforcing Article 102 TFEU, should facilitate Google in justifying its conduct and business strategies in court. Google is constantly providing more advanced technologies for free to consumers and competition law does not protect competitors but consumers. Furthermore, we should keep in mind that, in Europe, the fine imposed by the EU Commission does not pay back damaged consumers and companies; rather Google is likely to pass the costs of that fine on to its consumers.

On April 15, 2015, the EU Commission opened another antitrust investigation against Google, alleging that Google was abusing its dominant position in the smartphone operating system market through its Google Android operating system. On July 18, 2018, the EU Commission fined Google EUR 4.34 billion for illegal practices in the smartphone operating system market. According to the EU Commission, Google used Android "to cement its dominant position in general internet search,"[476] although it is doubtful that Google Android is an ancillary product of Google Search. Google Android is an open source operating system based on Linux kernel and written in Java language which, in 2005, was acquired by Google and soon became one of the most important smartphone operating system platforms.

In summary, in recent Google cases the EU Commission seems to favor a formal approach rather than an economic one by giving preference to prohibition decisions and fines versus commitment decisions and tailored remedies grounded in economics.

In light of the Intel ruling, European judges might reverse both Google decisions and the European Competition Law could continue to approach the U.S. antitrust enforcement mechanism. If that is the case, similarly to the U.S. in Europe the practice of antitrust settlements based on remedies regulatory in nature is likely to increase in importance.[477]

474. *See* Farhad Manjoo, *Here's the Conversation We Really Need to Have about Bias at Google*, New York Times (Aug. 30, 2018).
475. Rochelle Toplensky, *Google Appeals €2.4bn EU Antitrust Fine*, Financial Times, https://www.ft.com/content/8016cf66-9f97-3ce4-8d40-9b9dc16c7459 (Sep. 11, 2017).
476. EU Commission, Antitrust: Commission Fines Google €4.34 billion for Illegal Practices Regarding Android Mobile Devices to Strengthen Dominance of Google's Search Engine, Press Release IP/18/4581 (Jul. 18, 2018).
477. *See* 1 Botteman & Patsa, *supra* n. 321, at 347, 352.

## §3.03 CONCLUSIONS

The study of antitrust settlements in the U.S. and EU gives us the opportunity to get a deeper understanding of antitrust law in each framework. The role of antitrust settlements and antitrust law are not separate issues. The brief explanation of the history and ideology of antitrust settlements framework, U.S. and EU antitrust law provided in this Chapter is necessary to understand the evolution and the development of the protagonist of this book and its application in both the U.S. and EU context.

Antitrust law originated in the U.S. as a tool of economic democracy while, in Europe, competition law served as a tool to integrate the markets of its Member States. Europe needed to create a single European economy before increasing competition within the market. Only in the 1990s, once the goal of creating a single European market was achieved, did European Competition Law start adopting an economic approach and increasingly resemble U.S. antitrust law. This rapprochement led to the introduction of the antitrust settlements practice which was formalized in 2003 when Mario Monti was the EU Commission Commissioner for Competition. EU commitment decisions soon became a valuable tool to regulate EU markets when traditional rules of regulation were not able to intervene in highly concentrated markets. Despite initial enthusiasm of the EU Commission for EU commitment decisions, the recent Intel and Google EU Commission prohibition decisions indicate a return of the European agency toward a more formalistic approach and a tendency to impose huge fines rather than settlements. By doing so, the effort made over the past thirty years for EU competition law to increasingly resemble U.S. antitrust law seems fruitless.

Again, the evolution of antitrust settlements is strictly related to the antitrust law and antitrust agencies' approach in enforcing antitrust law. It is difficult to see a significant use of antitrust settlements if an antitrust agency abandons an economic approach and the use of economic analysis in assessing a firm's conduct. Antitrust law is explicitly grounded in economics. The adoption of antitrust settlements that define remedies based on economic analysis and reasoning shared with the companies subject to investigations seems to be the right way forward.

PART II

# Do Antitrust Settlements Make Economic Sense? An Economic Analysis of Consent Decrees and Commitment Decisions

"[J]udges simply do not *talk* like Ronald Coase"[478]
(Frank H. Easterbrook & Daniel R. Fischel)

Judges and lawyers deal with law, economists deal with markets and economic analysis. Antitrust law evolved from a blend of law and economics, dispelling the myth that the formalistic nature of law and the shifting nature of economic models are incompatible. This marriage, however, has not been a perfect relationship. In the context of both U.S. and EU antitrust law, the role of law and economics has been constantly shifting, giving rise to the need for the marriage to adapt. In the last twenty years, especially in the U.S., economics and economic analysis has dominated the antitrust enforcement mechanism. Economics and economic analysis are basically driving the U.S. antitrust enforcers' action.[479]

The increase in the adoption of consent decrees supports this trend.[480] Through antitrust settlements (U.S. consent decrees and EU commitment decisions), instead of requiring adjudication by the courts, antitrust agencies can seek market efficiency goals directly by concluding antitrust investigations through the imposition of procompetitive remedies grounded in economics. Is that good or bad for competition, consumers, markets and the economy overall?

478. Frank H. Easterbrook & Daniel R. Fischel, *Contract and Fiduciary Duty*, 36 J. L. Econ. 425, 429 (1993).
479. *See* Michael R. Baye & Joshua D. Wright, *Is Antitrust Too Complicated for Generalist Judges? The Impact of Economic Complexity and Judicial Training on Appeal*, 54 J. L. & Econ. 1, 2 (2011).
480. Wright & Ginsburg, *supra* n. 7, at 1.

Part II scrutinizes the economic effects of both consent decrees and commitment decisions. Part II engages in qualitative empirical research with respect to the functioning of the consensual bargaining process, as well as an investigation of the outcome of such agreements in terms of firm behavior and agency practice going forward. Part II also compares *pros* and *cons* of a bargaining solution with the *pros* and *cons* of a conviction for an antitrust violation in the U.S.. Part II is divided into three chapters.

Chapter 4 considers when and in what cases the U.S. antitrust agencies have resorted to a consensual settlement, investigating the outcomes of antitrust settlements in terms of firm behavior and agency practice going forward. In other words, this chapter examines both the FTC's and DOJ's investigations settled by means of consent decrees in the last five years by assessing: (*i*) the timing from the filing of an antitrust complain to the issue of the consent decrees; (*ii*) the main markets/industries involved; (*iii*) the kind of remedies adopted in each industry; (*iv*) the evolution of the affected markets after the adoption of remedies enshrined in some consent decrees. Criteria used to evaluate the pro-competitive effects of such remedies are price, the development of potential substitute products/technologies, and market share structure (when this data is available) within the affected industries.

Chapter 5 engages in the same empirical analysis on the use of commitment decisions by the EU Commission. This chapter examines the EU Commission's investigations settled by means of commitment decision in the last five years by assessing: (*i*) the timing from the filing of the EU Commission's complain to the issue of the commitment decision; (*ii*) the main markets/industries involved; (*iii*) the kind of remedies adopted in each industry; (*iv*) the evolution of the affected markets after the adoption of remedies enshrined in the commitment decision. Through this analysis, the chapter emphasizes the evolution and the differences between EU commitment decisions and U.S. consent decrees and draws some conclusions.

Chapter 6 investigates the differing economic effects between the adoption of consent decrees in the U.S. and commitment decisions in EU by analyzing a single case that was settled with an antitrust settlement in both jurisdictions. Chapter 6 also compares the consequences of settling an antitrust case in the U.S. by means of an antitrust settlement with a conviction. In particular, this chapter examines the Ebook case settled by means of a settlement solution both in the U.S. and in Europe by investigating the different economic outcomes in the U.S. and EU markets. In the U.S., the Ebook case has been settled with the publishers such as Harper Collins Publishers L.L.C. and Penguin Group Inc. while Apple was the only investigated company that decided to proceed to trial and that has been convicted for antitrust violation. Therefore, the Ebook case is the perfect case to study for comparing U.S. consent decrees with EU commitment decisions, and assessing the *pros* and *cons* of a bargain solution in the U.S. relative to the *pros* and *cons* of a conviction for an antitrust violation.

# CHAPTER 4
# An Economic Analysis of the Consent Decrees Practice

From more than a century, the United States' experience in enforcing antitrust law provided a lesson to be learned: how to use antitrust as an arm of regulation[481] by means of consent decrees which are grounded in economics. The interaction between antitrust law and regulation has always been clear to the antitrust community; the Sherman Act, as a "legal weapon for the control of business",[482] soon became an "instrument in the arsenal of regulation."[483] The regulatory effects of antitrust settlements are undisputed as the FTC was designed as a regulatory agency to supplement the work of the DOJ (Antitrust Division)—the prosecutor.[484]

In contrast to the FCC which is a regulator that regulates a specific industry,[485] Section 5 of the FTC Act[486] gave the FTC a wide range of discretion in regulating any markets/industries.[487] Although the DOJ is the antitrust prosecutor (not a regulator), the DOJ's consent decrees have the same regulatory effects as the FTC's consent

481. Herbert Hovenkamp, *Progressive Antitrust* (2018). Faculty Scholarship. 1764. https://scholarship.law.upenn.edu/cgi/viewcontent.cgi?article = 2766&context = faculty_scholarship.
482. Hamilton & Till, *supra* n. 10, at 24.
483. *Ibid.*
484. The FTC "was meant to practice preventive law through administrative and regulatory activities as well as by the initiation and conduct of adversary proceedings ... Both agencies were to work in the same field, but with different tools." Hon. Edward F. Howrey, *The Federal Trade Commission and the Administrative Process* (Section of Antitrust law of NY ABA, Jan. 28, 1954) at 1.
485. Ronald Coase, *The Federal Communications Commission*, 56 J. L. & Econ. 879, 883, 884 (2013). ("The Commission was [...] provided with massive powers to regulate the radio industry ... In 1934 the powers exercised by the Federal Radio Commission were transferred to the Federal Communications Commission, which was also made responsible for the regulation of the telephone and telegraph industries.") *Ibid.*
486. Under Section 5 of the FTC Act, the FTC regulates "unfair methods of competition ... and unfair or deceptive acts or practices." 15 U.S.C. §45(a).
487. Howrey, *supra* n. 484, at 1.

orders—thus, both the FTC's and the DOJ's consent decrees regulate markets in a similar way.

However, the law and economics doctrine is silent on the economic effects of consent decrees/orders. Professor Joshua D. Wright and Judge Douglas H. Ginsburg have recently brought the issue to light, arguing that consent decrees represent a fundamental antitrust tool for resolving antitrust disputes[488] which need a full economic analysis to be effective. They do not, however, provide any economic analysis or empirical studies and merely scratch the surface of this issue.[489]

In summary, this chapter represents an effort to define a common practice in the adoption of consent decrees, in addition, to examine their economic effects to determine whether remedies enshrined in consent decrees make economic sense. Through an empirical analysis on the functioning of consensual bargaining process in the U.S. antitrust framework, this chapter emphasizes the practice in terms of firm behavior and agency practice going forward. Chapter 4 also examines the economic effects of consent decrees and draws some conclusions on governing markets through the *antitrust consent*.[490]

The sample of my analysis considers FTC and DOJ consent decrees issued in the last five years to settle U.S. antitrust civil no-merger cases. The analysis investigates the timing from the filing of an antitrust complaint to the issue of the consent decrees, the main markets/industries involved, and the kind of remedies adopted in each industry. This study also examines the economic effects of those remedies through the analysis of price and the development of substitute products in the affected markets/industries when this data is available. Cases used to conduct the latter analysis might be older than 2013, as a minimum time frame is necessary to access the economic effects of an antitrust decision and the required data (price and market shares) are not always available, especially for very narrowly defined markets of relevance.

## §4.01 HOW CONSENT DECREES REGULATED U.S. MARKETS IN THE LAST FIVE YEARS

"The food here is so terrible. Yeah, and always such small portions."[491]

Professor Steven P. Croley used Woody Allen's joke about two complaining inhabitants of a retirement home to express today's attitude toward modern regulation. The same joke fits perfectly for the modern debate over antitrust regulation. Despite the fact that antitrust regulation is often criticized,[492] the trend in the adoption of consent decrees

488. Wright & Ginsburg, *supra* n. 7.
489. *Ibid.*
490. *Ibid.*
491. Steven P. Croley, *Regulation and Public Interests, the Possibility of Good Regulatory Government*, 10 (Princeton U. Press, 2008).
492. *See*, e.g., Assistant Attorney General Makan Delrahim Delivers Remarks at the Antitrust Division's Second Roundtable on Competition and Deregulation (Washington, DC, Apr. 26,

that are regulatory in nature has increased over the years. Judge Douglas H. Ginsburg and Professor Joshua D. Wright observed that "[o]ver the last 35 years, the United States Federal Trade Commission and the Antitrust Division of the Department of Justice have shifted dramatically toward greater reliance upon consent decrees than upon litigation to resolve antitrust disputes."[493]

As outlined below, antitrust regulatory intervention by means of consent decrees does not prevent market failures. Rather, antitrust agencies act through consent decrees as a doctor in an emergency room, rapidly intervening to correct market failures as they occur.[494] Consent decrees are regulatory antitrust tools in nature that cure markets as an antibiotic cures ill patients. Both government interventions can improve, as well as harm, markets. Remedies enshrined in consent decrees diverge from traditional governments' rules of regulation, like an antibiotic divergent from a vaccine that seeks to prevent the disease.

As seductive as antitrust regulation by means of consent decrees has proven to be, it masks complicated economic and legal issues explored here. Starting from the analysis of the DOJ and FTC consent decrees practice, this study concludes with a discussion of some potential policy implications from the following findings.

## [A] The DOJ

While generally 10 percent of civil trial cases on any legal issue filed by the DOJ are settled,[495] in the context of antitrust law, approximately 90 percent of civil antitrust cases are settled by means of an agreement. This raises the question of why settlements are so attractive in the context of antitrust relative to other legal actions. Should this trend in the adoption of consent decrees continue, or does it need to be reexamined with more scrutiny? And if so, why? As Judge Ginsburg and Professor Wright correctly observed: "a full economic analysis of reliance primarily upon consent decrees is necessary."

This part engages in an empirical analysis focused on the DOJ's consent decrees enacted in the last five years. First, this analysis considers the time frame from the beginning of the formal civil no merger antitrust proceeding to the final judgment, and the affected markets/industries. Second, this study investigates the remedies enshrined in such consent decrees by evaluating the economic effects of those remedies in an attempt to provide some policy insights for the future. From October 1, 2013, to October 31, 2018, the DOJ closed eighteen civil no merger cases.[496] Fourteen proceedings out of eighteen were settled by means of a consent decree.

---

2018) ("I believe antitrust enforcers should approach using consent decrees consistent with a view of the Antitrust Division as law enforcement agencies, not a regulatory one.")

493. Wright & Ginsburg, *supra* n. 7.
494. Massarotto, *supra* n. 302.
495. U.S. Department, United States Attorneys Annual Statistical Report (2013) 24 https://www.justice.gov/sites/default/files/usao/legacy/2014/09/22/13statrpt.pdf.
496. DOJ, Antitrust Division, *Antitrust Case Filings*, https://www.justice.gov/atr/antitrust-case-filings?field_case_type_value=civil_non_merger&field_brief_federal_court_value=All&field_case_violation_tid=All&industry-code= (accessed Oct. 31, 2018).

### *[1] Timing and Markets/Industries Involved*

With respect to the time frame from the filing of an antitrust complaint to the issue of the final judgment, five out of fourteen proceedings settled through a consent decree the date of the final judgment corresponds to the date of the filing.[497] In one case, *U.S. and State of Michigan v. Hillsdale Community Health Center, W.A. Foote Memorial Hospital, D/B/A Allegiance Health, Community Health Center of Branch County, and Promedica Health Systems, Inc.*, the final consent decree was issued 1,061 days after the DOJ's complaint was filed on June 25, 2015. On May 31, 2017, having denied a summary judgment, the federal judge ruled that the suit between the DOJ and the State of Michigan against *W.A. Foote Memorial Hospital and Allegiance Health* needed to proceed to trial.[498] The trial ended with a consent decree on May 21, 2018.[499]

The average days between the filing of the formal antitrust complain and the issuance of the final judgment is about one-hundred sixty-seven days. The following chart shows the exact time frame between the filing of the antitrust complaint to the issuing of the final judgment per each case settled by means of consent decrees in the last five years. Excluding the 1,061 days necessary to settle the dispute with *W.A. Foote Memorial Hospital and Allegiance Health* (the extreme outlier), the average number of days from the filing of the complaint to the final approval of the consent decree is about ninety-eight days (Figure 4.1). In any of the other four cases not settled by means of consent decrees, the DOJ won the trial, a case is still ongoing,[500] and one case has been dismissed.[501] While in the *US v. BMI*, ASCAP and BMI required the DOJ to review the terms of the ASCAP and BMI consent decree of 1941. The DOJ concluded that "the ASCAP and BMI consent decrees continue to serve the purpose for which they were put in place in 1941"[502] urging "the development of a comprehensive legislative solution that ensures a competitive marketplace and obviates the need for continued Division of the PROs."[503] In *Pandora Media, Inc. v. American Society of Composers*,[504] the court discussed the terms of the ASCAP and IBM consent decrees. The Second Circuit upheld the district court decision, ruling in favor of Pandora by recognizing that the language

497. *Ibid. See* Goldfein & Pak, *supra* n. 224, at 214. ("Similar to DOJ consents, most FTC consents are agreed to during the FTC's investigation phase and prior to the commencement of any administrative adjudication.") *Ibid.*
498. Lisl J. Dunlop & Shoshana S. Speiser, *Suit over Hospitals' Alleged Anticompetitive Marketing Sent to Trial* (Lexology, Jun. 22, 2017), https://www.lexology.com/library/detail.aspx?g=37b10619-7944-4476-a95b-3ad70a5d3b25.
499. *U.S. and State of Michigan v. W.A. Foote Memorial Hospital, D/B/A Allegiance Health* 5:15-cv-12311-JEL-DRG (May 21, 2018).
500. *U.S. v. Bethlehem Steel Corporation, et al.*, https://www.justice.gov/atr/case/us-v-bethlehem-steel-corporation-et-al (updated Apr. 19, 2018).
501. *U.S. v. United Continental Holdings, Inc., and Delta Air Lines Inc.*, Case 2:15-cv-07992-WHW-CLW, Stipulation of Dismissal (D.C.N.Y., Apr. 6, 2016).
502. DOJ, Statement of the DOJ on the Closing of the Antitrust Division's Review of the ASCAP and BMI Consent Decrees, 22 (Aug. 4, 2016), https://www.justice.gov/atr/file/882101/download.
503. *Ibid.*
504. *Pandora Media, Inc. v. American Society of Composers* (Update Jul. 9, 2015), https://www.justice.gov/atr/case/pandora-media-inc-v-american-society-composers-authors-and-publishers.

of the consent decree precluded ASCAP from accepting partial withdrawals from the licensing scheme.[505] The DOJ agreed with the district court ruling.[506]

*Figure 4.1 Days from the Filing of an Antitrust Complaint to the Issue of the Consent Decrees*

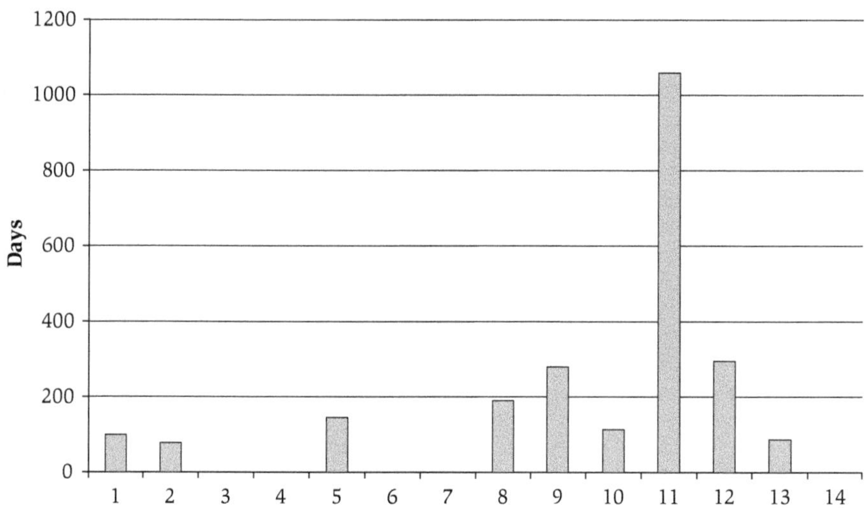


With respect to the affected markets/industries, the analyzed cases involved communication/telecom, healthcare, financial and transportation markets (Figure 4.2). The following chart depicts the exact proportion of cases per each affected industry considering the eighteen civil no merger cases. Five cases involved the communication industries. Two cases concerned the finance, transportation and healthcare industry showing the specific DOJ and FTC expertise in those industries.[507]

505. *Ibid.*, at 2.
506. DOJ, *Letter Brief, Pandora Media, Inc., v. American Society of Composers,* Authors and Publishers, 2d Cir. Nos. 14-1158-cv(L), 14-1161, 14-1246 (Mar. 6, 2015) https://www.justice.gov/atr/case-document/file/628831/download. ("The district court concluded that the ASCAP Consent Decree, as amended in 2001 and known as the Second Amended Final Judgment or AFJ2, requires ASCAP to provide Pandora with a license to all of the works in its repertory. The Department agrees.") *Ibid.*, at 2.
507. Donald A. Torres, *Handbook of Federal Police and Investigative Agencies,* 163 (Greenwood Press, 1985).

*Figure 4.2 Most Affected Industries*

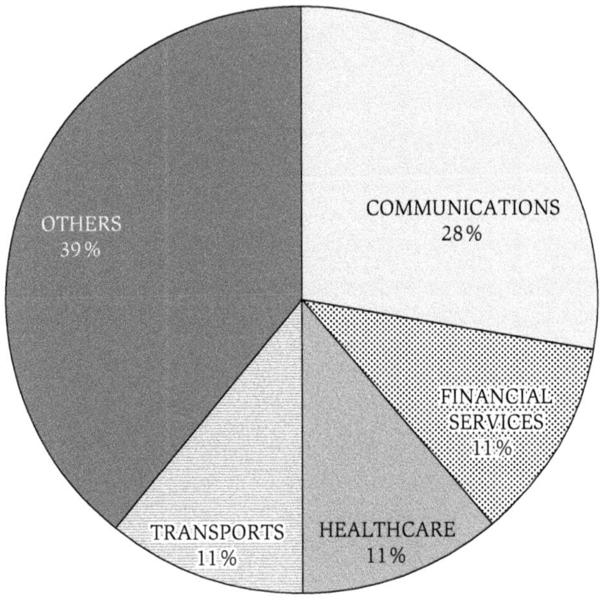


### *[2] Adopted Remedies*

Ten out of the eighteen civil proceedings initiated by the DOJ concern a failure to notify regarding a merger under the Hart-Scott-Rodino Act, in violation of Section 7A of the Clayton Act. All of those ten proceedings were settled by means of a consent solution. Thus, ten out of the fourteen total cases ended with an antitrust settlement concerning a failure to notify the antitrust enforcers of a merger. Nine of those cases imposed a civil penalty on the defendant.

In *U.S. v. Fayez Sarofim*, for example, the defendant was condemned to pay USD 720,000 in civil penalty.[508] In *U.S. v. Flakeboard America Limited et. Others*, the consent decree condemned the defendant to pay a USD 3.8 million civil penalty and USD 1.15 million in disgorgement to the United States in addition to maintaining an antitrust compliance program that designates an Antitrust Compliance Officer responsible for achieving compliance with the final order.[509] Only in *U.S. v. Third Point Offshore Fund, LTD., Third Point Ultra, Ltd., Third Point Partners Qualified L.P., and Third Point, LLC* did the final decision require the defendant the mere implementation

508. *US v. Fayez Sarofim*, Case 1:16-cv-02156 at 2 (D.C.D.C., 2016).
509. *U.S. v. Flakeboard America Limited et. Others* Case 3:14-cv-04949-VC (N. D. Cal., 2015).

of a compliance provision.[510] Specifically, the defendants had to designate a Compliance Officer responsible for achieving compliance with the final consent order.[511]

The other four cases settled by means of consent decrees concerned the violation of Section 1 of the Sherman Act, 15 U.S.C. § 1. In *U.S. and State of Michigan v. Hillsdale Community Health Center, W.A. Foote Memorial Hospital, D/B/A Allegiance Health, Community Health Center of Branch County, and Promedica Health Systems, Inc.*[512] Here, in addition to Section 1 of the Sherman Act it was considered the violation of the Michigan Antitrust Reform Act, MCL 445.772.

In all four cases, consent decrees imposed only behavioral remedies. Specifically, in *U.S. v. Knorr-Bremse AG and Westinghouse Air Brake Technologies Corp.*,[513] the parties agreed to not enter, maintain or enforce any No-Poach agreements or No-Poach provision. In addition, the consent decree required each defendant to appoint an Antitrust Compliance Officer.[514] Defendants needed also to "furnish notice of [this antitrust] action to the rail industry"[515] by both placing an advertisement and creating a website pages linked to Knorr and Wabtec's websites.

In *U.S. v. Directv Group Holdings, LLC and AT&T, Inc.*,[516] Directv was accused of exchanging competitively sensitive information with Cox, Charter and AT&T during the companies' negotiations for the right to telecast SportsNet LA (the "Dodgers Channel") in violation of Section 1 of the Sherman act. The case was settled after one-hundred forty-five days from the filing date through a consent decree which required the defendants to implement a training and antitrust compliance program. The compliance program aimed to instruct both the defendants' executives and employees responsible for, or participating in, content carriage negotiations that included the communication of sensitive information.[517] Furthermore, such a program foresees the designation of an Antitrust Compliance Officer responsible for adopting the training and antitrust compliance program and ensuring its full compliance with the consent order, which expires in five years.[518]

The *U.S. v. Charleston Area Medical Center, Inc. and ST. Mary's Medical Center, Inc.* case was settled through a consent decrees one-hundred ninety days from the filing of the complaint (without calculating the end day). According to DOJ's allegations, the defendants limited competition among themselves by allocating territories for the marketing of competing healthcare services in violation of Section 1 of the Sherman

510. *U.S. v. Third Point Offshore Fund, LTD., Third Point Ultra, Ltd., Third Point Partners Qualified L.P., and Third Point, LLC*, Case 1:15-cv-01366-KBJ (D. D. C., 2015).
511. *Ibid.*, at 5-7.
512. *U.S. and State of Michigan v. Hillsdale Community Health Center, W.A. Foote Memorial Hospital, D/B/A Allegiance Health, Community Health Center of Branch County, and Promedica Health Systems, Inc.*, 2:15-cv-12311-JEL-DRG (D.E. Mich., 2015).
513. *U.S. v. Knorr-Bremse AG and Westinghouse Air Brake Technologies Corp.*, Case 1:18-cv-00747-CKK, Final judgment (Jul. 11, 2018).
514. *Ibid.*, at 5.
515. *Ibid.*, at 7.
516. *U.S. v. Directv Group Holdings, LLC and AT&T, Inc.*, Case 2:16-cv-08150, Complaint (D. C. Cal., 2016).
517. *U.S. v. Directv Group Holdings, LLC and AT&T, Inc.*, Case 2:16-cv-08150-MWF-E, Final Judgment, at 5 (D. C. Cal., 2017).
518. *Ibid.*, at 5-8.

Act.[519] To remove any possible violation, the decree prohibits each defendant to enter, maintain or enforce agreements with other medical centers that limit or prohibit marketing, or "allocates any service, customer, or geographic market or territory"[520] unless such agreement is reasonably necessary to aim procompetitive purposes through joint ventures or other joint activity among healthcare centers/providers.[521] All communications among defendants about any defendant's marketing activity as defined in the decree[522] are not allowed. There are some exceptions, such as exchanging information related to the defined joint venture activities or due diligence during a merger, acquisition and joint venture.[523] In addition, each defendant needs to appoint an Antitrust Compliance Officer who has specific duties including providing a copy of the consent decree along with the Competitive Impact Statement to defendants' officers, directors, and Marketing managers and receiving from them a certification of compliance with the decree.[524]

Finally, in *U.S. and State of Michigan v. Hillsdale Community Health Center, W.A. Foote Memorial Hospital, D/B/A Allegiance Health, Community Health Center of Branch County, and Promedica Health Systems, Inc.*, defendants were sued for entering into unlawful agreements to allocate territories for the marketing of competing healthcare services. The same day that the DOJ filed the complaint on June 25, 2015 defendants other than Allegiance agreed to settle the case through a consent solution.[525] The agreement ratified by the court prohibited the defendants from entering into any future agreements to allocate marketing territories in addition to adopting compliance measures to prevent similar violations. The antitrust case proceeding against Allegiance continued to trial.[526] On May 21, 2018, the case had been settled through a consent decree which, similar to the consent decree of June 2015, prohibits Allegiance from agreeing with other hospitals and health care providers to limit marketing or to allocate customers, markets, or territories between providers. The settlement also prohibits improper communications between the defendant and competitors about

519. *U.S. v. Charleston Area Medical Center, Inc. and ST. Mary's Medical Center, Inc.*, Case 2:16-cv-03664, Complaint (Apr. 14, 2016).
520. *U.S. v. Charleston Area Medical Center, Inc. and ST. Mary's Medical Center, Inc.*, Case 2:16-cv-03664, Final Judgment, at 4 (Oct. 21, 2016).
521. The decree specifies that "'Join Provisions of Services' means any past, present, or future joint health education campaign or coordinated delivery of any healthcare services by two or more healthcare providers, including a clinical affiliation, joint venture, management agreement, accountable care organization, clinically integrated network, group purchasing organization, management services organization, or physician hospital organization.") *Ibid.*, at 2.
522. *Ibid.*, at 2, 3. ("'Marketing' means any past, present, or future activities that are involved in making persons aware of the services or products of the hospital or of physicians employed or with privileges at the hospital, including advertising, communications, public relations, provider network development, outreach to employers or physicians, and promotions, such as free health screenings and education.") *Ibid.*
523. *Ibid.*, at 4.
524. *Ibid.*, at 5.
525. *U.S. and State of Michigan v. Hillsdale Community Health Center, W.A. Foote Memorial Hospital, D/B/A Allegiance Health, Community Health Center of Branch County, and Promedica Health Systems, Inc.*, 2:15-cv-12311-JEL-DRG (Jun. 25, 2015).
526. Lisl J. Dunlop & Shoshana S. Speiser, *Suit over Hospitals' Alleged Anticompetitive Marketing Sent to Trial* (Jun. 22, 2017), https://www.lexology.com/library/detail.aspx?g=37b10619-7944-4476-a95b-3ad70a5d3b25.

marketing efforts, the designation of an Antitrust Compliance Officer and grants rights of inspection to DOJ and Michigan Attorney General staff.[527] Furthermore, Allegiance agreed to pay USD 5,000.00 per pretrial litigation costs to the United Stated and USD 35,000.00 to the State of Michigan to partially cover litigation costs.[528]

In summary, in all of consent decrees (excluding those adopted in a failure to notify agencies of a merger under Section 7 of the Clayton Act and the Hart-Scott-Rodino Act) required that companies merely refrain from engaging in the investigated anticompetitive conduct. In some cases, to ensure the compliance of the antitrust order, the DOJ required the company to designate an Antitrust Compliance Officer or specify the DOJ's rights of conducting inspections against the company.

### *[3] Economic Effects of Remedies*

Similar to the government's regulation, the economic effects of consent decrees can be assessed through the analysis of relevant economic variables including prices and the evolution of affected markets. Since the required data for this analysis (like price and market shares) are not always available (especially for very narrow relevant markets), part *[3]* considers an antitrust case settled through a consent decree in 2000, along with a case that is part of our previous sample.

Specifically, on December 6, 2000, the District Court for the District of Columbia enacted a consent decree between the DOJ and the American Stock Exchange LLC, Chicago Board Options Exchange, Incorporated; Pacific Exchange Inc. and Philadelphia Stock Exchange Inc.[529] The decree concerns the stock exchange market, a regulated market by the Security Exchange Commission (SEC) where data is usually available to the public. The second consent decree analyzed is the one which involved Directv Group Holdings LLC and other operators active in the distribution of professional video programming services in the Los Angeles area.[530]

#### *[a] U.S. Stock Exchange Market after the Consent Decree of 2000*

On September 11, 2000, the DOJ filed a civil antitrust complaint against American Stock Exchange LLC, Chicago Board Options Exchange Incorporated, Pacific Exchange Inc. and Philadelphia Stock Exchange Inc., alleging that these companies violated Section 1 of the Sherman Act, 15 U.S.C. § 1. According to the DOJ complaint, from 1990 "the defendants and their co-conspirators maintained an agreement pursuant to which many frequently-traded equity options were traded only on one exchange, resulting in

527. *U.S. and State of Michigan v. W.A. Foote Memorial Hospital, D/B/A Allegiance Health*, No. 5:15-cv-12311-JEL-DRG, Final Judgement (D. E. Mich., May 21, 2015).
528. *Ibid.*, at 11.
529. *U.S. v. American Stock Exchange, LLC, et al.*, No. 1:00CV02174, Final Judgment (D.C. Circ., Dec. 6, 2010).
530. *U.S. v. Directv Group Holdings, LLC, et al.*, No. 2:16-cv-08150-MWF-E, Stipulation and Order (D.C. Cal., 2017).

some investors paying more when buying options and receiving less when selling options, and being denied the other benefits of competition."[531]

On December 6, 2000, the District Court for the District of Columbia issued a decree which was the result of the agreement between the DOJ and the defendants to settle the case. The consent decree basically enjoined and restrained each defendant from agreeing with any other exchange to limit competition by not listing options that are already listed on another exchange.[532] The decree did not apply when the conduct was expressively permitted by statute, SEC orders or exchange rules that got the specific approval by the SEC.[533] Furthermore, each defendant had to introduce and maintain an antitrust compliance program which required the company to design an Antitrust Compliance Officer in charge of establishing and ensuring the compliance of the program. Among their duties, the Antitrust Compliance Officer has to distribute a copy of the final judgment to a variety of company officers, including members of the board of directors. The Antitrust Compliance Officer would obtain from each of these people an annual written certification specifying that he or she "(a) has read and agrees to abide by the terms of [the] Final Judgment; and (b) has been advised and understands that noncompliance with this Final Judgment may result in his or her being found in civil or criminal contempt of court."[534]

That agreement was subject to the competitive impact assessment in the relevant market of trading options on exchanges before becoming final on December 6, 2000.[535] As the competitive impact statement specified, "[e]xchanges compete for orders by, among other things, offering lower transaction fees and higher quality services, including quicker execution and greater liquidity, than their competitors."[536] The price to buy an option on an exchange is known as "bid", while the price to sell an option is called "ask." In the U.S., both prices are transmitted to an authority called Options Price Reporting Authority, which transmits price information to third parties for processing and distribution.

Exchanges mainly compete with each other by offering the best bid or ask in a particular option and the difference between the price to buy and sell the same option is called spread. Competition between exchanges for the business of investors results in narrowing spreads.[537] Consequently, such spreads are here considered in the evaluation of the competitive effects of remedies enshrined in the consent decree.

531. *U.S. v. American Stock Exchange, LLC, et al.*, No. 1:00CV02174, Complaint at § 2 (D. D. C., 2000).
532. *U.S. v. American Stock Exchange, LLC, et al.*, Final Judgment at IV (hereinafter "*American Stock Exchange consent decree*"). ("[E]ach defendant is enjoined and restrained from, directly or indirectly: 1. Agreeing with any other exchange that any equity option class shall be traded exclusively on any one exchange; 2. Agreeing with any other exchange to allocate trading of any equity option class or classes between or among exchanges; and 3. Agreeing with any other exchange to require, prevent, or limit the listing, delisting or trading of any equity option class.") *Ibid.*
533. *Ibid.*, at V.
534. *Ibid.*, at VI. D.
535. *U.S. v. American Stock Exchange, LLC, et al.*, Competitive Impact Statement (D. D. C., 2000).
536. *Ibid.*, at 4.
537. *Ibid.*

Professor Hans R. Stoll analyzed changes in bid-ask spreads from January 1, 1993, to January 1, 2002, by providing the daily average quoted and effective half-spreads in that time frame for two listed companies: Microsoft and IBM.[538] While the quoted half-spread is half the difference between the best bid and the best ask, the effective half-spread is the difference between the transaction price and the midpoint of the quoted spread.

Professor Stoll observed that, in 1993, the Microsoft's quoted half-spread[539] (which is generally used to measure trading costs) was over sixteen cents. In January 2002, that quoted half-spread declined to under two cents.[540] Similarly, in 1993 the quoted half-spread in IBM options averaged about eight cents, declining to about two cents in January 2002.[541] As other researches emphasized,[542] in the U.S., spreads and generally trade execution costs steadily declined from 1999. These costs are significant indicators of market competition and quality.

The DOJ consent decree is not the only explanation for such a decline. In 2000, the SEC issued an order that required the same defendants to comply with several rules in order to increase transparency on of activities. Defendants agreed to get the SEC's approval for any practice or procedure "by which any market makers trading any particular option class determine by agreement the spreads or option prices at which any particular option class, or the allocation of orders in an option class."[543]

In addition, electronic trading has significantly reduced the transaction costs and increased the accuracy of price signals, ultimately improving the efficiency of stock markets.[544]

### [b] *The Distribution of Professional Video Programming Services after the Direct TV Decision of 2017*

The second case concerns the multichannel video programming distributors (MVPDs) market within the telecommunication industry. MVPDs buy from video programmers the rights to transmit content and distribute that content to subscribers. MVPDs compete with each other to attract subscribers through the prices that they charge and the programming content offered. On November 2, 2016, the DOJ filed an antitrust complaint[545] accusing DirecTv of exchanging competitively sensitive information

---

538. Hans R. Stoll, *Electronic Trading in Stock Markets*, 20 J. Econ. Perspectives 153, 164 (2006).
539. The quoted half-spread if half the difference between the ask and the bid, averaged over the day.
540. Stoll, *supra* n. 538, at 164.
541. *Ibid.*, at 165.
542. Ekkehart Boehmer, *Dimensions of Execution Quality: Recent Evidence for US Equity Markets*, 78 J. Financial Econ. 553 (2005); Kumar Venkararaman, *Bid-Ask Spreads: Measuring Trade Execution Costs in Financial Markets* at 12 (2009), available at https://www.researchgate.net/publication/254354745_Bid-Ask_Spreads_Measuring_Trade_Execution_Costs_in_Financial_Markets.
543. Competitive Impact Statement, *supra* n. 535, at 22.
544. Stoll, *supra* n. 538, at 172, 173.
545. *U.S. v. Directv Group Holdings, LLC, and AT&T*, No. 2:16-cv-08150-MWF-E, Complaint (D.C. Cal., 2016).

during the companies' negotiations for the right to telecast SportsNet LA (the "Dodgers Channel") with competitors, including Cox, Charter and AT&T. According to the complaint, the relevant product market was the market for the distribution of professional video programming services to residential or business customers. In 2014, Directv was the second-largest MVPD in the United States. In 2015, AT&T bought Directv, making AT&T the largest cable provider in the United States. In 2014, Charter was the third-largest U.S. cable company, which in 2016 merged with the second Cable Company that owned the rights to the Dodgers Channel—Time Warner Cable. In 2014, Time Warner Cable signed a twenty-five-year agreement to buy the exclusive rights of Dodgers broadcasts for USD 8.35 billion. This agreement led to the creation of a new sport channel—SportsNet LA. This channel is entirely dedicated to the Dodgers, including all Dodgers game, news, interview and documentaries on the baseball team and was only broadcasted by Time Warner/Charter. Time Warner asked the others cable companies, including Directv and AT&T, to pay USD 4.8 a month per subscriber to broadcast the SportsNet LA channel. Neither Directv nor any other cable providers were willing to accept this offer and charge their customers that extra amount of money for SportsNet LA. The channel's limited distribution caused Time Warner Cable to lose more than USD 100 million a year.[546] From 2013 to June 2017, the SportsNet LA viewership for Dodgers games had dropped 49 percent.[547] The antitrust concern here was that Directv engaged in an unlawful exchange of competitively sensitive information with AT&T, Charter and Cox Communications to carry SportsNet LA and reduce the risk "that they would lose subscribers if they decided not to carry the channel but a competitor chose to do so."[548]

The case was settled on October 2, 2017, by means of a consent decree requiring the defendants to implement an antitrust training and compliance program. The compliance program has the specific aim to make defendants' executives and employees aware of their responsibility for or participation in negotiations that included the communication of sensitive information with competing MVPD.[549] According to the program, defendants had to designate an Antitrust Compliance Officer responsible for the adoption of the training and antitrust compliance program and for the full compliance with the consent order.[550]

How did the market of MVPDs react to such remedies? There is still no agreement among cable companies and Charter to broadcast SportsNet LA channel. However, AT&T—which bought Directv in 2016—also bought Time Warner in June 2018, and the Dodgers' rights along with it. Despite the time that has passed since the DOJ's consent decree, the competitive dynamics of the affected market did not really change.

546. *See* Meg James, Charter to carry Dodgers channel, SportsNet LA, beginning Tuesday (Jun. 4, 2015), https://www.latimes.com/entertainment/envelope/cotown/la-et-ct-charter-to-carry-dodger-channel-june-9-20150604-story.html.
547. John Ourand, *On a New RSN, Dodgers see TV Numbers Dive* (Jul. 14, 2014), https://www.sportsbusinessdaily.com/Journal/Issues/2014/07/14/Media/MLB-RSNs.aspx.
548. Linda O'Brien, *Justice Department sues DirecTV for Unlawful Information-Sharing*, Antitrust Law Daily (Nov. 2, 2016).
549. *U.S. v. Directv Group Holdings, LLC, et al.*, No. 2:16-cv-08150-MWF-E, Proposed Final Judgment at V (D.C. Cal 2017).
550. *Ibid.*

Instead of having an exchange of sensitive information concerning price among different cable providers, now we deal with only one Cable Company instead of three.

In summary, we want to know if the entire antitrust case was necessary and, from an economic perspective, useful. Or did it basically lead cable companies to merge with each other instead of continuing to compete? The reality is that there is a steady decline in subscriptions on cable television.[551] Video streaming services are cheaper and come without commercial interruptions. Netflix is probably the most well-known example of a streaming video service that has benefitted from the trend toward streaming video services and away from cable television in the last years.

Netflix is acquiring even more subscribers, increasing its market share in the market of broadcasting video programs. However, AT&T has acquired the main cable providers and all of the programs, shows, and sports rights owned by these cable companies. AT&T is also the main U.S. Internet Service Provider (ISP) which, thanks to the repeal of the U.S. net neutrality regulation, now can charge different prices for video streaming services depending on the Internet speed required. As discussed in Chapter 1, the DOJ took almost a century to break-up the AT&T monopoly era by means of the 1982 consent decree. At this moment, the likely scenario after AT&T's acquisition of Time Warner and the repeal of net neutrality regulation[552] is that the AT&T monopoly will soon be back in the telecommunication industry, owning everything from the Internet infrastructure to final consumer goods such as programs and shows.

### [B] The FTC

This section examines the FTC cases under Section 5 of the FTC Act settled from January 2013 to November 2018. In that time frame, the FTC had closed and opened forty-three no-merger cases in total. Thirty-three cases were settled by consent decree and four cases went to trial ending with a conviction. Five out of forty-three cases are still ongoing up to November 2018, and one case concerned a modification of a previous FTC order.[553] This means that nearly 90 percent of FTC no-merger cases are settled by means of consent decrees if we exclude the ongoing cases and the modification of a previous order.

Considering the sample of thirty-eight no-merger cases closed by the FTC in the last five years, the following subsections analyze *[1]* the timing from the filing of the FTC antitrust complaint to the issue of the consent decrees or a different final order, the markets/industries which were more involved. Subsection *[2]* investigates the kind of remedies adopted in each industry, and subsection *[3]* examines the evolution of the affected markets after the adoption of the agreed remedies. Criteria used to evaluate the

551. Gerry Smith, *Who Killed the Great American Cable-TV Bundle*, Bloomberg (Aug. 8, 2018).
552. *See* Brian Fung, *The FCC's Net Neutrality Rules Are Officially Repealed Today. Here's What That Really Means*, The Washington Post (Jun. 11, 2018).
553. FTC Approves Toys "R" Us Petition to Reopen and Modify 1998 Final Commission Order, Press Release (Apr. 15, 2014), https://www.ftc.gov/news-events/press-releases/2014/04/ftc-approves-toys-r-us-petition-reopen-modify-1998-final.

pro-competitive effects of such remedies are the price and the evolution of the affected markets, focusing on the offering of new substitute products at lower price or higher quality.

### *[1] Timing and Markets/Industries Involved*

This analysis always includes the end date in the calculation of days from the filing of the FTC complaint to the final judgment/order. By analyzing cases settled by consent decrees, it turns out that in twenty-six out of thirty-three the date that the FTC complaint was filed coincides with the date of the issuing of the consent decree. Therefore, most of FTC consent orders are defined prior to the begin of any administrative decision during the FTC's investigations.
In the sample of the analyzed decisions it detects an outlier. In *Federal Trade Commission v. Cephalon Inc.* the consent decree was issued 2,682 days after the filing of the FTC complaint. In *the Matter of Ferrellgas Partners, L.P., Ferrellgas L.P., AmeriGas Partners, L.P., and UGI corporation*, the consent decree was issued two hundred eighty-seven days after the complaint was filed. In *Federal Trade Commission v. Allergan plc, Allergan Finance LLC, Watson Laboratories, Inc., Endo International plc, and Endo Pharmaceuticals Inc.*, from the filing of the complaint to the issuing of the consent decree, one hundred seventy-five days passed. In another case, *Federal Trade Commission, Plaintiff v. Endo Pharmaceuticals, Inc., Endo International plc, Teikoku Pharma USA, Inc., Teikoku Seiyaku Co., Ltd., Watson Laboratories, Inc., Allergan plc, and Impax Labs, Inc.*, only Teikoko Pharma USA and Teikoku Seiyaku Co. Ltd. settled the case through a consent decree after thirty days from the filing the complaint. In the remaining three cases, the consent decrees were issued less than fourteen days from the formal filing of the FTC complaint.

If we consider all thirty-three FTC cases settled through consent decrees, the average number of days between the filing of the complaint in court to the issue of the consent decree is about one ninety-six days. The four FTC cases that ended with a different judgment lasted much longer. The average number of days from the filing of the FTC complaint to the final judgment is about one thousand five hundred twelve. Therefore, this analysis confirms that both the FTC and the companies involved save time in settling a case by means of consent decrees.

With respect to the affected industries most affected in the forty-three cases analyzed, the great majority (seventeen out of forty-three cases) concern healthcare markets including the pharmaceutical industry and medical devices industry. Ten out of forty-three cases affected professional/trade associations, three affected the media and telecommunication industry, and two out of forty-three the sport industry. The remaining cases each concern a different industry including the industry of propane, barcodes and animal breeding. The following chart (Figure 4.3) depicts the proportion of cases per each industry.

*Figure 4.3 Main Affected Industries*

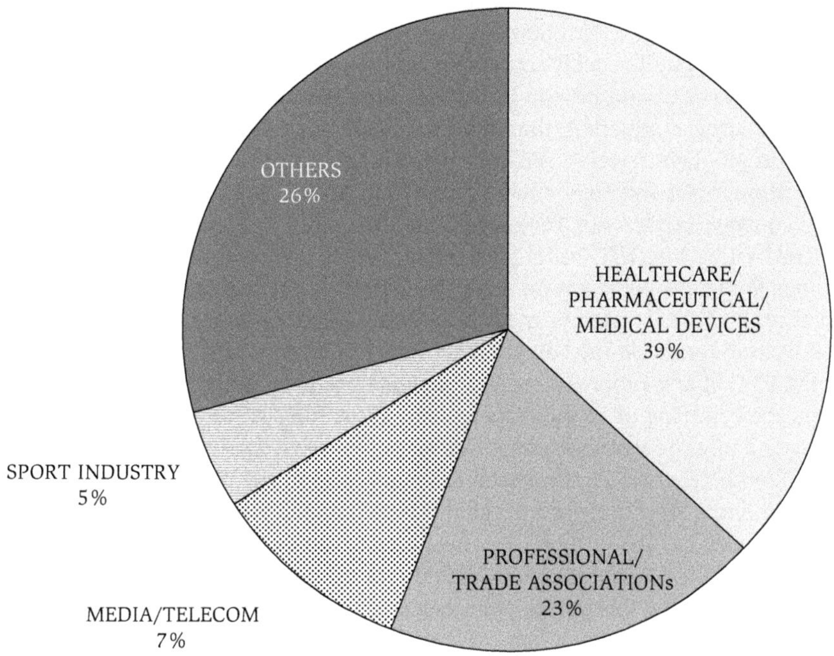


### *[2] Adopted Remedies*

Subsection *[2]* analyzes the kind of remedies adopted in each industry to define the practice followed by the FTC and companies in defining remedies enshrined in FTC consent decrees. As outlined above, the FTC antitrust enforcement focused on healthcare, including the pharmaceutical and medical devices industries.

#### *[a] Healthcare/Pharmaceutical*

In the pharmaceutical industry, the most common antitrust practice is the *pay for delay agreement* or *reverse payment agreement* between the brand and the generic drug company to delay the entry of a generic drug into the market.[554] By doing so, the brand name drug company protects its patent monopoly over the drug. From January 2013 to November 2018, the FTC settled three *pay for delay* cases through the consent of the pharmaceutical firms. Two cases concern the same conduct but they have been filed on

554. *See* FTC, Pay for Delay: When Drug Companies Agree not to Compete, https://www.ftc.gov/news-events/media-resources/mergers-competition/pay-delay.

different dates. On March 31, 2016, the FTC filed a complaint against Endo Pharmaceuticals, Inc., Endo International plc (hereinafter "Endo"), Teikoku Pharma USA, Inc., Teikoku Seiyaku Co., Ltd., Watson Laboratories, Inc., Allergan plc, and Impax Labs, Inc.[555] According to the FTC, Endo and the others defendants engaged in an antitrust violation by using pay-for-delay settlements to impede consumers' access to lower-cost generic versions of Opana ER and Lidoderm. In particular, Endo would have paid the first generic drug companies that filed for Food and Drug Administration (FDA) approval (Impax Laboratories, Inc. and Watson Laboratories, Inc.) to prevent the risk of competition for Opana ER and Lidoderm.[556] On April 7, 2016, the case was settled by means a consent decree with Teikoku Pharma USA and Teikoku Seiyaku Co. (hereinafter "Teikoku"). The FTC order prohibited Teikoku from entering in the same or similar *pay for delay* agreement for any period of time unless an agreement receives the approval of the FTC.[557] Each year for nine years, Teikoku has to submit to the FTC a verified written report on the compliance of the FTC order. Teikoku is also required to notify the FTC of any proposed merger, acquisition, consolidation or dissolution that concerns the company or its subsidiaries and allow the FTC to access and inspect the company and interview officers, directors or employees regarding any such matters.[558] In November 2016, the FTC dismissed the complaint in this investigation against the others defendants after the court granted the defendants' severance motion.[559]

On January 23, 2017, the FTC re-filed a complaint against Allergan plc, Allergan Finance LLC, Watson Laboratories Inc., Endo International plc, and Endo Pharmaceuticals Inc., arguing that these companies engaged in a *pay for delay* agreement.[560] Endo paid Watson Laboratories, Inc. to stifle competition for its brand name drug—Lidoderm. On July 11, 2017, the FTC authorized the appointment of a monitor with the power to determine whether defendants' agreements comply with the FTC order, which barred the defendants from entering into the *pay for delay* agreement.[561]

555. *FTC v. Endo Pharmaceuticals, Inc., Endo Pharmaceutical Inc., Endo International plc, Teikoku Pharma USA, Inc., Teikoku Seiyaku Co., Ltd., Watson Laboratories, Inc., Allergan plc, and Impax Labs, Inc.*, No. Case 2:16-cv-01440-PD, Complaint (D.C.E. Pen., 2016).
556. FTC Sues Endo Pharmaceuticals Inc. and Others for Illegally Blocking Lower-Cost Generic Versions of the Branded Drugs Opana ER and Lidoderm, Press Release (Mar. 31, 2016) https://www.ftc.gov/news-events/press-releases/2016/03/ftc-sues-endo-pharmaceuticals-inc-others-illegally-blocking-lower.
557. *FTC v. Teikoku Pharma USA, Inc., Teikoku Seiyaku Co., Ltd.*, No. Case 2:16-cv-01440-PD, Stipulated Order for Permanent Injunction (D.C. E. Pen., 2016).
558. *Ibid.*
559. FTC, Endo Pharmaceuticals/Impax Lab, Case Summary (Mar. 31, 2016), https://www.ftc.gov/enforcement/cases-proceedings/141-0004/endo-pharmaceuticals-impax-labs.
560. FTC, Endo Pharmaceuticals Inc. Agrees to Abandon Anticompetitive Pay-for-Delay Agreements to Settle FTC Charges; FTC Refiles Suits Against Generic Defendants, Press Release (Jan. 23, 2017), https://www.ftc.gov/news-events/press-releases/2017/01/endo-pharmaceuticals-inc-agrees-abandon-anticompetitive-pay-delay.
561. FTC Approves Appointment of Monitor in Pay-for-Delay Case against Endo Pharmaceuticals Inc., Press Release (Jul. 11, 2017), https://www.ftc.gov/news-events/press-releases/2017/07/federal-trade-commission-approves-appointment-monitor-pay-delay.

On February 13, 2008, the FTC sued Cephalon Inc. for preventing competition to its branded drug Provigil.[562] According to the FTC complaint, Cephalon paid four pharmaceutical companies to avoid their entry into the Provigil market with a cheaper generic version. On June 17, 2015, the case was settled by a consent decree, which, surprisingly required the defendant to pay USD 1.2 billion to compensate purchasers who overpaid for the drug at hand.[563] The decree also prohibited the defendant from entering in certain types of *pay for delay* agreements. This case would be further analyzed in paragraph *[a]* of the following Section *[3]*.

In the healthcare industry, the FTC settled nine other cases by the consent of defendants between January 2013 and November 2018. On July 31, 2018, the FTC filed a complaint against Your Therapy Source, LLC (which provides therapist staffing services), and Neeraj Jindal, Sheri Yarbray ("the two owners" of a competing staffing company) for possible collusive practices. According to the FTC's complaint, Your Therapy Source and the two owners not only agreed to lower their therapist pay rates, but also invited a number of their competitors to lower such rates (hence to collude). The case was settled the same day through a consent decree under which the parties were barred from colluding or inviting to collude on therapist pay rates and entering into or organizing agreements with any person that aim to the same anticompetitive conduct. On January 18, 2017, the FTC filed a complaint against Mallinckrodt ARD Inc. (formerly known as Questcor Pharmaceuticals, Inc.) and its parent company, Mallinckrodt plc, alleging that Questcor illegally bought the U.S. right to Synacthen Depot, a drug which jeopardized its monopoly for adrenocorticotropic hormone drugs in the U.S. market. To settle the antitrust charges, Mallinckrodt agreed to pay USD 100 million and agreed that Questcor needed to grant a license to develop Synacthen Depot.[564]

On February 27, 2017, the FTC charged the Cooperativa de Médicos Oftalmólogos de Puerto Rico (OFTACOOP) to coordinate an agreement among competing ophthalmologists to refuse to deal with a health plan, MCS Advantage, Inc., and its network administrator, Eye Management of Puerto Rico, LLC. OFTACOOP also forced MCS to maintain its then-current reimbursement rates paid to ophthalmologists without justification. The FTC consent order barred OFTACOOP from making or encouraging agreements among ophthalmologists "(1) to refuse to deal, or threaten to refuse to deal,

562. FTC, FTC Sues Cephalon, Inc. for Unlawfully Blocking Sale of Lower-Cost Generic Versions of Branded Drug Until 2012 (Feb. 13, 2008), https://www.ftc.gov/news-events/press-releases/2008/02/ftc-sues-cephalon-inc-unlawfully-blocking-sale-lower-cost-generic.

563. Two FTC Commissioners, Maureen K. Ohlhausen and Joshua D. Wright, wrote a separate statement to explain "why disgorgement is appropriate in this case" and "to convey [their] continuing concerns about the lack of guidance the Commission has provided on the pursuit of this extraordinary remedy in competition cases." Separate Statement of Commissioners Maureen K. Ohlhausen & Joshua D. Wright *Federal Trade Commission v. Cephalon, Inc.* (May 28, 2015) available at https://www.ftc.gov/system/files/documents/public_statements/645501/150528cephalonohlhausenwright1.pdf.

564. FTC, Mallinckrodt Will Pay $ 100 Million to Settle FTC, State Charges It Illegally Maintained its Monopoly of Specialty Drug Used to Treat Infants (Jan. 18, 2017), https://www.ftc.gov/news-events/press-releases/2017/01/mallinckrodt-will-pay-100-million-settle-ftc-state-charges-it.

with any payor regarding any term, including price terms, or (2) not to deal individually with any payor, or not to deal with any payor other than through OFTACOOP;"[565] in addition to exchange information aimed to facilitate the prohibited behavior.

On July 13, 2016, the FTC accused Invibio Limited, Invibio, Inc. ("Invibio"), and the parent company Victrex plc of exclusive contracting practices. Solvay Specialty Polymers LLC and Evonik Corporation were potentially excluded from competing with them in the implant-grade Polyether Etherketone (PEEK) market.[566] The investigation ended the same day by means of a consent decree which prohibited Invibio and its parent company from entering into exclusive supply contracts. Moreover, the FTC banned the companies from restricting current customers from employing in new products alternative source of PEEK.[567]

On October 30, 2015, the FTC filed a complaint against Concordia Pharmaceuticals Inc. ("Concordia") and Par Pharmaceutical, Inc. ("Par"), arguing that the pharmaceutical companies agreed not to compete in the market of generic versions of Kapvay.[568] The antitrust settlement barred Concordia and Par from enforcing the anticompetitive provisions of the agreement.[569] Defendants also agreed to provide notice to the FTC of any patent settlement they make that restricted entry of an authorized generic drug for ten years and to establish a compliance program for employees who are in a position to violate the order's provisions.[570]

On April 20, 2015, the Commission accused Cardinal Health Inc. of preventing a number of potential firms from entering the affected radiopharmaceuticals markets. According to the FTC, Cardinal (which owned the nation's largest chain of radiopharmacies) induced the only producers of radiopharmaceuticals HPAs, Bristol-Myers Squibb and General Electric Co., to refuse to grant distribution rights for HPAs to new competitors. HPAs were considered "key inputs for a financially viable radiopharmacy business,"[571] thus necessary to enter a new radiopharmaceuticals market. By doing so, the FTC argued that Cardinal became *de facto* the exclusive distributor of HPAs. Cardinal agreed to pay USD 26.8 million as disgorgement of its unlawful gains and to stop entering into exclusive agreements with producers of the same radiopharmaceutical product or obtaining through retaliation or coercion exclusivity rights. Cardinal

565. FTC, Cooperativa de Médicos Oftalmólogos de Puerto Rico (Jan. 30, 2017), https://www.ftc.gov/enforcement/cases-proceedings/141-0194/cooperativa-de-medicos-oftalmologos-de-puerto-rico.
566. FTC, *In the Matter of* Victrex plc Corp., Invibio Limited Corp. and Invibio (Aug. 5, 2016) https://www.ftc.gov/enforcement/cases-proceedings/141-0042/victrex-plc-et-al-matter.
567. *Ibid.*
568. *In the Matter of* Concordia Pharmaceuticals Inc., Concordia Healthcare Corp., Par Pharmaceutical Inc., Par Pharmaceutical Holding, No. C-4553 and C-4554, Complaint (2015).
569. FTC, FTC Issues Final Orders Settling Charges of Illegal Agreement not to Compete, Press Release (Oct. 30, 2015) https://www.ftc.gov/news-events/press-releases/2015/10/ftc-issues-final-orders-settling-charges-illegal-agreement-not.
570. *In the Matter of* Concordia Pharmaceuticals Inc., Concordia Healthcare Corp., Par Pharmaceutical Inc., Par Pharmaceutical Holding, No. C-4553 and C-4554, Decision and Order (2015).
571. FTC, Cardinal Health Agrees to Pay $ 26.8 Million to Settle Charges It Monopolized 25 Markets for the Sale of Radiopharmaceuticals to Hospitals and Clinics, Press Release (Apr. 20, 2015), https://www.ftc.gov/news-events/press-releases/2015/04/cardinal-health-agrees-pay-268-million-settle-charges-it.

also agreed to notify the FTC of any new exclusive distribution agreements or the acquisition of any radiopharmacy assets when such an acquisition was not subject to the notification requirements of the Hart-Scott Rodino Act.[572]

In the *Matter of Bosley, Inc., Aderans America Holdings, Inc., and Aderans Co., Ltd.*, the defendants agreed to settle FTC charges of exchanging competitively sensitive nonpublic information about its business operations with rivals by requiring parties to stop communicating such information and adopting an antitrust compliance program.[573] On May 1, 2013, the FTC settled another complaint[574] by prohibiting the defendants from engaging in the alleged antitrust conduct in the future and specifically imposed notification requirements to prevent the violation of the consent order.

On February 11, 2013, the last pharmaceutical case of my sample was settled. The defendant was accused of monopolizing the market where it exerted market power by engaging in exclusionary conduct. The FTC prohibited the defendant from entering into exclusive distribution agreements with the main distributors of its product.[575] The FTC also imposed some notification duties and its right to access all facilities and all company records related to the compliance of its order.

In summary, within in the pharmaceutical sector, the main antitrust conduct is the *pay for delay* agreements prosecuted by the FTC by means of agreements that usually require, in addition to stopping the alleged anticompetitive practice, the implementation of an antitrust compliance program. In the most serious cases, the FTC has also required pharmaceutical companies to pay a disgorgement.

### *[b] Professional/Trade Associations*

The FTC shows a lot of interest in professional and trade associations, opening ten investigations against different associations in the last five years. Eight of these investigations ended with consent decrees and two went to trial. Most cases concerned the codes of ethics of those associations, which, according to the FTC, contained anticompetitive provisions. Eight out of ten cases affected professional associations, while two investigations were opened against the National Association of Animal Breeders (NAAB). On November 2, 2015, the FTC filed its first complaint against the NAAB, alleging that some provisions of its Code of Ethic stifled competition by restricting the ability of its members to disclose truthful and non-deceptive information.[576] Such provisions also prevented its members from advertising by comparing their products to the products of other members. The NAAB agreed to remove the

572. *Ibid.*
573. FTC Approves Final Order Settling Charges that Bosley, Inc., Illegally Exchanged Competitively Sensitive Business Information With Hair Club (Jun. 5, 2013), https://www.ftc.gov/news-events/press-releases/2013/06/ftc-approves-final-order-settling-charges-bosley-inc-illegally.
574. *In the Matter of* Práxedes E. Alvarez Santiago, M.D., Daniel Pérez Brisebois, M.D., Jorge Grillasca Palou, M.D., Rafael Garcia Nieves, M.D., Francis M. Vázquez Roura, M.D., Angel B. Rivera Santos, M.D., Cosme D. Santos Torres, M.D., and Juan L. Vilaró Chardón, M.D., C-4402, Decision and Order (May 1, 2013).
575. *In the Matter of* IDEXX Laboratories, Inc., No. C-4383, Decision and Order (Feb. 11, 2013).
576. *In the Matter of* National Association of Animal Breeders, Inc., No. C-4558, Complaint (2015).

challenged provisions of its Code of Ethics and to cease certain advertising restrictions, in addition to publishing and distributing an announcement on the consent decree and the resulting changes to the Code. The NAAB also agreed to implement an antitrust compliance program. On September 26, 2017, the FTC filed a new complaint and issued a consent decree against the NAAB.[577] The FTC order prohibited the NAAB from restraining price-related competition among its members relating to the sale or acquisition of bulls or bull semen. It also required NAAB to implement an antitrust compliance program and to meet certain compliance and reporting standards.

Similarly, in *the Matter of National Association of Residential Property Managers, Inc.* (NARP), the NARP agreed to eliminate provisions in its Code of Ethics that the FTC considered anticompetitive and to adopt an antitrust compliance program.[578] On the same day of the NARP consent decree, the FTC issued a consent decree to settle the antitrust changes against the National Association of Teachers of Singing, Inc (NATS).[579] The FTC order required the NATS to eliminate those provisions in its Code of Ethics which restrained competition among its members and acquire from each of its chapters a certification that the chapter is not engaged in any prohibited practices. The FTC also ordered NATS to adopt an antitrust compliance program. On April 3, 2014, the FTC settled *In the Matter of California Association of Legal Support Professionals,*[580] and *In the Matter of Music Teachers National Association, Inc* through consent decrees.[581] Both consent orders required the two associations to remove provisions in their codes of ethics that stifled competition among their members and implement a compliance program.

On March 3, 2015 the FTC filed a complaint and settled its charges against an association of skating teachers (*In the Matter of* Professional Skaters Association, Inc.). Similar to the previous cases, the professional skaters association agreed to eliminate potential anticompetitive provisions in its bylaws and to implement an antitrust compliance program. The association was also barred from restraining its member from soliciting work.

Finally, on May 26, 2018, the FTC settled *In the Matter of American Guild of Organists*, requiring also the American Guild of Organists to eliminate the guild's rules that restrained competition and to stop issuing guidance, compensation schedules, or model contract provisions for members to adopt to determinate compensation. Also in

577. *In the Matter of* National Association of Animal Breeders, Inc., No. C-4623, Complaint (Sep. 26, 2017).
578. FTC, FTC Approves Final Orders Requiring Two Professional Associations to Eliminate Rules that Restrict Competition among Their Members, Press Release (Oct. 10, 2014), https://www.ftc.gov/news-events/press-releases/2014/10/ftc-approves-final-orders-requiring-two-professional-associations.
579. *In the Matter of* National Association of Teachers of Singing, Inc., No. C-4491, Decision and Order (Oct. 1, 2014).
580. *In the Matter of* California Association of Legal Support Professionals, No. C-4447, Decision and Order (Apr. 3, 2014).
581. *In the Matter of* Music Teachers National Association, Inc., No. C-4448, Decision and Order (Apr. 3, 2014).

this case, the FTC required the defendant to implement an antitrust compliance program.[582]

### *[c] Media/Telecommunication Industry*

Three out of the forty-three analyzed FTC cases concerned the media/telecommunication industry. One of these cases is still ongoing and the other two have been settled by means a consent decree

On July 23, 2013, the FTC settled *In the Matter of Motorola Mobility LLC* and *Google Inc.* case concerning Motorola's standard essential patents (SEPs). The consent order barred Google from seeking injunctions against a willing licensee, either in federal court or at the International Trade Commission (ITC), to block the use of any standard-essential patents that the firm has previously committed to license on FRAND (Fair Reasonable and Non-Discriminatory) terms.[583] Under a separate commitment, the FTC ordered Google to delete restrictions on the use of its online search advertising platform, AdWords, and to allow all websites to keep their content out of Google's vertical search offerings. In any case, websites would have still appeared in Google's general, or "organic," web search results.

On April 24, 2018, *In the Matter of Oregon Lithoprint, Inc.* the FTC filed a complaint and issued the consent decree on against Oregon Lithoprint Inc.[584] According to the FTC complaint, Oregon Lithoprint Inc. engaged in an invitation to collude in violation of Section 5 of the FTC Act. The FTC order basically barred the defendant from making or attempting to make any agreement aimed to collude; namely to stop the alleged conduct.

### *[d] Other Industries*

Unsurprisingly, in the remaining cases, remedies enshrined in consent decrees merely required companies to stop engaging in the alleged antitrust conduct. Only sometimes did the FTC required companies to adopt a compliance program and comply with reporting/notification obligations. In *the Matter of Fortiline, LLC*, for example, the FTC prohibited Fontiline from entering into or attempting to enter into any agreement with any rival to raise or fix prices, allocate markets or customers. Thus, the FTC seems to order something that antitrust law prohibits of any company—engaging in cartels. In

582. FTC, American Guild of Organists, Case Summary (May 26, 2017), https://www.ftc.gov/enforcement/cases-proceedings/151-0159/american-guild-organists.
583. FTC, FTC Finalizes Settlement in Google Motorola Mobility Case (Jul. 24, 2013), https://www.ftc.gov/news-events/press-releases/2013/07/ftc-finalizes-settlement-google-motorola-mobility-case.
584. FTC, FTC Approves Final Order with Community Newspaper Owner Oregon Lithoprint Inc. (Apr. 27, 2018) https://www.ftc.gov/news-events/press-releases/2018/04/ftc-approves-final-order-community-newspaper-owner-oregon.

the *Matter of Tecnica Group S.p.A.* and *Volkl*, the FTC merely bared both companies from engaging in the alleged anticompetitive conduct in the future.[585]

### *[3] Economic Effects of Remedies*

This part investigates the Cephalon case settled by means of a consent decree in 2015 after seven years of investigation. The particularity of this consent decree is not only the long period required to reach an agreement, but also the fact that such an agreement covered a variety of litigations and required companies to pay a disgorgement of USD 1.2 billion. Having described the main facts of such a complex case (which concerns a *pay for delay* agreement in the pharmaceutical industry) my analysis focuses on the evolution of price and the development of substitute products in the market of Provigil/Modafinil to assess the pro-competitive effects of the consent solution.

#### *[a] Cephalon Case*

*In the Matter of Cephalon* is certainly one of the most interesting cases settled by the FTC in the last five years. In contrast to the majority of consent orders, Cephalon and its parent company Teva Pharmaceutical agreed to pay USD 1.2 billion as equitable relief (the so-called "Settlement Fund Disbursement Agreement").[586] The amount set forth in such a settlement was deposited into a specific Settlement Account and the money was used to satisfy any settlement or judgment in a related case. For related cases, the order means "any of the following cases, or any case consolidated with or merged into the following case: *King Drug Co., et. Al. v. Celaphon, Inc., at al.*, No. 06-1797 (E.D. Pa.) ('Direct Purchaser Class Case'); *Vista Healthplan, Inc, et al. v. Cephalon Inc et al.*, No. 06-1833 (E.D. Pa.) ('End Pyor Class Case'); *Apotex, Inc. v. Cephalon, Inc., et al.*, No. 06-2768 (E.D. Pa.); *Ride Aid Corp. v. Cephalon, Inc.*, et al., No. 09-3820 (E.D. Pa.); *Walgreen Co. v. Cephalon*, Inc. et al. No. 09-3956 (E.D. Pa.); and *Giant Eagle, Inc. v. Cephalon, Inc*, et al. No. 10-5164 (E.D. Pa.); or (b) any other government investigation or litigation that is threatened in writing or filed that seeks to recover damages or equitable monetary relief based on alleged anticompetitive or other unlawful practices by the Cephalon Parties in connection with (i) the procurement, listing or enforcement of patents related to the drug Provigil®, (ii) FDA exclusivities related to the drug Provigil®, or (iii) settling litigation related to the drug Provigil®."[587] In summary, the FTC agreement affected all litigations related to drug Provigil, including patent and antitrust litigations. According to the FTC Complaint, Cephalon engaged in a *pay for delay* agreement by paying four generic pharmaceutical companies to avoid their entry into the Provigil market with a cheaper generic version.

585. In the Matter of Tecnica Group (Jul. 9, 2014), https://www.ftc.gov/enforcement/cases-proceedings/121-0004/tecnica-group-matter.
586. *FTC v. Cephalon*, No. 2:08-cv-2141, Stipulated Order for Permanent Injunction and Equitable Monetary Relief (D. C. E. D. Pen., 2015).
587. *Ibid.*, at §22.

### [i] The Facts

The Cephalon consent decree affected several litigations, thus, a deeper analysis of the facts of this case is necessary before assessing the economic effects of remedies enshrined in the consent solution. Provigil, the brand name of the drug subject to the reverse payment agreement, was originally developed in France under the name Modiodal by the French company Lafon. In 1998, Lafon leased the rights to Cephalon to market Modiodal in the U.S. under the name of Provigil.[588] In 2001, Cephalon acquired Lafon for USD 450 million.[589] In 2002, Cephalon' sales doubled and "Cephalon's five year annualized sales growth of 102 percent ma[de] it the fastest-growing biotech in the U.S" journalists noted.[590]

In December 2002, some generic drug manufactures, Teva Pharmaceuticals USA Inc. (Teva), Ranbaxy Pharmaceuticals Inc. (Ranbaxy); Mylan Pharmaceuticals Inc. (Mylan), Barr Laboratories Inc. (Barr) applied to the FDA to start producing and marketing a generic form of Provigil (known as Modafinil in Europe). According to these generic drug companies, Cephalon's patent was both invalid and not applicable to their drug version.[591] Between 2005 and 2006 Cephalon entered into an agreement with these generics manufacturers (Teva, Ranbaxy, Mylan and Barr) to delay the market of the generic version of Provigil until April 2012 (namely the *pay for delay agreement*), said the FTC. The FTC argued that Cephalon paid each generic company "more than $200 million collectively"[592] to delay their entering the market until April 2012 and extend its patent protection for six more years.[593]

In that time frame, the price of Provigil exponentially increased. From December 31, 2005, to December 31, 2013, the price of Provigil 200 mg tablets increased by 476.6 percent.[594] In doing so, Cephalon seems to have maintained its monopoly at the expenses of patients and consumers by denying them the opportunity to buy Provigil's (lower cost) generic versions and increasing the price of the only version available in

588. In 1998, the U.S. Food and Drug Administration approved Provigil for the treatment of narcolepsy. *See* FDA, NDA 20-717 Provigil (modafinil)—FDA Approved Draft Labeling 12/98, available at https://www.accessdata.fda.gov/drugsatfda_docs/label/1998/20717lbl.pdf. *See also Apotex Inc. v. Cephalon, Inc.* Action No. 06-cv-2768, 2011 WL 6090676 (E.D. Pa. 2011). ("Cephalon obtained approval from the FDA to market its Provigil® product by a New Drug Application ('NDA') 20-717 on December 24, 1998, and began selling Provigil® shortly thereafter.") *Ibid.*, at 5.
589. *Apotex INC. v. Cephalon*, Inc., No. 2:06-cv-2768 (D. C. E. D. Pen., 2011).
590. Forbes, Matthew Herper, What Keeps Cephalon Awake at Night? (Apr. 9, 2003), https://www.forbes.com/2003/04/09/cx_mh_0409ceph.html#b278f32613e4.
591. *Federal Trade Commission v. Cephalon Inc.*, 551 F. Supp. 2d 21, Complaint (D. C. C, 2008) at §36.
592. *Ibid.*, at §3.
593. "As Cephalon's CEO observed shortly after entering these agreements: 'We were able to get six more years of patent protection. That's $4 billion in sales that no one expected.'" *Ibid.*, at §4.
594. Stephen W. Schondelmeyer & Leigh Puris, *Trends in Retail Prices of Specialty Prescription Drugs Widely Used by Older Americans*, 2006 to 2013 (Public Policy Institute, November 2015) at 13. ("Provigil 200 mg tablets had a price increase of 476.6 percent over the 8-year study period ending in 2013.") *Ibid.*

the market.[595] Moreover, in *Apotex Inc. v. Cephalon, Inc.*,[596] the district court stated that, in obtaining the Provigil patent, Cephalon engaged in inequitable practice before the U.S. Patent & Trademark Office and the patent was unenforceable.[597]

In May 2011, Teva (the largest generic drug manufacture in the world[598] involved in the *pay for delay* agreement) acquired Cephalon for USD 6.8 billion.[599] The FTC's approval of the acquisition was subject to the condition that Teva would have divested to Par Pharmaceutical Inc. (Par) "all of Teva's rights and assets relating to its generic transmucosal fentanyl citrate lozenges ('fentanyl citrate') and generic extended release cyclobenzaprine hydrochloride capsules ('cyclobenzaprine hydrochloride')."[600] In addition, Teva had to allow Par to sell generic Modafinil for a period of at least a year through a supply agreement.[601] Surprisingly, Par does not appear listed in the *FDA Approved Drug Products* for Provigil or any generic versions of Modafinil.[602] In 2015, Endo Pharmaceutical Plc (Endo) bought Par for USD 8.05 billion.[603] Endo, as outlined in Section *[2][a]*, was and is presently investigated for several *pay for delay* agreements in the pharmaceutical sector.[604]

#### [ii] The FTC Consent Order

In May 2015, the FTC closed the antitrust investigation that was opened in 2008 against Cephalon and its parent company Teva for engaging in the agreement with generic drug manufactures to delay the generic versions of Provigil until April 2012—the *pay for delay agreement*. In this FTC consent order a special emphasis has been placed on the use of disgorgement as FTC remedy. FTC's Commissioners Maureen K. Ohlhausen and Joshua D. Wright wrote a Separated Statement where they emphasized the proper use of disgorgement in that case, along with the lack of guidance in using similar

595. FTC, FTC Settlement of Cephalon Pay for Delay Case Ensures $1.2 Billion in Ill-Gotten Gains Relinquished; Refunds Will Go To Purchasers Affected By Anticompetitive Tactics, Press Release (May 28, 2015), https://www.ftc.gov/news-events/press-releases/2015/05/ftc-settlement-cephalon-pay-delay-case-ensures-12-billion-ill.
596. *Apotex Inc. v. Cephalon, Inc.*, Action No. 06-cv-2768, 2011 WL 6090676, at *28 (E.D. Pa. 2011).
597. *Ibid.*
598. Teva Generic, Frequently Asked Questions, https://www.tevagenerics.com/patients/frequently-asked-questions/#q-1-1.
599. Teva Pharmaceutical Industries Ltd., Teva to Acquire Cephalon in USD 6.8 Billion Transaction (May 2, 2011), https://www.tevapharm.com/news/teva_to_acquire_cephalon_in_6_8_billion_transaction_05_11.aspx.
600. FTC, Analysis of Agreement Containing Consent Orders to Aid Public Comment, In the Matter of Teva Pharmaceutical Industries Ltd. And Cephalon, Inc., File No. 111-0166.
601. *Ibid.*
602. U.S. Food and Drug Administration, Drugs@FDA: FDA Approved Drug Products, https://www.accessdata.fda.gov/scripts/cder/daf/index.cfm?event = overview.process&ApplNo = 020717 (last visited Dec. 7, 2018).
603. Cision PR Newswire, Endo Completes Acquisition of Par Pharmaceutical and Provides Financial Guidance (Sep. 28, 2015) https://www.prnewswire.com/news-releases/endo-completes-acquisition-of-par-pharmaceutical-and-provides-financial-guidance-300149703.html.
604. According to the FTC, Endo and the others defendants engaged in an antitrust violation by using pay-for-delay settlements to impede consumers' access to lower-cost generic versions of Opana ER and Lidoderm.

remedies in FTC antitrust cases.[605] According to the FTC Policy Statement,[606] the FTC can order the disgorgement if the violation is clear, a "reasonable basis for calculating the amount of a remedial payment" exists, and "the value of seeking monetary relief in light of any other remedies available in the matter, including private actions and criminal proceedings."[607]

In the case at hand, as the FTC's Commissioners emphasized, the violation was clear as the settlement concerned fraudulent procured patents, and there was reason to believe that Cephalon knew about the antitrust violation when it entered into the *pay for delay* agreement.[608] With respect to the amount of the disgorgement, Commissioner Wright observed that penalties "should be set at a level to induce offenders to internalize the full social cost of their violation."[609] The amount of USD 1.2 billion set forth in such a settlement is remarkable, but we have to consider both the gravity of the company's behavior and the several lawsuits that such a settlement has covered.

### [iii] The Economic Effects of the Consent Order

To assess the economic affects of the FTC consent decree of 2015, I evaluate the price of Provigil from 2013 to date, as well as generic versions of Provigil now available by Cephalon and Teva's competitors.

In 2013, the retail price of a package of thirty Provigil 200 mg tablets was USD 38.46.[610] Nowadays, there are a variety of drug producers that offer brand name or generic versions of Provigil, such as Alertec, Modiodal, Modapro, Modvigil, Modafinil, Modanil and Modasomil.[611] The price of that drug appears to be increased since 2013. Today, the cheapest version of this drug—to be Modvigil—ranges in price "from $0.49 USD to $2.99 USD depending on the quantity,"[612] while the "brand name modafinil (Provigil®) can cost as much as 50 times the off-brand versions like Modvigil or

605. Separate Statement of Commissioners Maureen K. Ohlhausen and Joshua D. Wright, *Federal Trade Commission v. Cephalon, Inc.*, May 18, 2015.
606. Fed. Trade Comm'n, Policy Statement on Monetary Equitable Remedies in Competition Cases, 68 Fed. Reg. 45820 (Aug. 4, 2003).
607. *Ibid.*, at 45821.
608. Separate Statement of Commissioners Maureen K. Ohlhausen and Joshua D. Wright, *Federal Trade Commission v. Cephalon, Inc.*, May 18, 2015, at 2.
609. *Ibid.*, at 3.
610. Schondelmeyer & Puris, *supra* n. 594, at 17.
611. *See*, e.g., U.S. Food and Drug Administration, Drugs@FDA: FDA Approved Drug Products, https://www.accessdata.fda.gov/scripts/cder/daf/index.cfm?event = overview.process&App lNo = 020717 (last visited Dec. 7, 2018); Drug.com, Modafinil, U.S. Food and Drug Administration, Drugs@FDA: FDA Approved Drug Products, https://www.accessdata.fda.gov/scripts /cder/daf/index.cfm?event = overview.process&ApplNo = 020717 (last visited Dec. 7, 2018). Pharmacompass, Modafinil, https://www.pharmacompass.com/manufacturers-suppliers-exporters/modafinil (last visited Dec. 7, 2018).
612. *See* Modafinil.org, *Beginners Guide to Modvigil, the Costs of Modvigil*, https://modafinil.org/ modvigil/ (Jul. 29, 2018). ("Brand name modafinil (Provigil®) can cost as much as 50 times the off-brand versions like Modvigil or Modalert."). *Ibid.*

Modalert."[613] Now, the cost of a package of thirty Modafilin/Provigil 200 mg tablets starts from USD 260.48.[614]

In doing the analysis of price for generic versions of Provigil now available, we need to consider that Provigil/Modafinil is a prescribed drug not legally saleable online in the U.S., Canada and Europe. In 2017, the AARP Public Policy Institute analyzed trends in retail prices of prescription drugs and recognized a consistent increase in price of prescription drugs that could not be justified by general inflation.[615] Generic versions of this drug—like the cheapest one, Modvigil—are offered in online/traditional markets without a medical prescription in countries like India that do not classify that drug as a prescription-only medication.

## §4.02 SOME CONSIDERATIONS

The conclusions to derive from this analysis are as follows. The DOJ and FTC were created with very different characteristics and tasks, but through the increase in the adoption of consent decrees such differences began to fade away. Both agencies can regulate and shape the U.S. markets through the adoption of remedies enshrined in consent decrees. However, in contrast to the leading consent decrees examined in Chapter I (including AT&T and Microsoft consent decrees) in the last five years, remedies imposed through consent solutions by both the FTC and DOJ appear quite soft. Generally, both agencies merely required the companies subject to investigation to stop engaging in the alleged anticompetitive conduct. In some cases, the FTC and DOJ also imposed the adoption of a compliance program, some specific reporting duties and/or rights of inspection of the agency. In the few cases where the agency imposed a disgorgement such as the Cephalon case, the price of the affected product seems to be increased after the antitrust decision.

In summary, antitrust remedies enshrined in consent decrees do not seem as effective as in the past. The magnitude of consent decrees, as outlined in Chapter 1, is enormous, but like any powerful tool, consent decrees and their remedies need to be used appropriately or else it can create more harm than benefit. Consumers and markets overall would only benefit from an economic analysis, both before and after the adoption of antitrust remedies.

613. *Ibid.*
614. Drug.com, *Modafinil Prices, Coupons and Patient Assistance Programs*, https://www.drugs.com/price-guide/modafinil (last visited Dec. 9, 2018).
615. AARP, Trends in Retail Prices of Prescription Drugs Widely Used by Older Americans: 2006 to 2015 (December 2017), available at https://www.aarp.org/content/dam/aarp/ppi/2017/11/trends-in-retail-prices-of-prescription-drugs-widely-used-by-older-americans-december.pdf.

CHAPTER 5

# An Economic Analysis of Commitment Decisions

EU competition law has always had the primary goal of creating and maintaining a single European market before increasing market efficiency and consumer welfare. As Professor Richard Whish and David Bailey observed, the EU Commission and EU Courts enforce EU competition law "very much with the issue of single market integration in mind"[616] and this also needs to be remembered in the practice of investigating EU commitment decisions.

In 2003, when the procedure of commitment decisions was formalized and the goal of creating a single European market was largely achieved, EU competition law went through a profound process of modernization. As will be explored in the following, the practice of commitment decisions was not consistent, but changed over the years, reflecting the favor of the EU Commission for an economic or formalistic approach in enforcing antitrust provisions. The commitment decisions practice, for example, was largely adopted in 2013 at which point 40 percent of all of 101 and 102 TFEU cases were settled through commitment decisions. By 2015, the percent of cases settled by means of a commitment decision had fallen to 37 percent,[617] and in 2017 only a case out of eleven (hence 9 percent) ended with commitments.[618]

Similar to the investigation conducted in Chapter 4 on U.S. antitrust context, Chapter 5 engages in an empirical analysis on the use of commitment decisions by the EU Commission and one National Competition Authority (NCA). I picked the Italian Antitrust Authority, *Autorita' Garante della Concorrenza e del Mercato* (AGCM) as it represents a very recent example in one of Europe's largest economies. This chapter

616. Richard Whish & David Bailey, *Competition Law* §2.09 (Oxford U. Press, 2015).
617. EU Commission, Competition, Cases, http://ec.europa.eu/competition/elojade/isef/index.cfm?fuseaction=dsp_result (last visited Apr. 10, 2016).
618. In 2017, the Ebook/Amazon case was the only one settled by means of a commitment decisions in 2017. Case COMP/AT.40153, E-book MFNs and related matters (Amazon) Commission Decision of 4 May 2017, 2017 C (2017) 2876 final.

examines EU Commission and AGCM's investigations settled by means of commitment decisions from January 2013 to the end of 2018 by assessing: (*i*) the timing from the opening of the antitrust investigation (Preliminary Assessment or Statement of Objection)[619] to the enactment of the commitment decision; (*ii*) the main markets/industries involved; (*iii*) the kind of remedies adopted in each industry; (*iv*) the evolution of the affected markets after the adoption of remedies enshrined in the commitment decision. Through this analysis, the chapter assesses the practice and evolution of EU commitment decisions, drawing some conclusions.

This Chapter assesses when and in what circumstances the EU Commission and AGCM have resorted to a consensual settlement, investigating the outcomes of commitment decisions in terms of firm behavior and agency practice going forward. We will use case examples from January 2013 to October 2018. This analysis allows us to determine the EU common practice (both at European and national levels) with commitment decisions by focusing on the timing to reach a consensus on remedies and the kind of remedies adopted for each main affected industry. The economic effects of some commitment decisions are also explored to assess *pros* and *cons* of such remedies from an economic and consumer welfare perspective.

## §5.01 THE EU COMMISSION'S COMMITMENT DECISIONS PRACTICE

From January 1, 2013, to October 31, 2018 the EU Commission decided seventy-four cases concerning Articles 101 and 102 of the TFEU. The following analysis considers only a sample of fifty-four cases ended with commitments or a prohibition decision without considering those closed, for example, with a rejection decision. Twelve out of fifty-four cases were settled by means of commitment decisions, forty ended with a prohibition decision. In one case the EU Commission re-adopted a cartel decision (the General Court for procedural grounds annulled the EU Commission's decision of 2010 in December 2015),[620] and another case concerned an amending decision.[621]

619. *See* Chapter 2, §2.02, [A] Preliminary Assessment at 42. ("Instead of the Statement of Objection, commitment decisions foresee a simpler step, the Preliminary Assessment. However, when the parties have already received a Statement of Objections, the EU Commission can still accept the parties' commitments.") *Ibid. See also*, EU Commission, Antitrust Manual of Procedures, *supra* n. 251, at 177.

620. Antitrust: Commission re-adopts decision and fines air cargo carriers EUR 776 million for price-fixing cartel, Press Release (Mar. 17, 2017), http://europa.eu/rapid/press-release_IP-17-661_en.htm.

621. Case n. 38238, Raw Tabacco (Jun. 16, 2017). ("By judgment of 8 March 2011, the General Court partly granted WWTE's application for annulment and fixed its fine at EUR 1,579,500, reducing the fine imposed on it by EUR 243,000 as a consequence of increasing WWTE's leniency reduction from 25 percent to 35 percent. This judgment was confirmed by the Court of Justice on 3 May 2012 in Case C-240/11 P.") On 16 June 2017, the European Commission amended its decision C(2004) 4030 (final) of 20 Oct. 2004. EU Commission, Prohibition Decision amending Decision C(2004) 4030 (final) of 20 October 2004 relating to a proceeding under Article 81(1) of the EC Treaty, §(4) (Jun. 6, 2017).

Commitment decisions were concentrated in 2013, 2015, and 2016. In 2014, 2017 and 2018 the EU Commission adopted only one commitment decision each year.[622]

### [A] Timing and Markets/Industries Involved

In the analysis of the timing from the opening of EU Commission investigation (by means of a Preliminary Assessment or a Statement of Objection) and the EU Commission's final decision,[623] it turns out that there is not a significant difference between a decision under Article 9 and under Article 7 of the Reg. 1/2003. The average number of days from the opening of the EU Commission's investigation to the final decision is around 1,197 days. If we consider only commitment decisions, the average number of days from the beginning of the investigation to a commitment decision is 1,129. Conversely, the average number of days from the beginning of the EU Commission's case to the prohibition decision under Article 7 is about 1,217 days. This means that the EU Commission save less than 8 percent of time through the adoption of commitment decisions. However, this analysis does not consider the eventual trial after the EU Commission's decision, which will likely come after a prohibition decision.

Case n. 39745, *Information Market case* (*CDS*), which lasted 1,919 days, is the longest EU case settled by means of commitment decision. On April 20, 2011, the EU Commission started its formal investigation[624] which ended with a commitment decision on July 20, 2016. The fastest cases settled with a commitment decision took five hundred fifty-four days: Case 39731, *Deutsche Bahn II* and Case n. 39678, *Deutsche Bahn I*.[625]

In the analysis of prohibition decisions under Article 7, the longest case seems to be Case n. 39792, *Steel Abrasives*, which started with unannounced inspections between June 15 and 17, 2010 and closed with a prohibition decision on May 25, 2016.[626] On the contrary, one of the fastest cases (Case n. 40055, *Parking Heaters*) started on July 24, 2013, and ended with a prohibition decision on June 17, 2015.

This analysis always includes the end date in the calculation of days from the opening of the EU Commission investigation to the final decision. In the sample of analyzed decisions, I have excluded the decision of modification of a previous decision, and the decision taken after the reopening of a previous case.

---

622. Gazprom (2018), Ebook/Amazon (2017), Samsung—Enforcement of UMTS standard essential patents (2014).
623. *See* Chapter 2, at 42.
624. The investigation was opened in 2011, but on Jul. 1, 2013 the Commission adopted a Statement of Objections against the International Swaps and Derivatives Association (ISDA), Markit, and the ISDA and 13 investment banks. "The Statement of Objections raised preliminary concerns that all parties had coordinated to foreclose from the credit default swaps market Deutsche Börse in 2007 and Chicago Mercantile Exchange in 2008." EU Commission, Antitrust: Commission closes proceedings against 13 investment banks in credit default swaps case, Press Release (Dec. 4, 2015) http://ec.europa.eu/competition/antitrust/cases/dec_docs/39745/39745_13719_14.pdf.
625. EU Commission, Deutsche Bahn I (AT.39678), Deutsche Bahn II (AT.39731), Commitment Decision (Dec. 18, 2013).
626. EU Commission, Steel Abrasives (AT.39792), Prohibition Decision (May 25, 2016).

With respect to the primarily affected industries in the fifty-four analyzed cases, the majority concern the industry of transportation. Fifteen percent of the EU Commission's cases affect the media/communication industry and another 15 percent the market of accessories or parts for cars or motor vehicles. Eleven percent of the EU Commission's cases affected the market of electronic components. The following chart better depicts the exact proportion of cases for each industry (Figure 5.1).

*Figure 5.1 Main Affected Industries*

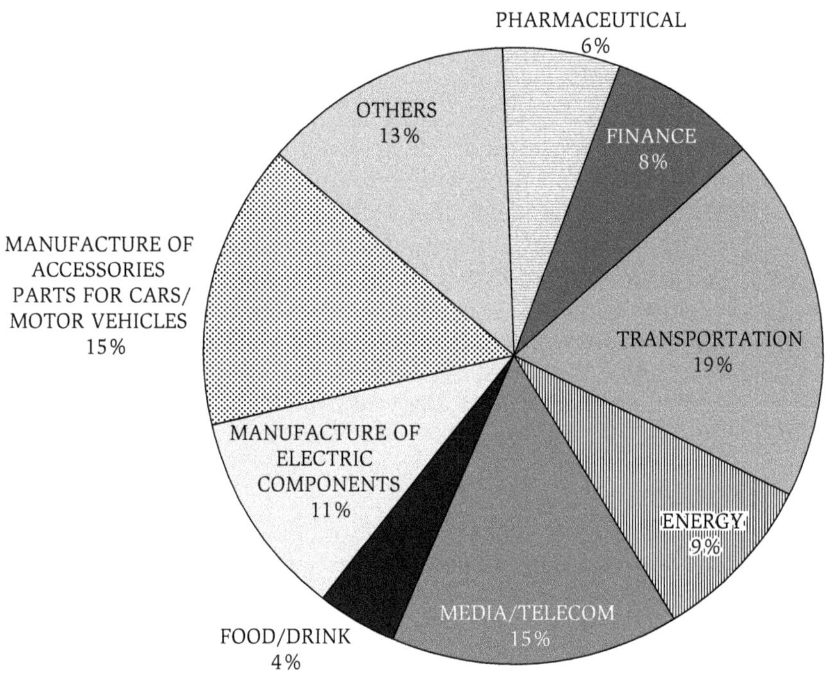


## [B] Adopted Remedies

This Section [B] investigates the kind of remedies enshrined in commitment decisions in the industries most affected in order to define the EU Commission's practice in determining and accepting commitment decisions. As outlined in the previous Section [A], the EU Commission antitrust enforcement focuses on the transportation and media/communication industries and on the markets of electronic and vehicle component manufacturing.

### *[1] Transportation Industry*

Ten cases out of fifty-four concerned the Transportation Industry, five of which ended with a commitment decision. In Case n. 39595, *Continental/United/Lufthansa/Air*

*Canada*, the EU Commission accepted the commitments offered by parties to settle the case without finding of liability and fine ex Article 101 TFEU.[627] On April 17, 2009, the EU Commission opened a proceeding against these airlines companies for a possible Article 101 TFEU violation by means of a revenue-sharing joint venture. The EU Commission discerned that these airline companies constituted a join venture to coordinate their conduct and to increase the price for premium passengers on the Frankfurt-New York route. The parties "offered to make slots available at Frankfurt and New York airports and to enter into agreements with competitors, allowing them to offer more attractive services"[628] improving competition on the Frankfurt-New York route. Such commitments became legally binding for a period of ten years on the three airlines.

In case n. 39964, *AF-KL/DL/AZ*, the EU Commission accepted the commitments offered by the airline companies subject to an investigation under Article 101 of TFEU. Similar to the previous case n. 39595, the airlines companies participated in a metal-neutral profit/loss-sharing join venture on the route Paris-New York and Rome-New York routes in relation to premium and non-premium passengers. To address the EU Commission's concerns, the airlines companies agreed to "make arrival and departure slot pairs available at Amsterdam airport and/or New York JFK/Newark Liberty airports, as well as at Rome airport and/or New York JFK/Newark Liberty airports—at the competitor's choice."[629] The airline companies also agreed to "enter into fare combinability agreements [and special prorate agreements] with competitors for all classes of passengers on each Route of Concern, except on Paris-New York, where the agreements will cover premium passengers only."[630] The parties offered to appoint a trustee to oversee the application of the commitments.

On June 13, 2012, the EU Commission opened case n. 39678/39731, *Deutsche Bahn (DB) I and II*, to investigate a possible abuse of dominant position through a discount practice of DB in the German railroad industry. The EU Commission was concerned about the pricing system (including its discounts) which DB Energie applies to railway companies active in Germany for the supply of traction current, which is the specific electricity used by locomotives to propel trains. On December 18, 2013, the EU Commission accepted the commitments offered by DB to close the investigation.[631] DB agreed to charge a price approved by the German regulatory authority (Bundesnetzagentur) for the traction current and to grant access to its traction current

627. EU Commission, Continental/United/Lufthansa/Air Canada (Case n. 39595), Commitment Decision (May 23, 2013).
628. EU Commission, Antitrust: Commission renders legally binding commitments from Star alliance members Air Canada, United and Lufthansa on transatlantic air transport passenger market, Press Release (May 23, 2013).
629. Summary of Commission Decision of 12 May 2015 relating to a proceeding under Article 101 of the Treaty on the Functioning of the European Union (Case AT.39964—Air France/KLM/Alitalia/Delta) (notified under document number C(2015) 3125) OJ C 212, 27.6.2015, at §10(a).
630. *Ibid.*, at 10(b).
631. EU Commission, Deutsche Bahn I (AT.39678), Deutsche Bahn II (AT.39731), Commitment Decision (Dec. 18, 2013) (hereinafter Deutsche Bahn I and Deutsche Bahn II).

network to third parties.[632] By doing so, DB would have charged the same price to all railway companies without discounts for its own railway companies. The companies not belonging to DB group would also have received a one-time payment of 4 percent of their yearly traction current invoice, based on the period of one year before the entry into the new pricing system. DB agreed to appoint a trustee in charge of monitoring its compliance with the commitments. The commitments lasted five years.

On November 21, 2013, the EU Commission opened another investigation in the transportation section—Case n. 39850, *Container Shipping*.[633] The EU Commission expressed concerns about the General Rate Increase Announcements (GRI Announcements) known in the industry, which indicated the increase in U.S.-Dollars per transported container unit (twenty-foot equivalent). In the Preliminary Assessment on November 26, 2015, the EU Commission argued that GRI Announcements may be of little value for customers as they do not inform said customers of the new full future price they will have to pay.[634] Moreover, GRI Announcements may have only limited committal value that does not allow customers to rely on them. On July 7, 2016, the EU Commission made legally binding the commitments offered by the parties subject to the investigation. The fourteen container liner shipping companies involved agreed to stop publishing and transmitting GRI announcements and that if they want to communicate their price, their announcements need to enable purchasers to rely on such announcements.[635]

### *[2] Media/Communication*

On January 31, 2012, the EU Commission started investigating Samsung's conduct in licensing the Universal Mobile Telecommunications System (UMTS) SEPs on fair, reasonable and non-discriminatory (so-called "FRAND") terms and enforcing such licensing agreements and FRAND terms by seeking an injunction. The EU Commission argued that, in the context of SEPs, seeking an injunction (which is a legitimate remedy for patent holders in patent infringement cases) could engage Samsung in an abuse of dominant position conduct under Article 102 of TFEU. To address the EU Commission's concerns, Samsung committed to "not seek injunctions in Europe on the basis of its standard-essential patents (SEPs) for smartphones and tablets against licensees who sign up to a specified licensing framework."[636] Any dispute over FRAND terms for the

632. EU Commission, Antitrust: Commission accepts legally binding commitments from Deutsche Bahn concerning pricing of traction current in Germany, Press Release (Dec. 18, 2013), http://europa.eu/rapid/press-release_IP-13-1289_en.htm.
633. EU Commission, Container Shipping (AT.39850), Opening Proceeding (Nov. 21, 2013), http://ec.europa.eu/competition/antitrust/cases/dec_docs/39850/39850_2081_6.pdf.
634. EU Commission Decision, Container Shipping, Commitment Decision (AT.39850), at 9, http://ec.europa.eu/competition/antitrust/cases/dec_docs/39850/39850_3377_3.pdf.
635. *Ibid.*
636. EU Commission, Antitrust: Commission accepts legally binding commitments by Samsung Electronics on standard essential patent injunctions (Apr. 29, 2014), https://europa.eu/rapid/press-release_IP-14-490_en.htm.. *See also*, EU Commission, Samsung—Enforcement of UMTS Standard Essential Patents (AT.39939), Commitment Decision (Apr. 29, 2014), http://ec.europa.eu/competition/antitrust/cases/dec_docs/39939/39939_1501_5.pdf.

SEPs at hand will be decided by a court or alternatively, if both parties agree, by an arbitrator. On April 29, 2014, these commitments became legally binding.

In January 2014 the EU Commission opened an investigation against some paid TV providers, ultimately sending them a Statement of Objection (SO) on July 2015 which expressed the EU Commission's antitrust concerns related to some contractual obligations under Article 101 TFEU. In particular, the EU Commission argued that certain contract obligations in Paramount's agreements with Sky UK Limited had prevented Sky "from providing its retail pay-TV services in response to unsolicited requests from consumers residing or located in the European Economic Area ('EEA') but outside the United Kingdom and the Republic of Ireland."[637] In contrast, other contract obligations required "Paramount to prohibit or limit pay-TV broadcasters located within the EEA, but outside the United Kingdom and the Republic of Ireland, from providing their retail pay-TV services in response to unsolicited requests from consumers residing or located in the United Kingdom and the Republic of Ireland."[638] On July 26, 2016, the investigation was closed with the commitments offered by the parties to remove all clauses "in any new pay-TV output license agreement, extension or renewal between Paramount and pay-TV broadcasters located in the EEA"[639] which led to antitrust concerns. Paramount also agreed not to seek to enforce or honor the existing concern clauses in the established contracts enforced in the EEA with pay-TV broadcasters.

On June 11, 2015, the EU Commission opened an investigation into Amazon's eBook distribution agreements which seemed to have clauses referred to as "Most Favored Nation" (MFN clauses). These clauses required publishers "to offer Amazon similar (or better) terms and conditions as those offered to its competitors and/or to inform Amazon about more favourable or alternative terms given to Amazon's competitors."[640] On May 4, 2017, the EU Commission made legally binding the commitments offered by Amazon including Amazon's commitment not to enforce "(i) relevant clauses requiring publishers to offer Amazon similar non-price and price terms and conditions as those offered to Amazon's competitors or ii) any such clauses requiring publishers to inform Amazon about such terms and conditions."[641] The commitments covered clauses regarding "alternative/new business models, release date and catalogue of e-books, features of e-books, promotions, agency price, agency commission and wholesale price."[642]

---

637. EU Commission, Cross-border access to pay-TV (AT.40023), Summary of Commission Decision of July 2016 §13 (Nov. 25, 2016).
638. *Ibid.*
639. *Ibid.*, at § 24.
640. EU Commission, Antitrust: Commission accepts commitments from Amazon on e-books, Press Release (May 4, 2017), http://europa.eu/rapid/press-release_IP-17-1223_en.htm.
641. *Ibid.*
642. *Ibid.*

### [3] Energy Sector

On July 11, 2011, the EU Commission opened an investigation in the energy sector which ended with commitments. The EU Commission suspected that the Czech company ČEZ engaged in anticompetitive practices, such as excluding competitors and raising prices in the Czech wholesale electricity market to enhance its dominant position.[643] To address the EU Commission's concerns, ČEZ offered to sell a number of generation assets in the Czech Republic to allow new entrants in the Czech market for the creation and wholesale supply of energy. The buyers would have needed the Commission's approval to proceed with the acquisition.[644] On April 10, 2013, the Commission made binding the ČEZ's commitments.

The *Bulgaria* case also examined in Chapter 2 concerns an antirust proceeding settled by the EU Commission with similar structural remedies in the energy sector. In *Bulgaria*, the EU Commission investigated possible territorial restrictions in violation of Article 102 TFEU in the Bulgaria market of both electricity and gas production, supply and transmission.[645] On December 10, 2015, the EU Commission accepted the commitments that Bulgaria offered. In particular, Bulgaria agreed to divest the ownership of the only Bulgaria licensed power exchange administrator (IBEX EAD)—implementing a structural unbundling remedy.[646]

In September 2012, the EU Commission started investigating the Russian company Gazprom and three possible anticompetitive practices in Eastern and Central Europe. The EU Commission suspected that Gazprom would have "divided gas markets by hindering the free flow of gas across"[647] European countries, preventing diversification of supply of gas. In addition, Gazprom "may have imposed unfair prices on its customers by linking the price of gas to oil prices,"[648] harming EU consumers. On May 25, 2018, the EU Commission closed the case, making legally binding Gazprom's commitments according to which Gazprom had to implement a set of new rules which significantly changed its way to sell gas in Central and Eastern Europe. Gazprom had to remove any restrictions imposed on customers to re-sell gas cross-border and to "enable gas flow to and from parts of Central and Eastern Europe that are still isolated from other Member States due to lack of interconnectors, namely the Baltic States and Bulgaria."[649]

643. EU Commission, Web notice—ČEZ & others: opening of proceedings (Jul. 11, 2011), http://ec.europa.eu/competition/antitrust/cases/dec_docs/39727/39727_614_3.pdf.
644. EU Commission, ČEZ (AT/39727), Commitment Decision (Apr. 10, 2013) (hereinafter ČEZ).
645. EU Commission, Antitrust: Commission Opens Proceedings against Bulgaria Energy Holding, Press Release IP/12/1307 (Dec. 3, 2012).
646. EU Commission, BEH Electricity (AT.39767), Commitment Decision (Dec. 10, 2015) (hereinafter BEH).
647. EU Commission, Antitrust: Commission opens proceedings against Gazprom, Press Release (Sep. 4, 2012) http://europa.eu/rapid/press-release_IP-12-937_en.htm (hereinafter Gazprom).
648. *Ibid.*
649. EU Commission, Antitrust: Commission imposes binding obligations on Gazprom to enable free flow of gas at competitive prices in Central and Eastern European gas markets, Press Release (May 24, 2018) http://europa.eu/rapid/press-release_IP-18-3921_en.htm.

### *[4] Other Industries*

On April 20, 2011, the EU Commission opened a case in the market for the exchange trading of unfunded credit derivatives (in particular of credit default swaps "CDS"). On July 1, 2013, the EU Commission sent an SO against Markit, the ISDA and thirteen investment banks for a possible Article 101 TFEU violation. The EU Commission discerned that these companies and association coordinated to "foreclose from the credit default swaps market Deutsche Börse in 2007 and Chicago Mercantile Exchange in 2008."[650]

On July 20, 2016, the EU Commission accepted the commitments offered by ISDA under which the Association agreed to license "the Final Price for the exchange trading on fair, reasonable and non-discriminatory (FRAND) terms."[651] In addition, ISDA agreed to appoint a Monitoring Trustee to oversee its compliance with commitments. These and other similar commitments became valid for a period of ten years from the date of notification of the commitment decision to the association.

## [C] Economic Effects of Remedies

This section explores the economic effects of remedies enshrined in the *Bulgaria*[652] and *Deutsche Bahn I and II*[653] commitment decisions. *Bulgaria* concerns the Bulgarian's incumbent in the electricity market and *Deutsche Bahn I and II* the German railway incumbent.

In both cases, I investigate the affected markets by assessing how the price of products and the level of competition changed after the adoption of the commitment decisions.

### *[1] BEH and the European/Bulgarian Electricity Market*

Electricity is one of the most crucial markets for the European single market where the EU Commission focused its attention. In 2005, DGCom launched an inquiry to assess competition in gas and electricity markets,[654] the findings of which were released in

650. EU Commission, Antitrust: Commission closes proceedings against 13 investment banks in credit default swaps case, Press Release (Dec. 4, 2015) http://ec.europa.eu/competition/antitrust/cases/dec_docs/39745/39745_13719_14.pdf.
651. EU Commission, Antitrust: Commission accepts commitments by ISDA and Markit on credit default swaps, Press Release (Jul. 20, 2016), http://europa.eu/rapid/press-release_IP-16-2586_en.htm.
652. Case n. 39767-BEH Electricity, *supra* n. 646.
653. Case n. 39678; 39731, *supra* n. 631.
654. EU Commission, Competition, Energy and Environment, Sector Inquiry, http://ec.europa.eu/competition/sectors/energy/2005_inquiry/index_en.html. *See also* Neelie Kroes, *Improving Competition in European Energy Markets Through Effective Unbundling*, 31 Fordham Intern'l L. J. 1387, 1402 (2007). ("In 2005, the Commission launched the Sector Inquiry into the European gas and electricity sectors, which was the largest ever exercise in information gathering and analysis of the EU energy markets. It aimed at identifying the obstacles that were holding back effective competition.") *Ibid. See also* Hofmann, *supra* n. 264.

September 2007.[655] The EU Commission expressed its concern on the still high levels of concentration in the energy market, where incumbents seldom lose market power generating vertical foreclosure.[656] Further, lack of transparency about operations in the energy market, as well as a low level of cross-border trade,[657] appeared to make meaningful competition an unattainable goal. The key proposal of the Commission was a full unbundling, which would have addressed the main competition concerns in the energy sector.

The third EU Energy Package of September 2009 was a modest result for the EU Commission, which partially achieved what it asked for. The EU directives on the energy sector were, indeed, a great compromise among Member States, which had to perform unbundling measures in the energy sector but not exactly in the terms proposed by the DGCom.[658] EU Member States had three ways to implement unbundling: (1) full ownership unbundling; (2) independent system operator (ISO); (3) independent transmission operator (ITO).[659]

The full ownership option requires companies that generate and produce energy to not hold a majority share or interfere in the transmission/supply system operator (TSO). With the ITO option, the vertically integrated company owns the TSO but the entire operation of the network, including the maintenance and investment in the grid, is left to an independent company. Finally, the ITO allows the ownership of the TSO to remain vertically integrated but, in that case, the company must comply with rules to ensure the independence between the supply and the generation activities. Thus, although the new legislation required unbundling measures, incumbents were able to secure their vertical structure.[660]

From 2008 to 2012 the DG COMP opened a number of investigations concerning energy companies,[661] including the Bulgarian incumbent—Bulgarian Energy Holding (BEH or *Bulgaria*). Bulgaria complied with the EU Energy Package by adopting the ITO unbundling model.[662] NEK, a wholly-owned subsidiary of the state-owned BEH EAD, owned the electricity transmission grid network which was managed by one of its

655. EU Commission, Neelie Kroes, More Competitive Energy Markets: Building on the Findings of the Sector Inquire to Shape the Right Policy Solutions, Press Release SPEECH/07/547 (Sep. 19, 2007).
656. *Ibid.*
657. *Ibid.*
658. EU Commission, Energy, Market Legislation, https://ec.europa.eu/energy/en/topics/markets-and-consumers/market-legislation (last access May 21, 2019).
659. *Ibid.*
660. Kroes, *supra* n. 654, at 1417. ("[T]he Commission has [] proposed a possible derogation to [the full] form of unbundling, i.e., the ISO model.") *See also* Niamh Dunne, *Commitment Decisions in EU Competition Law*, 10 J. Competition L. & Econ. 399 (2014).
661. *See also* EU Commission, Distrigaz (AT.37.966) Summary of Commission Decision (Oct. 11, 2007); EU Commission, ČEZ, *supra* n. 644; EU Commission, Long Term Electricity Contracts France (COMP/39.386) Commitment Decision (Mar. 17, 2010) (hereinafter EDF); EU Commission, E.On Gas Foreclosure (AT.39317), Summary Decision (Oct. 15, 2010) (hereinafter E.On Gas); EU Commission, Gaz de France, Opening Proceeding (May 16, 2008) (hereinafter Gaz de France).
662. Herbert Smith Freehills, The European Energy Handbook 52 (February 2015), https://www.schoenherr.eu/uploads/tx_news/1180E_European_energy_handbook_2015_WEB.PDF.

subsidiaries–the Electricity System Operator (ESO) EAD. In December 2013 the Regulatory Commission issued a decision allowing the spin-off of ESO from NEK and the transfer of the transmission grid network of NEK to ESO which started its restructuring to comply with the unbundling requirements of the ITO model.[663] Since September 2008, BEH has owned 100 percent of the capital of NEK, NPP Kozloduy and TPP Maritsa East 2 and the Independent Bulgaria Power Exchange EAD (IBEX). Throughout the period of the Commission's investigation, BEH's production subsidiaries TPP Maritsa East 2 and NPP Kozloduy held "for up to [70-75] % (in 2012) of the share of supply on the market for the wholesale supply of electricity at freely negotiated prices in Bulgaria."[664]

With respect to the wholesale and retail electricity market, a hybrid model governs the supply of electricity at wholesale and retail levels. The Bulgarian Energy Act establishes that a Public Provider buys a share of the electricity output quantities generated by different producers for protected consumers at regulated prices. NEK (the BEH's subsidiary) owns the only license in Bulgaria as a public provider.[665] The rest of the electricity output can be sold on liberalized market.

The Bulgaria State owns 100 percent of BEH's capital and the Minister of Energy exercises the rights of BEH, which is the successor to the state-owned oil and gas organization.[666] BEH is the parent company of a group of leading companies in Bulgarian electricity generation, as well as the electricity and gas supply and transmission markets. On November 27, 2012, the EU Commission started a formal investigation on BEH to determine whether *Bulgaria* was abusing its dominant position in the wholesale electricity market in Bulgaria.[667]

According to the EU Commission, *Bulgaria* hindered competition in the wholesale electricity market in Bulgaria and neighboring Member States through some territorial restrictions in violation of Article 102 TFEU. Such competition concerns were later confirmed in a Statement of Objections, according to which the Bulgarian incumbent imposed territorial restrictions through the majority of its contracts that limited traders to resell energy. The EU Commission stated that *Bulgaria*'s contracts also imposed mechanisms to control and sanction customers that did not comply with its territorial restrictions.

On June 19, 2015, *Bulgaria* proposed some commitments to address the EU Commission's concerns.[668] Such commitments were not limited to the removal of territorial restrictions. *Bulgaria* also offered to "divest the ownership of IBEX EAD from

663. *Ibid.*
664. EC commitment decisions (BHE) 2015 at § 39.
665. *Ibid.*, at § 25.
666. Case AT.39767-BEH Electricity, *supra* n. 646, § 4.
667. EU Commission, Antitrust: Commission Opens Proceedings against Bulgaria Energy Holding, Press Release IP/12/1307 (Dec. 3, 2012). In particular, on November 27, 2012, the Commission decided to initiate antitrust proceedings in case 39767- BEH electricity.
668. Commitments Submitted by Bulgarian Energy Holding Ead Natsionalna Elektricheska Kompania EAD Thermal Power Plant Maritsa East 2 EAD Nuclear Power Plant Kozloduy EAD, AT.39767-BEH Electricity (Jun. 19, 2015), available at http://ec.europa.eu/competition/antitrust/cases/dec_docs/39767/39767_1505_3.pdf.

its structure ... and transfer the capital of IBEX EAD to the Ministry of Finance."[669] In addition, *Bulgaria* undertook action to ensure full support in the IBEX EAD activities "towards establishing an operational DAM Platform and to continue to provide IBEX EAD with the necessary funding and Key Personnel that have the necessary competence and knowledge for establishing the DAM Platform until the end of the Divestiture period [of six months]."[670] The commitment period was five years. In other words, *Bulgaria*'s commitments focused on ensuring the independence of the power exchange by implementing a structural unbundling remedy. On December 10, 2015, the EU Commission was satisfied with the commitments' terms and made those terms legally binding.[671]

After the commitment decision in December 2015[672], the price of electricity in Bulgaria decreased from 2016 to 2017, then slightly increased from 2017 to 2018. According to Eurostat, from January to June 2016 the price of electricity in Bulgaria was EUR 0,0956 per kWh for household consumers. This rate decreased in the first semester of 2017 to 0,0955. In the first semester of 2018, the price of electricity for households increased to 0,0979. Eurostat reported a similar trend for the price of electricity for non-households which decreased from EUR 0,1002 per kWh in the first January to June of 2016 to 0,073 in the first semester of 2017 then slightly increasing in the first semester of 2018 to EUR 0,0810 per kWh.[673] Bulgarian journals reported that "Bulgaria is in the middle ground but pays [for electricity] more than the leading countries as well as the rapidly developing Baltic States of the EU."[674]

In January 2018, the EU Commission observed that "Bulgaria has incorrectly transposed several unbundling requirements concerning the ownership unbundling model, the independent transmission operator unbundling model and the distribution system operator."[675] The EU Commission gave Bulgaria two months to fully comply with the Third Energy Package Directives by correctly transposing the required unbundling requirements. Bulgaria needs to do more to fully liberalize its energy markets.[676]

669. *Ibid.*, § 2.8.
670. *Ibid.*, § 2.5.
671. EU Commission, Antitrust: Commission Accepts Commitments by Bulgaria Energy Holding to Open up Bulgarian Wholesale Electricity Market, Press Release IP/15/6289 (Dec. 10, 2015).
672. *Ibid.*
673. In the first half of 2018 the price of household consumers in Bulgaria increased less than 5 percent (Eurostad Report, Electricity price statistics at 6, https://ec.europa.eu/eurostat/statistics-explained/index.php/Electricity_price_statistics), while more than 5 percent for non -household consumers. *Ibid.*, at 10.
674. Sofia News Agency, Electricity in Bulgaria is more Expensive than in Germany and Denmark (May 4, 2018) https://www.novinite.com/articles/189884/Electricity + in + Bulgaria + is + more + Expensive + than + in + Germany + and + Denmark.
675. EU Commission, January infringements package: key decisions (Jan. 25, 2018). http://europa.eu/rapid/press-release_MEMO-18-349_en.htm.
676. Novinite Insider, Bulgaria Must do More to Liberalise its Energy Markets (Jul. 29, 2018), https://www.novinite.com/articles/191340/Bulgaria + Must + do + More + to + Liberalise + its + Energy + Markets.

In sum, the DGCom's commitment decision seems insufficient to guarantee the unbundling requirements in Bulgaria's electricity market, requiring other regulatory and sanctioning interventions against the Bulgarian incumbent.

### *[2] Deutsche Bahn and the German Railway Market*

At first glance, the Deutsche Bahn (DB) commitment decision seems a successful story. The EU Commissioner Margrethe Vestager praised the DB commitment decision issued in December 2013. According to the EU Commissioner this was a "good example of how commitment decisions can quickly and effectively open up markets, ensure a level playing field and lead to more competition and lower prices for consumers and businesses."[677] Is this truly a happy ending for the German railway industry?

Historically the European railway system is structurally fragmented. Each Member State locally established its own rail system and national industries, along with railway corporations, implemented their own operational and technical standards.[678] The European legislator understood the importance of creating a Single European Railway Area built on an integrated infrastructure and interoperable equipment by enacting a number of Directives, Regulations and Decisions. The most important legislation is the Directive 2012/34/EU. This directive merged previously separated directives to address the lack of competition, low levels of investment, poor regulatory oversight and ultimately establish a single European railway area.[679]

At the same time, the EU Commission opened a number of antitrust investigations as one of the main concerns was the lack of competition in the railway industry. As outlined above, on June 13, 2012, the EU Commission opened two cases against the German incumbent in the railway industry—*Deutsche Bahn* (DB). These investigations focused on the price of traction current charged by a DB's subsidiary, DB Energie, to railway companies (*see* IP/12/597).[680] Traction current is the specific electricity used by locomotives to propel trains. According to the EU Commission, DB Energie was applying certain discounts only to DB's own subsidiaries, raising a concern about a possible margin squeeze for DB's competitors. To close the investigation without a fine and a prohibition decision, DB agreed to charge the same price to all railways companies without discounts for its railways companies. The price would have to be approved by the German regulatory authority (Bundesnetzagentur). DB also agreed to grant companies not belonging to DB group a one-time payment of 4 percent of their yearly traction invoice, calculated on the period of one year before the entry of the new pricing system comes into force. This might be perceived as an innovative compensatory remedy that DB offered to repair its conduct. Finally, DB agreed to appoint a

677. EU Commission, Antitrust: successful market opening allows early termination of commitments in Deutsche Bahn case, Press Release (Apr. 8, 2016), http://europa.eu/rapid/press-release_IP-16-1322_en.
678. EU Commission, COM(2010) 474 final, § 1 (Sep. 17, 2010).
679. Summaries of EU Legislation, Development of a single railway area, https://eur-lex.europa.eu/legal-content/EN/TXT/?uri=LEGISSUM%3Atr0041.
680. *See also*, Itai Rabinovici, *The Application of EU Competition Rules in the Transport Sector*, 9 J. Eur. Competition L. & Practice 282-289 (2018).

trustee for ensuring the compliance with such commitments that would have lasted five years.[681] On December 18, 2013, the EU Commission accepted such commitments and closed the investigation.[682]

On April 8, 2016, the EU Commission relieved DB from their commitments ahead of schedule. The EU Commission's commitments decision specifically provided that such commitments could "cease prematurely in the event that, for the period of calendar year, at least 25 percent of the combined demand of Traction Current of all railway undertakings in Germany which are not affiliated with DB ML or DB Energie and/or the affiliated companies of DB ML and DB Energie is purchased from one or several Third Party Suppliers."[683] Because this condition was met, the EU Commission alleged that the commitments could cease and the appointed Trustee be discharged from their duty.[684]

To assess the economic effects of this decision, I evaluate both the barriers of entry (thus the access in the market of new players), and the price changes for traction current and track access. The German regulator of the railway industry, Bundesnetzagentur, releases each year a Market Analysis of the railway. In 2017, the report identified that "more than 16 percent of the transaction current in the traction power network was ordered from providers other than DB Energie,"[685] and "11 energy suppliers besides DB Energie operated in the transaction current market."[686] In sum, from 25 percent in 2016, the demand of traction current by providers other than DB Energie seems to decrease by almost 10 percent.

With respect to the price, there are special rules that govern the setting of charges levied by infrastructure managers. The main rule is explained in Section 14(4) of the General Railway Act (AEG). The determination of the track access charges is defined in this section of the AEG as well as additional rules enshrined in the Rail Infrastructure Usage Regulations. As the Bundesnetzagentur emphasizes, *infrastructure managers* must adhere to the imposed requirements that define the limits applicable to pricing.[687] The railway infrastructure manager is "any body or undertaking that is responsible in particular for establishing and maintaining railway infrastructure." This "may also include the management of infrastructure control and safety systems. The functions of

681. EU Commission, Deutsche Bahn I (AT.39678), Deutsche Bahn II (AT.39731), Summary of Commission Decision (Dec. 18, 2013).
682. *Ibid.*
683. EU Commission, Deutsche Bahn I/II (AT.39678/AT.39731), Commission Decision (Apr. 4, 2016), http://ec.europa.eu/competition/antitrust/cases/dec_docs/39678/39678_2648_8.pdf at § 4.
684. *Ibid.*, § 7.
685. *Bundesnetzagentur*, Market Analysis 2017 Railway, https://www.bundesnetzagentur.de/SharedDocs/Downloads/EN/BNetzA/PressSection/ReportsPublications/2017/MarketAnalysesRailway2017.pdf?__blob=publicationFile&v=1, at 37.
686. *Ibid.*
687. Bundesnetzagentur, Charges. Price Regulation in the Railway Sector, https://www.bundesnetzagentur.de/EN/Areas/Rail/Companies/Charges/Charges_note.html.

the infrastructure manager on a network or part of a network may be allocated to different bodies or undertakings."[688]

The 2017 Market Analysis Report from the Bundesnetzagentur indicates that, between 2012 and 2017, track access charges increased steadily: "the track access charges railway undertakings had to pay increased by more than 16 percent in the long-distance passenger rail transport segment, by approximately 14 percent in the short-distance passenger rail transport segment and by a little more than 12 percent in the rail freight segment."[689] As the same German Authority noted, these increases appear remarkably higher than those for important benchmark indicators, including both the consumer price index (CPI) and the producer price index. The CPI, for example, "rose by only five percent while the producer price index for industrial products actually fell by two percent during the reporting period."[690]

The rating for price performance of traction current, however, improved over the last five years. The Bundesnetzagentur reported that, in 2012, the development of the infrastructure managers' price-performance ratios in the traction current was 3.3, while in 2017 that figure decreased to 2.8.[691]

According to the Federal Network Agency's Railway Market Analysis, the fact that over the last years "track access charges rose by an average of 13 percent for freight, 14 percent for regional passenger"[692] is mainly related to the increase of station charges that between 2011 and 2015 rose by about 10 percent.[693] In summary, the traction current price seems to decrease while the overall track access charges appear to significantly increase due to the rising prices of other track access components.

### [D] Conclusions

In Europe seven cases out of twelve settled with commitment decisions concerned Article 102 TFEU; the Ebook case concerned both Articles 101 and 102 TFEU. With respect to the timing to close an antitrust case, there is not much difference between commitment decisions and prohibition decisions. The average number days from the opening of the EU Commission's investigation to a commitment decision is about 1,129 days, while the average number days from the opening of the EU Commission's proceeding to a prohibition decision is about 1,217 days. The most affected industries are transportation, media/telecommunication, energy and the market for accessories or parts for cars or motor vehicles.

With respect to the type of solutions enacted, structural remedies are rarely used. There is no trace of such remedies except for the Bulgaria and ČEZ cases where

688. Article 3(b) of the Directive 2004/49/EC European Parliament and of the Council 29 April 2004, OJ L 164, 30.04.2004, at 44-113.
689. *Bundesnetzagentur*, Market Analysis 2017 Railway, *supra* n. 685, at 61.
690. *Ibid.*
691. *Ibid.*, at 64.
692. Keith Barrow, *German Monopoly Commission Challenges DB Dominance*, International Railway J. (Sep. 1, 2017), https://www.railjournal.com/in_depth/german-monopoly-commission-challenges-db-dominance.
693. *Ibid.*

companies agreed to implement divestiture remedies. However, both behavioral and structural remedies have had the effects of regulating markets replicating what takes place in the U.S. Analysis of the procompetitive effects of two EU commitment decisions showed that antitrust intervention alone is often not sufficient to regulate industries and ensure competition.

## §5.02 THE ITALIAN ANTITRUST AUTHORITY COMMITMENT DECISIONS PRACTICE

Each European Member State has a National Competition Authority (NCA) which needs to comply with the European regulation and maintain consistency with the EU Commission's practices. As explored in Chapter 2, during Monti's term as Commissioner for competition, the European competition law system went through a modernization process. In addition to formalizing the practice of commitment decisions, Regulation 1/2003 required NCAs and Member States' courts to apply Articles 101 and 102 TFEU to all cases where trade between Member States could be affected by anticompetitive conduct as defined by Articles 101 and 102 TFEU.[694] As Professor Giorgio Monti noted, "the Community moved from having one competition authority (DG Competition) to twenty-[eight],"[695] which included all NCAs.

In this Section §5.02, I explore the Italian Competition Authority's (ICA)—called AGCM—history with commitment decisions to investigate similarities and differences between the European practice and an NCA's practice with commitment decisions. Similar to the previous §5.01, this section investigates when and in what cases the AGCM settled cases with commitment decisions, analyzing the timing to reach a consensus on commitments and the types of remedies adopted in different industries. The economic effects of antitrust remedies adopted in a specific case will also be examined.

The sample of my analysis includes all no-merger AGCM's antitrust decisions under Articles 101 and 102 of the TFEU, Articles 2 and 3 of the law n. 287/1990 adopted from January 2013 to December 2018. In this time frame, the AGCM decided one hundred eleven cases, of which twenty-six ended with a commitment decision and fifty-two resulted with a prohibition decision. Ten cases out of one hundred eleven ended with a decision that revaluated a fine previously imposed and three with a decision of no compliance with commitments or order and one case concerned a modification of previous remedies. In the remaining nineteen cases, the AGCM

694. Council Regulation (EC) No. 1/2003 establishes at Article 5 that "[t]he competition authorities of the Member States shall have the power to apply Articles 81 and 82 of the Treaty in individual cases. For this purpose, acting on their own initiative or on a complaint, they may take the following decisions: requiring that an infringement be brought to an end, ordering interim measures, accepting commitments, imposing fines, periodic penalty payments or any other penalty provided for in their national law." Ioannis Lianos & Ioannis Kokkoris, *The Reform of EC Competition Law*, 56 (Wolters, 2010); Office of Fair Trading, Modernisation. Understanding Competition Law, 2 (December 2004) available at https://www.gov.uk/government/uploads/system/uploads/attachment_data/file/284432/oft442.pdf.

695. Monti, *supra* n. 396, at 394.

discerned that no liability was found: in fifteen cases the AGCM argued that there was no violation, and in four cases the agency dismissed the cases because the law was not applicable.

The Italian trend in the adoption of commitment decisions was not steady; it significantly changed from 2014 to the next years. The following chart (Figure 5.2) considers both the AGCM's commitments and total decisions taken each year from January 2014 to December 2018.

*Figure 5.2 Italian Adoption of Commitment Decisions*

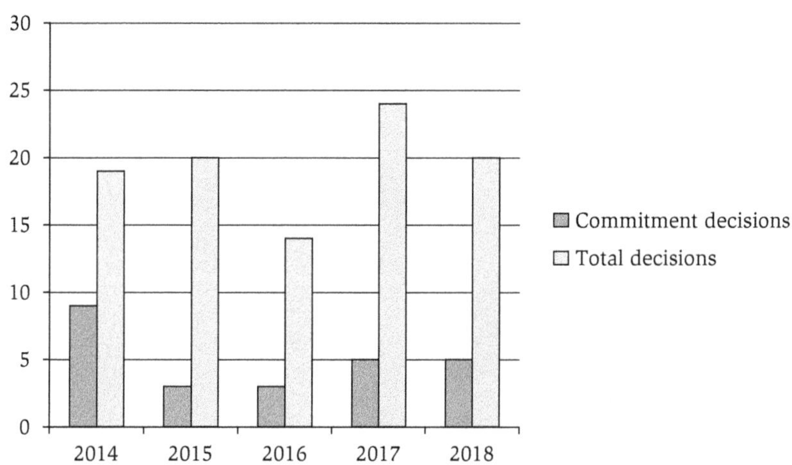


In 2014, nine out of nineteen cases were closed with commitments, while in 2015 the AGCM closed only three cases out of twenty with commitment decisions. In sum, in 2014 more than 47 percent of proceedings ended with commitment decisions and in only one year this fallen to 15 percent. As the chart above shows, from 2015 to 2018, the trend in the adoption of commitment decisions in Italy seems to be quite steady. In 2017, five out of twenty-four cases were settled by means of commitment decisions while in 2018 only five out of twenty cases were.

### [A] Timing and Markets/Industries Involved

In examining the time frame from the opening of the AGCM's investigation in January 2013 and the AGCM's final decision in December 2018, the difference between a prohibition and a commitment decision is significant. The average days between the opening of investigations and commitment decisions is about three hundred fifty-three days, while the average days between the opening of investigations and prohibition decisions is about five hundred twenty-three days. In summary, in Italy companies subjected to an antitrust investigation usually save one hundred seventy days in settling the proceeding with a commitment decision.

If we consider only commitment decisions, the longest proceeding took eight hundred twenty days while the shortest required one hundred ninety days. The *Wind-Fastweb/condotte Telecom Italia*[696] is the longest proceeding that ended with a prohibition decision. The AGCM closed the investigation, fining the companies after 1,051 days. The *Tariffario minimo per gli amministratori professionisti di condominio-legge 4/2013* was closed in two hundred thirty-eight days, resulting in the shortest case ending with a prohibition decision.[697]

The following chart (Figure 5.3) depicts the breakdown of industries affected by antitrust investigations from January 2013 to December 2018 to better visualize where the ICA focused its attention.

*Figure 5.3 Main Affected Industries*

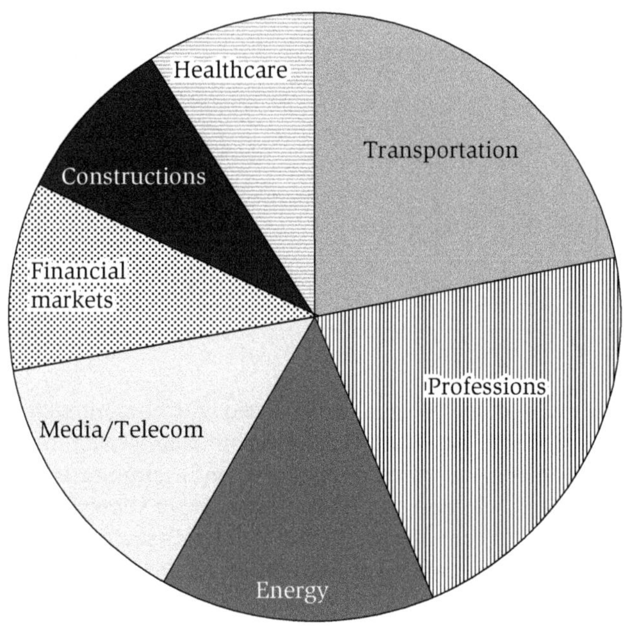


The chart does not consider thirty-three cases that concerned extremely varied markets, allowing the analysis to focus on the seven industries primarily affected by antitrust investigations.

As the chart shows, the Italian Antitrust Authority focused on professional services and the transportation industry, opening seventeen cases in each sector in the time frame being considered. The AGCM opened eleven proceedings, both in the media/telecommunication and the energy industry. In the same time frame (January

696. AGCM, A428—Wind-Fastweb/Condotte Telecom Italia, Prohibition Decision (May 5, 2013).
697. AGCM, I774—Tariffario Minimo per gli amministratori professionisti di condominio-Legge 4/2013, Prohibition decision (Nov. 5, 2014).

2013 to December 2018), the financial sector was affected by eight cases, and healthcare/pharmaceutical industry by seven.

### [B] Adopted Remedies

This subsection [B] investigates the adopted remedies in the most affected industries, which include professional services, transportations, media and telecommunications, energy, finance services, healthcare and construction.

In the sector of professional services, only one case out of seventeen culminated with a commitment decision that concerned the sole agents in the insurance industry. On June 5, 2013, the AGCM opened the investigation[698] that ended with a commitment decision on May 20, 2014.[699] The AGCM discerned that some clauses in the agency contracts were capable of discouraging multi-agencies in the insurance industry. To deal with the AGCM's antitrust concerns, the affected insurance companies eliminated any exclusive clauses from their agency's contracts. Some insurance companies also agreed to eliminate the duty of the agent to notify the acquisition of work from competitors,[700] and others permitted agents to use their offices to work for different companies.[701] Other commitments focused on the use of the software/hardware by the insurance company to work for rivals and using the same bank account to manage the insurance premiums of different companies.[702]

In the transportation industry, three out of seventeen cases were settled by means of commitment decisions: *A442-Assofort/ADR-Servizi aeroportuali*,[703] *A507-Servizio Rifornimento Carburante Avio Aeroporto di Bergamo*,[704] and *A443—NTV/FS/Ostacoli all'accesso nel mercato dei servizi di trasporto ferroviario passeggeri ad alta velocita'*.[705] All of these cases concern an investigation for abuse of dominant position conduct and were closed by means of behavior commitments. *NTV/FS/Ostacoli all'accesso nel mercato dei servizi di trasporto ferroviario passeggeri ad alta velocita'*, which concerned the Italian incumbent rail operator (*FS*) and the main railway company (*Trenitalia*), is probably the most relevant. According to Nuovo Trasporto Viaggiatori (NTV), which is basically the only competitor to *Trenitalia* in the passenger high-speed rail (HSR) market, *FS* engaged in margin squeeze conduct by significantly increasing the cost for NTV to enter the HSR market.[706] In addition, *FS* and *Trenitalia* would have delayed access to railway infrastructure through a number of practices to ensure *Trenitalia*

698. AGCM, I702—Agenti Monomandanti, Opening Proceeding (Jun. 5, 2013).
699. AGCM, I702—Agenti Monomandanti, Commitment Decision (May 20, 2014).
700. *Ibid.*, §§18-22.
701. *Ibid.*, §§28-29.
702. OCSE, *Annual Report on Competition Policy Developments in Italy-2014* § 33 (Oct. 17-28, 2015) available at http://en.agcm.it/dotcmsDOC/annual-reports/AnnualReport2014.pdf (*Annual Report 2014*).
703. AGCM, A442—Assofort/ADR-Servizi Aeroportuali, Commitment Decision (Jan. 31, 2013).
704. AGCM, A507—Servizio Rifornimento Carburante Avio Aeroporto di Bergamo, Commitment Decision (Mar. 14, 2018).
705. AGCM, A443—NTV/FS/Ostacoli all'Accesso nel Mercato dei Servizi di Trasporto Ferroviario Passeggeri ad Alta Velocita', Commitment Decision (Feb. 19, 2014).
706. *Ibid. See also*, *Annual Report 2014* § 43.

maintains its dominant position in the passenger HSR market. To close the investigation without finding an antitrust violation and imposing a fine, FS and Trenitalia offered "to open up access to train routes, to reduce the cost of railway access by 15 per cent and to provide rival rail operators with more space within stations."[707] Such commitments became legally binding on February 19, 2014.

In the telecommunication and media industry, two cases were settled by means of commitment decisions between January of 2013 and December 2018: *I757-Ostacoli all'accesso al mercato di un nuovo operatore di telefonia mobile*[708] and *I799-TIM-Fastweb-Realizzazione rete in fibra.*[709] Both investigations concerned agreements in restrain of trade under Article 101 of TFEU. On September 12, 2012 the AGCM opened an investigation against the mobile operators, *Telecom Italia S.p.A.*, *Vodafone Omnitel N.V.*, and *Wind Telecommunication S.p.A.*, regarding certain clauses in their contracts with multi-brand dealers that included extra-discounts and/or contractual benefits.[710] The AGCM noted that such clauses could have foreclosed new entrants in the mobile markets and restrained competition.

To address the ICA's competition concerns, the mobile operators agreed to remove from their distribution agreements the challenged exclusivity clause under which dealers agreed "not to sell goods or services of operators other than those the already part of the commercial distribution agreement with the buyer [...]."[711] On December 11, 2014, the AGCM closed the investigation making the commitments offered by the mobile operators legally binding. The ICA considered such commitments sufficient to address the possible risk of vertical integration in the distribution agreements that were under antitrust scrutiny.

The other case in the telecommunication industry involves a joint venture between *Telecom Italia Sp.A.* (Telecom) and *Fastweb S.p.A.* (Fastweb)—two vertically integrated operators in the telecommunication industry.[712] The joint venture named Flash Fiber s.r.l. (FF), which aimed to build a new Internet infrastructure of ultra-wideband Fiber-to-the-home access networks, raised antitrust concerns under Article 101 of the TFEU. Telecom and Fastweb's rivals were concerned that such a joint venture could create structural and long-run cooperation between Telecom and Fastweb at their expense. The ICA accepted the commitments offered by the two operators subject to investigation under which:

(a) the construction of the new ultra-wideband network will end by 2020;

707. *Annual Report 2014* § 43.
708. AGCM, I757—Ostacoli all'Accesso al Mercato di un Nuovo Operatore di Telefonia Mobile, Commitment Decision (Dec. 11, 2014).
709. AGCM, I799—TIM-Fastweb-Realizzazione Rete in Fibra, Commitment Decision (Mar. 28, 2018).
710. AGCM, I757—Ostacoli all'Accesso al Mercato di un Nuovo Operatore di Telefonia Mobile, Opening Proceeding (Sep. 12, 2012).
711. *Annual Report 2014* § 34.
712. AGCM, I799—TIM-Fastweb-Realizzazione rete in fibra, Commitment Decision (Mar. 28, 2018). Telecom holds a 96 percent of market share in the market for fixed broadband wholesale access, while Telecom and Fastweb own a market share of forty and twenty seven in the retail market of broadband and ultrafast-broadband.

(b) the pre-emptive right of Telecom and Fastweb on the network capacity of FF will be removed;
(c) the duration of FF will be reduced to what is strictly necessary to recover the investments made;
(d) Telecom and Fastweb agreed to negotiate dealings with third parties, requiring—for up to thirty years—reciprocal access to the respective infrastructures in terms of the transfer of the indefeasible right of use;
(e) FF committed to adopt suitable remedies to prevent the exchange of any commercially sensitive information between Telecom and Fastweb. In addition, the parties agreed to adopt an antitrust compliance manual and appoint a person in charge of monitoring the compliance with said manual.[713]

With respect to the Energy industry, the ICA ended four cases out of eleven by means of commitment decisions: (1) *I766B-Inverter Solari ed Eolici-Imposizione prezzi minimi*; (2) *A486-Enel distribuzione-Rimozione coatta dispositivi smart metering*; (3) *A498A-Enel-Prezzi servizi di dispacciamento area brindisi*; and (4) *A507-Servizio di rifornimento carburante avio aereoporto di Bergamo*. Three of these cases concerned an abuse of dominant position ex Article 102 of the TFEU and a case a possible agreement in restraint of trade under Article 101 of the TFEU. The following analysis focuses on the first (under Article 101 of the TFEU) and the second case (under Article 102 of TFEU).

On October 22, 2013 the AGCM opened an investigation against Power-One Italia S.p.A. (Power One) for a possible vertical agreement regarding restraint of trade in the market of production and distribution of renewable energy inverters.[714] Specifically, the ICA expressed concern about the structure of minimum resale prices that existed between Power One (which sells renewable energy converters) and its Italian distributors.

To address the antitrust concerns, Power One offered to eliminate from its contracts the retail price maintenance clause within the EU area. Power One also agreed to include in new contracts, for a three-year period from the AGCM's decision, any provisions regarding product and territorial exclusivity.[715] After that time frame, Power One would be able to include similar provisions only for passive sales. On July 2, 2014, the AGCM closed the proceeding by accepting those commitments as they were deemed sufficient to address its antitrust concerns.[716]

The others analyzed remedies concerning the energy industry involves Enel, the Italian incumbent in the electricity sector, and its subsidiary Enel Distribution SpA (ED). According to the ICA, Enel, through exclusionary practices, could hinder competitors in the service of monitoring electricity consumption. Enel was investigated for denying physical access to their meters to install pulse-count devices of the

713. *Ibid.*
714. AGCM, I766—Inverter Solari ed Eolici—Imposizione Prezzi Minimi, Commitment Decision (Jul. 2, 2014).
715. *Ibid.*
716. *Ibid.*

reporting party and engaging in numerous incidents of detaching such pulse-count devices of the reporting party. ED's commitments to address the AGCM's concerns focused on:

(1) Limiting removals of LED-based devices from meters, except if it is strictly necessary, guaranteeing the "transfer to the market of information about the second-generation electronic meter installation program the company will active in coming years."[717]
(2) Providing meters located inside sealed housing "free of charge, within a maximum number of monthly interventions, Signal Emitters ('SE') for advanced consumption monitoring services."[718]
(3) Providing "on request an Original Equipment Manufacturer module ('OEM') to be added to third-party in-home devices, making available on request its own in-home device called Smart info, in a generic version, in both cases at cost price."[719]

In the financial markets, three cases out of seven were settled by means of consent decrees: *A482—E-Class/Borsa Italiana;*[720] *A499-Assicurazioni Agricole/Comportamenti Escludenti Codipra*; and *I773D-Consorzio Bancomat-Commissioni Bill Payments*.

On April 8, 2015, the AGCM opened an investigation against Borsa Italiana S.p.A. (BIT) and BIT Market Services S.p.A. (BIMS)—both controlled by the London Stock Exchange Group Holding Italia S.p.A.—for a possible abuse of dominant position conduct. BIT and BIMS are "respectively active in the upstream market for the management of trading platforms and in the downstream market for the provision of financial information services to investors and brokers."[721] According to the complaint filed by BIMS's competitor, e-Class, BIM might apply some contractual provisions related to the access and the use of its financial data in a discriminatory way to favor its sister company in the downstream market. Such contract clauses could exclude vendors from the market for the supply of financial data services. To close the investigation, BIT and BIMS agreed to divest the business branch of BIMS that supplied financial data services, ending the vertical integration between the owner of the financial information and the service provider. In addition to this structural remedy, BIT and BIMS agreed to perform some behavioral remedies to guarantee functional separation in the transition period.[722]

In *I773D-Consorzio Bancomat-Commissioni Bill Payments*, the ICA agreed to revise previous commitments offered by *Consorzio Bancomat* which became legally

717. AGCM, A486 Antitrust Authority Accepts E-Distribuzione and Enel SPA Commitments: more Competition and Transparency in "Smart Meters," Press Release (Sep. 8, 2016).
718. *Ibid.*
719. *Ibid.*
720. AGCM, A482—E-Class/Borsa Italiana, Commitment Decision (Feb. 3, 2016).
721. OCSE, *Annual Report on Competition Policy Developments in Italy-2016* §36 (Nov. 27, 2017).
722. *Ibid.*, at §39.

binding on September 20, 2018, to close an investigation for a possible agreement in restrain of trade conduct.[723]

### [C] Economic Effects of Remedies

In 2016, a study of the Organisation for Economic Co-operation and Development (OECD) praised Italy for open access competition in the HSR.[724] This Section *iii* analyses the economic effects of remedies related to the commitment decision adopted on February 19, 2014, in that market—*NTV/FS/Ostacoli all'accesso nel mercato dei servizi di trasporto ferroviario passeggeri ad alta velocita'*. As outlined above, this commitment decision concerned possible margin squeeze conduct by the incumbent Italian rail operator (*FS*) to favor its subsidiary *Trenitalia* (the main railway company), effectively harming Trenitalia's competitors. FS agreed "to open up access to train routes, to reduce the cost of railway access by 15 per cent and to provide rival rail operators with more space within stations."[725]

From 2014 to 2015, the Italian Transport Regulatory Authority (ITRA or ART) reported encouraging data, citing increases in efficiency and consumer welfare in the Italian railway market. From 2014 to 2015, the traffic of passengers-kilometers had increased by 1.4 percent[726] and the traffic of freight by 2.2 percent.[727] Specifically, the number of passengers increased that year from 864.122.591 to 872.622.910. In 2016, the traffic of passengers per kilometer slightly fell to 869.199.286, while the traffic of freight rose to 9.3 percent.[728] NTR, *Trenitalia's* main competitor, increased revenue and market share from 2014 to 2015. In 2014, NTV generated EUR 270 million and in 2015, EUR 308 million in revenue. In 2016, OECD[729] study reported that NTV carried more than nine million passengers "an increase of 40 percent compared with 2014." NTV market share in the HSR market increased from about 23 percent in 2014 to almost 26 percent in 2015.[730]

With respect to prices, since 2015 the ITRA establishes annual fees to access the railway infrastructure[731] turning into a process of non-price competition.[732] The ART's

723. AGCM, I773D—Consorzio Bancomat-Commissioni Bill Payments, Commitment Decision (Sep. 20, 2018).
724. OECD, High Speed Rail Competition in Italy, A Major Railway Reform with a "Win-Win Game?" (2016), available at https://www.itf-oecd.org/sites/default/files/docs/high-speed-rail-competition-italy.pdf.
725. *Annual Report 2014* §43.
726. ART, Annual Relation 2017 at 112, available at https://www.autorita-trasporti.it/wp-content/uploads/2017/07/ART-Quarto-Rapporto-Annuale-2017.pdf.
727. *Ibid.*, at 113.
728. ART, Annual Relation 2018, available at https://www.autorita-trasporti.it/wp-content/uploads/2018/09/RA-ART_2018_ART_Errata_corrige_05-09-2018.pdf, at 120, 123.
729. OECD, High Speed Rail Competition in Italy, A Major Railway Reform with a "Win-Win Game?" (2016), *supra* n. 724, at 17.
730. *Ibid.*
731. ART, Delibera n. 96/2015 (Criteri per la determinazione dei canoni di accesso e utilizzo dell'infrastruttura ferroviaria).
732. *See* Richard A. Posner, *Economic Analysis of Law*, 399 (Wolters Kluwer, 9th ed., 2014). *See also* ART, Annual Relation 2017 at 30.

regulation also includes the monitoring of the incumbent (FS)'s imposition of fees to access the infrastructure.

The AGCM's commitment decision is not the only explanation for such an apparent increase in competition in the HSR market. The Italian Railway industry passed through a radical reformation and the legislative and regulatory framework has significantly changed over the last five years. Both the AGCM and ART's interventions seem to be primarily responsible for the improvement of efficiency in the Italian railway industry.

In summary, these Italian commitment decisions have allowed both the antitrust agencies and the companies subject to investigation to save time and money compared to prohibition decisions. The economic effects of commitment decisions appear to be positive when antitrust commitments are adopted within an appropriate regulatory framework. However, in Italy the practice of commitment decisions significantly decreased from 2014 to 2018, becoming a residual settlement solution tool to enforce competition law at the national level.

CHAPTER 6

# Consent Decrees Versus Commitment Decisions: Antitrust Settlements Versus Antitrust Convictions—Ebook Case

*Ebook* is the perfect case study to examine for comparing the effects of consent decrees with commitment decisions as it includes three consent decrees, a commitment decision and a conviction. In the U.S., the *Ebook* case was settled through a consent decree with the publishers subject to investigation (Verlagsgruppe Georg von Holtzbrinck GMBH & Holtzbrinck Publishers, LLC d/b/a MacMillan, Hachette Book Group Inc., HarperCollins Publishers L.L.C., the Penguin Group, a division of Pearson plc, Penguin Group (USA), Inc., Simon&Schuster Inc.) and it proceeded with Apple to trial. Conversely, in Europe the EU Commission closed the case by means of commitment decisions with each of the publishers involved (Hachette Livre (Lagardère Publishing, France), Harper Collins (News Corp., USA), Simon & Schuster (CBS Corp., USA), Penguin (Pearson Group, United Kingdom) and Verlagsgruppe Georg von Holzbrinck (owner of inter alia Macmillan, Germany)) and Apple.

Through the analysis of the *Ebook* case, Chapter 6 examines the differing results of settling an antitrust case in the U.S. by means of an antitrust settlement with a conviction. Chapter 6 compares the adoption of consent decrees in the U.S. and commitment decisions in EU through the investigation of the *EBook* case in both contexts.

## §6.01 THE U.S. EBOOK CASE

On April 11, 2012, the DOJ filed a complaint against Apple and several publishers: Verlagsgruppe Georg von Holtzbrinck GMBH & Holtzbrinck Publishers, LLC d/b/a MacMillan (collectively "MacMillan"), the Penguin Group, a division of Pearson plc and Penguin Group (USA), Inc. (collectively "Penguin"), Hachette Book Group Inc. ("Hachette"), HarperCollins Publishers L.L.C. ("HarperCollins"), and Simon&Schuster

Inc. ("Simon&Schuster") (collectively "Hachette", "HarperCollins", "MacMillan", "Penguin", and "Simon&Schuster" are referred to as "*Publisher Defendants*"). The DOJ argued that Apple conspired with the *Publisher Defendants* to raise the USD 9.99 Amazon's ebook price in violation of Section 1 of the Sherman Act.[733] On September 6, 2012, Simon&Schuster, Hachette and HarperCollins settled the case by means of a consent decree. On May 17, 2013, Penguin also reached an agreement with the DOJ. On August 12, 2013, Macmillan was the last *Publisher Defendant* to settle the antitrust proceeding with a consent solution. In contrast, Apple proceeded to try the case and ultimately reached the Supreme Court in 2015.[734]

Before dealing with the terms and remedies enshrined in each settlement and the Apple trial, a brief explanation of the ebook market is necessary.

### [A] The Ebook Market

On November 19, 2007, Amazon released the first *ereader* in the ebook market—Amazon's Kindle. In 2007, the ebook market was in its infancy: in North America the ebook revenue was USD 70 million, which, compared with about USD 30 billion revenue from the physical trade books, was a quite small amount. Still, the ebook market was growing; by 2008 the ebook industry revenue had doubled.[735] In 2009, Amazon sold 90 percent of ebooks on the market.[736]

Similar to print books, Amazon adopted a "wholesale" business model: publishers recommended a digital list price that was about 20 percent lower than the print list price and received from Amazon a wholesale price for each ebook sold.[737] Despite the recommended list price, Amazon was basically free to set the retail price of publishers' ebooks. Amazon started selling all *ebooks* at a price of USD 9.99, which was the same or slightly lower than the wholesale price Amazon paid to the publishers.

Amazon's at/below cost price strategy did not discourage entry into the ebook retail market. In November 2009, Barnes & Noble launched its ereader, Nook, and Google Inc. ("Google") planned to enter the market as early as 2007.[738]

Amazon's lower-priced ebook concerned publishers as it would make it more challenging for them to sell print books: hardcover copies of new releases were often sold "at thirty dollars or more."[739] The "Big Six" publishers, which included Hachette, HarperCollins, Macmillan, Penguin and Simon & Schuster, discussed joint strategies to contrast Amazon's USD 9.99 ebook price, such as building an alternative ebook

733. *United States v. Apple Inc., et al.*, Complaint (S.D.N.Y., 2012).
734. *United States v. Apple Inc.*, 952 F. Supp. 2d 638 (S.D.N.Y. 2013), aff'd, 791 F.3d 290 (2d Cir. 2015), cert. denied, 136 S. Ct. 1376 (2016).
735. Francoise Behmou, *Fair Use and Fair Competition for Digitalized Cultural Goods: The Case of eBooks*, 39 J. Cult. Econ. 123, 124 (2015). The U.S. market of ebooks exponentially grew in a few years representing "0.6% of the total trade market in 2008, 6.4% in 2010 and 22% in 2012." *Ibid.*
736. *United States v. Apple, Inc.*, 791 F.3d 290, 299 (2d Circ., 2015).
737. *Ibid.*
738. *Ibid.*
739. Apple, 952 F. Supp. 2d 638, 649 (S.D.N.Y., 2013).

platform or "eliminating the discounted wholesale price for ebook."[740] At the end of 2009, the announced launch of Apple's iPad raised the morale of publishers who saw in Apple's entry into the ebook market a way to gain leverage in their negotiations with Amazon.[741]

Publishers' discontentment with Amazon's USD 9.99 price point was clear to Apple, who proposed to them a switch from a wholesale model to an agency model by which the publishers would be able to set and raise the ebooks' retail prices. However, Apple would collect a commission of 30 percent on all e-book sales revenue and avoid Amazon's competition on price by means of an MFN clause.[742] The MFN provision also forced the publishers to switch from a wholesale model to an agency model with Amazon in June 2010.[743] Otherwise, publishers would have to sell ebooks on the Apple iBookstore at USD 9.99 to match Amazon's retail price, making less than USD 7 on each ebook sold versus the USD 13 they collected from each ebook sold by Amazon.

Apple also recommended *price ceilings*: "$14.99 for hardcover books with list prices above $35; $12.99 for hardcover books with list prices below $35; and $9.99 for all other trade book,"[744] to prevent the publishers from setting prices too high. In January 2010, the *Publisher Defendants* signed the Apple Agency Agreement. As a result of the price increases, consumers had to pay higher prices for e-books and the *Publisher Defendants*' sales of e-books declined to 14.5 percent.[745] In summary, the Apple Agency Agreement and the new agency model adopted to sell ebooks seemed to reduce competition in the newborn ebook market, harming consumers. Antitrust agencies, both in the U.S. and in Europe, started investigations into the ebook market.

### [B] The Consent Decrees with Publishers

On April 11, 2012, the U.S. ebook case formally started with the DOJ filing a complaint against Apple and the *Publisher Defendants*. According to the Complaint, Apple and the *Publisher Defendants* conspired to prevent retail price competition in the ebook market through the Apple Agency Contract. The DOJ estimated damage of millions of dollars against consumers who had to pay higher prices for ebooks.

By August 2013, all *Publisher Defendants* settled the U.S. antitrust proceeding through consent decrees whose terms were almost identical to each other and were considered sufficient to restore competition in the ebook industry.

740. *United States v. Apple, Inc.*, 791 F.3d 290, 300 (2dCir. 2015).
741. Apple, 952 F. Supp. 2d at 659. *See also United States v. Apple Inc.*, 952 F.Supp.2d 638 Competitive Impact Statement (S.D.N.Y., 2013) at 3. ("Apple's entry into the e-book business provided a perfect opportunity to coordinate the Publisher Defendants' collective action to raise e-book price.") *Ibid.*
742. *United States v. Apple, Inc.*, 791 F.3d at 304.
743. *Ibid.*, at 305. *See also,* Zachary C. Flood, *Antitrust Enforcement in the Developing E-Book Market: Apple, Amazon, and the Future of the Publishing Industry*, 31 Berkeley Tech. L. J. 879, 887 (2016).
744. *United States v. Apple, Inc.*, 791 F.3d at 304.
745. *Ibid*,. at 310.

### *[1] Simon & Schuster, Hachette and HarperCollins Consent Decree*

Simon & Schuster, Hachette and HarperCollins were the first publishers to settle the case. The terms of Simon & Schuster's, Hachette's and HarperCollins' consent decree are very similar to those analyzed in Chapter 4. These terms required the publishers to refrain from engaging in the investigated anticompetitive conduct and to appoint an Antitrust Compliance Officer.

Specifically, Simon & Schuster, Hachette and HarperCollins agreed to:

(1) Terminate any agreement with Apple regarding E-book sales[746] and those agreements with other ebook retailers which contained an MFN clause or that limited, restricted or impeded the ebook retailers' capability to set the retail price.

(2) Not enter into any agreements of point 1) for a two year period which runs separately for each ebook retailer and at the preference of the publisher from either: (a) the termination of the agreement between the publisher and the E-book retailer; (b) or, the date on which the publisher notifies the ebook retailers of any restrictive terms that impede or limit the retailer in setting the retail price will not be enforced.

(3) Not enter, for two years, into agreements with ebook retailers that provide an MFN clause.[747]

(4) Notify the DOJ (at least sixty days in advance) of "the formation or material modification of any join venture or other business arrangement relating to the Sale, development, or promotion of E-Books in the United States in which"[748] one of the *Publisher Defendants* were participants or owners.

(5) Provide the DOJ "one complete copy of each agreement, executed, renewed, or extended [related to ebook sales] on or after January 1, 2012"[749] with any other ebook retailers within seven days from the entry of the consent decree.

(6) Appoint a general counsel, legal officer, or someone that is reporting directly to the general counsel or chief legal officer as Antitrust Compliance Officer responsible for the company's compliance with the terms of the decree. The Antitrust Compliance Officer receives a minimum of four hours of training annually and is in charge of: *(a)* providing a copy of the consent decree to each defendant's officers, directors and employees involved in the ebook distribution and selling; *(b)* obtaining from each of people of point *(a)* an annual written certification specifying that he or she "has read, understands, and agrees to abide by the terms"[750] of the decree and "is not aware of any violation"[751] related to the decree; *(c)* "conducting an annual antitrust

746. *United States v. Apple Inc. et al.*, Final Judgment as to Defendants Hachette, HarperCollins, and Simon & Schuster (S.D.N.Y., 2012), at 8.
747. *Ibid.*, at 11.
748. *Ibid.* at 8.
749. *Ibid.*, at 10.
750. *Ibid.*, at 15.
751. *Ibid.*

compliance audit"[752] which concerns each person of point *(a)*; *(d)* tell to the publisher's employees that they can report to him any information related to potential violations of the antitrust law or the terms of the consent decree; *(e)* taking the necessary actions in case he receives credible information on a potential or actual violation of the consent decree. The Antitrust Compliance Officer has to act within three days and report to the DOJ within seven days of his intervention; *(f)* providing the DOJ "on a quarterly basis electronic copies of any non-privileged communications with any [p]erson containing allegations of Settling Defendants' noncompliance with any"[753] terms of the consent decree; *(g)* furnishing annually the DOJ a written statement regarding the compliance with the terms of the consent decrees related to the required and prohibited conduct, besides the antitrust compliance program.

The consent decree will be in force for five years from the date of its entry.[754]

### *[2] Penguin Consent Decree*

On December 18, 2012, the DOJ announced to have reached another consent solution with Penguin. The language and remedies contained in the proposed agreement were almost identical to the language and remedies used in the Simon & Schuster, Hachette and HarperCollins consent decree. In short, Penguin would stop from engaging in the investigated anticompetitive conduct and would adopt an antitrust compliance program overseen by an Antitrust Compliance Officer.

The settlement was subject to public comments until March 5, 2013.[755] On January 7, 2013, the District Court issued an order under which the DOJ would file the public comments and its response to the comments by April 5, 2013. Considering the terms of the agreement appropriate, on April 18, 2013, the DOJ moved the Court for entry of the settlement, closing the proceeding against Penguin.

On May 17, 2013, the District Court for the Southern District of New York considered the settlement between the DOJ and Penguin in compliance with the public interest and approved the terms of the consent decree.

### *[3] Macmillan Consent Decree*

The remaining publisher subject to the antitrust investigation—Macmillan—offered remedies to settle the investigation that were published for public comments on February 8, 2013.[756] The terms of the proposed settlement were essentially the same of

752. *Ibid.*
753. *Ibid.*
754. *Ibid.*, at 18.
755. *United States v. Apple Inc. et al.*, Final Judgment as to Defendants The Penguin Group, A Division Of Pearson PLC, And Penguin Group (USA), Inc. (S.D.N.Y., 2013).
756. [PROPOSED] Final Judgment as to Defendants Verlagsgruppe Georg Von Holtzbrinck GMBH & Holtzbrinck Holtzbrinck Publishers, LLC D/B/A Macmillan (Feb. 8, 2013).

those contained in the final judgments of Simon & Schuster, Hachette and HarperCollins and Penguin. Macmillian would be barred from engaging in the anticompetitive practices specified in the Complaint and would implement an antitrust compliance program appointing an Antitrust Compliance Officer to monitor its continued compliance.

In contrast to consent decrees settled with Penguin, Simon & Schuster, Hachette, and HarperCollins, Macmillan would immediately stop "enforcing restrictions on discounting or promotions contained in its contracts with [ebook] retailers."[757] Conversely, the agreement reached with the other publishers allowed each publisher "to choose whether to immediately allow discounting or, alternatively, to permit discounting only after the Court's approval of the settlement and the orderly termination of the publisher's existing contracts with retailers."[758] The proposed agreement did not give Macmillan an option to ensure a more prompt relief to consumers.

Even if Macmillan had not formalized new agreements with ebook retailers, it had to allow them an opportunity to discount the price within three days of agreeing to the settlement.[759] For Macmillan, the two-year cooling-off period would begin on December 18, 2012 (the same day on which Penguin signed its settlement).[760] The agreement between the DOJ and Macmillan did not include the termination of the existing contract with Apple as Macmillan had already terminated its Apple agency agreement when the other publishers settled their proceedings with the DOJ.

In addition, the Macmillan agreement "expressly carve[d] out the sale of electronic versions of academic textbook from its requirements and prohibitions,"[761] since the Complaint did not concern the ebook versions of academic textbooks. The agreement also made clear that Macmillan's German parent company (Verlagsgruppe Georg von Holtzbrink) was subject to all terms of the settlement.

The Final judgment related to Macmillan was entered on August 12, 2013 after the court determined the compliance of the terms with the public interest.

### *[4] Competitive Impact Statement*

This section examines the DOJ's considerations expressed in the Competitive Impact Statement released for each proposed settlement/consent decree before becoming final. These considerations are collectively analyzed, as the terms of the three antitrust settlements were largely identical. Generally, the DOJ considered the requirements and prohibitions stated in the proposed settlements sufficient to eliminate the *Publisher Defendants*' antitrust conduct and to prevent recurrence of the same or similar behavior.

757. *United States v. Apple Inc. et al.*, Competitive Impact Statement (S.D.N.Y., Feb. 8, 2013), https://www.justice.gov/atr/case-document/file/486801/download, at 6.
758. *Ibid.*
759. *Ibid.*
760. This term was included to persuade Macmillan to accept the more stringer terms of its settlement. *Ibid.*
761. *Ibid.*, at 7. ("Unlike the other Publisher Defendants, which publish only trade e-books, Macmillan also publishes e-textbooks.") *Ibid.*

Specifically, the requirement under which the publishers would immediately terminate the Apple Agency Agreements will allow the parties to reset their contractual relationships with Apple in a way that would be legal. Similarly, the publishers would terminate all contracts with major e-book retailers that contain restrictive terms that impede or limit the retailer in setting the retail price or that include an MFN clause. The fact that, in new contracts with retailers, the publishers could not include prohibitions on retailer discounting for at least two years or an MFN clause will prevent the new contracts to be set under similar collusive terms defined in the Apple Agency Agreement.[762] The new provisions stated in the antitrust settlements would enable most retailers to discount ebooks and to set the ebooks' retail price to gain market share and benefit consumers.[763] The terms of the reached antitrust settlements would also ban the kind of agreements among the publishers that led to the increase in ebook prices.

The ban on directly or indirectly conveying confidential or competitively sensitive information to any other e-book publisher has been considered fundamental to contrast the risk of collusive agreements. The adoption of a detailed antitrust compliance program and the appointment of an Antitrust Compliance Officer were also recognized as necessary. The DOJ argued that the extensive communication among competitors' CEOs facilitated the collusive conduct among the *Publisher Defendants*.[764]

In summary, the DOJ has positively embraced the terms and conditions defined in the proposed agreements which would eliminate the publishers' illegal conduct, likely lowering ebook prices of most *Publisher Defendants* titles.[765] All three agreements became final by August 2013, after the court approved the proposed Final Judgment. Apple remained the only active defendant in the U.S. *Ebook* case.

## [C] Apple Trial

### *[1] District Court*

As the New York Times reported, the "*Trial on Ebook price-fixing Puts Apple in the Spotlight.*"[766] Apple was left alone in the courtroom as all the other Defendants settled the case through consent decrees.

Apple's defense focused on showing that:

762. *United States v. Apple Inc. et al.*, Competitive Impact Statement ( S.D.N.Y., Apr. 11, 2012) at 10.
763. *Ibid.*, at 12.
764. *Ibid.*
765. *United States v. Apple Inc. et al.*, Competitive Impact Statement (Dist. Court S.D.N.Y., Dec. 18, 2012) (Penguin) at 4.
766. Brian X. Chen & Julie Bosman, *Trial on E-Book Price-Fixing Puts Apple in Spotlight*, The New York Times (Jun. 2, 2013), https://www.nytimes.com/2013/06/03/technology/e-book-antitrust-case-against-apple-to-begin.html.

(a) The evidence did not "tend to exclude" the possibility that Apple acted lawfully by pursuing its own independent business interests, and that, relying on (calling) *Monsanto* ruling,[767] Apple should be acquitted.
(b) Apple did not intend to conspire.[768]
(c) The Plaintiffs failed to prove that the *Publisher Defendants* increased the ebook prices.
(d) Its conduct needed to be scrutinized under *the rule of reason* rather than the *per se* rule.[769]

The District Court rejected all Apple's arguments, recognizing that:

(a) Apple misunderstood the Monsanto ruling which does not state that the antitrust liability depends on the fact that conspiracy is "the more likely explanation" for the prosecuted conduct. The fact that Apple's conduct was motivated by independent business reasons did not excuse Apple from conspiring with the *Publisher Defendants* to raise ebook prices. In *Monsanto,* the Supreme Court stated that a plaintiff needed to provide evidence that goes beyond the mere complaints to show the price fixing. Specifically, there "must be evidence that tends to exclude the possibility that the manufacturer and nonterminated distributors were acting independently."[770] In *Matsushita,* the Supreme Court further recognized that the evidence has to "'tend to exclude the possibility' that the accused engaged in legitimate behavior rather than engaging in 'an economically senseless conspiracy'."[771] However, it has never been stated that a cartel's participant is not liable for conspiracy if it acted also in its own independent business interests.
(b) The District Court found a variety of evidence that showed that Apple knew and "intentionally participated in and facilitated"[772] the horizontal agreement to raise the ebooks' retail prices and to remove price competition. The District Court recognized that "[f]rom its very first meetings with the Publishers, Apple appealed to their desire to raise prices and offered them a vision of how

767. 465 U.S. 752.
768. *United States v. Apple Inc., et al.* (*Apple I*), 1:12-cv-02826-DLC (S.D.N.Y., 2013). Apple argued that "it never intended to conspire with the Publisher Defendants to raise the retail prices of e-books. Apple emphasizes that it was the Publisher Defendants who raised the prices, and Apple should not be found liable just because those Publishers used Apple's Agreements as a tool to force an industry change to the agency model and then used their newly acquired price-setting authority to raise the retail prices of e-books." *Ibid.*, at 135.
769. *Apple I* at 152.
770. *Ibid.*, at 126. ("In sum, Apple business reasons for creating an e-bookstore and for adopting an agency model to do so have not created any ambiguity in the evidentiary record that should require hesitation before finding Apple liable.") *Ibid.* at 134.
771. *Ibid. citing* Matsushita at 127-128. The Second Circuit emphasized the importance of not misleading Matsushita as the Supreme Court "was simply requiring sufficient evidence to allow a reasonable fact-finder to infer that the conspiratorial explanation is more likely than not." *Ibid.*, at 128. Publ'n Paper, 690 F.3d at 63.
772. *Apple I* at 129.

they could reach that objective."[773] Apple, indeed, built a specific strategy and conditions that enabled the publishers to act together, completely removing retail price competition for ebooks. The District Court found the evidence of Apple's intent in the collusive conduct "overwhelming."[774]

(c) The District Court found Apple's argument that their entry into the ebook market "meant that ebooks were now available at $14.99 and $12.99,"[775] instead of not being available at all—totally creative. There was no evidence that publishers were actually considering withholding ebooks from Amazon. Those that announced that possibility would have represented merely thirty-seven titles. It was also ironic, alleged the Court, that Apple claimed credit for stopping the windowing when Apple encouraged the *Publisher Defendants* "to present Amazon with a blanket threat of windowing for a seven month period."[776]

Voluminous documentation showed Apple's intention to join the publishers in removing any retail price competition raising the e-book prices. Apple's founder, Steve Jobs, declared that "Amazon's $9.99 price for new releases [was] eroding the value perception of their product" and that Apple was "willing to try at the [$12.99 and $14.99] prices" sharing the publishers' necessity to raise ebook prices.

(d) Because Apple "directly participated in a horizontal price-fixing conspiracy,"[777] Apple's conduct was *per se* illegal. Apple actively encouraged and assisted the *Publisher Defendants* in the collusion scheme to raise e-book price. The increase of ebook prices was not the result of regular market forces, but of a perfectly orchestrated strategy by Apple.[778]

For the reasons outlined above, on September 5, 2013 (after a three-week trial) the District Court found Apple guilty of conspiring to restrain trade in violation of Section 1 of the Sherman act. The District Court forbade Apple from enforcing the MFN clause and any agreements with the publishers that restricted retail ebook prices in any way. The District Court order also required Apple to adopt an antitrust compliance program and a court-appointed external compliance monitor.

### *[2] The Second Circuit*

Apple and two of the *Publisher Defendants* (Macmillan and Simon&Schuster) appealed the decision, but without obtaining the expected results. The Second Circuit Court affirmed the lower court's ruling, recognizing that "Apple violated § 1 of the Sherman Act by orchestrating a horizontal conspiracy amongst the Publisher Defendants to raise

773. *Ibid.*, at 136.
774. *Ibid.*, at 137.
775. *Ibid.*, at 140.
776. *Ibid.*, at 142.
777. *Ibid.*, at 153.
778. *Ibid.*, at 9.

ebook prices."[779] Apple contended that its conduct should be scrutinized under the *rule of reason* rather than the *per se rule* as its relation with the publishers consisted of vertical and not horizontal or *per se* illegal agreements. Apple emphasized the pro-competitive effects linked to its entry into the ebook retail market, which antitrust enforcers needed to consider in assessing its conduct.[780] But the Second Circuit did not condemn the contract signed between Apple and each publisher under the *per se* rule, rather, it condemned Apple's central role in the horizontal price-fixing conspiracy. As Professor Richard A. Epstein observed, the vertical arrangement assisted the horizontal one, increasing the odds of the horizontal scheme, which is *per se* illegal.[781]

In conclusion, the Court of Appeal recognized that "Apple orchestrated a conspiracy among the [publishers] to raise the price,"[782] violating § 1 of the Sherman Act, and not the specific vertical agreements between Apple and the publishers.

### *[3] The Supreme Court*

Apple filed a petition for a writ of *certiorari* with the U.S. Supreme Court to reverse the Second Circuit court's ruling, but the Court declined to hear the case and Apple's arguments against the Court of Appeal's decision. The Supreme Court noted that the petitioner did not dispute that the publishers engaged in a horizontal price-fixing agreement and it "knowingly participated" in such an illegal conspiracy scheme. According to the Supreme Court, the fact that Apple "stood in a vertical relationship to its conspirators"[783] did not affect Apple's illegal conduct.

The Supreme Court's denial of the *certiorari* made the lower court decisions final.[784] As a consequence, Apple had to pay USD 450 million to ebook purchasers as part of the settlement reached in July 2014 among Apple, the attorneys general of thirty-three states, and a private class of ebook purchasers. In November 2014 Judge Denise L. Cote of Federal District Court in Manhattan endorsed the settlement under which Apple agreed to pay consumers USD 400 million plus an additional USD 50 million to lawyers. This settlement was not enforced until the Supreme Court ruled on Apple's *certiorari*.

In total, ebook purchasers received USD 566 million when considering the USD 166 million previously paid by the *Publisher Defendants* to end the antitrust allegations against them.[785]

779. *United States v. Apple, Inc.* (*Apple II*), 791 F.3d 290, 340 (2d Cir. 2015). *See also* Flood, *supra* n. 743, at 888.
780. *Appellant Apple Inc.'s Opening Brief, Apple v. United States*, 731 F.3d 290 (2d Cir. 2015) (2014 WL 3556301), 50-52.
781. Richard A. Epstein, *Epstein on the Apple E-books Case: The Hidden Traps in the Apple ebook Case* (Feb. 15, 2016).
782. *Apple II*, at 297.
783. *Apple, Inc. v. US*, 136 S. Ct. 1376 (2016), Brief for the United States in Opposition, https://www.justice.gov/atr/file/809946/download at 17.
784. DOJ, Supreme Court Rejects Apple's Request to Review E-Books Antitrust Conspiracy Findings (Mar. 7, 2016) https://www.justice.gov/opa/pr/supreme-court-rejects-apples-request-review-e-books-antitrust-conspiracy-findings.
785. *Ibid.*

### [D] Consent Decree Versus Antitrust Conviction

Having analyzed the different antitrust solutions, namely, the three consent decrees with the *Publisher Defendants* and the conviction with Apple, some conclusions can be drawn.

In 2010, Amazon sold ebooks at USD 9.99 and held ninety percent of market share in the ebook market before it fell to sixty percent in 2012.[786] In 2013, when *Publisher Defendants* settled the ebook case, Amazon market share increased to sixty-seven percent.[787] In February 2017, Amazon sold eighty-two percent of ebooks in the U.S.[788] leading someone to think that free price monopolies are reinforced through antitrust intervention.[789]

In the U.S., the sales of ebook decreased from 242 million in 2013 to 234 million in 2014 and then to 204 million in 2015. The number of e-books sold increased to 221 million units in 2016, and eventually reached 266 million units in 2017.[790] Therefore, in the U.S. from the first year of the antitrust settlements with the publishers to 2017, the sales of ebooks increased. However, if we analyzed the trend in year-over-year sales, we would notice significant changes from one year to another.

If we analyze the distribution of trade book sales in the United States by format from the 1st half of 2013 to the 1st half of 2017, there was a significant decrease in ebook sales. In the first half of 2013, ebook formats in the United States made up 24.5 percent of total trade book sales.[791] This percentage decreased to 23.6 percent in the first half of 2015 and then to 17 percent in 2017. Surprisingly though, there was an increase of paperbacks from 29.8 percent of trade book sales in the first half of 2013 to 34.3 percent in the first half of 2017.[792] In the United States, the estimated revenue generated by publishers from ebooks decreased from 2013 to 2017. In 2013, the U.S. ebook industry generated USD 3.24 billion in revenues which declined to USD 3.20 billion in 2014. The Association of American Publishers reported a double-digit declined in ebook sales. In 2015, revenues collected from ebooks amounted to USD 2.84 billion[793] and in 2016 to USD 1.157 billion.[794]

---

786. Françoise Behamou, *Fair Use and Fair Competition for Digitized Cultural Goods: The Case of Ebooks*, 39 J. Cult. Econ. 123, 129 (2015) citing (source: Publishers Weekly).
787. *Ibid.*
788. AuthorEarnings, Big, Bad, Wide & International Report: covering Amazon, Apple, B&N, and Kobo ebook sales in the US, UK, Canada, Australia, and New Zealand (February 2017), https://www.thepassivevoice.com/big-bad-wide-international-report-covering-amazon-apple-bn-and-kobo-ebook-sales-in-the-us-uk-canada-australia-and-new-zealand/; Kinga Jentetics, *Amazon Ebook Market Share 2017—Is It Big Enough?* (Publishdrive Jan. 4, 2018), https://publishdrive.com/amazon-ebook-market-share/.
789. Behamou, *supra* n. 786, at 129.
790. Statista, E-books in the U.S., 7 (2017).
791. *Ibid.*, at 9.
792. *Ibid.*
793. Association of American Publishers, U.S. Publishing Industry's Annual Survey Reveals Nearly USD 28 Billion in Revenue in 2015 (Jul. 11, 2016) https://newsroom.publishers.org/us-publishing-industrys-annual-survey-reveals-nearly-28-billion-in-revenue-in-2015.
794. US Publishers' StatShot 2017 Report: Fifth Year of Double-Digit Audiobooks Growth (May 9, 2018) https://publishingperspectives.com/2018/05/american-publishers-statshot-revenue-2017-report/.

The price of ebooks increased from 2010 until 2013 mainly due to Apple's entry into the ebook market. As outlined above, Apple recommended *price ceilings* to the publishers: "$14.99 for hardcover books with list prices above $35; $12.99 for hardcover books with list prices below $35; and $9.99 for all other trade book,"[795] and imposed an MFN clause to ensure that the ebooks sold on iBookstore were the cheapest ones. As the price of ebooks increased, the *Publisher Defendants*' sales of e-books declined to 14.5 percent before the antitrust settlements.[796]

In 2016, statistic analysis showed that ebooks of NY Times bestsellers were priced USD 12.44, twenty-two percent less than hardcover price.[797] Meanwhile, the average price of a Big Five ebook from January 2016 dropped from USD 10.31 to USD 8.67 in May 2016.[798] Thus, from 2013 to 2016, ebook prices generally decreased.

In summary, the first three antitrust settlements and Apple's later conviction lead to: (1) a general reduction of ebook prices; (2) an increase of both ebook sales and Amazon's market share.

Particularly encouraging is the data from 2015 to 2017, after Apple's final conviction which required Apple to change its agency contract agreements with the publishers and payback consumers affected by its anticompetitive practice.

## §6.02 THE EU EBOOK CASE

### [A] Main Facts

On December 6, 2011 the EU Commission opened a formal investigation in the EU ebook market against Hachette Livre (Lagardère Publishing, France), Harper Collins (News Corp., USA), Simon & Schuster (CBS Corp., USA), Penguin (Pearson Group, UK), Verlagsgruppe Georg von Holzbrinck (which owns *inter alia* Macmillan, Germany) and Apple.[799] Similar to the U.S. proceedings, the EU Commission expressed concerned that Apple and the main EU publishers conspired to raise the ebook retail prices in the European Economic Area (EEA). In the Preliminary Assessment, the EU Commission observed that the global strategy of Apple and the publishers could violate Article 101 of the TFEU and Article 53 of the Agreement of the European Economic Area (EU Area).

In September 2012 Harper Collins, Hachette Livre, Simon & Schuster, Verlagsgruppe Georg von Holzbrinck (the four publishers) and Apple submitted some commitments to address the EU Commission's antitrust concerns.[800] These initial

795. *United States v. Apple, Inc.*, 791 F.3d at 304.
796. *Ibid.*, at 310.
797. Statista, eBook Pricing Around the World, https://www.statista.com/chart/6361/ebook-pricing/.
798. May 2016 Author Earnings Report: the Definitive Million-title Study of US Author Earings (Jun. 2, 2016) https://www.thepassivevoice.com/may-2016-author-earnings-report-the-definitive-million-title-study-of-us-author-earnings/.
799. EU Commission, Antitrust: Commission Opens Formal Proceedings to Investigate Sales of e-book, Press Release (Dec. 6, 2011).
800. EU Commission, Case COMP/AT.39847-E-books (Dec. 12, 2012) [*Ebook commitments I*].

commitments were modified after receiving observations from third parties. On December 12, 2012, the commitments became final, closing the EU antitrust proceeding against Harper Collins, Hachette Livre, Simon & Schuster, Verlagsgruppe Georg von Holtzbrinck and Apple (*Ebook commitments I*). On July 25, 2013, Penguin also closed the investigation by offering similar commitments. During the European antitrust investigation, Penguin was involved in a transaction to create the joint venture *Penguin Random House*, which was completed on July 1, 2013.[801] Only after completing that transaction was Penguin able to settle the antitrust investigation by means of commitments (*Ebook commitments II*).

### [B] EU Commitment Decisions

Between May and August in 2010, the five publishers and Apple signed an agency agreement related to the EU Area which contained the same key pricing terms as their respective U.S. agreements: "the retail price MFN clause, maximum retail price grids, and the payment of a commission to Apple equal to 30 % of the retail price."[802] According to the EU Commission, there was parallel behavior in the United States and the European Economic Area between Apple and the publishers, which lead to agency contracts containing the same key clauses.[803]

In its preliminary view, the EU Commission recognized that the direct contacts between Apple and the investigated publishers eliminated the risks of competition and lead to the signing of the Apple Agency agreements, first in the U.S. and then in Europe.[804] According to the EU Commission, the collective shift of the publishers from a wholesale model to an agency model, with the same key pricing terms on a global scale, was the result of a concerned practice in violation of Article 101 of TFEU and Article 53 of the EEA Agreement.

To address the EU Commission's antitrust concerns, the four publishers and Apple offered some commitments. The initial commitments proposed in September 2012 were modified after the market test and receiving observations from the third parties. The initial commitments included:

(1) The termination of agency agreements for sale of ebooks in the EU Area between Apple and the four publishers.

801. EU Commission, Case COMP/AT.39847-E-books, Commission Decision (Jul 25, 2013), http://ec.europa.eu/competition/antitrust/cases/dec_docs/39847/39847_27536_4.pdf. ("On 1 July 2013, the Transaction was completed. As a result, Penguin Group (USA), Inc. has changed its name to Penguin Group (USA), LLC and The Penguin Publishing Company Limited has changed its name to Penguin Random House Limited. The Penguin Group (a division of Pearson plc) has ceased to exist and its assets have been or shortly will be transferred to Penguin Random House Limited or Penguin Group (USA), LLC. The publishing assets of Dorling Kindersley Holdings Limited have been transferred to Penguin Random House Limited or its subsidiaries (over which Penguin Random House Limited exercises decisive influence"). *Ibid.*, at 6.

802. *Ebook commitment decision I* at 12.

803. *Ibid.*, at 16.

804. *Ibid.*, at 18.

(2) Besides Apple, each of the four publishers will offer retailers to end any agency agreements concluded for the sale of e-books that: "(i) restrict, limit or impede the retailer's ability to set, alter or reduce the retail price, or to offer any other form of promotions; or (ii) contain a price MFN clause as defined in the four publishers' initial commitments."[805]
(3) Each of the four publishers will not restrict, impede or limit—for a period of two years (the cooling-off period)—the ability of ebook retailers to set, alter or reduce both retail prices for e-books and/or discounts or other form of promotions.
(4) For five years, neither Apple nor the four publishers will enter into agreements that include any kind of MFN clause for the sale of ebooks in the EU Area.

The EU Commission received comments from fourteen third parties, which mainly concerned: (a) the termination of existing agency agreements; (b) the scope of the prohibition on price MFN clauses as stated in the Initial Commitments; (c) the definition of "eBook" and "Online eBook Store Provider."[806]

The final draft of commitments, which became legally binging on December 12, 2012, included Apple's alignment with the definition of "eBook" used by the four publishers and the removal of the ban on business model MFN clauses. In July 2013, the EU Commission adopted a decision which made legally binding similar commitments offered by Peguin (*Ebook commitments II*).

### [C] The EU Ebook Market from 2012 to Date

Now that we know the remedies enshrined in the EU ebook commitment decisions, it might be interesting to explore the evolution of the ebook markets in Europe and European Member States to assess the economic effects of such remedies.

In 2013, 4.3 percent of books sold in Europe were ebooks. By 2017, ebook sales increased to 21 percent.[807] If we consider only the German market over the same time period, ebook market revenue increased from EUR 609 to 1.332 million.[808] In Germany, the price of e-books decreased between 2013 and 2017 from EUR 7.58 to 6.38.[809]

In Italy, the ebook market value increased from EUR 32.1 million in 2013 to EUR 64 million in 2017. Similar to Germany, the price of ebooks decreased.[810] In 2012, the average cover price of and ebook was EUR 9.02, which in 2015 decreased to EUR

805. Summary of Commission Decision of 12 December 2012 relating to a proceeding under Article 101 of the Treaty on the Functioning of the European Union and Article 53 of the EEA Agreement at §19 (Mar. 3, 2013) https://eur-lex.europa.eu/legal-content/EN/TXT/PDF/?uri=CELEX:52013XC0313(03)&from=EN.
806. *Ebook commitment decision I* at 23.
807. Statista, *E-book Market Share in Europe in 2013 and 2017* (2018).
808. Statista, *Print v. E-book: Book Market Revenue in Germany from 2011 to 2020 (in million euros)* (2018).
809. Statista, *Average E-book Price in Germany from 2010 to 2017 (in euros)* (2018).
810. Statista, *E-book Market Value in Italy from 2011 to 2017(in 1,000 euros)* (2018).

6.65.[811] This trend appears to be similar in Spain. The revenue of the digital book industry increased from EUR 80.3 million in 2013 to EUR 119.1 million in 2017.[812] In 2013, ebook sales represented 3.7 percent of the total books published digitally in Spain, and in 2016 ebook sales reached 5 percent.[813]

In summary, looking at ebook revenues and prices in Europe and in some of the main European countries, it appears that the *Ebook commitments I and II* have positively affected the European ebook market. Total revenues have increased while price of ebook has generally decreased, indicating an increase in competition and consumer welfare in the EU ebook markets.

## §6.03 U.S. CONSENT DECREES VERSUS EU COMMITMENT DECISIONS IN THE EBOOK CASE

In the analysis of U.S. consent decrees and EU commitment decisions that occurred in the U.S. and European ebook markets, reveals that both *antitrust consent* solutions remedies required the termination of agreements between Apple and the publishers subject to investigation. Both settlements also included prohibition from entering into future agreements that would restrict, limit or impede the ability of e-book retailers to set, alter or reduce the prices of ebooks, and any agreements that include an MFN clause. With respect to the prohibition of the MFN clause, the EU commitment decisions extended the prohibition to five years instead of two as it was established in the U.S. consent decrees. Other differences between the two antitrust settlements concerned the termination, only in Europe, of all agency agreements, and the appointment—in the U.S.—of an Antitrust Compliance Officer who has specific and detailed tasks that assure continued compliance to the agreed upon remedies.

If we consider the time frame from the filing of the U.S. antitrust complaint and the opening of the antitrust investigation in EU to the issuance of the final settlement, the settlement occurred in about a year and half in both contexts. In the U.S., the complaint was filed on April 11, 2012, and the last consent decree became final on August 12, 2013. In the EU, the EU Commission opened the case on December 6, 2011, and reached the final agreement with the last publisher on July 1, 2013.

In summary, both the terms and the time frames to close the antitrust investigation are quite similar between the two contexts. Both the U.S. and EU antitrust settlements required the companies in the proceeding to refrain from engaging in the investigated anticompetitive conduct, extending the prohibition from entering into the suspected contracts to all e-book retailers, not only Apple. The main difference between the U.S. and EU settlements concerned the request in the U.S. to the publishers to adopt an antitrust compliance program and to appoint an Antitrust Compliance Officer. Besides that, remedies defined to settle the ebook case were basically the same in both jurisdictions.

811. Statista, *Average Cover Price of E-book in Italy from 2010 to 2015* (2018).
812. Statista, *Revenue of the Digital Book Industry in Spain from 2009 to 2017 (in million euros)* (2018).
813. Statista, *Market Share of Books Published Digitally in Spain from 2009 to 2016* (2018).

# Conclusions of Part II

The results of the analysis conducted in Part II are straightforward. In the U.S., the DOJ and FTC settle almost all antitrust civil no merger cases by means of consent decrees. In contrast to past decrees, they do not seem to include structural or effective behavioral remedies. The pro competitive effects related to an antitrust conviction seem to exceed those resulted from remedies enshrined in consent decrees (*U.S. v. Apple*). Time is saved through a consent solution but at price of consumer welfare.

In Europe the initial enthusiasm in adopting commitment decisions slowed from 2014 to 2018. The EU Commission and companies subject to investigations do not save significant time through commitment decisions. But we have to consider that prohibition decisions are likely to be challenged in courts. EU commitments often required structural or incisive behavioral changes that might not be cost-effective for companies without an appropriate regulatory framework.

The truth is that the consent solutions have the potential to be the most effective antitrust tool if appropriately used. As the U.S. Intel case analyzed in Chapter 1 reveals, antitrust remedies enshrined in consent decrees can be cost-effective and benefit overall consumers and markets much more than a conviction. Conversely, if such remedies are limited to end the investigated conduct they do not seem to be sufficient in restoring competition and increasing consumer welfare.

Perhaps antitrust agencies should consider including more effective remedies into antitrust settlements and benefiting from both the U.S. and EU experience in the determination of the most appropriate remedies on a case-by-case basis. Although the U.S. and EU antitrust frameworks are very different from each other, there is much to learn from the knowledge and experience of both antitrust enforcement mechanisms. In the future, U.S. and EU antitrust agencies will face even more challenging situations, and can only benefit from collaborating with each other to deal with similar cases and situations.

Antitrust enforcers need to be proactive and get every company engaged in achieving market efficiency goals as companies have the best knowledge and resources to increase the efficiency of the very markets that they have created. The consent solution is a remarkable tool to enforce antitrust principles and likely the best, as remedies enshrined in antitrust settlements are offered and reviewed by the same market players.

Let me be clear: the *antitrust consent* is not a perfect antitrust tool but it has potential to be the most appropriate one to deal with markets. Antitrust settlements are a win-win solution. Antitrust agencies and regulators can only benefit from companies' collaboration—through the *antitrust consent*—and companies can only benefit from the guidance of antitrust and regulatory agencies.

## Part III

# Antitrust Settlements in the Digital and Blockchain Era

"The fact that a firm innovates should not insulate it from antitrust scrutiny or license it to take anticompetitive actions."[814]

(Franklin M. Fisher)

A common tendency in academia is to see things as more complex than they are—antitrust is no exception. Nowadays, antitrust enforcers and scholars emphasize the complexity of enforcing antitrust principles in digital two-sided markets[815] and dealing with issues such as big data and the development of artificial intelligence.[816] But the real solution might be easier than we think and the issues not so complex.

Part III explores the role of antitrust settlements in even more dynamic *data-driven* markets. Like never before, large tech companies as Google and Facebook are legally dominating global markets built on data—the so-called *Data Industry*—as this industry is characterized by network effects which favor market concentration. But, as explained in Chapter 9, this situation might change soon thanks to a new platform built on blockchain technology and antitrust remedies enshrined in *smart contracts*.

Data-driven markets governed by large tech companies represent an important issue for antitrust enforcers. The adoption of antitrust settlements along with unlocking the complexity of blockchain technology and *smart contracts* can be the key in the future.

---

814. Franklin M. Fisher, *Antitrust and Innovative Industries*, 68 Antitrust L. J. 559 (2000).
815. Douglas A. Melamed, *Network Industries and Antitrust*, 23 Harv. J. L. & Pub. Pol'y 147 (1999); Davis S. Evans, *Antitrust Issues Raised by the Emerging Global Internet Economy*, 102 Northwestern Univ. L. Rev. 285 (2008); Daniel L. Rubinfeld, *Antitrust Enforcement in Dynamic Network Industries*, 43 Antitrust Bull. 859, 860 (1998); Daniel J. Gifford & Robert T. Kudrle, *Antitrust Approaches to Dynamically Competitive Industries in the United States and the European Union*, 7 J. Comp. L. & Econ. 695, 700 (2011).
816. *See*, e.g., Ariel Ezrachi & Maurice E. Stucke, *Artificial Intelligence and Collusion: When Computers Inhibit Competition*, 5 U. Ill. L. Rev. 1775 (2017).

Part III is divided into three chapters. Chapter 7 examines the main antitrust issues related to digital markets in the U.S. by analyzing the Google cases and proceeds with the exploration of employing antitrust remedies enshrined in consent decrees to address such antitrust concerns. Chapter 7 analyses the adoption of the same antitrust remedies enshrined in the AT&T consent decree of 1982 to deal with present antitrust concerns that affect the most powerful company in the data industry—Google. Chapter 7 seeks to anticipate the outcomes of using some specific tailored antitrust remedies, such as Google break-up and behavior remedies, in the regulatory framework of today's most valuable resource—*data*.

Chapter 8 explores the future of the EU commitment decisions and their role in enforcing European competition law in the digital era. As explored in Chapter 5, the EU Commission and European antitrust agencies significantly decreased the adoption of commitment decisions in setting antitrust proceedings. Is this justified? Or, should European enforcers trust this flexible antitrust tool to face even more dynamic and unpredictable markets? Should the role of commitment decisions diverge or converge with the role of U.S. consent decrees in the future enforcement of antitrust principles? In other words, this chapter seeks to answer whether or not European enforcers should favor the adoption of commitment rather than prohibition decisions in regulating modern digital markets. Furthermore, we explore how the use of such a bargaining tool can be improved in Europe by looking at the U.S.'s century of experience with antitrust settlements.

Chapter 9, investigates blockchain technology and the use of *smart contracts* to enforce remedies enshrined in antitrust settlements in future markets. Blockchain technology is in its infancy, but it is likely to revolutionize markets as the Internet did twenty years ago. As will be explored in Chapter 9, antitrust does not need new tools. Antitrust law needs to employ tradition tools—U.S. consent decrees and EU commitment decisions—by means of cutting edge technologies (e.g., *smart contracts* and blockchain technology) to be effective in present and future markets.

CHAPTER 7

# U.S. Consent Decrees in Driving the Data Industry

While Professors Whish and Bailey stressed that EU competition law is enforced having the single European market in mind, this book has repeatedly stressed the fact that antitrust law was born in the U.S. as an arm of regulation[817] in what was the most powerful market of all—the oil market.[818] In the 1860s, the railroads allowed people to trade oil and other goods all over the United States creating all kinds of new market opportunities in the U.S. In the 1990s, the Internet has enabled people to easily share and trade data all over the world.

Rockefeller wisely understood how to govern the oil market in the 1860s, buying oil refineries all over the U.S. and making *a trust agreement* with the railroad.[819] At that time there was no federal antitrust law: hence, Rockefeller was not breaching any laws. The U.S. legislator later considered it a necessary form of market regulation to prevent the most precious resources of the U.S. to fall completely in the hands of a private entity. Antitrust law represents a remarkable tool of *economic democracy*.

Similar to Standard Oil, Google has found a creative way to control and profit from the new oil—*data*—without violating any laws because Google offers goods and services free of charge to consumers by collecting money from advertisers. Google now governs most of the data traded on a global scale by means of their Search and Android platforms which are installed for free in almost all Internet and digital devices. In summary, today's large tech companies such as Google and Facebook have found a way to control data markets without violating any apparent antitrust laws as consumer welfare is preserved through the free offering of their goods and services.

---

817. Hovenkamp, *supra* n. 481, at 71. ("[A]ntitrust policy is an extended arm of regulation.")
818. Giovanna Massarotto, *From Standard Oil to Google: How the Role of Antitrust Law Has Changed*, 41 World Competition 395 (2018).
819. *Ibid. See also* John D. Clark, The Federal Trust Policy (1931), available at http://babel.hathitrust.org/cgi/pt?id=coo.31924013937473;view=1up;seq=5, at 17; Amato, *supra* n. 332.

For more than ten years the antitrust community focused its attention on how to enforce antitrust principles in today's data markets without finding a real solution. Some scholars called for a *"paradox"*,[820] as in today's consumer welfare standard, based on decreasing price and increasing quality of goods may have become meaningfulness. The first question we should ask: should antitrust agencies intervene in today's data and digital markets? Or, are Google and other large corporations the ideal regulators of the *data industry*?

Chapter 7 investigates today's antitrust challenges in dealing with data-driven markets and how remedies enshrined in consent decrees can drive these markets. Remedies of this analysis include Google's break-up and other behavior remedies to deal with one of the most emblematic cases affecting the industry—the Google Search case.

## §7.01 INTRODUCTION

Particularly in the U.S., antitrust enforcers are emphasizing the complexity of today's data-driven markets to justify their lack of intervention and address the criticism of being lax.[821] But making things complex does not help the antitrust community to find a solution, nor does it provide an excuse for antitrust enforcers not to intervene. The whole concept of punishment is a complex one because a wrongful punishment can damage consumers more than a violation left unpunished. But Judge Frank J. Easterbrook's recognition[822] is not an alibi for antitrust agencies to take no actions in today's uncertain and complex digital markets.[823] Otherwise the legislator, and legal system in general, should give up any time that the result of a legislative intervention or judicial ruling is unpredictable—which means most of the time.

In understanding the main antitrust and regulatory challenges in the data industry, Daniel L. Rubinfeld and Michal S. Gal's article, *Access Barriers to Big Data,* was informative. Rubinfeld and Gal emphasized the importance of big data in today's economy and the potentially crucial role of antitrust and regulation in creating the path for the data industry.[824] Data is a double-edged sword as it creates new business

820. Khan, *supra* n. 400.

821. *See* FTC Hearing of Sep. 13, 2018, https://www.ftc.gov/news-events/events-calendar/2018/09/ftc-hearing-1-competition-consumer-protection-21st-century.

822. Frank J. Easterbrook explained how the false positive and false negative terms used by social scientists could be applied in the framework of antitrust law to limit government intervention in economic life. The false positive occurs when a judge or general law maker erroneously punishes an efficient (or at the very minimum not inefficient) business conduct. Conversely, the false negative transpires if the judge/law maker wrongly excuses harmful behaviour toward consumers. According to this theory, the false positive is far worse than false negative for consumers. Frank H. Easterbrook, *Comparative Advantage and Antitrust Law,* 75 Cal. L. Rev. 983, 985 (1987).

823. Easterbrook, *supra* n. 382. Geoffrey A. Manne & Joshua D. Wright, *Google and the Limits of Antitrust: The Case Against the Case Against Google,* 34 Harv. J. L. & Pub. Pol'y 171, 176-180 (2011).

824. Daniel L. Rubinfeld & Michal S. Gal, *Access Barriers to Big Data,* 59 Ariz. L. Rev. 339 (2017). *See also,* John D. Kelleher & Brendan Tierney, *Data Science,* 149 (MIT Press, 2018). ("[I]n the near future, data usage and privacy regulations may affect the selection of ML algorithms.") *Ibid.*

opportunities and a breeding ground for engaging in abusive conduct as the collection of data favors market concentration.

Antitrust issues related to data range from data protection to technological barriers and make data markets complex and challenging to regulate. Arguably the most fascinating issue is the existence of a permanent "tension between the advantages of free-ride (greater competition, synergies) and the disadvantages (reduce incentive to innovate, market power)"[825] in data industry.

Section §7.02 explores the main antitrust concerns around the data industry and provides some possible solutions. Section §7.03 investigates the adoption of the same antitrust remedies for the Google case as were employed in the AT&T case. Tailored and flexible remedies defined with the consent of the companies subject to antitrust investigations might effectively regulate the data industry and drive the *data economy*.[826]

## §7.02 GOOGLE AND THE DATA INDUSTRY

Section §7.02 examines the main antitrust issues related to data markets through the analysis of Google cases, as these cases exemplify the current challenges related to antitrust in the data industry.

### [A] Google Antitrust Cases

Today, Google[827]—like Standard Oil in the 1890s—exerts monopoly power in the most powerful industry—the data industry. However, in contrast to Standard Oil, Google acts in digital markets that are increasingly dynamic (hence unpredictable) and two-sided, thus complex and uncertain.[828] Google also notably provides services for free to users and collects money for advertisers.[829]

Up to the writing of this book, both the DOJ and FTC have been reluctant to take any antitrust intervention against Google. In 2011, the FTC sent a complaint to Google opening an antitrust investigation for possible monopolization conduct. According to the FTC, Google might have intentionally manipulated its algorithm by altering both organic and paid search results to favor its own services at the expense of rivals.[830] This

825. Rubinfeld & Gal, *supra* n. 824, at 374. ("The collection and analysis of big data has undoubtedly increased social welfare. However, big data markets are also often characterized by entry barriers which, in turn, have the potential to create durable market power in data-related markets or to serve as a basis for anti-competitive conduct.") *Ibid.*, at 381.
826. Massarotto, *From Standard Oil to Google: How the Role of Antitrust Law Has Changed*, *supra* n. 818.
827. *See* Charles Duhigg, *The Case Against Google* (N. Y. Times, Feb. 20, 2018).
828. *See*, e.g., Manne & Wright, *supra* n. 823, at 171.
829. Lapo Filistrucchi, Damien Geradin, Eric van Damme & Pauline Affeldt, *Market Definition in Two-Sided Markets: Theory and Practice*, 10 J. Competition L. & Econ. 293, 295 (2014).
830. *See*, e.g., *In the Matter of* Google Inc., Statement of the Federal Trade Commission Regarding Google's Search Practices. FTC File No. 111-0163 Jan. 3, 2013 at 2; Ratliff & Rubinfeld, *supra* n. 471.

case is known as *Google Search Bias*.[831] On January 3, 2013, the FTC said that Google's conduct in the search bias investigation was the result of "competition on the merit" and the "competitive process that the law encourages."[832] The FTC further observed that any negative effect was accidental,[833] and closed the case without action.[834] While the FTC has taken no action alleging that Google's conduct was a by-product of "competition on the merit"[835] in Europe, as further explored in Chapter 8, the EU Commission fined Google EUR 2.42 billion for abusing its dominant position in the search engine market.[836]

Besides Google Search, Google owns the Android platform and many other products and services, including a variety of smartphone applications. Android is an open-source operating system that, in only a few years, was installed in about 85 percent of total smartphones.[837] Through Google Android, which is free of charge, Google was able to install its smartphone applications, including Google Maps, YouTube, and Google Chrome, and collect fees from advertisements. Android is not only free but also an open-source software which anybody (at least in theory) can install and modify. Actually, Google Android cannot be modified, as Google requires smartphone manufacturers to sign anti-fragmentation agreements to prevent the creation of Android forks (different versions of Google Android).[838]

On May 1, 2014, Google users filed a class action against Google in the California Federal Court. According to the complaint, "[b]y way of Google's coercive and exclusionary practice with Android OS device manufacturers ... Google restrains and

831. *Ibid.* EU Commission, Antitrust: Commission probes allegations of antitrust violations by Google, Press Release IP/10/1624, *supra* n. 470.
832. *In the Matter of* Google Inc, Statement of the Federal Trade Commission Regarding Google's Search Practices, *supra* n. 830, at 2.
833. *Ibid.*
834. *Ibid.* More recently, on Jan. 29, 2016, the Attorney General for the State of both Utah and the District of Columbia urged the FTC to consider new evidence about the Google Search engine and Google Android. According to both Utah and the District of Columbia Attorney Generals, the FTC should revisit its investigation on the *Google Search Bias*, which was closed in 2013, in the light of the new evidence collected domestically and internationally during the past three years. However, as of January 2016 the FTC has not formally reopened its investigations on the *Google Search Bias* case or any investigations with respect to the evidence recalled in such a letter, avoiding any comments on the issue. Melissa Lipman, *Utah, DC AGs Push FTC to Revive Google Search Bias Probe*, Law360, https://www.law360.com/articles/754017/utah-dc-ags-push-ftc-to-revive-google-search-bias-probe (Feb. 2, 2016). *See also* David McLaughlin, *Google Search Probe by U.S. Should Get New Look, Utah Says*, Bloomberg Technology (Feb. 2, 2016), http://www.bloomberg.com/news/articles/2016-02-02/google-search-bias-probe-by-u-s-should-get-new-look-utah-says.
835. *In the Matter of* Google Inc, Statement of the Federal Trade Commission Regarding Google's Search Practices, *supra* n. 830, at 2.
836. EU Commission, Antitrust: Commission fines Google €2.42 for abusing dominance as search engine by giving illegal advantage to own comparison shopping service, Press Release IP/17/1784 (Jun. 27, 2017), http://europa.eu/rapid/press-release_IP-17-1784_en.htm.
837. IDC, Smartshone OS Market Share, 2015 Q2, http://www.idc.com/prodserv/smartphone-os-market-share.jsp.
838. Seth Rosenblatt, *What Google Really Means When It Calls Android "Open"*, C|net (Feb. 14, 2014, 7:49 AM), http://www.cnet.com/news/what-google-really-means-when-it-calls-android-open/.

quashes competition for default search engine status before it can even begin."[839] The class further alleged that "Google's practice is a pure power play designed to maintain and extend its monopoly in handheld general search."[840] In February 2015, the district court dismissed the class action. The FTC seems to have started an informal antitrust investigation against Google Android in the smartphone applications market, but no formal complaint has yet been filed.[841] In 2019, the DOJ and more than thirty U.S. State of Attorneys General, such as the Texas Attorney General, appear to be investigating Google for possible antitrust violations as well.

### [B] The U.S. Non-intervention Strategy

Possible justifications behind U.S. non-intervention are:

(1) Google digital markets concern big data and data protection—matters that go beyond antitrust concerns.[842]
(2) Google markets involve network effects and the issue of *standardization versus fragmentation* which are hard to regulate and self-regulation might be ideal.
(3) Google acts in new and unpredictable markets which require new antitrust tools to be effective;[843] traditional antitrust tools or antitrust regulation appear unadapt.

Each of these points is further developed in the following.

#### *[1] Antitrust Versus Data Protection*

The fact that Google markets affect data and privacy issues, subjects that might go beyond antitrust matters, does not seem to be a sufficient justification for a lack of antitrust intervention. In 2000, the FTC enacted the Telemarketing Act and the Do not

839. Class Action Complaint, *Feitelson v. Google Inc.*, No. 5:14-cv-02007-HRL, ¶38 (N.D. Cal. May 1, 2014), ECF No. 1.
840. *Ibid.*
841. Jack Nicas & Brent Kendall, *FTC Extends Probe into Google's Android*, The Wall Street J. (Apr. 26, 2016, 3:33 PM) http://www.wsj.com/articles/ftc-extends-probe-into-googles-android-1461699217.
842. *See*, e.g., Daniel D. Sokol & Roisin E. Comerford, *Antitrust and Regulating Big Data*, 23 Geo. Mason L. Rev. 1,129 (2015). ("Commentators generally are split into two camps: one in favor of more proactive antitrust enforcement in the Big Data realm, and one opposing such intervention, considering antitrust inappropriate for regulation of Big Data.") *Ibid. See also*, Andres V. Lerner, *The Role of "Big Data" in Online Platform Competition*, 62 (Aug. 26, 2014). Available at SSRN: https://ssrn.com/abstract=2482780; Giuseppe Colangelo & Mariateresa Maggiolino, *Data Protection in Attention Markets: Protecting Privacy through Competition?*, 8 J. Eur. Competition L. & Practice 363 (2017).
843. *See*, e.g., Ezrachi & Stucke, *supra* n. 816.

Call regulation to protect consumers' privacy from abusive patterns of calls.[844] Thus, the FTC dealt with and regulated *privacy* before the development of digital markets.

Big data "is a game changer"[845] — as the vast volume of data now available, thanks to the Internet platform, has led to the creation of new, increasingly high-quality products[846] that benefit consumers. Digital personal assistants, such as Alexa, are only one example. These new products generate big data themselves, increasing the need to regulate the data flow. The first question we should ask is: *Are antitrust enforcers and regulation the appropriate tool to regulate such a flow of data?* As Part III will reveal, the likely answer is affirmative.

As investigated in Chapter 8, the German antitrust agency (the Bundeskartellamt) has recently taken the approach of adopting antitrust decisions that are regulatory in nature. On February 6, 2019, for example, the Bundeskartellamt took a controversial antitrust action against Facebook. It was controversial because it was original in both the EU and U.S. antitrust enforcement contexts. The Bundeskartellamt ultimately required Facebook to change some of its terms and conditions.[847]

According to the current terms and conditions, Facebook can collect all data exchanged on Facebook-owned services, including Instagram, WhatsApp and third party websites, and combine and assign this data to the Facebook user's account.[848] After the German Agency's decision under Section 19(1) of the German Competition law (which prohibits the abuse of dominant position),[849] Facebook can keep doing that practice only if there is the voluntary consent of its users.[850] In the event that the user does not give consent, Facebook "will have to substantially restrict its collection and combining data."[851] In the U.S., there is no trace of similar antitrust decisions which

844. Steve Croley, *Regulation and the Public Interest: The Possibility of Good Regulatory Government*, 179 (Princeton U. Press, 2008). Fed. Trade Comm'n, Par III, FTC, 16 CFR Part 310 Telemarketing Sales Rule; Final Rule (Jan. 29, 2003) https://www.ftc.gov/sites/default/files/documents/federal_register_notices/telemarketing-sales-rule-16-cfr-part-310/030129telemar ketingsales.pdf.

845. Rubinfeld & Gal, *supra* n. 824, at 341.

846. *Ibid. See also*, Sokol & Comerford, *supra* n. 842.

847. Bundeskartellamt, Case Summary: Facebook, Exploitative Business Terms Pursuant to Section 19(1) GWB for Inadequate Data Processing (Feb. 15, 2019).

848. Bundeskartellamt, Bundeskartellamt Prohibits Facebook from Combining User Data from Different Sources, Press Release (Feb. 7, 2019), available at https://www.bundeskartellamt.de/SharedDocs/Meldung/EN/Pressemitteilungen/2019/07_02_2019_Facebook.html?nn=359 1568.

849. Bundeskarltellamt, Act against Restraints of Competition (Competition Act— GWB) last amended by Article 10(9) of the Act of 30 October 2017, available at https://www.bundeskartellamt.de/SharedDocs/Publikation/EN/Others/GWB.pdf?__blob=publicationFile &v=6).

850. Bundeskartellamt, Bundeskartellamt Prohibits Facebook from Combining User Data from Different Sources, Press Release, *supra* n. 848, "(i) Facebook-owned services like WhatsApp and Instagram can continue to collect data. However, assigning the data to Facebook user accounts will only be possible subject to the users' voluntary consent. Where consent is not given, the data must remain with the respective service and cannot be proceed in combination with Facebook data." *Ibid.*

851. *Ibid.*

have the effect of regulating privacy through tailored antitrust remedies until greater forms of regulation are in place.[852]

In the context of mergers and acquisitions, an antitrust regulation in the data industry appears to be even easier and more organic as U.S. antitrust enforcers have the power to condition mergers and acquisitions with the adoption of specific antitrust remedies.[853] But, in December 2007 during the notable *Google/DoubleClick* transaction, the FTC did not take any action to recognize that "Google's proposed acquisition of DoubleClick [was] unlikely to substantially lessen competition."[854] Similar to Google, DoubleClick is active in online advertising. The FTC also observed that "[t]he markets within the online advertising space continue to quickly evolve, and predicting their future course is not a simple task."[855]

On August 22, 2012, the FTC green-lighted the Facebook acquisition of Instagram, although that acquisition substantially increased Facebook's power on several data markets.[856] On April 10, 2014, the FTC took passive action on Facebook's acquisition of WhatsApp by requiring WhatsApp to maintain its privacy promises to consumers despite Facebook's acquisition.[857]

In 2011, in Google's launch of Buzz, the FTC's action was more proactive, requiring the parties to adopt a comprehensive privacy program.[858] According to the former FTC Chairman Jon Leibowitz, that was the result of a "tough settlement that ensures that Google will honor its commitments to consumers and build strong privacy protection into all of its operations."[859] Thus, in such a context, the FTC changed its approach, moving from a no-intervention strategy in dealing with privacy (e.g., *Google/DoubleClick*) to a more proactive approach (e.g., *Google Buzz*).

852. *See*, e.g., Martin Taschdjian, *From Open Networks to Open Markets: How Public Policy Affects Infrastructure Investment Decisions*, 33 (November 2000), available at http://www.pirp.harvard.edu/.
853. *See*, e.g., DOJ, Antitrust Division Policy Guide To Merger Remedies (October 2004), available at https://www.justice.gov/atr/antitrust-division-policy-guide-merger-remedies-october-2004.
854. FTC, Federal Trade Commission Closes Google/DoubleClick Investigation, Proposed Acquisition Unlikely to Substantially Lessen Competition, Press Release (Dec. 20, 2007), https://www.ftc.gov/news-events/press-releases/2007/12/federal-trade-commission-closes-googledoubleclick-investigation.
855. *Ibid.*
856. FTC, FTC Closes Its Investigation Into Facebook's Proposed Acquisition of Instagram Photo Sharing Program, Press Release (Aug. 22, 2012) https://www.ftc.gov/news-events/press-releases/2012/08/ftc-closes-its-investigation-facebooks-proposed-acquisition.
857. FTC, FTC Notifies Facebook, WhatsApp of Privacy Obligations in Light of Proposed Acquisition, Press Release (Apr. 10, 2014) https://www.ftc.gov/news-events/press-releases/2014/04/ftc-notifiesfacebook-whatsapp-privacy-obligations-light-proposed. Bureau Director of the FTC, Jessica Rich, made it clear that "regardless of the acquisition, WhatsApp must continue to honor [its] promises to consumers. Further, if the acquisition is completed and WhatsApp fails to honor these promises, both companies could be in violation of Section 5 of the Federal Trade Commission (FTC) Act and, potentially, the FTC's order against Facebook." *Ibid.*
858. *In the Matter of* Google Inc., Decision and Order, File No. 102-3136, Dkt No. C-4336 (F.T.C., 2011) at 3.
859. FTC, FTC Charges Deceptive Privacy Practices in Googles Rollout of Its Buzz Social Network (Mar. 30, 2011), https://www.ftc.gov/news-events/press-releases/2011/03/ftc-charges-deceptive-privacy-practices-googles-rollout-its-buzz.

In summary, the fact that the data industry *implies* data and privacy protection issues should not limit the action of antitrust enforcers. Privacy can represent an important factor to compete[860] and when there is no regulation at all, antitrust appears to be the only government body that has the authority to enforce rules.[861] As it occurred in Germany, U.S. antitrust enforcers can effectively regulate data-driven markets and privacy issues by means of specific behavioral or structural antitrust remedies, although in the German Facebook case they were neither shared nor enshrined in a settlement.

### *[2] Network Industries and the Standardization Phenomena*

The data industry is characterized by network effects that lead to high barriers to entry and substantial concentration. This begs the question of whether or not antitrust and regulation should intervene, as these phenomena seem to be the natural consequences of network effects. There is also the risk that antitrust intervention leads to fragmentation of current platforms and technologies and increases consumers' switching costs.[862]

The proliferation of products that exhibit network effects puts emphasis on the issue of standardization and compatibility (more concentrated markets) versus fragmentation (less concentrated markets). If you have a social network where you can find most of your friends, this social network will likely attract more users as they benefit from the fact that they can communicate with each other through a unique platform. On the other hand, this platform becomes increasingly relevant and, in some cases, might turn out to be essential.

Network effects, which characterize both the data and telecommunication industry,[863] are very similar to the concept of economies of scale that existed since the

---

860. Allen P. Grunes & Maurice E. Stucke, *No Mistake about It: The Important Role of Antitrust in the Era of Big Data*, 5 (Antitrust Source, April 2015). *See also* Pamela John Harbour, Comm'r, Fed. Trade Comm'n, Dissenting Statement Regarding In re Google/DoubleClick, FTC File No. 071-0170 at 12 (Dec. 20, 2007), available at https://www.ftc.gov/sites/default/files/documents/public_statements/statement-matter-google/doubleclick/071220harbour_0.pdf; Pamela Johnes Harbour & Tara Isa Koslow, *Section 2 in a Web 2.0 World: An Expanded Vision of Relevant Product Markets*, 76 Antitrust L. J. 769, 773 (2010).

861. Massarotto, *From Standard Oil to Google: How the Role of Antitrust Law Has Changed*, *supra* n. 818, at 416.

862. Rubinfeld, *supra* n. 815, at 861. ("Network industries are created by network effects, whereby each individual's demand for a product is positively related to the usage of other individuals.") *Ibid. See also,* Neil Gandal, *Compatibility, Standardization, & Network Effects: Some Policy Implications*, 18 Oxford Rev. Econ. Policy 80, 82 (2002).

863. *See* Carl Shapiro & Hal R. Varian, *Information Rules: A Strategic Guide to the Network Economy*, 45 (Harv. U. Press, 1998); Filistrucchi, Geradin, Damme & Affeldt, *supra* n. 829. *See also* David S. Evans, *The Antitrust Economics of Multi-Sided Platform Markets*, 20 Yale J. on Reg. 325 (2003); Jean-Charles Rochet & Jean Tirole, *Two-Sided Markets: A Progress Report*, 37 Rand J. Econ. 645 (2006); Jean-Charles Rochet & Jean Tirole, *Platform Competition in Two-Sided Markets*, 1 J. Eur. Econ. Ass'n 990, 990-991; Brief for *Amici Curiae* J. Gregory Sidak & Robert D. Willig in Support of Respondents, *State of Ohio v. American Express Co.*, No. 16-1454, Supreme Court of the United States (Jan. 23, 2018), 2018 WL 565325; J. Gregory Sidak & Robert

*Standard Oil* case.[864] In both economies of scale and network effects, utility garnered is related to the number of consumers or users. When consumers or users exponentially increase, it quickly translates into market power for the company.[865] Therefore, network effects, albeit complex, are something relatively new.

Similar to what happened in the telecommunication markets decades ago, in data driven-markets, network effects can easily lead to the situation where "a 'winner takes all' result where concentration is a likely outcome of market success."[866] This is not necessarily bad for competition and consumers, but the dominating incumbent firm might be tempted to engage in anticompetitive practices to keep its supremacy or to exert its monopoly power in ancillary markets.[867] Antitrust enforcers are necessary as the gatekeepers of markets to oversee that no one engages in anticompetitive conduct to profit beyond what is attainable in open and free markets.

The leading case for explaining the risk of anticompetitive practices in network industries is *Microsoft*, explored in Chapter 1, or the AT&T case, examined in both Chapter 1 and the following Section §7.03. In the late 1990s, Microsoft held monopoly power in the operating system for PC and was accused of engaging in an exclusive-dealing regime with OEMs and tying its operating system (Windows) to its browser (Internet Explorer).[868] Microsoft cases were closed with remedies enshrined in consent decrees that required Microsoft to modify its behavior. Although in the U.S. no antitrust violation was identified, the Microsoft cases clearly demonstrated that the temptation of a company to engage in anticompetitive practices in order to extend its monopoly power in secondary markets could be compelling.[869] Today, the same concerns exist regarding Google and Facebook developing monopoly power in a variety of data-driven markets.

Again, being a dominant incumbent firm with monopoly power is not unlawful as it might be a natural consequence of acting in a network industry and this can benefit markets and consumers in the end. An antitrust action against a dominant incumbent firm by default can discourage similar incumbent firms from continuing to invest in

---

D. Willing, *Two-Sided Market Definition and Competitive Effects for Credit Cards after United States v. American Express*, 1 Criterion J. on Innovation 1301 (2016).

864. *See* Massarotto, *From Standard Oil to Google: How the Role of Antitrust Law Has Changed*, *supra* n. 818; *Standard Oil Co. of NJ v. United States*, 221 U.S. 1, 50 (1911).

865. *See* Shapiro & Varian, *supra* n. 863, at 45; Giovanna Massarotto, *How a Simple Agreement Affects Digital Markets—An Antitrust Perspective*, Diritto Mercato Tecnologia 2, 4 (2017); Hanna Halaburda, Bruno Jullien & Yaroh Yehezkel, *Dynamic Competition with Network Externalities: Why History Matters* 8, Working Paper n. TSE-636, available at https://www.tse-fr.eu/sites/default/files/TSE/documents/doc/wp/2016/wp_636.pdf (March 2016). *See also* Nicholas Economides, *The Internet and Network Economics*, available at http://www.stern.nyu.edu/networks/Economides_Internet_and_Network_Economics.pdf, at 247.

866. OECD, Data-driven Innovation for Growth and Well-being 7 (October 2014) available at https://www.oecd.org/sti/inno/data-driven-innovation-interim-synthesis.pdf.

867. Rubinfeld, *supra* n. 815, at 860.

868. Rubinfeld, *supra* n. 73.

869. Rubinfeld, *supra* n. 815, at 874. ("Dynamic network industries present substantial opportunities for firms to manipulate standards for anticompetitive advantage.") *Ibid.*

new technologies and developing increasingly advanced products and services.[870] Alexander Bell was both the founder of AT&T (which maintained its monopoly on the U.S. telephone industry until the antitrust decision of 1982)[871] and the inventor of the telephone.[872]

However, the risk that large companies may engage in anticompetitive conduct is high, as they are the ones that have more to lose in the development of alternative products and platforms. Lack of intervention certainly does not discourage today's dominant incumbents with monopoly power from taking the short cut and engaging in potentially illegal conduct. One of the people most skeptical about regulation, Professor Alfred E. Kahn, recognized that the access to some facilities of newly deregulated monopoly utilities is required for the entry of competition.[873]

In summary, standardization and the creation of dominant incumbent firms in network industries such as Google is not bad for competition, but it is not a reason for antitrust agencies to turn a blind eye. A good compromise between the risk of wrongly punishing companies and no intervention at all might be that antitrust agencies provide companies with guidelines on how to limit the risk of anticompetitive practices. In the most challenging situations, antitrust authorities should require companies to adopt specific remedies. For example, the agency may ask a company to adopt a compliance program similar to that required by the FTC in *Google/ITA* merger.

When uncharted markets need rules, antitrust can serve as the most valuable market guidance. Antitrust remedies defined with the same companies subject to investigation and enshrined in consent decrees can be the best way to go forward in the data industry where the risk of wrongfully punishing conduct is high.

### *[3] Is Antitrust Adept to Tackle Data Markets?*

Antitrust agencies may think that, because Google acts in new, dynamic and unpredictable markets, traditional antitrust tools are not effective to deal with such markets.[874] Thus, antitrust would need new tools[875] or it remains simply unable to govern today's data-driven markets.

Most of today's digital markets are two-sided[876] and built on increasingly sophisticated algorithms (also known as *machine learning*).[877] Algorithms can enable computers to perform a variety of tasks, from how to play chess to how to collude

870. The Guardian, Revealed: Facebook's global lobbying against data privacy laws (Mar. 2, 2019), https://www.theguardian.com/technology/2019/mar/02/facebook-global-lobbying-campaign-against-data-privacy-laws-investment.
871. *United States v. American Tel. and Tel. Co.*, 552 F. Supp. 131 (D.D.C. 1982).
872. AT&T, Milestones in AT&T History, https://www.corp.att.com/history/milestones.html.
873. Alfred E. Kahn, *The Deregulatory Tar Baby: The Precarious Balance Between Regulation and Deregulation, 1970-2000 and Henceforward*, 21 J. Regulatory Econ. 35, 53 (2002).
874. *See*, e.g., Ezrachi & Stucke, *supra* n. 816.
875. *Ibid.*, at 1809.
876. Melamed, *supra* n. 815; Evans, *supra* n. 815; Rubinfeld, *supra* n. 815; Gifford & Kudrle, *supra* n. 815.
877. *See*, e.g., Ezrachi & Stucke, *supra* n. 816.

within markets.[878] Therefore, algorithms can, at the same time, improve the quality of goods and facilitate transparency and collusion in markets. As the OECD observed, pricing algorithms based on *machine learning* can benefit consumers.[879] A good example of this is the ride-sharing company, Uber, which developed a pricing algorithm that matches drivers to passengers seeking rides by means of a real-time pricing algorithm. A study estimated a consumer surplus of USD 2.9 billion was generated by Uber's algorithm (UberX) services in four U.S. cities.[880]

Adopting an entirely new mechanism to enforce antitrust law any time markets find new ways to engage in anticompetitive conduct seems extremely costly. Moreover, there is a lag required to implement such mechanisms and, during the time necessary to test such tools and to assess the related costs and benefits, companies might have changed techniques to conspire again. However, leaving data markets free to engage in anticompetitive conduct because companies found a new and more efficient way to do it by means of algorithms[881] does not seem appropriate. The fact that companies innovate "should not insulate [them] from antitrust scrutiny or license [them] to take anticompetitive actions,"[882] Professor Frank M. Fisher observed.

Antitrust law does not need to change its nature or tools. But, similar to companies, antitrust agencies might start using algorithms to assess pro and anticompetitive effects of, for example, pricing algorithms. Antitrust agencies may also require companies to implement within their software a command that instructs the computer to redo the process if collusion or other antitrust practices are detected. These issues are further explored in Chapter 9.

Meanwhile, the following economic analysis will predict the effects of implementing the same antitrust remedies enshrined in the AT&T consent decree of 1982 to the Google Search market. True telecommunication and search online advertisements markets might have several differences. But they are both characterized by network effects and both AT&T and Google platforms are perceived as essential in these markets.

---

878. Giovanna Massarotto, *From Digital to Blockchain Markets: What Role for Antitrust and Regulation* (Jan. 26, 2019) available at SSRN: https://ssrn.com/abstract=3323420 or http://dx.doi.org/10.2139/ssrn.3323420.
879. OECD, *Personalized Pricing in the Digital Era* (Nov. 28, 2018), http://www.oecd.org/officialdocuments/publicdisplaydocumentpdf/?cote=DAF/COMP(2018)13&docLanguage=En.
880. Peter Cohen, Robert Hahn, Jonathan Hall, Steven Levitt & Robert Metcalfe, *Using Big Data to Estimate Consumer Surplus: The Case of Uber* (Aug. 30, 2016), https://www.ftc.gov/system/files/documents/public_comments/2018/08/ftc-2018-0048-d-0124-155312.pdf.
881. Ezrachi & Stucke, *supra* n. 816, at 1809.
882. Fisher, *supra* n. 814, at 559.

## §7.03 AN ECONOMIC ANALYSIS OF GOOGLE'S CONSENT DECREE

### [A] Introduction

The main justifications behind a no antitrust intervention in Google markets (as outlined above)—are unconvincing.[883] In the following, I envisage the adoption of some specific behavioral and structural antitrust remedies enshrined in a consent decree to deal with *Google Search Bias* case described in Section §7.02. The adoption of both structural and behavioral remedies will be examined through an economic analysis, which aims to forecast the related economic effects on Google Search market by adopting a *yardstick* method.

In the context of antitrust, the "*yardstick*" method is usually adopted for calculating antitrust damages[884] by comparing the economic conditions of the company subject to an antitrust violation with those of a similar uninjured company.[885] The logic underlying the yardstick method in assessing antitrust damages is that "but for" the anticompetitive conduct, the company's business would have performed as the comparable firm.[886] In such an analysis it is fundamental that the yardstick company is comparable in all crucial respects to the harmed firm. The similarities between Google and AT&T are compelling: both companies were accused of monopolizing markets in the telecommunication and the data industry engaging in exclusionary conduct. As outlined in Section §7.02, significant network effects are present in both the telecommunication and data industries. Both Google and AT&T own a platform that is perceived as essential by market players; due to network effects such platforms enabled them to gain market power in vertical integrated markets. Google and AT&T acted in very concentrated markets that they have created and might have monopolized. AT&T will be the comparable company and the telecommunications industry the comparable industry of my analysis.

In addition, to determine antitrust damages, the *yardstick* approach is employed to forecast the efficiency of a regulation when the agency is lacking of sufficient information, such as market demand and costs[887]— "*yardstick regulation.*" The regulatory agency uses information on the performance of regulated firms active in distinct markets to lead to an efficient solution in other markets. Remedies enshrined in *antitrust consent* decrees are regulatory in nature and anticipating the efficiency of such remedies is the issue at hand. Here I will use AT&T remedies enshrined in the

883. *See* Fisher, *supra* n. 814, at 563. As Professor Fisher noted although "it is true that antitrust in innovative, quickly changing industries must be carefully applied" we cannot draw the conclusion that "antitrust has no place in innovative industries." *Ibid.*, at 564.

884. Justin McCrary & Daniel L. Rubinfeld, D. L., *Measuring Benchmark Damages in Antitrust Litigation*, 3 J. Econometric Methods 63 (2014); *See*, e.g., Areeda, Blair & Hovenkamp, *supra* n. 12, at 486 ¶ 391f. (2d ed., 2000).

885. Roger D. Blair & Amanda Kay Esquibel, *Yardstick Damages in Lost Profit Cases: An Econometric Approach*, 72 Denv. U. L. Rev. 113 (1994). *See also National Farmers' Org., Inc. v. Associated Milk Producers, Inc.*, 850 F.2d 1286 (8th Cir. 1988). *Home Placement Serv., Inc. v. Providence Journal Co.*, 819 F.2d 1199, 1206 (1st Cir. 1987).

886. Blair & Esquibel, *supra* n. 885, at 114.

887. Viscusi, Harrington & Vemon, *supra* n. 37, at 442.

consent decree of 1982 employed in the telecommunication markets to predict the efficiency of the same remedies in another market—Google's search engines markets.

The yardstick approach needs an economic technique to be put into practice and to provide useful economic results as is a general methodology. The chosen economic technique to anticipate the outcomes of both behavioral and structural remedies (such as Google *break-up*) enshrined in Google's consent decrees is the multi-regression analysis.[888]

Regression analysis is considered as the primary tool to deal with empirical research.[889] Put simply the regression analysis is a basic tool of econometrics useful in measuring the correlation of one or more economic variables—thus the precise relationship between two or more factors. For example, the regression analysis is used to examine wage discrimination against women,[890] therefore the possible impact of gender in determining the hourly wage. Here it will be used to measure the possible impact and efficiency of specific antitrust remedies, such as Google break-up, in Google's Search market.

The U.S. courts have widely recognized both the use of regression analysis[891] and the yardstick method[892] as admissible scientific evidence.

### [B] Google Search Bias Consent Decree

In *Google Search Bias* case, the main antitrust concern was that Google might have intentionally manipulated its algorithm by altering both organic and paid search results favoring its own services at the expense of rivals.[893]

Several of Google's search engine rivals have supported those antitrust allegations. In particular, between 2010 and 2011, a group of businesses and organizations called FairSearch[894] published two white papers[895] according to which Google has

888. Blair & Esquibel, *supra* n. 885, at 120.
889. William H. Greene, *Econometric Analysis* 7 (Prentice Hall 5th ed., 2003).
890. Franklin M. Fisher, *Multiple Regression in Legal Proceedings*, 80 Colum. L. Rev. 702, 721 (1980).
891. *See*, e.g., *Petruzzi's IGA Supermarkets v. Darling-Delaware Co.*, 998 F.2d 1224, 1238 (3d Cir. 1993), *cert. denied*, 510 U.S. 994 (1993); *LePage's, Inc. v. 3M*, 324 F 3d 141, 165 (3d Cir. 2003). *See also*, Daniel Rubinfeld, *Econometrics in Court*, 85 Colum. L. Rev. 1048 (1985). In court a "greater acceptance of statistics has opened the door to law-related econometrics studies, particularly in connection with the use of multiple regression models." *Ibid.*
892. 327 U.S. 251 (1946). *See also National Farmers' Org., Inc. v. Associated Milk Producers, Inc.*, 850 F.2d 1286 (8th Cir. 1988). *In re* Rubber Chem. Antitrust Litig., 232 F.R.D. 346, 354 (N.D. Cal., 2005).
893. *See*, e.g., *See*, e.g., *In the Matter of* Google Inc, Statement of the Federal Trade Commission Regarding Google's Search Practices, *supra* n. 830, at 2; Ratliff & Rubinfield, *supra* n. 471.
894. FairSearch members include Expedia, Tripadvisor, Nokia and Oracle, some of the most significant Google rivals.
895. Fairsearch, Can Search Discrimination by a Monopolist Violate U.S. Antitrust Laws? (2011), available at http://www.fairsearch.org/wp-content/uploads/2011/07/Can-Search-Discrimination-by-a-Monopolist-Violate-U.S.-Antitrust-Laws1.pdf.

"monopoly in Internet search and search advertising."[896] FairSearch observed that Google's search engine answers users' queries by first offering Google's products, such as Google Maps and YouTube, instead of providing pure organic results. In other words, before showing any results provided by rivals, Google would use, for example, Google Maps to provide location and direction information, or YouTube to provide video content by altering its algorithm.[897] According to FairSearch, Google would leverage "its dominance in search to subdue its rivals"[898] by means of exclusionary conduct.

Therefore the relevant markets considered in the analysis of *Google Search Bias* case appear to be:

(1) the market of horizontal search engines (e.g., Google Search Horizontal Platform);
(2) the market of vertical search engines (e.g., Google Flights, Booking, Expedia).[899]

Section [1] investigates AT&T consent decrees of 1982 with a focus on the economic effects of the adopted antitrust remedies in the telecommunication industry. A special emphasis will be put on the evolution of market shares, AT&T R&D expenditures, industry revenue and market concentration before and after the antitrust intervention.

Section [2] examines the economic effects in the adoption of the same remedies enshrined in AT&T consent decree of 1982 in Google and the search engine industry on which is sold digital advertising. A multi-regression model based on a yardstick method will allow anticipating the evolution of the market concentration in the digital search advertising (Google's Search market) through the assessment of the Herfindahl-Hirschman Index (HHI) index from 2019 to 2021.

Once I have determined the HHI, which is commonly used to measure competition in markets,[900] in Google Search's market, I can evaluate the pro or anticompetitive effects of the adopted remedies in Google Search's market. If the market concentration decreased after the antitrust intervention we can deduce that such remedies are effective. In the opposite scenario, if the HHI increases we can assume that the adopted remedies were anticompetitive or ineffective.

896. Fairsearch, Google's Transformation from Gateway to Gatekeeper: How Google's Exclusionary and Anticompetitive Conduct Restricts Innovation and Deceives Consumers, http://www.fairsearch.org/wp-content/uploads/2011/10/Googles-Transformation-from-Gateway-to-Gatekeeper.pdf.
897. *Ibid.*
898. Google Strategy: If You Can't Buy 'em, Use Your Dominance to Crush 'em, Fairsearch (Sep. 1, 2011), http://www.fairsearch.org/search-manipulation/google-strategy-if-you-cant-buy-em-useyour-dominance-to-crush-em/.
899. *See*, e.g., *In the Matter of* Google Inc, Statement of the Federal Trade Commission Regarding Google's Search Practices, *supra* n. 830, at 1.
900. The HHI is a commonly used measure of market concentration to determine competition in markets. It is calculated by squaring the market shares of the firms active in the same market.

### *[1] AT&T Break-up: The Effects on the Telecommunication Markets*

As explored in Chapter 1, AT&T is the telecommunication company founded on February 28, 1885, by the inventor of the telephone—Alexander Bell.[901] AT&T became the holding company of the so-called *Bell System*, which acted in the entire production chain of telephone services: long distance, local distance and telecommunication equipment markets.[902] The *Bell System* encompassed the parent company AT&T, Bell Telephone companies, Bell Telephone Laboratories, Inc., and Western Electric Co.[903] AT&T provided long-distance telephone lines through its subsidiary AT&T Long Lines, which owned the physical infrastructure. AT&T also offered local distance services for calls within a limited geographic area through twenty-two Bell System Operating Companies. Yet, AT&T provided telecommunication equipment necessary for consumers to enjoy telecommunication services by means of its subsidiaries Western Electric, Bell Laboratories, and American Bell.[904]

In summary, AT&T acted—until 1982 when the *antitrust consent* decree required AT&T to break-up—as a natural monopoly in the entire production chain of telephone services: long distance, local distance and telecommunication equipment markets.[905] The AT&T consent decree of 1982 is also referred to Modification of Final Judgment (MFJ) as it is the 1956 AT&T consent decree in its modified form. The AT&T consent decree of 1956 did not require any structural relief (only behavior remedies), while the MFJ required AT&T to divest seven subsidiaries that provided long-distance service, out of its twenty-two BOCs.

From 1975 to 1983, AT&T held a market share which ranged from 98.8 percent in 1975 to 92.1 percent in 1983.[906] The Figure 7.1 below depicts AT&T market share in the telecommunication industry before the AT&T break-up, which was never below 90 percent.

901. Massarotto, *From Standard Oil to Google: How the Role of Antitrust Law Has Changed*, *supra* n. 818; AT&T, Milestones in AT&T History, https://www.corp.att.com/history/milestones.html.
902. FTC, Measurements of Market Power in Long Distance Telecommunications (April 1995), available at https://www.ftc.gov/sites/default/files/documents/reports/measurements-market-power-long-distance-telecommunications/232316_0.pdf.
903. *Notes, Antitrust: Consent Decree: The History and Effect of Western Electric Co. v. United States, 1956 Trade Cas. 71,134* (D.C.N.J. 1956), 45 Cornell L. Q. 88 (1960).
904. *See*, e.g., Kevin G. Wilson, *Deregulating Telecommunications: U.S. and Canadian Telecommunications*, 1840-1997 (Rowman & Littlefield Pub., 2000).
905. FTC, Measurements of Market Power in Long Distance Telecommunications, *supra* n. 902.
906. *See* John E. Kwoka, *The Effects of Divestiture, Privatization, and Competition and Productivity in U.S. and U.K. Telecommunications*, 8 Rev. Industrial Organization 49, 54 (1993).

*Figure 7.1 AT&T Market Share Pre-AT&T Break-up*

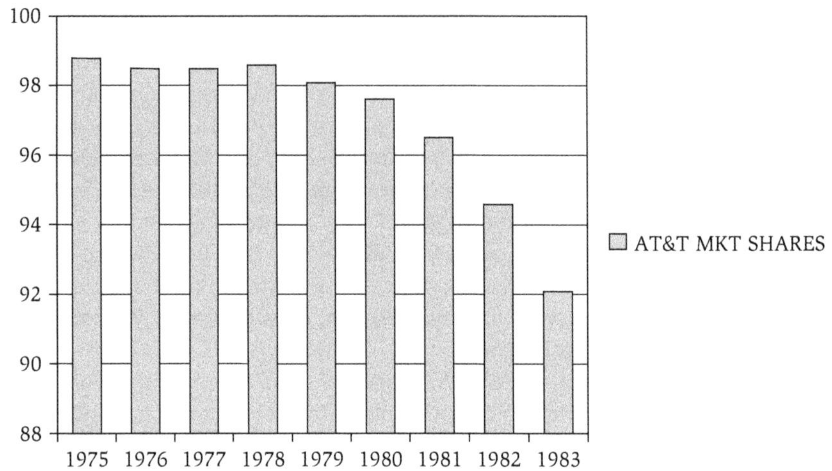


In 1982, the MFJ required AT&T to break-up into several companies.[907] On January 1, 1984, the AT&T divestiture formally occurred.[908]

The theory underpinning the *AT&T break-up* was the Baxter "quarantine theory,"[909] according to which the solution to the AT&T monopolization conduct was to "separate—quarantine—the competitive and potentially competitive from the monopoly portion of AT&T." According to this theory, AT&T needed to divest "[its] local exchange companies to provide all long-distance carriers equal access and service to their bottleneck local facilities."[910]

In addition to the divestiture, the MFJ forbid BOCs to provide "long distance services and information services, and from manufacturing equipment used in the telecommunications industry."[911] Moreover, it "specifically barred the divested telephone companies from manufacturing or marketing customer premises equipment, from providing long-distance service, from providing directory advertising such as the Yellow Pages, and from offering services where they controlled the information content."[912]

After the divestiture, AT&T continued to operate the long-distance and manufacturing units of its remaining BOCs. AT&T's structure pre and post divestiture is depicted in Figure 7.2.

907. Massarotto, *From Standard Oil to Google: How the Role of Antitrust Law Has Changed, supra* n. 818, at 400.
908. Paul W. MacAvoy & Kenneth Robinson, *Losing By Judicial Policymaking: The First Year of the AT&T Divestiture,* 2 Yale J. on Reg. 225 (1985).
909. *See*, e.g., Sidak & Spulber, *supra* n. 55; Shelanski & Sidak, *supra* n. 55; *see also* Baumol & Sidak, *supra* n. 55.
910. *See* Cole, *supra* n. 40, at 7.
911. *United States v. AT&T*, 522 F. Supp. 131 at 224.
912. Shooshan III, *supra* n. 57. *See also United States v. AT&T*, 522 F. Supp. 131 at 143.

*Figure 7.2 AT&T Pre and Post the Divestiture*

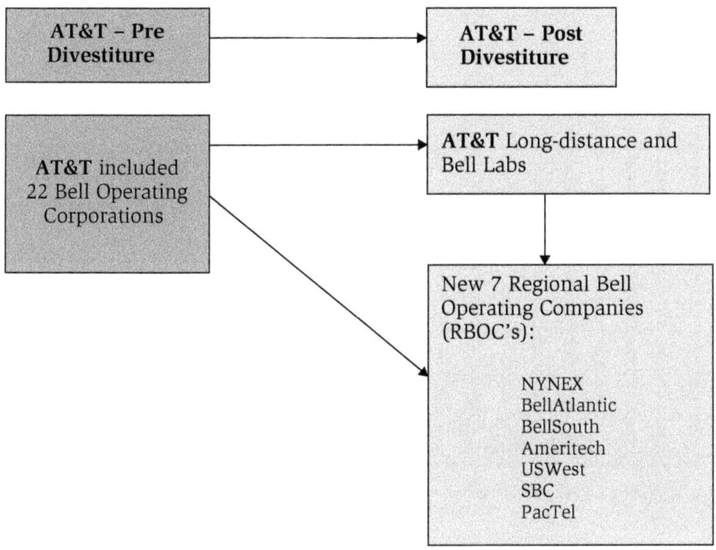


### *[a] Market Share*

Following the MFJ, AT&T's market share significantly decreased, and the telecommunications market never looked the same. As shown in Figure 7.3, in 1984 AT&T held a market share of 90 percent,[913] which decreased to around 47 percent[914] in 1996. In 2011, AT&T held a market share in the long-distance market of 24 percent.[915]

913. Here are considered market share based on revenues of long distance carriers only. *See* FTC, Statistics of Communications Common Carriers, Table 1.5 (1996), available at http://www.fcc.gov/reports/statistics-communications-common-carriers-1996.
914. *Ibid.*, at 8. Indeed, the Commission after the 1984 breakup of AT&T started to reduce long-distance rates and make cost recovery more efficient. Jerry Hausman & Howard Shelanskij, *Economic Welfare and Telecommunications Regulation: The E-Rate Policy for Universal-Service Subsidies*, 16 Yale J. on Reg. 19, 23 (1999).
915. Statista, Long distance telecom market share in the U.S. in 2011, by service provider, available at http://www.statista.com/statistics/214202/us-long-distance-telecom-market-shares-by-provider/.

*Figure 7.3 Telecommunications Industry: Long Distance Market Shares*

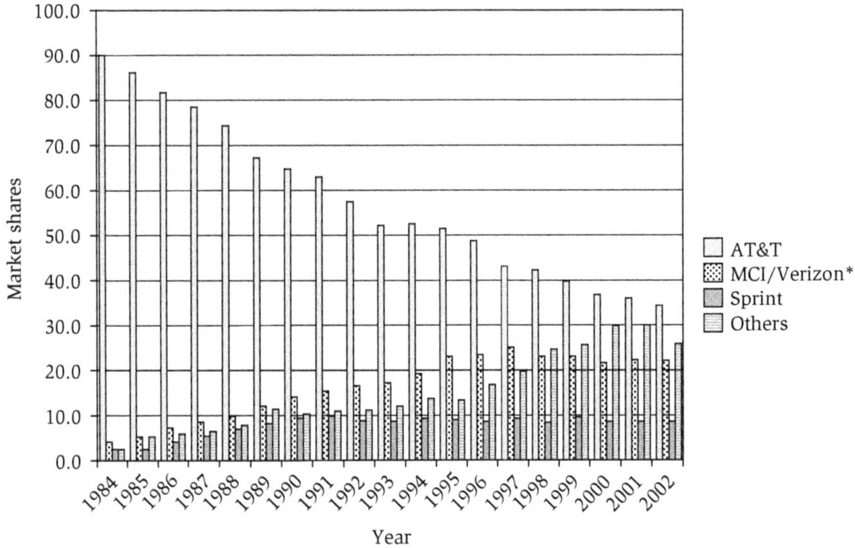


*Source: FCC Report 2003*[916] * MCI: It was founded in 1963 and it was purchased by WordCom in 2000 and in 2006 the company was bought by Verizon.

### *[b] U.S. Telecommunication Industry Revenues*

Despite the fact that the AT&T's market share has been decreasing, according to the FCC's 1995 study, AT&T increased its output, measured by the number of calling minutes, by two-thirds over 1984 levels.[917] In other words, since AT&T's break-up, industry output has nearly tripled. This does not imply that is all due to the consent decree as the market was expanding and more people began using telephone service, but it is likely that the decree has prompted such a growth. The number of telephone subscribers (households), for example, increased from 78.9 millions in 1984 to over 97.4 millions in 1998.[918]

The following Figure 7.4 shows the trend of the U.S. telecommunication industry revenue from 1978 to 1992, which increased steadily.

916. FCC, Federal Communications Commission Releases *Statistics of Communications Common Carriers, see Table 1.5* at 8 (October 2004), available at https://transition.fcc.gov/Bureaus/Common_Carrier/Reports/FCC-State_Link/SOCC/03socc.pdf.
917. FTC, Measurements of Market Power in Long Distance Telecommunications, *supra* n. 902, at 4.
918. *See* Industry Analysis Division, Common Carrier Bureau, *Trends in Telephone Service* (September 1999), at 17-3.

*Figure 7.4 U.S. Telecommunication Industry Revenues (in millions USD)*

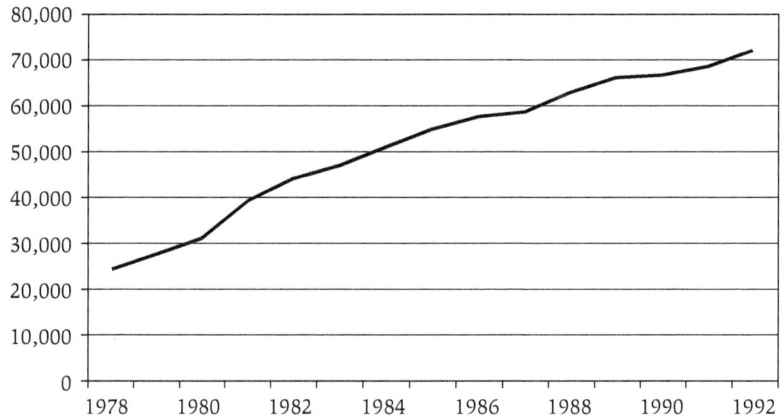


*Source: FCC Report 1997.*[919]

Furthermore, the AT&T divestiture reduced prices for customer equipment and services and of distance calls, which became more competitive.[920] According to the FCC, the price of a long-distance call dropped "from 32 cents per minute to 7 cents per minute," from 1984 to 2006, thus the price decrease was more than 85 percent.[921]

### *[c] R&D*

The AT&T R&D expenditures as a percentage of operating revenue increased "to an average of about 7 % between 1984 and 1994,"[922] while between 1962 and 1983 AT&T R&D expenditures as a percentage of operating revenue increased by an average of 2.6 percent (Figure 7.5).

919. Jim Lande & Linda Blake, *Trends in the U.S. International Telecommunications Industry*, 2 (1997) https://transition.fcc.gov/Bureaus/Common_Carrier/Reports/FCC-State_Link/Intl/itltrd97.pdf.
920. *Ibid.*
921. FCC, Trend in Telephone Industry—Industry Analysis and Technology Division Wireline Competition Bureau 13-1 available at https://apps.fcc.gov/edocs_public/attachmatch/DOC-284932A1.pdf. The FCC specified that "[t]he average price of 7 cents per minute represents a mix of international calling (10 cents per minute) and domestic interstate calling (6 cents per minute)." *Ibid.*
922. Anusua Datta, *Divestiture and Its Implications for Innovation and Productivity Growth in the U.S. Telecommunications*, 69 Southern Economic J. 644, 648 (2003).

*Figure 7.5 AT&T R&D Expenditures from 1974 to 1994 (Percentage of Operating Revenues %)*

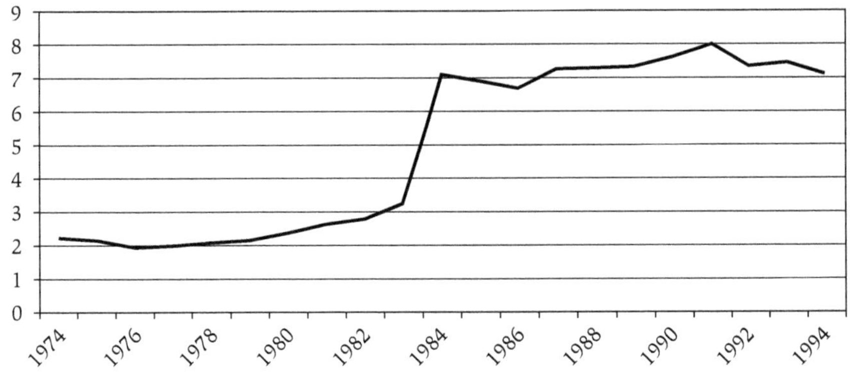


*Source: Annual Reports of AT&T and Western Electric Company, Moody's Public Utility Manual.*

### *[d] CPI for Telecommunication Services*

The CPI for the telecommunication services decreased after the AT&T consent decree. The CPI for telephone services is based on "*market basket*" of services purchase, which represents the telephone-related expenditures of a typical urban household, including land-line telephone service and wireless telephone service. Conversely, the overall CPI measures the impact of inflation on consumers. The following Figure 7.6 shows the trend of the CPI for telephone services from 1978 to 1992 along with the CPI related to all goods and services.[923]

923. *Universal Service Monitoring Report*, CC Docket No. 98-202, 2011 (Data Received Through October 2011), prepared by the Federal and State Staff for the Federal- State Joint Board on Universal Service in CC Docket No. 96-45, Table 4.2, at 4 - 4.

*Figure 7.6 CPI Telephone Services and All Items (Goods and Services) in %*

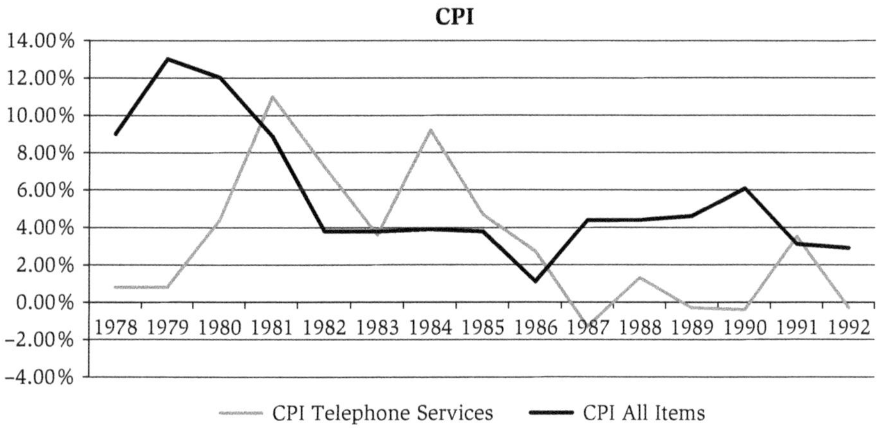


*Source: FCC Report 2011.*[924]

From 1978 to 1988, the CPI index for telephone services tells us that there were two major rate shocks: (1) the first shock occurred from 1980-1982 (thus before the antitrust intervention); (2) the second one occurred from 1984 until 1986. As also Roger G. Noll & Susan R. Smart noted, the first shock have "little to do with federal policy changes,"[925] whereas the second rate shock was likely linked to both the *antitrust consent* decree of 1982 and FCC policies.[926]

### *[e] Market Concentration*

I use the HHI[927] to measure market concentration in the AT&T's market, which will be the dependent variable (Y) of my multi-regression model as the HHI is one of the most common criteria to determine market competitiveness. The HHI is the result of the sum of the square of market shares of the firms active in the market at hand. If there is only a firm in the market the HHI is 10,000; if there are thousands of firms the HHI is zero indicating that there is almost perfect competition in the market.

924. FCC data. *See*, FCC, Universal Service Monitoring Report, CC Docket No. 98-202, available at http://www.fcc.gov/reports/monitoring-report-december-2011 (October 2011), 4-4: FCC, Trend in Telephone Service 13-4 (September 1999), available at http://transition.fcc.gov/Bureaus/Common_Carrier/Reports/FCC-State_Link/IAD/trend199.pdf.
925. *See* Roger G. Noll & Susan R. Smart, *The Political Economics of State Responses to Divestiture and Federal Deregulation in Telecommunications*, in Barry Cole, ed., After the Breakup Assessing the New Post At&T Divestiture Era 189 (Columbia U. Press, 1991).
926. *Ibid.*, at 191.
927. The HHI is a commonly used measure of market concentration to determine competition in markets. It is calculated by squaring the market shares of the firms active in the same market.

The DOJ usually considers a market with an HHI of lower than 1,500 competitive and when the HHI is equal or greater than 2,500 it is highly concentrated.[928] In 1979, AT&T held 98 percent of the market and the square of AT&T market share is 9623.1. Thus, the AT&T market was considered to be a monopoly by the DOJ estimates.

In 1980 the HHI considering the AT&T market share slightly decreased to 9525.76 and in 1981 (the year before the antitrust intervention) was of 9312.25. In 1984, thus when the AT&T divestiture took place, the HHI was 8145.55, in 1985 it decreased to 7484.7 and in 1986 the HHI was 6783.86. From 1984 to 1992, the standard deviation of the HHI, which tells us the average of distance from the mean, is 1531.13. Figure 7.7 shows the HHI trend in AT&T market from 1979 to 1992.

*Figure 7.7 HHI in the Telecommunication Market*

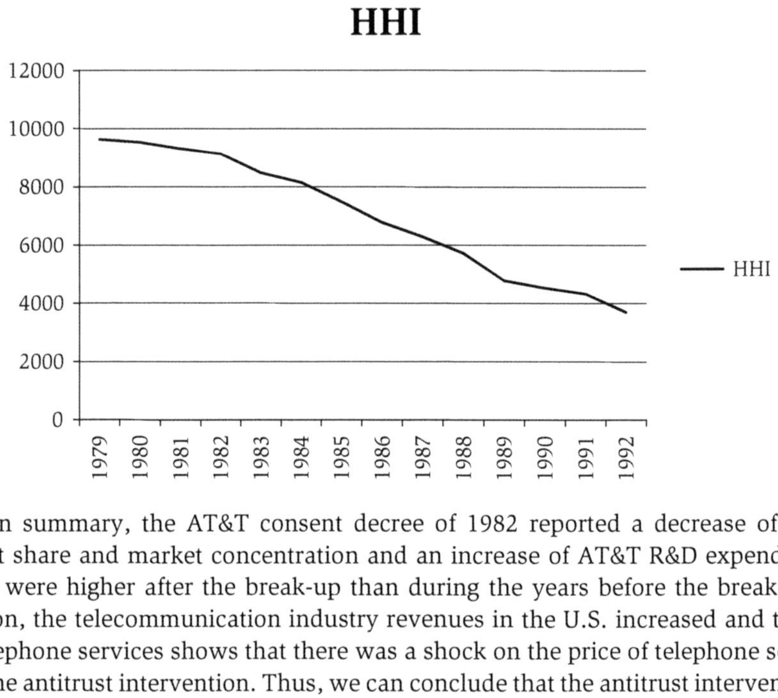


In summary, the AT&T consent decree of 1982 reported a decrease of AT&T market share and market concentration and an increase of AT&T R&D expenditures, which were higher after the break-up than during the years before the break-up. In addition, the telecommunication industry revenues in the U.S. increased and the CPI for telephone services shows that there was a shock on the price of telephone services after the antitrust intervention. Thus, we can conclude that the antitrust intervention in AT&T case of 1982 allowed competition to prevail in the long-distance market, and it is an important example that illustrates the procompetitive effects of antitrust structural remedies.[929]

According to Judge Richard A. Posner, there is no doubt that the divestiture increased competition in the long-distance telephone market, although other factors

928. DOJ, Herfindahl-Hirschman Index, https://www.justice.gov/atr/herfindahl-hirschman-index.
929. Posner, *supra* n. 63, at 110.

contributed. For example, we have to consider the introduction of new technologies and the deregulation that at that time occurred in the telecommunication industry.[930]

The MFJ might not be the best procompetitive relief, but it was time-sensitive and perhaps the only way to *de facto* interrupt a monopoly in one of the most fundamental markets.[931]

### *[2] Google Break-up*

Here I analyze the economic effects of the Google break-up and others behavioral remedies imposed by means of the AT&T consent decree of 1982, to deal with Google possible monopolization in both horizontal and vertical search engines markets. In the following analysis the envisaged consent decree imposes on Google the mandate to split into different corporations:

(1) Google Horizontal Search Engine (*Google platform*).
(2) Google Vertical Search Engines (*Google Search Products*, such as Google flights, Google shopping).

Google Search Horizontal Platform will be treated as the AT&T long-distance network and Google vertical search engines (e.g., Google Flights) as the Bell Companies that were locally active in the distribution of telecommunication services—hence in the vertical integrated market.

Google's structure pre and post divestiture is depicted in Figure 7.8.

930. *Ibid.*
931. Massarotto, *From Standard Oil to Google: How the Role of Antitrust Law Has Changed*, *supra* n. 818, at 401.

*Figure 7.8 Google Pre and Post the Divestiture*

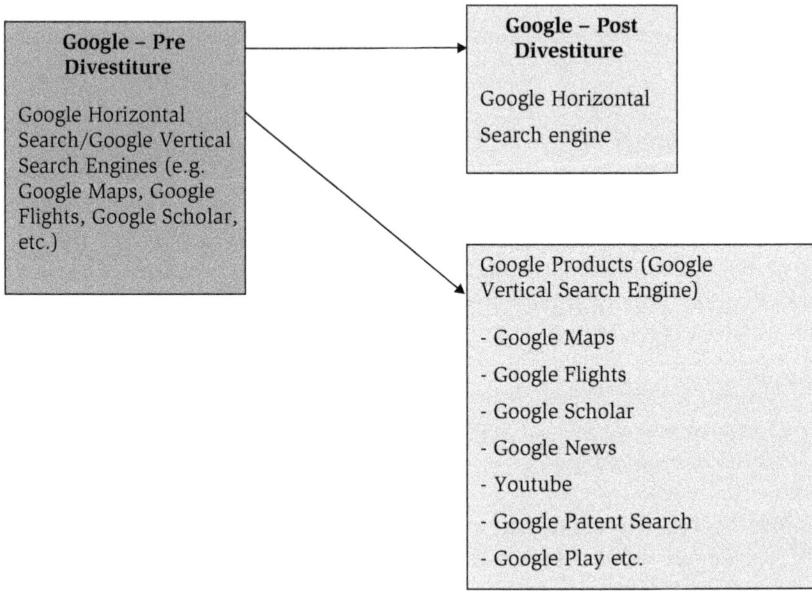


Similar to the AT&T consent decree of 1982, Google consent decree would also forbid Google companies active in the vertical search engines markets (Google products) to provide horizontal search engine and information services, and from providing accessories services used in the Search Engine industry.

Before performing a multi-regression analysis I examine the trend of Google Search market shares, Google R&D expenditures and the search digital advertising revenue from 2010 to 2018.

### *[a] Market Share*

Figure 7.9 shows the variation of Google's market shares from 2008 to 2018 in the horizontal search engines market in the United States.

*Figure 7.9 Search Engine Industry: Horizontal Search Engine Market Shares in the U.S.*

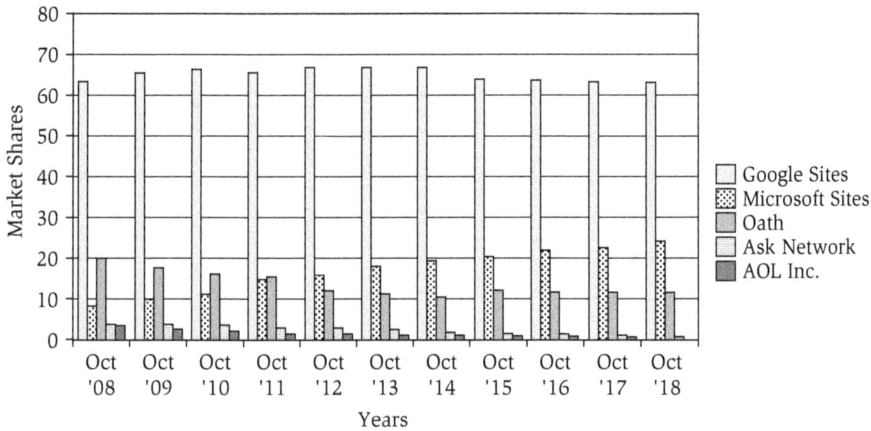


*Source: Statista 2019.*

From 2008 to 2018, Google's market share has varied from 63 percent to 67 percent. In 2016 Google market share was 63.6 percent, in 2017 it decreased to 63.4 percent and in 2018 it was 63.1 percent.

### *[b] R&D*

I examine the variance of research and development expenditures of Alphabet (Google's parent company) before the hypothetical antitrust intervention from 2014 to 2018. According to Nasdaq, in 2017 Alphabet spent 16.62 billion, which corresponds to 15 percent of its revenue in R&D.[932] In 2018, Alphabet reported revenues of USD 136.815 billion[933] and a total spending on R&D of USD 21.31 billion, again about 15 percent of the total Alphabet revenues.

The following Figure 7.10 reports the Alphabet R&D expenditure as a percentage of the total Alphabet revenues from 2014 to 2018.

932. Prableen Bajpai, *6 Companies Spending The Most on R&D*, Nasdaq (Aug. 8, 2018), https://www.nasdaq.com/article/6-companies-spending-the-most-on-rd-cm1004333.
933. *See* Statista 2019, https://www.statista.com/statistics/507742/alphabet-annual-global-revenue/.

*Figure 7.10 ALPHABET R&D Expenditures from 2014 to 2018 (Percentage of R&D Operating Revenues %)*

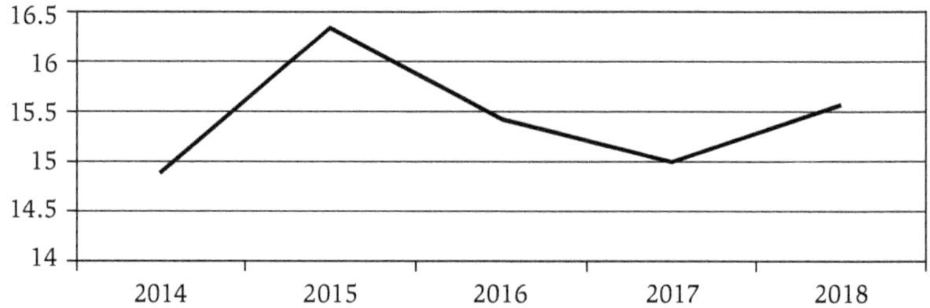


*Source: Statista 2019.*

As summarized in Figure 7.10, from 2014 to 2018 the percentage of spending on R&D in percentage of the total Alphabet revenue has remained between 14.9 percent and 15.5 percent. However, the multi-regression model shows that this variable is not particularly significant. Thus, the R&D will not be included among the explanatory variables in the following multi-regression model.

### *[c] Industry Revenue*

Now, I consider the variance of digital search advertising spending in the U.S. before the hypothetical *antitrust consent* decree. From 2010 to 2018, the digital search advertising spending in the U.S. has increased from 11.7 to 36.41 billion dollars—is almost three times (Figure 7.11).

*Figure 7.11 Digital Search Advertising Spending in the U.S. from 2010 to 2018 (in billion U.S. USD)*

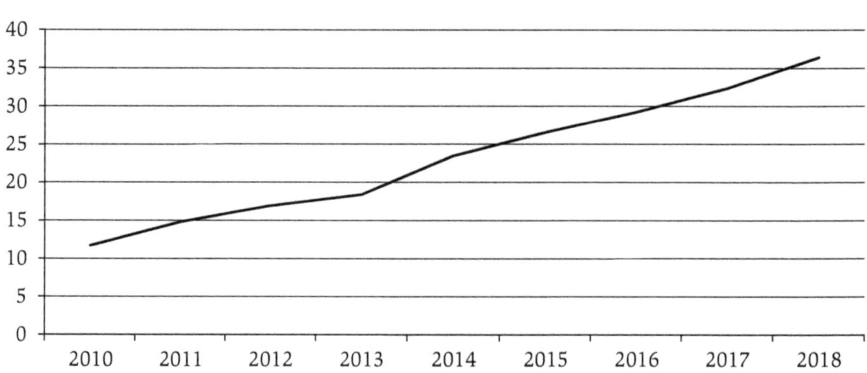


*Source: IAB and Statista data.* It is considered advertising that appears on laptop, desktop, mobile phones, tablets and other internet-connected devices.

### *[d] Consumer Price Index*

In contrast to traditional markets where a company sells its products to a group of consumers, Google Search acts in a two-sided market,[934] where companies (e.g., Google) sell services or products "to two different groups of consumers":[935] users and advertisers. Google profits only from advertisers (the second side of the market), but the price of advertisement on Google platform depends on the number of Google's users.

Hence, I have considered the cost that an advertiser or a firm usually pays per click **Cost Per Click** (CPC)[936] to advertise on search engines in the United States to calculate the consumer price index (CPI) related to the Google Search services. The CPC has basically tripled from 2008 to 2018. In 2008, the CPC was USD 0.71[937] which increased to 2.76 in 2018. In 2009, the related CPI was 1.45, which decreased to 1.3 in 2018.

### *[e] Multi-Regression Analysis*

As mentioned above, I now use the multi-regression analysis to predict the impact on competition of adopting the AT&T antitrust remedies in Google Search Engine market (the digital search advertising market). In practice, I use AT&T coefficients of my economic model to measure the effects of enforcing the same antitrust remedies enshrined in AT&T consent decree to Google Search before and after the antitrust intervention.

The HHI in the telecommunication industry before and after the AT&T consent decree of 1982 (from 1984 to 1992) is the independent variable of my model. My explanatory variables are:

(i) $X_1$ = AT&T market share from 1979 to 1992;
(ii) $X_2$ = a dummy variable (antitrust intervention/no antitrust intervention);
(iii) $X_3$ = CPI for telecommunication services;
(iv) $X_4$ = Telecom industry revenues in the U.S. from 1979 to 1992.

Although many other factors come into play, I have simplified the model for illustrative purposes. Table 1 shows the results of my regression model, while the regression statistics appear in Table 2.

---

934. Melamed, *supra* n. 815; Evans, *supra* n. 815; Rubinfeld, *supra* n. 815, at 859, 860; Gifford & Kudrle, *supra* n. 815.
935. Filistrucchi, Geradin, Damme & Affeldt, *supra* n. 829.
936. *See* Google Ads, Search Ads, https://ads.google.com/intl/en_sa/home/how-it-works/search-ads/.
937. *See* Jonathan Hochman, *The Cost of Pay-Per-Click (PPC) Advertising—Trends and Analysis*, available at https://www.hochmanconsultants.com/cost-of-ppc-advertising/.

*Table 1 AT&T Multi-Regression Model Summary*

| | *Coefficients* | *Standard Error* | *T-Statistic* |
|---|---|---|---|
| Intercept | -1,451 | 883.933 | -1.642 |
| Antitrust Intervention | -264 | 108.169 | -2.445 |
| Market Share | 118.41 | 6.792 | 17.433 |
| Telecom Revenues | -0.02 | 0.007 | -2.830 |
| CPI Telephone Services | 24.623 | 9.428 | 2.611 |

*Table 2 Regression Statistics*

| | |
|---|---|
| $R_2$ | 0.998 |
| Adjusted $R_2$ | 0.998 |
| Standard error | 94.29 |
| Observations | 14 |
| P-value | 0.00000 |

Now I estimate the HHI for Google digital search advertising market before and after the antitrust intervention by using the AT&T coefficients from my economic model. I have used the following formula:

$$HHI = \alpha + B_1 X_1 + B_2 X_2 + B_3 X_3 + B_4 X_4$$

$B_1$ is Google Search market share, $B_2$ is the digital search advertising spending in the U.S., $B_3$ is the antitrust intervention in Google Search (hence the dummy variable) and $B_4$ is the CPI related to the CPC.

I have estimated both the HHI on Google Search's market before and after the antitrust intervention with the AT&T coefficients. By using the described formula the HHI for Google Search's market in the U.S. decreased from 5,960 in 2012 to 5209 in 2019,[938] thus the year where I have envisaged the adoption of Google consent decree. In 2020 and 2021, I have assumed that Google Search's market share decreased by 0.3 percent per each year as that market share decreased of that percentage in the last four years. The CPI decreased of an average of -0.04 from 2014 to 2018 and I have considered that change in the forecast of the CPI from 2019 to 2021; while the digital search advertising spending will be increased by three million dollars in that range of time, according to Statista.[939]

The following Figure 7.12 shows the trend of the HHI in Google Search's Market before and after the antitrust intervention calculated by using the described above formula.

938. HHI (Google Search's market) = - 1,451 + (118.41 * 7436.148) + (-264.55 * 1) + (24.62 * 1.3) + (-0.02 * 39.14) = 5209.

939. Statista, Digital Advertising Spending in the United States from 2017 to 2023, by format (in million U.S. dollars).

*Figure 7.12 Trend of HHI in the U.S. Search Engine Market Before and after the Antitrust Intervention (from 2011 to 2021).*

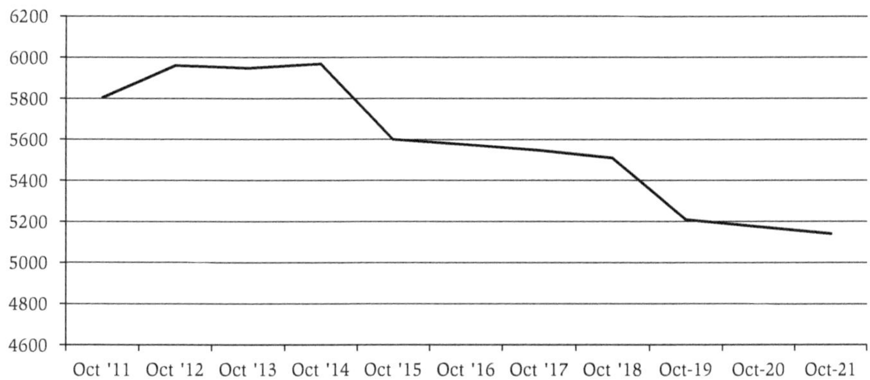


Figure 7.12 shows two significant decreases for the HHI at hand: one occurred in 2015 which is not related to the antitrust intervention and a second one in 2019, the year of the envisaged consent decree.

## §7.04 CONCLUSIONS

The estimated results lead to a number of conclusions. Chief among them is that the adoption of the AT&T remedies enshrined in the consent decree of 1982 on the *Google Search Bias* case would increase competition in the affected market. After the antitrust intervention, the market at hand appears to be less concentrated. However, a similar decrease in market concentration occurred in 2015 without an antitrust intervention, making it is hard to tell the necessity of using such intrusive remedies against Google Search. As Professor John E. Lopatka observed, a behavioral remedy that prohibits exclusionary practices may be more efficient, as is likely to "quickly extirpate any effects of the anticompetitive behavior while minimizing the risk to innovation."[940]

Similar economic analysis might be done considering other remedies adopted in the past, such as the Microsoft remedies and the more recent remedies adopted in the Intel case discussed in Chapter 1. Similar to the telecommunication industry at the end of the nineteenth century, today's privacy concerns within the data industry are relatively new. In contrast to the telecommunication industry and AT&T consent decree of 1982, we can now benefit from important case studies where different antitrust remedies were applied (the AT&T, Microsoft and Intel are only three examples). The data industry is complex and a deeper inquiry is required. However, as we have seen, there is much to learn from the telecommunication industry and the experience resulting from the AT&T case. This and other past consent decrees can be

940. John E. Lopatka, *United States v. IBM: A Monument of Arrogance*, 68 Antitrust L. J. 145, 160 (2000).

used to make predictions regarding the adoption of antitrust remedies enshrined in future consent decrees.

As emphasized in Section §7.02[B]*[2]*, being a dominant incumbent firm with monopoly power in a market is not unlawful and might be a natural consequence of acting in a network industry that can ultimately benefit both markets and consumers. Antitrust action against a dominant incumbent firm by default can discourage similar incumbent firms from continuing to invest in new technologies.[941] However, antitrust law protects competition (open and free markets) and needs to be enforced to remain effective.[942] As the analysis conducted in Chapter 1 revealed, the adoption of tailored antitrust remedies enshrined in consent decrees might turn out to be the best way forward.[943]

941. The Guardian, Revealed: Facebook's global lobbying against data privacy laws (Mar. 2, 2019), https://www.theguardian.com/technology/2019/mar/02/facebook-global-lobbying-campaign-against-data-privacy-laws-investment.

942. Massarotto, *supra* n. 878.

943. Massarotto, *supra* n. 818.

CHAPTER 8

# What Future for the EU Commitment Decisions

Chapter 8 investigates the role of EU commitment decisions in dealing with digital markets through exploring two different approaches: (1) the EU Commission approach; (2) the Bundeskartellamt approach. As Chapter 5 revealed, in Europe, the adoption of commitment decisions has generally decreased. In 2018, the EU Commission settled only one case by means of commitment decision.[944]

Chapter 8 scrutinizes the EU's Google cases to describe the EU Commission's favor for prohibition decisions in the context of digital markets. It proceeds with the investigation of the Bundeskartellamt's approach through the exploration of the Facebook case. Some reflections are conducted to evaluate whether the deterrence of EU competition law is preserved with an increase in the adoption of commitment decisions. Further conclusions are drawn on the adoption of commitment decisions to settle antitrust cases in today's digital markets and considers the U.S. approach with consent decrees.

A specific question we should ask is: *Should the role of commitment decisions resemble the role of U.S. consent decrees in the future enforcement of competition principles?* In other words, should European authorities enforce EU competition law by means of commitment decisions in the digital era? If the answer is yes, how could the use of commitment decisions be improved by looking at the United States' century of experience in the adoption of consent decrees? These questions are explored in the following chapter.

944. EU Commission, *Upstream gas supplies in Central and Eastern Europe* (AT39816), Commitment Decision (May 24, 2018) (Gazprom).

## §8.01 THE EU COMMISSION APPROACH WITH DIGITAL MARKETS

In contrast to U.S. enforcers, the EU Commission's approach with digital markets appears to be very interventionist. On the other hand, the EU Commission seems skeptical about enforcing competition principles by means of commitment decisions. As Chapter 5 revealed, the EU Commission clearly favors prohibition decisions and the imposition of fines relative to a settlement solution.

The Google cases (*Google Search Bias* and *Google Android*) explored in the following exemplify such an approach. In both cases, the EU Commission ended the antitrust investigation with a prohibition decision and the imposition of heavy fines. Let us also investigate some alternatives to employing such an approach.

### [A] Google Cases

The *Google Search Bias* and *Google Android* cases are interesting for two reasons: (i) both cases concern the data industry and two-sided markets, topics that currently worry antitrust enforcers the most; (ii) both cases reveal the EU Commission's approach in favor of a prohibition decision and the imposition of a heavy fine in dealing with digital markets.

In 2019, the EU Commission released a report on how to enforce competition policy in the digital era (*Report*),[945] summarizing the EU Commission's reasoning behind its decisions on digital markets and data industry, including EU Commission's decisions on Google cases. The EU Commission put "less emphasis on the analysis of market definition"[946] and instead focused on the theory of harm and identification of anticompetitive conduct. The EU Commission also identifies a special responsibility of dominant platforms "to ensure that their rules do not impede free, undistorted and vigorous competition;"[947] thus, assuring anyone can benefit from the platform.

Different from the U.S. approach, the EU Commission proposes "to translate general insights in error costs into legal tests."[948] This approach is very interesting, but, as we will see, it is questionable in the Google cases how well the EU Commission puts this theory into practice.

#### *[1] Google Search Bias*

The facts of the *Google Search Bias* case have been described several times in the course of the book. Therefore, here you will find only the main ones with a focus on the rejected commitments that Google proposed.

On November 30, 2010, the EU Commission opened the related investigation, alleging that Google unfavorably treated rival services in their unpaid and sponsored

945. EU Commission, Competition Policy for the Digital Era (2019), available at http://ec.europa.eu/competition/publications/reports/kd0419345enn.pdf (EU Commission *Report*).
946. *Ibid.*, at 3.
947. *Ibid.*, at 6.
948. *Ibid.*, at 51.

search results;[949] the EU Commission issued the related preliminary assessment on March 13, 2013.[950] On April 3, 2013, the EU Commission released, for the *market test*, those commitments[951] proposed by Google to end the investigations without finding any antitrust liability on Google's conduct.[952]

Under the terms of these commitments, Google agreed for a period of five years to:

1) "label promoted links to its own specialized search services so that users can distinguish them from natural web search results, clearly separate these promoted links from other web search results by clear graphical features (such as a frame), and display links to three rival specialized search services close to its own services, in a place that is clearly visible to users;"[953]
2) "offer all websites the option to opt-out from the use of all content in Google's specialized search services, while ensuring that any opt-out does not unduly affect the ranking of those web sites in Google's general web search results, offer all specialized search websites that focus on product search or local search the option to mark certain categories of information in such a way that such information is not indexed or used by Google, provide newspaper publishers with a mechanism allowing them to control on a web page per web page basis the display of their content in Google News;"[954]
3) "no longer include in its agreements with publishers any written or unwritten obligations that would require them to source online search advertisements exclusively from Google;"[955]
4) and "no longer impose obligations that would prevent advertisers from managing search advertising campaigns across competing advertising platform."[956]

The market test responded negatively to Google's proposed commitments. The EU Commission rejected such commitments, although initially the EU Commission had indicated a positive view of the proposed remedies.[957] The former EU Commissioner, Joaquin Almunia, observed that "[t]he feedback received from the market test was very negative"[958] and that the EU Commission required Google "to improve significantly"[959] its offered commitments.

949. EU Commission, Antitrust: Commission probes allegations of antitrust violations by Google, Press Release IP/10/1624 (Nov. 30, 2010).
950. *See* EU Commission, *Foundem and others* (AT.39.740), Commitment Decision (Apr. 3, 2013), http://ec.europa.eu/competition/antitrust/cases/dec_docs/39740/39740_8608_5.pdf.
951. EU Commission, Antitrust: Commission seeks feedback on commitments offered by Google to address competition concerns, Press Release (Apr. 25, 2013).
952. *Ibid.*
953. EU Commission, Antitrust: Commission probes allegations of antitrust violations by Google, Press Release IP/10/1624 (Nov. 30, 2010).
954. *Ibid.*
955. *Ibid.*
956. *Ibid.*
957. According to the EU Commission, "the commitments proposed by Google provide a satisfactory solution to the Commission's competition concerns, the Commission may adopt a decision to make them legally binding on Google (under Article 9 of the EU's antitrust Regulation 1/2003)." *Ibid.*
958. EU Commission, Joaquin Almunia, The Google Antitrust Case: What Is at Stake?, Press Release (Oct. 1, 2013), http://europa.eu/rapid/press-release_SPEECH-13-768_en.htm.
959. *Ibid.*

In February 2014, Google offered an improved commitment proposal, accepting terms to display the services of three rivals along with its own specialized search services on its web pages.[960] This meant that Google would have displayed three rival services prominently on the search pages along with Google's own specialized search services; all of these services would have been clearly visible to users.[961]

Although Joaquin Almunia recognized that the new version of Google's commitments "address[ed] the competition concerns,"[962] on April 15, 2015, the EU Commission formally accused Google of abusing its dominant position in the search engine market by releasing a Statement of Objections. According to the current Commissioner for Competition, Margrethe Vestager, Google "has given an unfair advantage to its own comparison shopping service, in breach of EU antitrust rules."[963] The new Commissioner sent a revised Statement of Objections to Google on July 14, 2016, reinforcing the EU Commission's concern about Google's abuse of dominant position in the search engine market.[964] As was easily foreseeable, on June 27, 2017 (after about seven years of investigation), Google was found liable of abusing its dominant position in the European Internet search markets and was fined EUR 2.42 billion.[965]

According to the prohibition decision, Google infringed on Article 102 of TFEU by giving preference to its own comparison services in the position and display of search results at the expense of its rivals' services.[966] Specifically, Google held a dominant position in each national market for general services[967] and abused such a position because "[t]he prospects of commercial success of Google's comparison shopping service [were] enhanced not because of the merits of that service."[968] Rather, Google had exploited its dominant platform (Google Search) to exclude its rivals in the comparison services market.

Rather than challenging the Commission's assumption under which Google needed to treat equally any comparison services in its platform. Google's defense focused on showing the Commission that there was no manipulation of its algorithm to favor its own comparison services. According to the EU Commission, Google failed to show that its conduct was objectively indispensable and the anticompetitive effects of

960. EU Commission, Antitrust: Commission Obtains from Google Comparable Display of Specialised Search Rivals, Press Release (Feb. 5, 2014).
961. EU Commission, Antitrust: Statement on the Google Investigation, Press Release (Feb. 5, 2014), http://europa.eu/rapid/press-release_SPEECH-14-93_en.htm.
962. *Ibid.*
963. EU Commission, Antitrust: Commission sends Statement of Objections to Google on comparison shopping service; opens separate formal investigation on Android, Press Release (Apr. 15, 2015), https://europa.eu/rapid/press-release_IP-15-4780_en.htm.
964. EU Commission, Antitrust: Commission takes further steps in investigations alleging Google's comparison shopping and advertising-related practices breach EU rules, Press Release (Jul. 14, 2016), http://europa.eu/rapid/press-release_IP-16-2532_en.htm.
965. EU Commission, Antitrust: Commission fines Google EUR 2.42 billion for abusing dominance as search engine by giving illegal advantage to own comparison shopping service, Press Release (Jun. 27, 2017), https://europa.eu/rapid/press-release_IP-17-1784_en.htm.
966. EU Commission, Case AT.39740, Google Search (Shopping), Jun. 27, 2017, at 7.
967. *Ibid.*, at § 271.
968. *Ibid.*, at § 600. Google would have applied "different underlying mechanisms on the basis of the advantages provided to it by its dominant position in the national markets for general search services." *Ibid.*

its conduct were counterbalanced by gains in efficiency for consumers and markets overall.[969]

In practice, the EU Commission seems to treat Google Search as an essential facility as it is the dominant search engine all over Europe. Because of that, Google would have a special responsibility, which implies enabling everyone to benefit from Google Search's platform under the same conditions. Such theory has been reaffirmed in the mentioned *Report* above, which defines dominant platforms, such as Google Search—as *regulators*. Dominant platforms are perceived as necessary for vertically integrated businesses such as Booking and Expedia; the conduct of the horizontally dominant platform inevitably affects all the others.[970] The first question we should ask is: Was Google aware of such a specific responsibility as regulator?

It is true in the context of antitrust companies who have a dominant position have a special responsibility requiring them not to engage in specific conduct, including exclusive conduct.[971] However, there is no specific provision related to special responsibility of dominant platforms. What one might recall is the unbundling policy implemented in the European telecommunication and energy industry following a specific regulatory intervention.[972]

Requiring Google Search to allow anyone to offer its comparison services at the same conditions on its platform may be the right way forward to increase competition in Google's vertical search services. But it might not be appropriate that Google Search is punished by default for not having complied with *non expressed* provision, only because it makes sense in the light of the public interest. This is particularly true if we think that Google has practically created the online search advertising platform. Furthermore, the definition of digital markets as the same EU Commission's recognized is challenging.[973]

In contrast to the EU Microsoft case, Google seems not to have refused its rivals to access to Google Search platform;[974] rather, it seems that Google put—by default—the results of the rivals' comparison services after it own comparison services' results. It sounds similar to the situation of entering in a Whole Foods supermarket and first seeing Whole Food's own products before other brands'. Should a similar conduct be condemned by default?

---

969. *Ibid.*, at § 653. The EU Commission also recognized that "Google has failed to demonstrate that it cannot use the same underlying process and methods in deciding the positioning and diplay of the results of its own comparison shopping service and for those of competing comparison shopping services." *Ibid.*, at § 671.
970. *Ibid.*, at 6.
971. *See* Judgment of the Court of 9 November 1983 in Case 322/81, *Michelin v. Commision* [1983] ECR3461, at para. 57.
972. *See*, e.g., Pierre-Andre' Buigues, European Policy on Local Loop Unbundling Competition Law Background and Problems of Implementation, http://ec.europa.eu/competition/speeches/text /sp2001_043_en.pdf.
973. EU Commission *Report* at 49.
974. EU Commission, Case COMP/C-3/37.792 Microsoft, C(2004)900 final. Specifically, in Microsoft the EU Commission fined Microsoft for refusing to provide interoperability information to Sun and others software developers as this information was necessary to develop software compatible with Windows operating system, which at that time was installed over about 90 percent of PC. *Ibid.*, at 560 and 784.

In the context of Internet services, for example, both in EU and the U.S., a regulation has been implemented to guarantee non-discrimination among market players and to prevent a paid prioritized Internet Speed. The U.S. Net Neutrality and the EU Open Internet regulation[975] have allowed corporations to act without the interference of the big Internet providers, creating a "*neutral*" environment where each company can benefit from the same Internet speed, and grow indiscriminately.[976] In 2018 the U.S. Net Neutrality regulation was repealed, allowing Internet providers[977] such as AT&T and Comcast to slow access to the Internet or charge for faster access. Google in the U.S. has built its own Internet platform.[978]

In summary, the Net Neutrality and Open Internet regulation are two examples of how, through specific forms of regulation, the government can impose non-discrimination policies and ensure that all market players in vertically integrated markets benefit from a dominant platform under the same conditions. Without similar forms of regulation, as the recent repeal of the U.S. Net Neutrality reveals, ISPs have no duty to provide the Internet service at the same conditions to businesses active in secondary markets.

Google has appealed the EU Commission's decision resulting from its *Google Search Bias* case,[979] and up to the writing of this book, the appeal is still pending. However, some conclusions can already be drawn. Google does not seem to have refused rivals access to Google Search in the comparison services market and no provisions seem to specifically require Google not to discriminate among comparison services providers. Specific forms of regulation might have been legally implemented through the adoption of commitments that were regulatory in nature. A commitment decision that prevented Google from discriminating against its rivals in vertical search markets could have been the best way to proceed, preventing the risk of (1) reducing the incentive that companies have to innovate and (2) losing the appeal after seven years of investigation.

### *[2] Google Android*

In addition to Google Search, Google owns Android, an open-source operating system installed on about 80 percent of the smartphones worldwide.[980] As outlined in Chapter 7, through the Android platform Google was able to install its smartphone applications, including Google Maps, YouTube, and Google Chrome, and collect fees from advertisements. As an open-source operating system, anyone should be able to install and

975. EU Commission, Open Internet (last update Jun. 18, 2018), https://ec.europa.eu/digital-single-market/en/open-internet-net-neutrality.
976. *See*, e.g., Nicholas Economides & Joacim Tåg, *Network Neutrality on the Internet: A Two-Sided Market Analysis*, 24 Information Economics and Policy 91–104 (2012).
977. *See* Fung, *supra* n. 552.
978. Google Fiber, *Faster, Fairer, Kinder Internet*, https://fiber.google.com/about/.
979. Toplensky, *supra* n. 475.
980. IDC, Smartshone OS Market Share, 2015 Q2, http://www.idc.com/prodserv/smartphone-os-market-share.jsp.

modify Android.[981] However, Google Android cannot be modified as Google requires smartphone manufacturers to sign anti-fragmentation agreements to prevent the creation of different versions of Google Android.[982]

There is a significant difference between Google's Android products and Android forks. Samsung, for example, uses Android source code as the base of several of its products, such as the development of smartphone applications. Conversely, Amazon has used the Android source to develop an independent project (namely an Android fork) for its Kindle Fire line, which diverges from Google Android.[983] As Google requires smartphone manufacturers to sign anti-fragmentation agreements to prevent the creation of Android forks, the question becomes whether Android is, in fact, an "open source."[984] Moreover, if most smartphone manufacturers install Android and sign an Anti-fragmentation agreement, in practice, Android forks are not saleable.

As examined in Chapter 7, the U.S. antitrust enforcers did not open any antitrust proceedings against Google Android. On April 20, 2016, the EU Commission sent a statement of objection to Google related to Google Android's violation of Article 102 of TFEU.[985] On July 18, 2018, the EU Commission fined Google EUR 4.34 billion for abusing, through Android operating systems, its dominant position under Article 102 of the TFEU. Despite the fact that the EU Commission's full decision is, up to the writing of this book, not publicly available, the EU Commission has specified that Google would "cement its dominant position in general internet search"[986] in its *Press Release*. In sum, Android seems to be the means through which Google strengthened its dominant position on Google Search.

The most interesting part of the *Press Release* concerns the fact that, according to the EU Commission, Apple IOS is not a sufficient competitor of Google Android. The EU Commission observed that "[a]s a licensable operating system, Android is different from operating systems exclusively used by vertically integrated developers (like Apple iOS or Blackberry)"[987] and they "are not part of the same market."[988] It will be interesting to see the definition of the relevant market provided by the EU Commission's full and final decision on Google Android. The *Report* that the EU Commission has recently released seems to provide a justification in the market definition within the digital industry.

In Google Android, there is no trace of commitments offered by Google to settle the case before the prohibition decision of July 2018. Thus, we may ask whether the

981. *See* Giovanna Massarotto, *Open Source Paradigm: Beyond the Solution to the Software Patentability Debate,* 15 J. Marshall Rev. Intell. Prop. L. 999, 1016 (2016); Opensource.com, What is Open Source? (last visited Sep. 5, 2016) https://opensource.com/resources/what-open-source.
982. Rosenblatt, *supra* n. 838.
983. Jerry Hildenbrand, *What the Fork Is a "Fork?,"* Androidcentral (Apr. 6, 2013, 9:32 AM) http://www.androidcentral.com/what-fork-fork.
984. Rosenblatt, *supra* n. 838.
985. EU Commission, Antitrust: Commission Sends Statement of Objections to Google on Android operating system and applications, Press Release (Apr. 20, 2016).
986. EU Commission, Antitrust: Commission fines Google EUR 4.34 billion for illegal practices regarding Android mobile devices to strengthen dominance of Google's search engine, Press Release (Jul. 18, 2018).
987. *Ibid.*
988. *Ibid.*

previous experience with Google Search investigation and the EU Commission's approach with commitment decisions disincentivized Google from trying the consent solution before being condemned. Certainly, no incentives seem to have been provided to repair market inefficiency in related markets through a settlement solution. The appeal against this decision is also pending up to the writing of this book. If the EU Commission loses the case, it will have missed another opportunity to efficiently regulate another crucial digital market through remedies tailored by specific antitrust concerns.

## §8.02 THE BUNDESKARTELLAMT REGULATION OF DIGITAL MARKETS

The Bundeskartellamt approach to enforcing competition principles in digital markets seems to fall between the United States' non-intervention style and the EU intervention approach with the imposition of heavy fines. The German Antitrust Agency holds that, in cases related to abuse of dominant position, forms of administrative proceedings are more appropriate than fine proceedings[989] as they concern challenging situations where an "interpretation of law in a (new) case constellation"[990] is required. In abuse of dominance proceedings, re-establishing pro-competitive conditions is preferred relative to the imposition of a fine. The German Antitrust Authority has also specified that its power is not limited to enforcing competition law provisions. Following German case law, the Bundeskartellamt is empowered to enforce data protection provisions as well as civil law principles.[991]

The recent Facebook case, examined in the following section, exemplifies that unique approach to enforcing competition law in digital markets.

### [A] Facebook case

In March 2016, the Bundeskartellamt opened an investigation against Facebook concerning its collection of data when other apps, third-party websites and corporate services are used and data combines with Facebook user data.[992] As the German antitrust agency noted, businesses and associations can also benefit from the Facebook platform by using the network to advertise their products or services.[993] Facebook based their business models on reaching more users to increase advertisers' demand.[994] The advertisements match profiles of individual Facebook users based on

989. Bundeskartellamt, Background Information on the Facebook Proceeding, 1 (Dec. 19, 2017).
990. *Ibid.*
991. *Ibid.*, at 4.
992. Bundeskartellamt, Case Summary: Facebook, Exploitative Business Terms Pursuant to Section 19(1) GWB for Inadequate Data Processing (Date of Decision, Feb. 6, 2019). (*Bundeskartellamt, Facebook Case Summary*).
993. *Ibid.*, at 2.
994. Simon P. Anderson & Jean J. Gabszewicz, *The Media and Advertising: A Tale of Two-Sided Markets* (August 2005), http://economics.virginia.edu/sites/economics.virginia.edu/files/anderson/fullfinaltale_0.pdf. Two sided-market paradigm is applied to all media markets.

their exemplified interests and personal commercial behavior. This is called *targeted advertising*.

### *[1] Facebook Conduct*

Facebook owns both Facebook and Instagram—the leading online social networks—as well as WhatsApp, which offers a free service for users to send and receive text messages, photos, documents, videos, voice message and phone calls. Up to the writing of this book, WhatsApp has not been used to make money from advertising.

People that want to benefit from a Facebook account have to agree to the terms of service, entering into a contract to get the service. Such terms of service imply that Facebook collects users' data in addition to "their devices outside of Facebook-related activities via Facebook Business Tools integrated by advertisers, app developers and publishers."[995]

### *[2] Market Definition*

In the Facebook case, the Bundeskartellamt defined the relevant market to exam the possible anticompetitive conduct, pursuant Section 18(2a) and (3a) of the German Competition Act (GCA) as modified in 2017.[996]

Such provisions are quite unique in the context of antitrust as they include specifics on multi-sided markets and network effects. Section 18(2a) of the GCA specifies that "[t]he assumption of a market shall not be invalidated by the fact that a good or service is provided free of charge."[997] While Section 18(3a) concerns the case of multi-sided markets and networks, stating that "in assessing the market position of an undertaking account shall also be taken of:

(1) direct and indirect network effects;
(2) the parallel use of services from different providers and the switching costs for users;
(3) the undertaking's economies of scale arising in connection with network effects;
(4) the undertaking's access to data relevant for competition;
(5) innovation-driven competitive pressure."[998]

The Bundeskartellamt considered relevant the national market for private users of social networks looking at "an overall assessment of all factors of market power."[999]

995. *Bundeskartellamt, Facebook Case Summary*, at 3.
996. The GCA was amended on Jun. 1, 2017 (Federal Law Gazette I, p. 1416). An English updated version of the GCA is available at this link http://www.gesetze-im-internet.de/englisch_gwb/index.html#gl_p0057.
997. *Ibid.* Section 18(2a).
998. *Ibid.* Section 18(3a).
999. *Bundeskartellamt, Facebook Case Summary*, at 5.

The agency focused on "the high degree of product differentiation of social media and the various overlaps of their functionality"[1000] besides the robust direct network effects. WhatsApp was considered part of a separate market as its technical characteristics and applications diverge from those of Facebook and Instagram. The investigation led to define the German market as the geographic boundary of the service mainly used to connect people from their country.

### *[3] Facebook Abuse of Dominance*

Facebook's market share in the German market for private users of social networks exceeded 95 percent among daily active users.[1001] Therefore, Facebook's dominance was clear and was characterized by high switching costs and "the strong direct network effects of Facebook's business model."[1002] The agency also noted that "the strong identity-based network effects lead to a lock-in effect which makes it difficult for users or prevents them from switching to another social network."[1003] The barriers to market entry were increased due to the indirect network effects with Facebook.

The Bundeskartellamt recognized that Facebook abused its dominant position in the German social network market through its data policy, which enables Facebook to collect users' data from sources outside of Facebook and combine such data with those collected on Facebook. By doing this, Facebook violated Section 19(1) of the GCA.

What is most interesting about this decision is the explanation of the relation between data protection and competition law. As the Bundeskartellamt observed, these two regulations are strongly interconnected with each other[1004] and it is in the view of the authority that the European data protection regulation needs to be considered within the antitrust scrutiny. Data protection rules "do not suspend abuse control,"[1005] observed the German antitrust agency, although such rules do not specifically include provisions on abusive practices engaged by dominant firms. Throughout the entire Facebook investigation the Bundeskartellamt worked close to the German authorities in charge of enforcing data protection regulations, which, since the beginning supported the antitrust agency's proceeding.[1006]

The same data protection body clarified that the enforcement of data protection rules alone is not sufficient to be effective against violations of data protection provisions and that antitrust law should also be enforced. Based on these legal grounds, the Bundeskartellamt held that Facebook's policy on the treatment of data violated the EU General Data Protection Regulation (GDPR) provisions and Facebook did not offer sufficient legal justification for its extended use of data. As Facebook holds

1000. *Ibid.*
1001. Because the success of a social network depends on the intensity of use, the German antitrust authority considered as the key indicator to measure market success and the network's competitive significance, the number of daily active users. *Ibid.*, at 6.
1002. *Ibid.*
1003. *Ibid.*
1004. *Ibid.*, at 8.
1005. *Ibid.*, at 9.
1006. *Ibid.*

a dominant position in the market of social media, the agency could not consider users consent to Facebook's terms and conditions adequate to ensure the free consent required by Article 6(a) of the GDPR.[1007] Facebook, indeed, has bargaining power over its users being the dominant company in the social network market and Facebook's users do not really have a choice if they want to access to the network. In both data protection and competition law, an unbalanced negotiation position is taken into account.

The Bundeskartellamt further observed the fact that Facebook processes "data from third-party sources to the extent determined by Facebook in its terms and conditions"[1008] that is not necessary for providing the social network or for monetizing the platform by means of targeting advertisement. On such grounds, the Bundeskartellamt, on February 7, 2019, "prohibited the data processing policy Facebook imposes on its users and its corresponding implementation pursuant to Section 19(1), 32 [GCA]"[1009] ordering the end of such a policy. It was also prohibited to implement Facebook's terms and conditions "in actual data processing procedures which Facebook performs based on its data and cookie policies."[1010] From the date of the Bundeskartellamt's decision, Facebook had twelve months to implement the necessary changes.

Facebook appealed the decision before the Dusseldorf Higher Regional Court.

### [B] Conclusions

The German antitrust approach in dealing with digital market has been shown through the exploration of the Facebook case. The Bundeskartellamt favors remedies that are regulatory in nature to settle abuse of dominance proceedings and to effectively ensure competition in data industry while retaining the power to enforce data protection. Different from the EU Commission's approach, market definition is no less emphasized in the context of digital markets.[1011] Rather, the German legislator adopted a market

1007. *Ibid.*, at 10.
1008. *Ibid.*
1009. *Ibid.*, at 12. Specifically, § 32 of the GCA (also known as GWB) states that: "(1) The competition authority may oblige undertakings or associations of undertakings to terminate an infringement of a provision of this Part or of Articles 101 or 102 of the Treaty on the Functioning of the European Union. (2) For this purpose, it may require them to take all necessary behavioural or structural remedies that are proportionate to the infringement identified and necessary to bring the infringement effectively to an end. Structural remedies may only be imposed if there is no behavioural remedy which would be equally effective, or if the behavioural remedy would entail a greater burden for the undertakings concerned than the structural remedies. (2a) In its order to terminate the infringement, the competition authority may order reimbursement of the benefits generated through the infringement. The amount of interest that is included in these benefits may be estimated. After expiry of the time limit for reimbursement of the benefits set in the order to terminate the infringement, the benefits generated up to such date shall bear interest in accordance with § 288(1) sentence 2 and § 289 sentence 1 of the German Civil Code. (3) To the extent that a legitimate interest exists, the competition authority may also declare that an infringement has been committed after the infringement has been terminated."
1010. *Bundeskartellamt, Facebook Case Summary*, at 12.
1011. *Ibid.*, at 3.

definition that considered multi-sided markets, network effects and the fact that products might be offered for free.[1012]

German case law recognizes the power of the Bunskartellamt to enforce data protection along with antitrust law provisions to make competition in digital markets effective.[1013]

In summary, the Bunskartellamt endorses the U.S. adoption of antitrust remedies regulatory along with the European interventionist approach in enforcing antitrust law in the data industry. However, such remedies are enshrined in a prohibition decision rather than a settlement solution reached with the consent of the company subject to an antitrust investigation. The German approach and experience certainly provide valuable insights on the future enforcement of EU competition law in increasingly dynamic markets to better preserve market efficiency and consumer welfare.

While Chapter 9 will investigate the use of remedies enshrined in antitrust settlements to deal with future markets in both the U.S. and EU antitrust framework, Chapter 8 proceeds with the analysis of an increase in the adoption of commitment decisions to deal with present digital markets and the investigation of related consequences.

## §8.03 COMMITMENT DECISIONS IN DIGITAL MARKETS

In Europe, another interesting approach to examine in enforcing competition principles in digital markets concerns the adoption of commitment decisions, now relegated to extreme situations. The adoption of a consent solution, as outlined through the course of this book, maybe the best way forward to deal with digital markets, which present very challenging situations. The market is difficult to define as it often concerns multi-sided markets along with strong network effects that naturally increase barriers to entry and market concentration.

Thus, prohibition decisions with the imposition of heavy fines may be easily challenged in court as the same antitrust agencies seem not to have a clear idea on how to apply competition principles in digital markets without compromising the incentives of companies to innovate. The German approach with Facebook is compelling, but the company subject to the investigation was not involved in defining the appropriate remedies and their risk of losing the case in Court seems high as well. However, the German decision on the Facebook case has started a lively debate on whether a similar approach might be extended in other jurisdictions, such as the EU and U.S.[1014] As some antitrust scholars observed, there are several legal issues that make it unlikely that the German approach will be slavishly followed in other states.[1015] For example, the Bunskartellamt does not seem to have met the EU test under Article 102 TFEU,

1012. *See* Section 18(2a) and Section 18(3a) of GCA as amended in June 2017.

1013. *Bundeskartellamt, Facebook Case Summary* at 7-8.

1014. Lexology, Data Exploring as an Abuse of Dominance: The German Facebook Decision (Mar. 4, 2019) available at https://www.lexology.com/library/detail.aspx?g=242876ec-4401-4771-80ce-480623c6423e.

1015. *See*, e.g., Renato Nazzini, *Privacy and Antitrust: Searching for the (Hopefully Not Yet Lost) Soul of Competition Law in the EU after the German Facebook Decision*, Competition Policy

requiring proof that harm caused by Facebook conduct is competitive harm linked to an abuse of dominant position.[1016] But the German Facebook case is still a remarkable example of how remedies that are regulatory in nature might be more effective than a fine in preserving competition in the data industry where only a few rules are now in place.

In Europe and the U.S., antitrust settlements are attractive in several ways. Antitrust cases are costly,[1017] complex, and time-consuming, and commitment decisions allow both antitrust agencies and companies subject to an investigation to save significant time and resources.[1018] Furthermore, commitment decisions are largely the result of negotiation (rather than litigation) between the antitrust agency and the investigated company, therefore the risk of appeal in such decisions is basically zero and markets benefit from a time-sensitive solution.

As simple and attractive as they seem, commitment decisions mask some complicated legal matters. For example, to protect and restore competition, antitrust agencies need to deter companies from engaging in anticompetitive conducts.[1019] Do commitment decisions achieve such a goal given that no fine is imposed? Furthermore, do commitment decisions sacrifice the public good of adjudication to say what the law is as no finding of liability is made? As is explained next, in Europe, greater reform of the present antitrust enforcement mechanism seems to be required before increasing the adoption of antitrust settlements.

### [A] Commitment Decisions and Deterrence

While Europe has twenty-eight competition law enforcers, in the U.S. any private party is incentivized to enforce antitrust law provisions.[1020] The U.S. antitrust enforcement

International (March 2019) available at https://www.competitionpolicyinternational.com/wp-content/uploads/2019/03/EU-News-Column-March-2019-4-Full.pdf.

1016. *Ibid.*, at 5.

1017. These costs reflect the working hours of economists, lawyers, and company personnel. For example, AT&T had predicted that full litigation of the lawsuit brought by the Government would have cost as much as USD 500 million to USD 1 billion. Instead, the cost involved in agreeing on a consent decree might well be far less than half the cost of litigation.

1018. Isenbergh & Rubin, *supra* n. 13, at 386, 387. *See also* Salop & White, *supra* n. 204. A settlement payment by the defendant to the plaintiff of an amount that is in the vicinity of this expected monetary value would allow both parties to save the litigation costs. Thus, on an expected-value basis (as a method of weighing up the probabilities), both parties would be better off with the settlement.

1019. Judgment 15 July 1970 in Case 41/69. *See also*, EU Commission, Fines for Breaking EU Competition Law 1 (November 2011) http://ec.europa.eu/competition/cartels/overview/factsheet_fines_en.pdf. *See also*, Wouter P.J. Wils, *The Optimal Enforcement of EC Antitrust Law*, Essays in Law & Economics 16 (Kluwer L. Int., 2002). In competition law deterrence prevails over prevention. *Ibid.*

1020. A. D. Neale & D. G. Goyder, *The Antitrust Laws of the United States of America* 1, 15 (Cambridge U. Press, 1980). "The enforcement of antitrust laws does not depend exclusively on the Department of Justice and the Federal Trade Commission. The Sherman and Clayton Acts permit any private person who suffers damage as a result of violations to sue offenders and recover 'threefold the damages by him sustained.'" *Ibid.*

mechanism is based on the assumption that antitrust law directly protects consumers[1021] and antitrust deterrence is exerted primarily by private actions[1022] through individual or collective actions (class actions).[1023] Class actions are generally used when the government does not take any intervention[1024] and the numerous damaged people would not claim for damages individually.

The U.S. public enforcement mechanism is also *de facto* more complex than the European one.[1025] Besides the FTC administrative intervention, both the DOJ[1026] and some individual states, such as New York,[1027] can prosecute antitrust conduct as economic crimes.[1028] In addition, the Hart-Scott-Rodino Antitrust Improvement (HSR) Act of 1976 empowered each State's Attorney General to bring a *parens patriae* suit[1029] on behalf of its residents asking for antitrust damages.[1030]

The European private antitrust enforcement mechanism is not as effective as in the U.S. In 2007, a study coordinated by Professor Andrea Renda[1031] revealed that, in

---

1021. *See*, e.g., Robert H. Bork, *The Antitrust Paradox: A Policy at War with Itself*, 66 (Free Press, 1978).

1022. Massarotto, *The Deterrent and Enunciating Effects of Consent Decrees*, *supra* n. 8.

1023. Bill Baer, *Public and Private Antitrust Enforcement in the United States, Remarks as Prepared for Delivery to European Competition Forum 2014*, 5 (Feb. 11, 2004); Lawrence J. Restieri Jr., *The Class Action Dilemma: The Certification of Classes Seeking Equitable Relief and Monetary Damages after Ticor Title Insurance Co. v. Brown*, 63 Fordham L. Rev. 1745 (1995). Class actions increased in importance after 1966 when the Advisory Committee substantially revised the procedural rules to facilitate antitrust class actions.

1024. In particular, class actions are used to seek private damages against cartels. Baer, *supra* n. 1023.

1025. *See* Baer, *supra* n. 1023. ("Since the 19th Century, the United States has relied on a combination of federal, state and private enforcers to combat anticompetitive conduct.")

1026. *See* Chapter 1.

1027. Attorney General Eric T. Schneiderman, *Antitrust Enforcement*, http://www.ag.ny.gov/antitrust/antitrust-enforcement (last visited Mar. 30, 2016).

1028. *See* Robert L. Hubbard & James Yoon, *How the Antitrust Modernization Commission Should View State Antitrust Enforcement*, 17 Loy. Consumer L. Rev. 497 (2005). "Under state law, many state attorneys general can prosecute antitrust violations as crimes and almost all have broad powers to investigate potential civil claims. In addition to the typical federal antitrust right to injunctive relief under Section 16 of the Clayton Act, state attorneys general can act as *parens patriae* to prevent actual or threatened harm to the state's general economy. Finally, state attorneys general represent consumers. State attorneys general pursue damages on behalf of state residents through *parens patriae* actions under federal antitrust law." *Ibid.*, at 503. Hence, the State Attorney General represents "an effective and ideal spokesman for the public in antitrust cases, because a primary duty of the State is to protect the health and welfare of its citizens. He is normally an elected and accountable and responsible public officer whose duty is to promote the public interest." *Ibid.*, at 515.

1029. *See* Richard A. Posner, *Federalism and the Enforcement of Antitrust Laws by State Attorneys General*, 2 Geo. J. L. & Pub. Pol'y 5 (2004). In particular, Richard A. Posner "turns now to antitrust enforcement by the states, beginning with the authority conferred in 1976 on state attorneys general by the Hart-Scott-Rodino Antitrust Improvements Act to bring suits (*parens patriae* suits) on behalf of the residents of their states under federal antitrust law." *Ibid.*, at 8. *See also*, Hovenkamp, *supra* n. 351, at 539. *See Louisiana v. Texas*, 176 U.S. 1 (1900). *See* Baer, *supra* n. 1023, at 2.

1030. Hovenkamp, *supra* n. 351, at 598. ABA Section of Antitrust Law, *State Antitrust Enforcement Handbook* 13 (ABA Book Pub., 2d ed., 2008).

1031. Andrea Renda et al., *Making Antitrust Damages Actions More Effective in the EU: Welfare Impact and Potential Scenarios* 42 (2007), available at http://ec.europa.eu/competition/antitrust/actionsdamages/files_white_paper/impact_study.pdf.

Europe, antitrust actions by private entities were *de facto* inexistent. Renda's study found that in the twenty-seven Member States between 2004 and 2007 privates filed just ninety-six antitrust damage actions.[1032] This data is even more critical if we consider the percentage of successful damage actions. In sixty-one cases involving vertical restrains there were no antitrust damages recognized and most of the total actions concerned "follow-on" actions, which have followed infringing decisions of competition agencies.[1033]

In 2005, the EU Commission developed a green paper followed by a white paper[1034] on damage actions for breaching EU competition law.[1035] Both the green and white papers confirmed negative data on the practical inexistence of private enforcement actions.[1036] As a result of these papers, the European Parliament, on a proposal from the Commission, enacted the EU Directive on antitrust private enforcement on November 26, 2014.[1037] However, the EU directive has not provided incentives like those offered by the U.S. private enforcement mechanism. Despite the fact that the same EU Commission noted that the main problem in EU antitrust private enforcement was the "undercompensation of victims of EU competition law,"[1038] the EU Directive explicitly prohibits forms of punitive damages, such as the U.S. treble damages rule. According to the EU Commission, punitive damages can overcompensate the injured parties, bringing about an abuse of private legal actions.[1039]

---

1032. *Ibid.*
1033. *Ibid.*, at 40, 42. *See also*, Folkert Wilman, *Private Enforcement of EU Law Before National Courts, The EU Legislative Framework*, 210 (Edward Elgar, 2015). The study carried out in the green paper on damages actions for antitrust violations pointed out that "by 2004 there were, EU-wide, only around 60 judged cases for damages actions for infringement of EU or national competition law, around half of which had led to an award of damages." *Ibid.*
1034. EU Commission, *White Paper on Damages Actions for Breach of the EC Antitrust Rules*, COM(2008) 165 final (Apr. 2, 2008), available at http://eur-lex.europa.eu/LexUriServ/LexUriServ.do?uri=COM:2008:0165:FIN:EN:PDF; EU Commission, *Green Paper—Damages Actions for Breach of the EC Antitrust Rules*, COM(2005) 672 final (Dec. 19, 2005), available at http://eur-lex.europa.eu/LexUriServ/LexUriServ.do?uri=COM:2005:0672:FIN:EN:PDF.
1035. *See* Lianos & Kokkoris, *supra* n. 694, at 17.
1036. Wilman, *supra* n. 1033.
1037. The European Parliament voted on Apr. 17, 2014 the directive on antitrust damages actions. Specifically, the Directive of the European Parliament and of the Council on certain rules governing actions for damages under national law for infringements of the competition law provisions of the Member States and of the European Union (Apr. 9, 2014), available at http://ec.europa.eu/competition/antitrust/actionsdamages/documents.html.
1038. EU Commission, Impact Assessment Report. Damages Actions for Breach of the EU antitrust Rules, COM(2013) 404 final, at 18.
1039. *See* the EU Directive on antitrust damages actions, at (13) ("This Directive should not require Member States to introduce collective redress mechanisms for the enforcement of Articles 101 and 102 TFEU. Without prejudice to compensation for loss of opportunity, full compensation under this Directive should not lead to overcompensation, whether by means of punitive, multiple or other damages.") *See also*, Article 3 on the *Right to full compensation*. ("1. Member States shall ensure that any natural or legal person who has suffered harm caused by an infringement of competition law is able to claim and to obtain full compensation for that harm. 2. Full compensation shall place a person who has suffered harm in the position in which that person would have been had the infringement of competition law not been committed. It shall therefore cover the right to compensation for actual loss and for loss of profit, plus the payment of interest. 3. Full compensation under this Directive shall not lead to overcompensation, whether by means of punitive, multiple or other types of damages.").

The main merit of the directive was striving to remove several practical difficulties that consumers face in seeking compensation for antitrust injury.[1040] Because competition law litigation is characterized by informational asymmetry, the EU Directive states the right of the claimant "to obtain the disclosure of evidence relevant to their claim,"[1041] but at the same time, the directive emphasizes the risk of compromising confidential information.

In 1959 Professor Hans B. Thorelli observed that "[a] striking common feature of Western European antitrust legislation is its emphasis on publicity,"[1042] and this still holds true today. The EU Commission's imposition of a huge fine is still the main mechanism of enforcing EU competition law, although there was an increase of private antitrust actions in most recent years.

As a consequence, the increasing adoption of commitment decisions (where no fine is imposed and no violation identified) would compromise in Europe competition law deterrence. To deal with that, the EU and State's Member legislators, along with antitrust agencies, may think of new incentives and/or simplify procedures to make private antitrust enforcement as effective as it is in the U.S.

### [B] The Enunciating Effects of Commitment Decisions

In one of my first articles, I explored the deterrent and enunciating effects of consent decrees and emphasized how, in the U.S., an increase in the adoption of antitrust settlements does not compromise antitrust deterrence. Again, in the U.S. deterrence is exerted primarily by private action. The risk of jeopardizing the public good of adjudication to say what the law is might be limited by requiring consent decrees to be enshrined in judges orders as it is in the U.S. when the plaintiff is the DOJ. Therefore, the European legislator may require that the terms of the antitrust settlements are reviewed by judges as foreseen for the DOJ's proceedings. In Europe, there is not similar judicial control for defining the terms of commitment decisions as Chapter 2 revealed.

Besides improving its private enforcement mechanism, Europe might follow the United States example in requiring a court to evaluate commitment decisions in order not to sacrifice a judicial interpretation of what the law is.[1043]

---

1040. EU Commission, *Proposal for a Directive of the European Parliament and of the Council*, COM(2013) 404 final (Jun. 11, 2013), available at http://eur-lex.europa.eu/LexUriServ/LexUriServ.do?uri=COM:2013:0404:FIN:EN:PDF.
1041. EU Directive on antitrust damages actions, at (15).
1042. Hans B. Thorelli, *Antitrust in Europe: National Policies after 1945*, 26 Univ. Chicago L. Rev., 222, 233 (1959). Hans B. Thorelli specified that such "feature [was] especially noteworthy because publicity about business relations [was] a great novelty in many of the nations in which business traditionally has been carried on behind a veil of secrecy." *Ibid.*
1043. *See* Massarotto, *The Deterrent and Enunciating Effects of Consent Decrees*, *supra* n. 8.

## §8.04 THE FUTURE OF EU COMMITMENT DECISIONS

Today an extensive use of commitment decisions to settle antitrust proceedings seems to be controversial. Commitment decisions sacrifice both competition law deterrence and the public good of adjudication. As outlined in Chapter 5, there is not a significant time saving in settling a case with commitment decisions versus through a prohibition decision.[1044] But, looking at the U.S. century of experience with antitrust settlements, Europe can easily figure out how to deal with these challenging legal issues. Private antitrust enforcement can be reinforced. Antitrust agencies may ask judges to review commitments before making them legally binding and reduce the time of investigations.

In summary, as mentioned earlier, a question we should ask is: *Should the role of commitment decisions resemble to the role of U.S. consent decrees in the future enforcement of antitrust principles?* I think the answer is "Yes". The potential for commitment decisions is enormous, but the success of these decisions largely depends on its framework, and the overall antitrust enforcement mechanism. Remedies enshrined in commitment decisions can be time sensitive and effectively restore competition through regulation in the data-driven markets where more sophisticated rules seem to be required.

Markets can naturally correct some antitrust concerns in today's increasingly digital structure. The anticompetitive practices that are not corrigible through self-regulation can be settled through structural or behavioral remedies tailored by specific antitrust concerns.[1045] The German Facebook case provides a valuable example by showing how antitrust should both: cooperate with other regulators and use remedies tailored by specific antitrust issues. In summary, tailored antitrust remedies can succeed where government's regulation and self-regulation fail.[1046] Instead of insisting on regulation to prevent foreseeable and unforeseeable anticompetitive practices, data-driven markets can better work through surgical and time-sensitive remedies defined with the same targeted companies.

Not to mention that an increase in the adoption of commitment decisions would lead to a *rapprochement* between U.S. and EU antitrust law. Thanks to the Internet and digital markets, we are living in an increasingly globalized world were goods and data are traded faster and cheaper every day. Today, the necessity of ending what Professor Eleonor M. Fox called *antitrust isolationism*[1047] is even more heartfelt.[1048] Antitrust

1044. *See* Chapter 5.
1045. Joshua D. Wright & Douglas H. Ginsburg, *The Costs and Benefits of Antitrust Consent*, George Mason University Law & Economics Research Paper Series 16-42, 18 (2016).
1046. Massarotto, *From Standard Oil to Google: How the Role of Antitrust Law Has Changed*, *supra* n. 818, at 418.
1047. Eleanor M. Fox, *The End of Antitrust Isolationism: The Vision of One World*, 1 University of Chicago Legal Forum 221 (1992).
1048. *See*, e.g., Douglas H. Ginsburg, *International Antitrust: 2000 and Beyond*, 68 Antitrust L. J. 571, 576 (2000).

isolationism implies the view that antitrust is both "separate from trade law"[1049] and "from other nation's antitrust law."[1050]

As explored in Chapter 3, European competition law seems to have little in common with U.S. antitrust law due to their different origins and approaches in enforcing competition principles. While an economic approach prevails in U.S. antitrust enforcement framework, a formalistic approach is favored by the EU Commission. These differences can end up in the two main antitrust jurisdictions through an increase in the adoption of antitrust settlements in Europe, along with an enforcement of antitrust more as regulatory policy than punitive policy.

In summary, now that the integration of the European market goal is achieved, competition law should closely resemble a tool of *economic democracy*.

1049. *Ibid.*
1050. *Ibid.*

## CHAPTER 9

# Antitrust Settlements in AI and Blockchain Era

"When you understand things, there's no more magic."
(Tim Berners-Lee)

On May 11, 1997, an IBM supercomputer known as *Deep Blue* made history by beating world champion Garry Kasparov at chess for the second time. The idea of building a machine programmed for chess stemmed from a primitive algorithm—the Turochamp—wrote in 1940s by Alan Turing (the father of computer science).[1051]

Actually, Turing started working on this algorithm before computers were capable of performing complicated calculations; Turochamp was able to think of only two moves in advance. But this cruel code inspired IBM computer engineers who, more than forty years later, built a supercomputer enabled to think of 200,000,000 moves per second.[1052] Today, anyone with a smart device benefits from these algorithms that assist us both at home and at work. Alexa and self-driving cars are just two familiar examples.

The story of *Deep Blue* is fascinating for two reasons: (1) algorithms and artificial intelligence (AI) increasingly concern antitrust agencies as companies seem to have recognized the potential to compete or collude; (2) it raises the issue of whether machines can increasingly learn to perform tasks better than humans, also in the field of antitrust. Thus, we should ask: *Will these new technologies make current methods of antitrust intervention insufficient or unnecessary?*

1051. Martin Stezano, *In 1950, Alan Turing Created a Chess Computer Program That Prefigured A.I.* (Aug. 29, 2017), https://www.history.com/news/in-1950-alan-turing-created-a-chess-computer-program-that-prefigured-a-i.

1052. The Conversation, Twenty years on from *Deep Blue v. Kasparov*: how a chess match started the big data revolution (May 11, 2017), http://theconversation.com/twenty-years-on-from-deep-blue-vs-kasparov-how-a-chess-match-started-the-big-data-revolution-76882.

As is explained throughout this Chapter, antitrust enforcers should not worry about algorithms and AI, rather, they should see both as an opportunity. In dealing with AI, antitrust agencies may use algorithms alone to assess pro and anticompetitive effects of pricing algorithms and to provide computer programmers some guidelines on how to prevent anticompetitive results while continuing to stimulate innovation.

Chapter 9 then proceeds with an investigation of blockchain technology, explaining why future markets are likely to shift from centralized to decentralized platforms based on blockchains and what the role of antitrust law will be. As we will see, this technology is in its infancy but has the potential to revolutionize markets yet again, building the grounds for new business models based on decentralized networks.

Remedies enshrined in what might appear as a simple agreement may be the best way forward also in dealing with future AI and blockchain markets. Rather than being the *death of antitrust*, as someone has envisaged,[1053] blockchain and antitrust remedies coded in *smart contracts* will be the key to preserving antitrust's primary goal—*economic democracy*.

## §9.01 ANTITRUST AND MACHINES

As is the case in any debate, there are three sides in the discussion over antitrust and algorithms. While one side is skeptical about the use of algorithms as a means to engage in anticompetitive conduct (Schwalbe),[1054] the other one put multiple warnings (Ezrachi-Stucke).[1055] The third side, instead, takes an intermediate position, noting that "we simply do not know enough"[1056] to endorse a specific policy recommendation (Calvano-Calzolari-Denicolo'-Pastorello). Perhaps, each side is partially right. Although in theory algorithms can enable companies to collude more efficiently,[1057] this is rare as the more sophisticated an algorithm is, the less likely that they are to cooperate (collude) with others algorithms (companies).[1058] Additionally, collusion is easy to detect if an algorithm is not sophisticated.

Machines are now learning the functionality of the human brain (artificial neural networks) from experience.[1059] Deep learning machines include several layers of connected artificial neurons to resemble the human brain where a number of neurons

1053. *See*, e.g., Thibault Schrepel, *Is Blockchain the Death of Antitrust Law? The Blockchain Antitrust Paradox*, 3 Geo. L. Tech. Rev. 281 (2019).
1054. Schwalbe, Ulrich, *Algorithms, Machine Learning, and Collusion* (Jun. 1, 2018). Available at SSRN: https://ssrn.com/abstract=3232631 or http://dx.doi.org/10.2139/ssrn.3232631.
1055. Ezrachi & Stucke, *supra* n. 816.
1056. Emilio Calvano, Giacomo Calzolari, Vincenzo Denicolo' & Sergio Pastorello, *Algorithmic Pricing: What Implications for Competition Policy?* (Jul. 7, 2018). Available at SSRN: https://ssrn.com/abstract=3209781.
1057. Ariel Ezrachi & Maurice E. Stucke, *Sustainable and Unchallenged Algorithmic Tacit Collusion* (Nov. 10, 2018). University of Tennessee Legal Studies Research Paper No. 366; Oxford Legal Studies Research Paper No. 16/2019. Available at SSRN: https://ssrn.com/abstract=3282235 or http://dx.doi.org/10.2139/ssrn.3282235.
1058. Schwalbe, *supra* n. 1054, at 17.
1059. *Ibid.*, at 10. *See also* Ethem Alpaydin, *Machine Learning* 85 (MIT Press, 2016).

are connected with each other through synapses.[1060] With little manual interference, these layers of neurons "are being automatically learned from large amount of data;"[1061] thus these machines can be used in a number of applications and are not built to learn only a single task. The same computer scientists who designed the machines are not able to predict with certainty what and how these machines will learn and we likely will not know enough to regulate them (*see* Calvano-Calzolari-Denicolo'-Pastorello).

In the context of antitrust, the main issue is if computer algorithms can learn to collude more efficiently than people[1062] and whether or not antitrust agencies are up to facing these challenges. Rather, do antitrust agencies have to change the way they enforce antitrust law?[1063] An argument is made in this section that they should neither revolutionize the way that they enforce competition principles nor give up before these challenges. What antitrust agencies should do to address these questions effectively is use algorithms as well and impose remedies on companies when collusion is detected.

### [A] Can Computers Collude?

A computer is as a paperweight, "it doesn't do anything;"[1064] it is the computer program written by a person that gives the computer instructions regarding what to do. Theoretically, a man can teach everything to a machine—to play chess, to speak English, and collude—by translating his human orders into computer language through software.[1065] This software is based on one or more algorithms. Thus, an algorithm teaches the computer to collude only if the person behind the computer decides so; this should be *per se* illegal and the person or company behind the computer

1060. Alpaydin, *supra* n. 1059, at 86.
1061. *Ibid.*, at 104.
1062. Professor Ariel Ezrachi and Maurice Stuker noted that big data, artificial intelligence and computer algorithms promise to benefit our lives, but in the long-run these technologies can also increase the price and decrease the quality of goods. Ezrachi & Stucke, *supra* n. 816, at 1809. *See also*, OECD, *Algorithms and Collusion—Note by the United States* (Jun. 21-23, 2017) at 6. An interesting issue is whether the competitors would be liable if they intentionally but unilaterally adopted the same algorithm knowing that this would make interdependent pricing more likely.
1063. *See*, e.g., OECD, Executive Summary of the Roundtable on Algorithms and Collusion (Jun. 21-23, 2017), available at https://one.oecd.org/document/DAF/COMP/M(2017)1/ANN3/FINAL/en/pdf; Remarks of FTC Chairman, Maureen K. Ohlhausen, at Concurrences Review Antitrust in the Financial Sector Conference (N.Y., May 23, 2017).
1064. Noam Chomsky, *Can Machine Think?*, YouTube (Feb. 7, 2017), https://www.youtube.com/watch?v=Ex9GbzX6tMo.
1065. *See* Massarotto, *Open Source Paradigm: Beyond the Solution to the Software Patentability Debate*, *supra* n. 986, at 647, 673.

condemned.[1066] A clear example of that is *U.S. v. David Topkins* where the defendant pleaded guilty for price-fixing through a pricing algorithm with his conspirators.[1067]

An algorithm is a set of instructions which transform an input to an output (both are known by the software designer). Collusion is easy to detect if an algorithm is not too complex. In the case of collusion, the input is likely a set of prices related to a specific product or service, while the output will be fixed prices.

In a more sophisticated scenario where we knows the input but we do not know how to transform it to the output, a computer engineer can instruct the computer to learn from experience—*machine learning*. The programmer collects a lot of data to learn general trends, ultimately building a model that makes predictions.[1068] The result of *machine learning*, therefore, might be unpredictable and potentially illegal. As outlined above, these *machine learning* techniques are increasingly sophisticated, resembling a human brain (*deep learning* or *neural networks*).

Condemning *machine learning* algorithms under the same *per se* rule does not seem appropriate as *machine learning* outcomes often benefit markets by increasing consumer welfare.[1069] Moreover, as Professor Ulrich Schwalbe noted, cooperation (thus collusion) is very unlikely in increasingly sophisticated algorithms such as deep learning algorithms. These algorithms increasingly evolve and communication among them is challenging as they learn at different speeds.[1070] Furthermore, the literature states that no algorithm can simultaneously learn how to perform the best response and "converge when associates' strategies converge,"[1071] Professor Jacob W. Crandall and Michael A. Goodrich observe.

### [B] Antitrust and AI

Anticipating the results of *machine learning* algorithms and asking whether such algorithms can collude or, more generally, harm consumers should not be the antitrust agencies' main concern. On the contrary, the investigation of how to regulate the results may be an interesting topic. A possible way forward would be for antitrust agencies to set specific antitrust remedies to enforce if the result of *machine learning* is collusion. For example, antitrust agencies can require that the company instruct the computer to automatically redo the process if collusion is detected.

---

1066. On this aspect is interesting the comments provided by Professor Williams on liability for animal "the atavistic idea is emerging that the animals are guilty and not the landowner." G.L. Williams, *Liability for Animals—An Account of the Development and Present Law of Tortious Liability for Animals, Distress Damage Feasant and the Duty to Fence, in Great Britain, Northern Ireland and the Common Law Dominions*, 243 (Cambridge U. Press, 1939).

1067. *U.S. v. David Topkins*, No. CR 15-0419 WHO, 3, 4 (N. D. Cal., 2015).

1068. Alpaydin, *supra* n. 1059.

1069. Schwalbe, *supra* n. 1054, at at 4.

1070. *Ibid.*, at 17. These algorithms are trained to increase their performance. *See* MIT News, *Machine-learning system processes sounds like humans do* (Apr. 19, 2018), http://news.mit.edu/2018/machine-learning-system-processes-sounds-humans-do-0419.

1071. Jacob W. Crandall & Michael A. Goodrich, *Learning to Compete, Coordinate and Cooperate in Repeated Games Using Reinforcement Learning* 281, 306-308, in Machine Learning (2011).

Should antitrust agencies change the way that they enforce antitrust law simply because computers have enabled companies to be more efficient in their anticompetitive conduct? Adopting an entirely new mechanism to enforce antitrust law any time markets find new ways to collude is extremely costly. Moreover, there is a lag required to implement such mechanisms and, during the time necessary to test such tools and assess related costs and benefits, companies might have changed techniques to conspire again. Traditional antitrust tools—such as remedies based on the *per se* rule and the *rule of reason* test—seem sufficient if they are applied to these new increasingly sophisticated economic situations.

Antitrust agencies should use their own algorithmic programs to assess pro and anticompetitive effects of pricing algorithms and detect any sign of collusion in machines learning patterns. Only if collusion is detected should agencies adopt specific remedies. I would recommend the condemnation of *per se* non-machine learning algorithms where the result of collusion was foreseeable. On the other hand, when the illegal result is unconscious, adopting tailored remedies to contrast collusion of *machine learning* under the *rule of reason* test seems logical.[1072] Furthermore, we need to consider that in today's data economy people found new ways to make use of data, creating more and more new useful products and services. This makes price-fixing not feasible as every product has different prices and characteristics.[1073]

In markets where innovation represents the main way to compete, condemning ex-ante—the use and improvement of algorithms—seems not worth the effort. An ex-post intervention by means of antitrust settlements appears more effective only if anticompetitive practices are detected.

## §9.02 ANTITRUST IN THE BLOCKCHAIN ERA

The study of AI and how AI can affect the antitrust enforcement mechanism is compelling. However, this discussion may become less relevant if markets change platforms and paradigms yet again. As explored in Chapter 1, antitrust law originated in the U.S. in 1890 as a tool to regulate the markets created through the development of a new platform—the railroad—thanks to which businesses were able to offer goods and services all over the continent.[1074] Today, markets are built mostly on the Internet platform rather than physical platforms and on increasingly sophisticated algorithms—the result of which, as we have seen, might be unpredictable.[1075] The Internet, like the railroads more than a century ago, has established a new paradigm of

1072. *See* Alfred E. Kahn, *Standards for Antitrust Policy*, 67 Harv. L. Rev. 28 (1953).
1073. George J. Stigler, *The Theory of Economic Regulation*, in Chicago Studies in Political Economy 218 (Univ. Chicago Press, 1988).
1074. Massarotto, *supra* n. 818. Clark, *supra* n. 332; Robert G. Albion & Harold F. Williamson, *The Growth of the American Economy, an Introduction to the Economic History of the United States* 16 (N. Y Prentice Hall, 1944). *See also* Amato, *supra* n. 332; Hovenkamp, *supra* n. 370, at 1029; Bork, *supra* n. 370, 9 J. L. & Econ. 14 (1966); 1 Areeda & Hovenkamp, *supra* n. 205, at 9.
1075. *See*, e.g., Massarotto, *From Digital to Blockchain Markets: What Role for Antitrust and Regulation*, *supra* n. 878; Rubinfeld, *supra* n. 815, at 859, 861.

markets and has revolutionized our world. Digital markets are becoming increasingly important as data represents what oil was a century ago—the most valuable resource.

What if a similar revolution happens yet again and companies continue finding a more sophisticated platform to do business? What may be the role of antitrust in markets built on such a new platform? Blockchain technology—as explored in the following—is built on the Internet network and has the potential to revolutionize markets yet again, establishing a new business paradigm. Remedies enshrined in *smart contracts* which run in a blockchain can turn out to be the best way to preserve competition in future blockchain markets.

Having explained the characteristics and functioning of blockchain, Section §9.02 proceeds with the investigation of the main antitrust issues and how antitrust remedies can be the solution to regulating future markets built on this innovative technology.

### [A] Blockchain Technology

A common tendency is to confuse Bitcoins with blockchain. Bitcoins are cryptocurrency and blockchain is the technology designed to store bitcoin transactions without the supervision of the banking system. In November 2008, Satoshi Nakamoto (which is a pseudonymous) introduced both bitcoins—a cryptocurrency—and blockchain—the decentralized database where bitcoin transactions are stored in the form of blocks. These transactions do not need of a third intermediary, which in the case of bitcoin is a bank, thanks to the blockchain.

What I find interesting are not bitcoins, whose future does not seem prosperous, but the adoption of blockchain technology which, though a consensus mechanism, bypasses third intermediaries making transactions cheaper and, as we will see, safer. Blockchain can execute and store transactions bypassing third intermediaries in a variety of different contexts, beyond the world of cryptocurrencies. Today, blockchain technology can be applied to many industries and situations: social applications, consumer goods and automotive industries are only three examples.[1076]

1076. For example in supply chain, blockchain networks enable companies to track and lodge the flow of goods in real time. *See, e.g.*, UCL Centre for Blockchain Technologies, *Distributed Ledger Technology in the Supply Chain* (2019), available at http://blockchain.cs.ucl.ac.uk/wp-content/uploads/2019/08/DLT-in-the-Supply-Chain_UCL-CBT.pdf. Blockchain technology is also valuable in the context of IP law where it can be used in providing creatorship, controlling and tracking the distribution of a registered IP, furnishing evidence of the first use, or registering and clearing IP rights. *See*, e.g., Birgit Clark, *Blockchain and IP Law: A Match Made in Crypto Heaven?* (February 2018), http://www.wipo.int/wipo_magazine/en/2018/01/article_0005.html; Governments could apply blockchain technology to make their databases more secure and transparent, and to better protect the privacy of their citizens *See* Brian Forde, *Using Blockchain to Keep Public Data Public*, Harv. Business Rev. (Mar. 31, 2017), https://hbr.org/2017/03/using-blockchain-to-keep-public-data-public; Melanie Swan, *Blockchain: Blueprint for a New Economy*, 44 (O'Reilly, 2015). Blockchain government is "the idea of using blockchain to provide services traditionally provided by nation-states in a decentralize, cheaper, more efficient, personalized manner ... The blockchain could become both the mechanism for governing in the present, and the deposit of all of a society's documents, records, and history for use in the future." *Ibid.*

Blockchain technology is based on a consensus mechanism and can be public or private.

### *[1] Consensus Mechanism*

The idea behind blockchain was to create a transaction system entirely self-governed through a consensus mechanism which incentives blockchain participants to work together rather than betray one another. Participants are also called validator nodes or bookkeepers, as they are the ones who validate and store blocks (which can include transactions or simply data) that form the chain. The participants need to agree to a set of rules—the consensus mechanism—which is hard-coded into *the protocol* of the blockchain network. If all participants follow the protocol, everyone wins and the blockchain network properly functions. In the case of bitcoins, the consensus mechanism is translated as follows: the bitcoin transaction is publicly announced to the network and the majority of participants need to agree on the order received before adding a new block in the chain.

There are different consensus mechanisms (consensus protocols). The bitcoin blockchain, for example, uses the *Proof of Work* (PoW)[1077] mechanism which is similar to Adam Back's Hashcash used to prevent spam in emails.[1078] The idea behind PoW is that, before being allowed to store a transaction (or perform any other service linked to the blockchain), the blockchain network needs to solve a complex mathematical problem which requires a lot of electric power.[1079] The first participant that solves the problem broadcasts the solution to the network; a new block is added to the chain only when fifty-one percent of the participants in the network agree on the solution.

Participants are usually rewarded through block rewards, transaction fees or network voting rights to incentivize them to be virtuous. Each time a bookkeeper is the first to solve the puzzle and to confirm the new block, the system can credit tokens into the bookkeeper's account, or the requester of the transaction pays a fee to the bookkeeper for recording that transaction. The concept of using PoW is to slow down the message or transaction sent to all participants, giving time for honest participants to agree on a common solution. This reduces the risk that the same money is spent twice (double-spending).

Another consensus mechanism is the *Proof of Stake* (PoS) where participants are not rewarded to solve a complex math problem but deterministically chosen to perform the transaction based on their wealth—or their total economic *stake* in the blockchain.

---

1077. *See* Marcella Atzori, *Blockchain Technology and Decentralized Governance: Is the State Still Necessary?*, 6 J. Governance & Regulation 45 (2017). ("Even if some nodes are unreliable, dishonest or malicious, the network is able to correctly verify the transactions and protect the ledger from tampering through a mathematical mechanism called proof of work, which makes human intervention or controlling authority unnecessary.") *Ibid.*

1078. What Hashcash does is to introduce CPU cost like a processing cost to engage something. In the context of emails, for example, when you send an email the receiver must first resolve that costs a bit of CPU. For a user this is a tiny difference, but for a spammer that used to send thousands of email per minute means a significant cost of time.

1079. The Economist Explains, Why Bitcoin Uses so much Energy (Jul. 9, 2018) https://www.economist.com/the-economist-explains/2018/07/09/why-bitcoin-uses-so-much-energy.

This mechanism allows saving the great amount of electric power required in the PoW to resolve the math puzzle. In blockchains based on PoW or PoS mechanisms, participants can pool their funds (stakes) or resolve the puzzle together to increase their chances of adding the block and being rewarded—*mining* or *proof of stake pools*. Participants of the pool will receive dividends if the pool is chosen or the math problem is solved, adding a block in the chain.

A blockchain engineer also introduced the *delegate proof of stake* (DPS) where blockchain participants vote the validator nodes (*delegates*) that will forge blocks for the chain. Each participant holds at least a token and one token corresponds to one vote. The DPS mechanism stimulates competition because users vote for people they trust more.

In short, it is consensus mechanism set in a blockchain (which as we have seen can assume different forms) that makes the services of third and centralized platforms and databases unnecessary.

### *[2] Blockchain Safety*

The blockchain is not only decentralized but also an immutable and transparent database that promises to better protect privacy and security.[1080] The possibility of losing blockchain information is zero, as the information is stored on several computer systems and synchronized ledger copies. In the bitcoin public blockchain, although a transaction is public announced, the name of the involved parties remains unknown thanks to the use of a form of cryptography called Public Key Infrastructure (PKI). The owner of a bitcoin, for example, receives a private key that creates a matched pair (one private key and a public key) through a complex mathematical algorithm. Although it is easy to generate a public key from a private key, the opposite is exceptionally difficult. The unique element of PKI is that the public key, visible to everybody, is never attached to a real-world owner. Thus, although all transactions are public and known by all participants, the actual parties within the transaction are kept secret. The recipient of a transaction or an order that use that blockchain can verify the signature (thus the identity of the sender) by checking whether the private key of the sender has effectively created the public key. If not, the public key of the recipient would not authenticate the private key of the sender.

### *[3] Public, Private and Permissioned Blockchains*

The bitcoin blockchain is a public blockchain. There are two macro categories of blockchain: public and private.[1081] In a public blockchain everyone can potentially participate, while a private blockchain clearly defines who can participate.[1082] This

1080. *Ibid.*
1081. Paolo Tasca & Claudio Tessone, *A Taxonomy of Blockchain Technologies: Principles of Identification and Classification*, 4 Ledger 1, 28 (2019).
1082. Tim Kozak, *Public v. Private Blockchain*, Intellectsoft (Feb. 28, 2018), https://blockchain.intellectsoft.net/blog/public-vs-private-blockchain/.

means that in private blockchains participants need to be invited and are only known to each other.[1083] Transaction security relies on the fact that participants have been previously screened by the other participants before joining the blockchain. Conversely, public blockchains are based on anonymity and consensus mechanisms reached, for example, through PoW or PoS.[1084]

The blockchain can set rules to clearly define what activities participants have the permission to perform—*permissioned blockchains*. In permissioned public blockchain, for example, all participants have "read" access, while the "write" and the "consensus management" is reserved to those who obtained the permission by a set of node, which is pre-selected.[1085] In permissioned private blockchains, both participation and the capability to write is limited to those participants that a central authority has authorized.[1086]

### [B] Antitrust and Blockchain

Blockchain can easily change the dynamics of both digital and non-digital markets by means of decentralized networks and challenge antitrust enforcers and regulators yet again. Blockchain technology, as outlined above, can make goods and services cheaper, better protecting the privacy and security of data. Some researchers have theorized the *death of antitrust* given the blockchain will likely reduce the market power of today's centralized platforms[1087] and make it difficult for antitrust enforcers to prosecute anticompetitive conduct without a regulatory intervention that allows antitrust agencies to infiltrate the chain (*regulatory humility*).[1088]

But, as outlined in the book, antitrust remedies enshrined in antitrust settlements both in the U.S. and EU are regulatory in nature. Blockchain will require greater and more diverse forms of antitrust surveillance and intervention to ensure the success of this technology.

The following section investigates these and other issues.

#### *[1] Blockchain and the Risk of Anticompetitive Conduct*

Although blockchain can reduce the market power of today's centralized platforms and better preserve the privacy and security of data, blockchain technology is far from perfect. Private blockchains can, for example, create the perfect conditions for companies to collude and for *smart contracts* to automatically punish deviations by participants.

1083. Rose Jacobs, *The Good and Bad of Blockchain* (Feb. 12, 2018), http://review.chicagobooth.edu/finance/2018/article/good-and-bad-blockchain.
1084. Proof of stake means that the creator of a new block is defined in a deterministic way, for example depending of its wealth (the so-called stake). *See* IBM, Blockchain for Dummies, 16 (John Wiley & Sons, 2 ed., 2018).
1085. Tasca & Tessone, *supra* n. 1081, at 28.
1086. *Ibid.*
1087. *See* Schrepel, *supra* n. 1053, at 50.
1088. *Ibid.*, at 43.

In a private blockchain, the validating power is usually assigned to previously verified and known parties who already regularly transact with one another, creating the potential for a transparent environment among their participants.[1089] In other words, participants know and trust each other and everything the blockchain does is totally private. This ease of communication can facilitate a quicker and more efficient collusion in markets, especially in oligopolies where only a few players control the markets.[1090] Moreover, the transparent environment can help the identification of deviations by cartel participants and *smart contracts*, which are self-executing agreements, automatize the punishment for any cartel's deviation.

*Smart contracts* are not exactly legal contracts, but they can become legal contracts if certain conditions are met.[1091] *Smart contracts* represent the "simplest form of decentralized automation"[1092] as they define standard rules through a digital protocol that are self-executed by a computer or a network of computers when the participants reach an agreement and its conditions. In other words, *smart contracts* are self-executing contractual states stored on a blockchain;[1093] contracts built into a code and enforced by a program.[1094] Thus, *smart contracts* can be used to establish "automated punishments"[1095] through a digital protocol for those who deviate from a cartel.

In summary, antitrust agencies worry that private blockchains and pricing algorithms examined above can basically have the same result as fixing goods and services' prices. Private blockchains can be more efficient than pricing algorithms in preserving confidentiality and punishing cartel's deviations by means of *smart contracts*.[1096]

Exclusionary conduct in private blockchains may also be possible, as the participation in those networks is by invitation only. As long as private blockchains encourage synergies there is no reason for concern and competition amongst blockchains can decrease the anticompetitive effects related to exclusionary conduct.[1097] But in the long run a single blockchain might become dominant and exclusionary strategies too effective; antitrust agencies should keep this in mind.

1089. Blockchainhub, *Blockchains & Distributed Ledger Technologies*, https://blockchainhub.net/blockchains-and-distributed-ledger-technologies-in-general/.

1090. *Ibid.*

1091. *See* Ai Deng, *Smart Contracts and Blockchains: Steroid for Collusion?* (Sep. 11, 2018) available at SSRN: https://ssrn.com/abstract=3187010 or http://dx.doi.org/10.2139/ssrn.3187010.

1092. Blockchainhub, *Smart Contracts*, https://blockchainhub.net/smart-contracts/.

1093. IBM, Blockchain for Dummies, *supra* n. 1084, at 32.

1094. *Ibid. See also* Massimo Bartoletti & Livio Pompianu, *An Empirical Analysis of Smart Contracts: Platforms, Applications, and Design Patterns* (Mar. 18, 2017), https://www.researchgate.net/publication/315454656_An_Empirical_Analysis_of_Smart_Contracts_Platforms_Applications_and_Design_Patterns.

1095. *See*, e.g., OECD, *Blockchain Technology and Competition Policy—Issues Paper by the Secretariat* 6 (Jun. 8, 2018), https://one.oecd.org/document/DAF/COMP/WD(2018)47/en/pdf.

1096. Lin W. Cong & Zhiguo He, *Blockchain Disruption and Smart Contracts* 27 (Dec. 27, 2018), available at https://papers.ssrn.com/sol3/papers.cfm?abstract_id=2985764.

1097. *Blockchain and smart contracts* "can improve both consumer surplus and welfare by encouraging entry and competition." *Ibid.*, at 26.

In public blockchains everyone can participate, alleviating the risk of collusion and exclusionary conduct. True, in public blockchain transactions data is distributed and stored in a vast number of computers (the decentralized blockchain ledger), which can make it easier for competitors to tacitly collude despite the parties being kept secret.[1098] However, the same OECD observed that the transparency of price information can increase consumer welfare.[1099] A good example of this that we have already explored is the ride-sharing company, Uber, which developed a pricing algorithm that increases consumer welfare. UberX matches drivers to consumers seeking rides by means of a real-time pricing algorithm. A study estimated a consumer surplus of USD 2.9 billion was generated by UberX service in four U.S. cities.[1100]

Furthermore, the risk of collusion should not be underestimated in mining pools and blockchains based on the DPS consensus mechanism that tend to concentrate power in the hands of a select group of participants. The concentration of votes or stakes can compromise the decentralization process and raises antitrust concerns related to collusion and the creation of cartels among blockchain participants or delegates.[1101] These topics will be further explored in some of my other articles.

### *[2] Antitrust Intervention in Blockchains*

Antitrust agencies need to be proactive in the development of conditions to limit both the collusion phenomena and exclusionary conduct, particularly in private blockchains that are significant in size with participants active in the same or secondary markets. Antitrust agencies might think of imposing remedies that are self-executed in *smart contracts* to prevent and punish collusive practices in blockchains where the risk of engaging in anticompetitive practices is high.

Similar to AI, prohibiting by default, for example, private blockchains because the risk of collusion tends to be high if some circumstances are met, does not seem appropriate. Not all private blockchains reach a size that raises antitrust concerns or are built among competitors or potential competitors. Private blockchain can be a crucial tool to increase efficiency of companies' performance, reducing costs of services and increasing their quality. As we will see, the use of private blockchains should be encouraged for antitrust agencies or any government's bodies as most information and documents need to be kept private and collusion is not an issue among government officials.

An effective antitrust intervention on private blockchains may include behavioral or structural antitrust remedies tailored for specific antitrust concerns. The antitrust

1098. *Ibid.*, at 4.

1099. OECD, *Personalized Pricing in the Digital Era*, 26 (Nov. 28, 2018), http://www.oecd.org/officialdocuments/publicdisplaydocumentpdf/?cote=DAF/COMP(2018)13&docLanguage=En.

1100. Cohen, Hahn & Hall, *supra* n. 880.

1101. Lisk-a blockchain owned by two cartels (Jul. 17, 2018) https://cryptogo.de/en/lisk-the-mafia-blockchain/. Paolo Tasca, The Hope and Betrayal of Blockchain, New York Times (Dec. 4, 2018), https://www.nytimes.com/2018/12/04/opinion/blockchain-bitcoin-technology-revolution.html.

agency, for example, may impose that blockchain participants hide prices or the name of parties in some transactions if the private blockchain meets both requirements: (*i*) reaches a significant size in the affected market/s; (*ii*) includes competitors or potential competitors. Similar remedies may be imposed on public blockchains that raise antitrust concerns as they include mining/proof of stake pools or the DPS mechanism.[1102] Here, the antitrust agency may define *ex ante* a special mining pools or delegates' responsibility which requires them not to engage in specific conduct if the same requirements (*i*) and (*ii*) are met in the single pool or group of delegates. Additional remedies may be imposed on these blockchains if considered as necessary in the specific situation to contrast actual or potential anticompetitive practices.

Again, these structural or behavioral remedies tailored to specific antitrust concerns, which can be similar to those explored through the book, should be enshrined in *smart contracts*. *Smart contracts* have the potential to become a remarkable legal and antitrust tool by replacing traditional antitrust settlements with agreements built into a code and enforced by a program.[1103] By doing so, *smart contracts* enable antitrust agencies to reduce monitoring costs and time-related to antitrust remedies that the agency decides to impose.

Antitrust agencies should benefit from blockchain technology as well. *Smart contracts* where antitrust remedies are written into a code might run in the antitrust authority's own (private) blockchain made up by its officials. This would make antitrust enforcement not only more effective but also more secure and transparent within the agency. The antitrust agency may also request to participate in those blockchains which raise antitrust concern. Everything is tracked in a blockchain making it easy for an agency part of the blockchain network to detect illegal activities turning the blockchain into a valuable antitrust tool itself.

Technology is not the driver of anticompetitive conduct, rather, new technologies represent the best way to compete as they increase the quality and reduce the price of products. Not only companies but also antitrust enforcers and any other government bodies should benefit from them to intervene effectively in current markets.[1104]

---

1102. *See* L.M. Bach, B. Mihaljevic & Zagar, *Comparative Analysis of Blockchain Consensus Algorithms, 41st International Convention on Information and Communication Technology, Electronics and Microelectronics (MIPRO)*, 1545, 1547 (2018). A bitcoin mining introduced the *delegate proof of stake* (DPS) to save electric power and time (usually ten minutes) required in blockchain transactions. In DPS one coin corresponds to one vote and users vote to select other users they trust called *witnesses*. Only the top tier of witnesses who have gathered the most votes has the right to validate transactions and are paid by the network as well as any miners in a PoW system. In addition to the vote of witnesses, users vote for *a group of delegates* that are responsible for governing and performance of the blockchain protocol. Delegates do not validate transactions nor do they produce blocks.

1103. *Ibid. See also* Bartoletti & Pompianu, *supra* n. 1094.

1104. Massarotto, *From Digital to Blockchain Markets: What Role for Antitrust and Regulation*, *supra* n. 878; *See also* Paul Michelman, *Seeing Beyond the Blockchain Hype*, 4 MIT Sloan Management Review 17, 18 (2017).

### [a] *Public Blockchain and the Internet*

The public blockchain is not merely a tool to increase efficiency of goods and services with less antitrust concerns than a private blockchain. A public blockchain has the potential to become, similar to the Web on the Internet—*universal*. The Internet is the infrastructure where information and data travel by means of languages known as protocols or standards; the Web is the language and protocol created by Tim Berners Lee in 1990, which became the universal language on the Internet network. Specifically, the Web includes the Hypertext Transfer Protocol (HTTP) and HyperText Markup Language (HTML).[1105] Other languages and protocols were initially used to transfer data. In 1995 for example, Microsoft launched the Microsoft Network (MSN), along with Windows 1995. The MSN was a centralized network built on the Internet infrastructure, which ran on protocols and software for Microsoft applications only.[1106] But, given the standardization of the Web by means of the HTTP and HTML, the MSN was converted to provide standard www applications.

The success of the Web was mainly due to the fact that HTTP and HTML were open, free and with "no central manager and no central data-base."[1107] People increasingly started to use it and the Web became the standard Internet language. Similar to the Web, a public blockchain is open, free and decentralized (no one owns a public blockchain as no one owns the Web). But data is more than merely transferred on a public blockchain—it is stored as the blockchain is a database. The founder of the Web wanted to create an open and decentralized infrastructure to freely transfer data on the Internet; the same can be accomplished by means of a public blockchain to conserve and protect data on the Internet.

Similar to what Tim Berners Lee made for the Web, someone could set a universal and open protocol in a public blockchain to create the universal infrastructure and network to store data. This universal public blockchain has the potential of restoring the Web's decentralization on the Internet platform. Initially, the Web was a decentralized platform. Over the last years, large technology companies, including Google and Facebook, found ways through centralized platforms to come between the users and the Web by making themselves an integral part of the process. Facebook, for example, created a social network on the Internet that has enabled it to connect people all over the world; more people that join the network the more attractive Facebook becomes for both users and advertisers. As a consequence, the Web became more centralized.[1108]

Today, large technology companies significantly control and affect the data industry by regulating most of the data flow. A decentralized universal public

1105. *See* W3C, Standards, https://www.w3.org/standards/.
1106. ISPs, http://alternatives.rzero.com/isp.html.
1107. The economist review of books: *Weaving the Web: The Original Design and Ultimate Destiny of the World Wide Web by Its inventor*, 353 The Economist S10 (Sep. 18, 1999).
1108. *See* Shannon Bond, *Google and Facebook Build Digital Ad Duopoly*, Financial Times (Mar. 14, 2017) https://www.ft.com/content/30c81d12-08c8-11e7-97d1-5e720a26771b; Lara O'Reilly, *The Race Is On to Challenge Google-Facebook "Duopoly" in Digital Advertising*, The Wall Street Journal (Jun. 19, 2017).

blockchain/database would track and store data of each person in multiple computers allowing everyone to have the same access to data. This would ensure an equal right to data. In this way each person would own and control their personal data through a PKI and everything would be tracked in such a blockchain. The same Tim Berners Lee recognized that the blockchain and the Web have the chance to "connect together in lots of interesting ways,"[1109] which may reduce the role of big tech companies and restore the Web's decentralization.[1110]

Similar to the Internet, the creation of a universal and single blockchain is feasible if such a blockchain can be kept free, open and subject to the supervision and regulation of neutral bodies—such as antitrust agencies—rather than private companies or a total *laissez-faire*. A single universal blockchain has the potential to be public in nature, requiring forms of regulation similar to the Internet and the telecommunication network. At this moment it might be difficult to elaborate specific forms of regulation for new markets that we cannot even envisage, but by focusing on antitrust's role, some insights can be drawn.

Antitrust agencies are necessary gatekeepers of markets to ensure the success of new technology like the cutting-edge blockchain. As outlined above, blockchain technology can make present centralized platforms unnecessary. As Professor William J. Baumol, Robert E. Litan and Carl J. Schramm observed, "breakthrough technologies can quickly make existing products and services obsolete and for that reason may be fiercely resisted within large organizations."[1111] Thus, antitrust enforcers need to be prepared for this resistance without compromising companies' incentives to innovate. This goal may be achieved through structural or behavioral remedies, tailored to specific antitrust concerns, that are self-executed by *smart contracts* which run through an antitrust agency's private blockchain.

In summary, antitrust enforcers must endorse and oversee the steps toward a decentralization of markets on behalf of the innovation process that increases market efficiency and consumer welfare. Antitrust enforcers will be crucial in the success of this new, cutting edge technology that can revolutionize markets and completely change the way to do business.

## §9.03 CONCLUSIONS

Part III has emphasized the importance of data for today's economy as data is the food to feed *machine learning* and algorithms in which are driving the economy today. This is true also in the context of antitrust. There is so much to learn that we can use from previous antitrust cases and history, which in the U.S. has more than a century and in Europe more than sixty years. Also in the context of antitrust, data left dormant is not

1109. Jeff J. Roberts, *Blockchain and the Web Are Coming Together, Says Berners-Lee*, The Fortune (Oct. 17, 2017), http://fortune.com/2017/10/17/blockchain-berners-lee/.
1110. *Ibid.*
1111. William J. Baumol, Robert E. Litan & Carl J. Schramm, *Good Capitalism, Bad Capitalism, and the Economics of Growth and Prosperity* 82 (Yale U. Press, 2008).

useful.[1112] *Machine learning* can perform a regression analysis that is much more sophisticated than the one performed for predicting antitrust remedies on the *Google Search Bias* case by using the AT&T consent decree of 1982.

Technology is neither the driver of anticompetitive conduct nor the *death of antitrust*. New, more advanced technologies should be endorsed in markets and in the context of antitrust as well. Past antitrust cases and precedents represent valuable resources[1113] for the antitrust enforcers of today to turn new technologies into useful tools.

Machines can learn everything, from playing chess to detecting and contrasting new advanced forms of anticompetitive conduct. This is not to say that antitrust will be governed by machines or computer scientists. Only lawyers and economists in the field of antitrust can recognize the importance of antitrust precedents and define antitrust concerns. Antitrust officers and anyone in the field of antitrust should not worry about losing their job. What is suggested for the field of antitrust, as well as other fields, is for people start learning how to use and exploit new technologies to perform their job and view them more as opportunities than a threat. True, a machine in 1997 beat the world chess champion, but it is also true that that machine would have never existed without computer scientists and chess players.

In summary, antitrust and innovation are not separate issues.[1114] The path of innovation largely depends on the actions of antitrust agencies that can determine the success or the failure of new technologies. Blockchain technology is the next testing grounds.

Antitrust enforcers are crucial in maintaining the delicate balance between controlling the actions of large players and keeping them incentivized to lead the creation of new technologies. The role of antitrust can be fully exploited through remedies tailored to specific antitrust concerns in any markets, whether they are tangible, on the Internet or on the blockchain platform.

---

1112. *Machine learning* algorithms investigate the past to predict the future; rather these algorithms from data determine and extract patterns to predict future outcomes.
1113. Kelleher & Tierney *supra* n. 824. "Data sets are intrinsically historic in the sense that data are representations of observations that were made in the past." *Ibid.*, at 150.
1114. Matthew Lane, *The History of Innovation in Antitrust Law* (Jun. 12, 2018), http://www.project-disco.org/competition/061218the-history-of-innovation-in-antitrust-law/#.WyJuwxm-m2w.

# PART IV
# Conclusions

In achieving a greater level of competition in markets *"we must make the act of faith and move as rapidly as possible"*[1115] in any way we can.

Since the origin of antitrust, scholars, politicians and economists have asked for change:[1116] either because antitrust is too interventionist, or because it is not enough. In 2019, the United States is accused of being too lax; in Europe, the opposite—too interventionist. This gives us the opportunity to explore both sides of the antitrust coin in primary antitrust jurisdictions and make some insights for the future.

In 1957 when Europe was created, diversity in approach to enforcing competition principles between Europe and the United States was justified. The single European market occurred *de facto* only in 1990s; until that time the crucial European industries were governed by state monopolies versus private monopolies in the U.S.. AT&T—which historically has concerned U.S. antitrust enforcers—exemplifies this point, as the inventor of the telephone, Alexander Bell, ran it and not a state-owned company.

In 1992, Professor Eleanor M. Fox wisely noted that antitrust isolationism—the concept of U.S. antitrust as separate from both trade law and the other antitrust law jurisdiction—needed to end[1117] as we are living in an increasingly globalized world. This is even truer today: the most valuable resource, *data*, is globally traded through the Internet platform, and only a few companies have found a way to control its trade worldwide.

Therefore, it is the time to decidedly remove antitrust from a national dimension and antitrust settlements is the key to globalize the way to enforce antitrust principles worldwide.

1115. Alfred E. Kahn, *Applying Economics to an Imperfect World*, 2 Regulation 17, 21 (1978).
1116. *See*, e.g., Kahn, *supra* n. 1072, at 35; Wesley J. Liebeler, Comments, 28 J. L. & Econ. 335 (1985); Khan, *supra* n. 400.
1117. Fox, *supra* n. 1047. "One World does mean an end to antitrust isolationism." *Ibid.*, at 240.

Throughout the book we have seen how what might appear as simple contracts—*antitrust settlements*—regulate the U.S. and EU markets, driving the economy with the participation and consensus of the same market players.

Economic regulation is "deeply imbedded"[1118] in economic models, which are perfect, despite the fact that markets are not.[1119] Antitrust settlements can be the "imperfect regulation"[1120] that achieves the "imperfect competition"[1121] that markets need. Antitrust settlements are *by definition* imperfect, being the result of a compromise between the antitrust agency and the company subject to an investigation rather than the adjudication by courts. Furthermore, antitrust agencies need to be "sufficiently flexible and creative to respond appropriately"[1122] to the new challenges that lie ahead.[1123] Markets based on increasingly sophisticated algorithms or blockchain technologies are only two examples. Antitrust settlements are flexible and tailored by mutable and specific market needs. Last but not least, the antitrust settlement procedure is usually much faster than a trial. There is a lag required to try a case in courts and, during the time necessary, markets might have changed again and made the ruling ineffective.

Antitrust settlements can be the perfect intersection between antitrust and trade law among all antitrust jurisdictions where competition principles are enforced for the sake of *economic democracy*.[1124] Antitrust settlements are the result of a bargaining process that brings us back to the foundation of markets. Adam Smith created the concept of markets to justify the "market price" that diverges from the natural price. The market price is the result of the bargaining process determined by competition.

As outlined in *Part III*, markets can naturally correct some antitrust concerns and remediate failures through the development of new technologies and the creation of new markets in competition with existing ones. Those anticompetitive practices and market failures that are not corrigible through self-regulation can require the intervention of antitrust settlements; in the most complex situations, greater forms of regulation.[1125]

As with any economic tool, antitrust settlements can result in market inefficiency and harm consumers if not appropriately used. As emphasized in *Part II*, an economic analysis pre and post *antitrust consent* is necessary. Antitrust settlements might be more than a contract or an agency/judge order, but a "device of economy"[1126]—where economic evaluations are required.

1118. Stigler, *supra* n. 1073.
1119. Kahn, *supra* n. 1072, at 18.
1120. Alfred E. Kahn, *The Economics of Regulation Principles and Institutions*, xxxvii (MIT Press, 1988).
1121. *Ibid.*
1122. Daniel L. Rubinfeld, *Antitrust Policy: Lessons from the US*, in International Encyclopedia of the Social & Behavioral Science 802 (Elsevier, 2d ed. 2015).
1123. *Ibid.*
1124. Massarotto, *From Standard Oil to Google: How the Role of Antitrust Law Has Changed*, *supra* n. 818, at 418; Hamilton & Till, *supra* n. 10, at 44.
1125. Massarotto, *From Digital to Blockchain Markets: What Role for Antitrust and Regulation*, *supra* n. 878.
1126. Hamilton & Till, *supra* n. 10, at 9.

In this "*perfect*" tool there remains an unresolved challenge for its success story, as was revealed at the beginning of this book. How do antitrust settlements that prevent judge's rulings preserve the enunciating effect of antitrust law? Again, legal rules are public goods, and private judges are not well suited to provide an authoritative interpretation or create law, but the answer may be easier than we think.

Antitrust is a tool in the arsenal of economic regulation rather than a law. Judges should evaluate the compliance of antitrust settlements with the required form, procedure and the public interest. In the U.S., some Professors found a different solution. Their suggestion was to train judges in antitrust economics.[1127] Professor Michael R. Baye and Joshua D. Wright examined antitrust litigations in federal and administrative courts from 1996 to 2006, concluding that antitrust was "too complicated for generalist judges."[1128] As attractive as this suggestion might be, in concrete terms it is unlikely to be an effective solution; training judges might address the problem superficially; acting as a painkiller that provides comfort without fighting the disease. Furthermore, as with individuals suffering a health crisis, quick care is needed in markets. In the lag required to train judges in antitrust economics, markets might have evolved. This brings us back to the same issue revealed with the trial—markets are time-sensitive.

Judges deal with law, economists deal with markets and economic regulation—*antitrust* is completely grounded in economics. Would it not make more sense to leave judges to create and interpret law and economists to grow our economy through the *consent* of the same market players? This might be contradicted by the study conducted by Baye and Wright, according to which FTC administrative decisions were appealed more frequently than the district courts' rulings. Thus, judges are more suitable than FTC economists in dealing with antitrust cases. But, apart from using the appeal rate,[1129] the same authors admitted that that conclusion can stem from "procedural and institutional differences between FTC administrative litigation and litigation in federal courts."[1130] Section 5 of the FTC act, as we have seen, is likely the most criticized provisions with content so vague and unclear, it represents a gift for any lawyer:

"*The power of the lawyer is in the uncertainty of the law*"
—recalls the judicial philosopher Jeremy Bentham

1127. Baye & Wright, *supra* n. 479.
1128. *Ibid.*
1129. To assess the quality of a decision an evaluation of the related economic effects may be more appropriate.
1130. Baye & Wright, *supra* n. 479, at 17.

In summary, it is time to remove judges from the economic playbook and limit their evaluation to the compliance of these settlements, both with the public interests and with the rights of parties during the proceeding. Antitrust settlements might not be the *perfect* tool—but markets are not perfect either:

Antitrust settlement is simply "*the instrument [of] faith.*"[1131]

1131. Hamilton & Till, *supra* n. 10, at 4.

# Index

## C

**D**

**E**



**F**

## INTERNATIONAL COMPETITION LAW SERIES

1. Ignacio De Leon, *Latin American Competition Law and Policy: A Policy in Search of Identity*, 2001 (ISBN 90-411-1542-0).
2. Wim Dejonghe & Wouter Van de Voorde (eds), *M & A in Belgium*, 2001 (ISBN 90-411-1594-3).
3. Yang-Ching Chao, Gee San, Changfa Lo & Jiming Ho (eds), *International and Comparative Competition Law and Policies*, 2001 (ISBN 90-411-1643-5).
4. Martin Mendelsohn & Stephen Rose, *Guide to the EC Block Exemption for Vertical Agreements*, 2002 (ISBN 90-411-9813-X).
5. Clifford A. Jones & Mitsuo Matsushita (eds), *Competition Policy in the Global Trading System: Perspectives from the EU, Japan and the USA*, 2002 (ISBN 90-411-1758-X).
6. Christian Koenig, Andreas Bartosch, Jens-Daniel Braun & Marion Romes (eds), *EC Competition and Telecommunications Law*. Second Edition, 2009 (ISBN 978-90-411-2564-4).
7. Jürgen Basedow (ed.), *Limits and Control of Competition with a View to International Harmonization*, 2002 (ISBN 90-411-1967-1).
8. Maureen Brunt, Economic Essays on Australian and New Zealand Competition Law, 2003 (ISBN 90-411-1991-4).
9. Ky P. Ewing, Jr., *Competition Rules for the 21st Century: Principles from America's Experience*, Second Edition, 2006 (ISBN 90-411-2477-2).
10. Joseph Wilson, *Globalization and the Limits of National Merger Control Laws*, 2003 (ISBN 90-411-1996-5).
11. Peter Verloop & Valérie Landes (eds), *Merger Control in Europe: EU, Member States and Accession States*, Fourth Edition, 2003 (ISBN 90-411-2056-4).
12. Themistoklis K. Giannakopoulos, *Safeguarding Companies' Rights in Competition and Anti-dumping/Anti-subsidies Proceedings*, Second Edition, 2011 (ISBN 978-90-411-3404-2).
13. Marjorie Holmes & Lesley Davey (eds), *A Practical Guide to National Competition Rules across Europe*, Second Edition, 2007 (ISBN 978-90- 411-2607-8).
14. Sigrid Stroux, *US and EU Oligopoly Control*, 2004 (ISBN 90-411-2296-6).
15. Tzong-Leh Hwang and Chiyuan Chen (eds), *The Future Development of Competition Framework*, 2004 (ISBN 90-411-2305-9).

16. Phedon Nicolaides, Mihalis Kekelekis and Maria Kleis, *State Aid Policy in the European Community: Principles and Practice,* Second Edition, 2008 (ISBN 978-90-411-2754-9).
17. Doris Hildebrand, *Economic Analyses of Vertical Agreements: A Self- Assessment*, 2005 (ISBN 90-411-2328-8).
18. Frauke Henning-Bodewig, *Unfair Competition Law: European Union and Member States*, 2005 (ISBN 90-411-2329-6).
19. Duarte Brito & Margarida Catalão-Lopes, *Mergers and Acquisitions: The Industrial Organization Perspective,* 2006 (ISBN 90-411-2451-9).
20. Nikos Th. Nikolinakos, *EU Competition Law and Regulation in the Converging Telecommunications, Media and IT Sectors*, 2006 (ISBN 90-411- 2469-1).
21. Mihalis Kekelekis, *The EC Merger Control Regulation: Rights of Defence. A Critical Analysis of DG COMP Practice and Community Courts' Jurisprudence*, 2006 (ISBN 90-411-2553-1).
22. Mark R. Joelson, *An International Antitrust Primer: A Guide to the Operation of United States, European Union and Other Key Competition Laws in the Global Economy*, Third Edition, 2006 (ISBN 90-411-2468-3).
23. Themistoklis K. Giannakopoulos, *A Concise Guide to the EU Anti-dumping/ Anti-subsidies Procedures*, 2006 (ISBN 90-411-2464-0).
24. George Cumming, Brad Spitz & Ruth Janal, *Civil Procedure Used for Enforcement of EC Competition Law by the English, French and German Civil Courts*, 2007 (ISBN 978-90-411-2471-5).
25. Jürgen Basedow (ed.), *Private Enforcement of EC Competition Law*, 2007 (ISBN 978-90-411-2613-9).
26. Jung Wook Cho, *Innovation and Competition in the Digital Network Economy: A Legal and Economic Assessment on Multi-tying Practices and Network Effects*, 2007 (ISBN 978-90-411-2574-3).
27. Akira Inoue, *Japanese Antitrust Law Manual: Law, Cases and Interpretation of the Japanese Antimonopoly Act*, 2007 (ISBN 978-90-411-2627-6).
28. René Barents, *Directory of EC Case Law on Competition*, 2007 (ISBN 978-90-411-2656-6).
29. Paul F. Nemitz (ed.), *The Effective Application of EU State Aid Procedures: The Role of National Law and Practice*, 2007 (ISBN 978-90-411-2657-3).
30. Jurian Langer, *Tying and Bundling as a Leveraging Concern under EC Competition Law*, 2007 (ISBN 978-90-411-2575-0).
31. Abel M. Mateus & Teresa Moreira (eds), *Competition Law and Economics – Advances in Competition Policy and Antitrust Enforcement*, 2007 (ISBN 978-90-411-2632-0).
32. Alberto Santa Maria, *Competition and State Aid: An Analysis of the EC Practice*, 2007 (ISBN 978-90-411-2617-7).
33. Barry J. Rodger (ed.), *Article 234 and Competition Law: An Analysis*, 2007 (ISBN 978-90-411-2605-4).

34. Alla Pozdnakova, *Liner Shipping and EU Competition Law*, 2008 (ISBN 978-90-411-2717-4).
35. Milena Stoyanova, *Competition Problems in Liberalized Telecommunications: Regulatory Solutions to Promote Effective Competition*, 2008 (ISBN 978-90-411-2736-5).
36. *EC State Aid Law/Le Droit des Aides d'Etat dans la CE. Liber Amicorum Francisco Santaolalla Gadea*, 2008 (ISBN 978-90-411-2774-7).
37. René Barents, *Directory of EC Case Law on State Aids*, 2008 (ISBN 978- 90-411-2732-7).
38. Ignacio De Leon, *An Institutional Assessment of Antitrust Policy: The Latin American Experience*, 2009 (ISBN 978-90-411-2478-4).
39. Doris Hildebrand, *The Role of Economic Analysis in EU Competition Law: The European School*, Fourth Edition, 2016 (ISBN 978-90-411-6245-8).
40. Eugène Buttigieg, *Competition Law: Safeguarding the Consumer Interest. A Comparative Analysis of US Antitrust Law and EC Competition Law*, 2009 (ISBN 978-90-411-3119-5).
41. Ioannis Lianos & Ioannis Kokkoris (eds), *The Reform of EC Competition Law: New Challenges*, 2010 (ISBN 978-90-411-2692-4).
42. George Cumming & Mirjam Freudenthal, *Civil Procedure in EU Competition Cases before the English and Dutch Courts*, 2010 (ISBN 978-90-411-3192-8).
43. A.E. Rodriguez & Ashok Menon, *The Limits of Competition Policy: The Shortcomings of Antitrust in Developing and Reforming Economies*, 2010 (ISBN 978-90-411-3177-5).
44. Mika Oinonen, *Does EU Merger Control Discriminate against Small Market Companies? Diagnosing the Argument with Conclusions*, 2010 (ISBN 978-90-411-3261-1).
45. Eirik Østerud, *Identifying Exclusionary Abuses by Dominant Undertakings under EU Competition Law: The Spectrum of Tests*, 2010 (ISBN 978-90-411-3271-0).
46. Marco Botta, *Merger Control Regimes in Emerging Economies: A Case Study on Brazil and Argentina*, 2011 (ISBN 978-90-411-3402-8).
47. Jürgen Basedow & Wolfgang Wurmnest (eds), *Structure and Effects in EU Competition Law: Studies on Exclusionary Conduct and State Aid*, 2011 (ISBN 978-90-411-3174-4).
48. George Cumming (ed.), *Merger Decisions and the Rules of Procedure of the European Community Courts*, 2012 (ISBN 978-90-411-3671-8).
49. Eduardo Molan Gaban & Juliana Oliveira Domingues (eds), *Antitrust Law in Brazil: Fighting Cartels*, 2012 (ISBN 978-90-411-3670-1).
50. Giandonato Caggiano, Gabriella Muscolo & Marina Tavassi (eds), *Competition Law and Intellectual Property: A European Perspective*, 2012 (ISBN 978-90-411-3447-9).
51. Ben Van Rompuy, *Economic Efficiency: The Sole Concern of Modern Antitrust Policy? Non-efficiency Considerations under Article 101 TFEU*, 2012 (ISBN 978-90-411-3870-5).

52. Liyang Hou, *Competition Law and Regulation of the EU Electronic Communications Sector: A Comparative Legal Approach*, 2012 (ISBN 978-90-411-4047-0).
53. Barry Rodger, *Landmark Cases in Competition Law: Around the World in Fourteen Stories*, 2012 (ISBN 978-90-411-3843-9).
54. Andreas Scordamaglia-Tousis, *EU Cartel Enforcement: Reconciling Effective Public Enforcement with Fundamental Rights*, 2013 (ISBN 978-90-411-4758-5).
55. Bernardo Cortese (ed.), *EU Competition Law: Between Public and Private Enforcement*, 2014 (ISBN 978-90-411-4677-9).
56. Barry Rodger (ed.), *Competition Law: Comparative Private Enforcement and Collective Redress across the EU*, 2014 (ISBN 978-90-411-4559-8).
57. Nada Ina Pauer, *The Single Economic Entity Doctrine and Corporate Group Responsibility in European Antitrust Law*, 2014 (ISBN 978-90-411-5262-6).
58. Urška Petrovčič, *Competition Law and Standard Essential Patents: A Transatlantic Perspective*, 2014 (ISBN 978-90-411-4960-2).
59. David Telyas, *The Interface between Competition Law, Patents and Technical Standards*, 2014 (ISBN 978-90-411-5418-7).
60. Katerina Maniadaki, *EU Competition Law, Regulation and the Internet: The Case of Net Neutrality*, 2014 (ISBN 978-90-411-4140-8).
61. Horacio Vedia Jerez, *Competition Law Enforcement and Compliance across the World: A Comparative Review*, 2015 (ISBN 978-90-411-5815-4).
62. Kadir Ba, *The Substantive Appraisal of Joint Ventures under the EU Merger Control Regime*, 2015 (ISBN 978-90-411-5816-1).
63. Alberto Santa Maria, *Competition and State Aid: An Analysis of the EU Practice*, Second Edition, 2015 (ISBN 978-90-411-5818-5).
64. Lúcio Tomé Feteira, *The Interplay between European and National Competition Law after Regulation 1/2003: "United (Should) We Stand?"*, 2016 (ISBN 978-90-411-5663-1).
65. Giovanni Pitruzzella & Gabriella Muscolo (eds), *Competition and Patent Law in the Pharmaceutical Sector: An International Perspective*, 2016 (ISBN 978-90-411-5927-4).
66. Małgorzata Cyndecka, *The Market Economy Investor Test in EU State Aid Law: Applicability and Application*, 2016 (ISBN 978-90-411-6102-4).
67. Damiano Canapa, *Trademarks and Brands in Merger Control: An Analysis of the European and Swiss Legal Orders*, 2016 (ISBN 978-90-411-6717-0).
68. Inge Graef, *EU Competition Law, Data Protection and Online Platforms: Data as Essential Facility*, 2016 (ISBN 978-90-411-8324-8).
69. Anders Jessen, *Exclusionary Abuse after the* Post Danmark I *Case: The Role of the Effects-Based Approach under Article 102 TFEU*, 2017 (ISBN 978-90-411-8996-7).
70. Baskaran Balasingham, *The EU Leniency Policy: Reconciling Effectiveness and Fairness*, 2017 (ISBN 978-90-411-8479-5).
71. Eugene Stuart & Iana Roginska-Green, *Sixty Years of EU State Aid Law and Policy: Analysis and Assessment*, 2018 (ISBN 978-90-411-8869-4).

72. Anna Renata Pisarkiewicz, *Margin Squeeze in the Electronic Communications Sector: Critical Analysis of the Decisional Practice and Case Law*, 2018 (ISBN 978-90-411-6246-5).
73. Ploykaew Porananond, *Competition Law in the ASEAN Countries: Regional Law and National Systems*, 2018 (ISBN 978-90-411-9102-1).
74. Corinne Ruechardt, *EU State Aid Control of Infrastructure Funding*, 2018 (ISBN 978-90-411-9099-4).
75. Amalia Athanasiadou, *Patent Settlements in the Pharmaceutical Industry under US Antitrust and EU Competition Law*, 2018 (ISBN 978-94-035-0113-0).
76. Miroslava Marinova, *Fidelity Rebates in Competition Law: Application of the 'As Efficient Competitor' Test*, 2018 (ISBN 978-94-035-0570-1).
77. Gabriella Muscolo & Marina Tavassi, *The Interplay Between Competition Law and Intellectual Property: An International Perspective*, 2019 (ISBN 978-90-411-8687-4).
78. Fevzi Toksoy, Bahadir Balki & Hanna Stakheyeva, *Merger Control in the EU and Turkey: A Comparative Guide*, 2019 (ISBN 978-94-035-0934-1).
79. Paulo Burnier da Silveira & William Evan Kovacic (eds), *Global Competition Enforcement: New Players, New Challenges*, 2019 (ISBN 978-94-035-0283-0).
80. Giovanna Massarotto, *Antitrust Settlements: How a Simple Agreement Can Drive the Economy*, 2019 (ISBN 978-94-035-1133-7).

www.ingramcontent.com/pod-product-compliance
Ingram Content Group UK Ltd.
Pitfield, Milton Keynes, MK11 3LW, UK
UKHW020807290926
15470UKWH00003B/1003

9 789403 511337